THE *ESSENTIALS* OF TEAMWORKING

THE *ESSENTIALS* OF TEAMWORKING
INTERNATIONAL PERSPECTIVES

Edited by

Michael A. West
*Professor of Organizational Psychology and
Head of Research, Aston Business School, UK*

Dean Tjosvold
Chair Professor of Management, Lingnan University, Hong Kong

and

Ken G. Smith
*Dean's Chaired Professor of Business Strategy,
Robert H. Smith School of Business, University of Maryland, USA*

WILEY

Copyright © 2005   John Wiley & Sons Ltd, The Atrium, Southern Gate, Chichester,
West Sussex PO19 8SQ, England

Telephone   (+44) 1243 779777

Email (for orders and customer service enquiries): cs-books@wiley.co.uk
Visit our Home Page on www.wiley.com

All Rights Reserved. No part of this publication may be reproduced, stored in a retrieval system or transmitted in any form or by any means, electronic, mechanical, photocopying, recording, scanning or otherwise, except under the terms of the Copyright, Designs and Patents Act 1988 or under the terms of a licence issued by the Copyright Licensing Agency Ltd, 90 Tottenham Court Road, London W1T 4LP, UK, without the permission in writing of the Publisher. Requests to the Publisher should be addressed to the Permissions Department, John Wiley & Sons Ltd, The Atrium, Southern Gate, Chichester, West Sussex PO19 8SQ, England, or emailed to permreq@wiley.co.uk, or faxed to (+44) 1243 770620.

Designations used by companies to distinguish their products are often claimed as trademarks. All brand names and product names used in this book are trade names, service marks, trademarks or registered trademarks of their respective owners. The Publisher is not associated with any product or vendor mentioned in this book.

This publication is designed to provide accurate and authoritative information in regard to the subject matter covered. It is sold on the understanding that the Publisher is not engaged in rendering professional services. If professional advice or other expert assistance is required, the services of a competent professional should be sought.

Other Wiley Editorial Offices

John Wiley & Sons Inc., 111 River Street, Hoboken, NJ 07030, USA

Jossey-Bass, 989 Market Street, San Francisco, CA 94103-1741, USA

Wiley-VCH Verlag GmbH, Boschstr. 12, D-69469 Weinheim, Germany

John Wiley & Sons Australia Ltd, 33 Park Road, Milton, Queensland 4064, Australia

John Wiley & Sons (Asia) Pte Ltd, 2 Clementi Loop #02-01, Jin Xing Distripark, Singapore 129809

John Wiley & Sons Canada Ltd, 22 Worcester Road, Etobicoke, Ontario, Canada M9W 1L1

Wiley also publishes its books in a variety of electronic formats. Some content that appears in print may not be available in electronic books.

Library of Congress Cataloging-in-Publication Data

The essentials of teamworking : international perspectives / edited by Michael A. West,
    Dean Tjosvold, and Ken G. Smith.
        p.   cm.
    Includes index.
    ISBN-13 978-0-470-01548-3 (alk. paper)
    ISBN-10 0-470-01548-9 (alk. paper)
    1. Teams in the workplace.   2. Conflict management.   3. Organizational behavior.   I. West, Michael A., 1951–   II. Tjosvold, Dean.   III. Smith, Ken G.
HD66 .E868   2005
658.4′022–dc22

                                  2005001256

British Library Cataloguing in Publication Data

A catalogue record for this book is available from the British Library

ISBN-13 978-0-470-01548-3 (pbk)
ISBN-10 0-470-01548-9 (pbk)

Typeset in 10/12pt Times and Helvetica by TechBooks Electronic Services, New Delhi, India
Printed and bound in Great Britain by Antony Rowe Ltd, Chippenham, Wiltshire
This book is printed on acid-free paper responsibly manufactured from sustainable forestry in which at least two trees are planted for each one used for paper production.

This book is dedicated to the memory of our co-authors Maureen Blyler and Dana Clyman.

Their unique and invaluable contributions to the academic and wider communities are cherished.

CONTENTS

About the Editors		ix
List of Contributors		xiii
Preface		xv

1. Cooperation and Conflict: A Personal Perspective on the History of the Social Psychological Study of Conflict Resolution — *Morton Deutsch* — 1

2. Trust, Identity, and Attachment: Promoting Individuals' Cooperation in Groups — *M. Audrey Korsgaard, Susan E. Brodt, and Harry J. Sapienza* — 37

3. A Contingency Theory of Task Conflict and Performance in Groups and Organizational Teams — *Carsten K. W. De Dreu and Laurie R. Weingart* — 55

4. The Role of Cognition in Managing Conflict to Maximize Team Effectiveness: A Team Member Schema Similarity Approach — *Joan R. Rentsch and Jacqueline A. Zelno* — 71

5. Skill Acquisition and the Development of a Team Mental Model: An Integrative Approach to Analysing Organizational Teams, Task, and Context — *Janice Langan-Fox* — 91

6. Training for Cooperative Group Work — *David W. Johnson and Roger T. Johnson* — 131

7. Team-based Organization: Creating an Environment for Team Success — *Cheryl L. Harris and Michael M. Beyerlein* — 149

8. Team Decision Making in Organizations — *Mary Ann Glynn and Pamela S. Barr* — 173

9. Social Loafing in Teams — *Christel G. Rutte* — 191

10. Power in Groups and Organizations — *Peter T. Coleman and Maxim Voronov* — 209

11	Managing the Risk of Learning: Psychological Safety in Work Teams *Amy C. Edmondson*	235
12	Cooperation and Teamwork for Innovation *Michael A. West and Giles Hirst*	257
13	When East and West Meet: Effective Teamwork across Cultures *Kwok Leung, Lin Lu, and Xiangfen Liang*	281

Index 303

ABOUT THE EDITORS

Michael A. West is Professor of Organizational Psychology and Head of Research at Aston Business School. He graduated from the University of Wales in 1973 and received his PhD in 1977. He then spent a year working in the coal mines of South Wales before beginning his academic career. He has authored, edited or co-edited 14 books including *Effective Teamwork* (2004, Blackwell), the first edition of which has been translated into 12 languages, *The Secrets of Successful Team Management* (2004, Duncan Baird), *Developing Team Based Organisations* (2004, Blackwell), *The International Handbook of Organizational Teamwork and Cooperative Working* (2003, Wiley), *Effective Top Management Teams* (2001, Blackhall), *Developing Creativity in Organizations* (1997, BPS) and the *Handbook of Workgroup Psychology* (1996, Wiley). He has also published over 150 articles for scientific and practitioner publications, as well as chapters in scholarly books. He is a Fellow of the British Psychological Society, the American Psychological Association (APA), the APA Society for Industrial/Organizational Psychology, and the Royal Society for the Encouragement of Arts, Manufactures and Commerce. His areas of research interest are team and organizational innovation and effectiveness, particularly in relation to the organization of health services.

Dean Tjosvold is Chair Professor of Management, Lingnan University in Hong Kong. After graduating from Princeton University, he earned his Master's Degree in History and his Ph.D. in the social psychology of organizations at the University of Minnesota, both in 1972. He has taught at Pennsylvania State University, Simon Fraser University, and was visiting professor at the National University of Singapore in 1983–84, the State University of Groningen in The Netherlands, 1991–92, Hong Kong University of Science and Technology, 1994–95, and the City University of Hong Kong, 1995–96.

In 1992, Simon Fraser University awarded him a University Professorship for his research contributions. He received the American Education Research Association's Outstanding Contribution to Cooperative Learning Award in 1998. His review of cooperative and competitive conflict was recognized as the best article in *Applied Psychology: An International Review* for 1998. He is past president of the International Association of Conflict Management. He has published over 200 articles on managing conflict, cooperation and competition, decision making, power, and other management issues. He has served on several editorial boards, including the *Academy of Management Review*, *Journal of Organizational Behavior*, *Journal of Management*, and *Small Group Research*.

He has written over 20 books which have been selected by *Fortune*, *Business Week*, Newbridge, and Executive Book Clubs and translated into Chinese and Spanish. These include: *Conflict Management in the Pacific Rim: Perspectives on International Business* (Wiley, 1998) (edited with Kwok Leung); *Psychology for Leaders: Using Motivation, Power, and Conflict to Manage More Effectively* (Wiley, 1995; Chinese Translation, Business Weekly Publication, 1999) (with Mary M. Tjosvold); *The Emerging Leader: Ways to a Stronger Team* (Lexington Books, 1993) (with Mary M. Tjosvold); *Learning to Manage Conflict: Getting People to Work Together Productively* (Lexington Books, 1993); *Teamwork for Customers: Building an Organization that Takes Pride in Serving* (Jossey-Bass, 1993); *Leading a Team Organization: How to Create an Enduring Competitive Advantage* (Lexington Books, 1991) (with Mary M. Tjosvold); *Team Organization: An Enduring Competitive Advantage* (Wiley, 1991); *The Conflict Positive Organization: Stimulate Diversity and Create Unity* (Addison-Wesley's OD series, 1991); *Working Together to Get Things Done: Managing for Organizational Productivity* (Lexington, 1986).

He has given invited seminars at universities in the US, Canada, Europe, and East Asia. He has consulted with large US banks, hotels in Asia Pacific, Canadian, US, and Hong Kong government agencies, family businesses, and organizations in other industries. He is a partner in his family health care business, which has 600 employees and is based in Minnesota.

Ken G. Smith is the Dean's Chaired Professor of Business Strategy in the Robert H. Smith School of Business at the University of Maryland at College Park. Dr Smith received his MBA in Organizational Behavior from the University of Rhode Island in 1972 and his Ph.D. from the University of Washington in Seattle in 1983. From 1972 to 1980 he was an entrepreneur and chief executive officer in the pump and marine products industries where he developed three separate and successful corporations.

The former editor of the *Academy of Management Review*, Dr Smith has served on a number of editorial boards, including *Academy of Management Journal* and *Academy of Management Executive*. He has published over 50 articles, in such journals as the *Academy of Management Journal*, *Administrative Science Quarterly*, *Strategic Management Journal*, *Management Science*, *Organization Science*, and *Organizational Behavior and Human Decision Processes*, and he has presented numerous papers at national and international meetings, and at many different universities around the world. In addition, he has also published two books: *The Dynamics of Competitive Strategy* (with Grimm and Gannon) (Sage Publishing, 1992); and *Strategy as Action: Industry Competition vs Cooperation* (with Grimm) (West Publishing, 1997).

Dr Smith's research interests in strategic management include strategic positioning, competitive advantage, and the dynamics of competitive and cooperative strategy. He is also a leader in the field of entrepreneurship where his research on the relationship between entrepreneurs and organizational innovation and growth is well known. His research has been supported by grants from the University of Maryland General Research, the National Science Foundation and the Small Business Administration.

In 1991 Dr Smith was a Fulbright Fellow in Strategic Management at the University of Limerick, Plassey, Ireland, and in Spring 2000 was Visiting Professor of Strategy, INSEAD, France. He was elected Fellow to the Academy of Management in 1998.

Professor Smith has participated in a wide variety of executive development programmes, and in 1987, 1990, and 1997 was awarded the Alan Krowe Award from the University of Maryland for teaching excellence. In 1996, Dr Smith was granted the University of Maryland Distinguished Scholar Teacher Award. Dr Smith has been a consultant to a variety of organizations, and is a member of the Academy of Management, the Strategic Management Society, and the Decision Sciences Institute.

LIST OF CONTRIBUTORS

Pamela S. Barr, *Robinson College of Business, Georgia State University, 35 Broad Street, Atlanta, GA 30303, USA*

Michael M. Beyerlein, *Department of Psychology, University of North Texas, PO Box 311280, Denton, TX 76203, USA*

Susan E. Brodt, *Fuqua School of Business, Duke University, Box 90120, Durham, NC 27708, USA*

Peter T. Coleman, *Teachers College, Columbia University, 525 West 120th St, New York 10027, USA*

Carsten K. W. De Dreu, *University of Amsterdam, Department of Psychology, Raetesstraat 15, 1018 WB, Amsterdam, The Netherlands*

Morton Deutsch, *Teachers College, Columbia University, 525 West 120th St, New York 10027, USA*

Amy C. Edmondson, *Associate Professor, Morgan Hall T-93, Harvard Business School, Boston, MA 02163, USA*

Mary Ann Glynn, *Goizueta Business School, Emory University, 1300 Clifton Road, Atlanta, GA 30322-2710, USA*

Cheryl L. Harris, *Department of Psychology, University of North Texas, PO Box 311280, Denton, TX 76203, USA*

Giles Hirst, *Aston University, Aston Business School, Birmingham B4 7ET, UK*

David W. Johnson, *Cooperative Learning Center, University of Minnesota, 60 Peik Hall, Minneapolis, MN 55455, USA*

Roger T. Johnson, *Cooperative Learning Center, University of Minnesota, 60 Peik Hall, Minneapolis, MN 55455, USA*

M. Audrey Korsgaard, *Associate Professor of Management, University of South Carolina, Moore School of Business, Columbia, SC 29208, USA*

Janice Langan-Fox, *Department of Psychology, University of Melbourne, Parkville 3010, Melbourne, Victoria, Australia*

Kwok Leung, *Department of Management, City University of Hong Kong, Tat Chee Avenue, Hong Kong, China*

Xiangfen Liang, *Department of Management, City University of Hong Kong, Tat Chee Avenue, Hong Kong, China*

Lin Lu, *Department of Management, City University of Hong Kong, Tat Chee Avenue, Hong Kong, China*

Joan R. Rentsch, *Associate Professor, Industrial/Organizational Psychology Program, Department of Management, 408 Stokely Management Center, The University of Tennessee, Knoxville, TN 37996-0545, USA*

Christel G. Rutte, *Eindhoven University of Technology, Department of Technology Management, PO Box 513, 5600 MB Eindhoven, The Netherlands*

Harry J. Sapienza, *University of Minnesota, Carlson School of Management, 321 19th Avenue South, Minneapolis, MN 55455, USA*

Maxim Voronov, *Teachers College, Columbia University, 525 West 120th St, New York 10027, USA*

Laurie R. Weingart, *Tepper School of Business, Carnegie Mellon University, 236A Posner Hall, Pittsburgh, PA 15213, USA*

Michael A. West, *Aston University, Aston Business School, Birmingham B4 7ET, UK*

Jacqueline A. Zelno, *Associate Professor, Industrial/Organizational Psychology Program, Department of Management, 408 Stokely Management Center, The University of Tennessee, Knoxville, TN 37996-0545, USA*

PREFACE

Human beings have worked in teams for over 200,000 years. During that time, we have honed our teamwork skills through practice in our childhood games and adult team sports as well as in organizations. By working in teams, we have discovered the structure of the human genome, built grand palaces, explored the beginnings and the outer reaches of our universe, and developed instruments to destroy vast numbers of our own species. Why then another scholarly book about teamworking?

In the last 200 years, we have developed complex, diverse organizations that were previously confined to religious and military institutions. Whereas organizations were typically small craft units of a few people (virtually never exceeding 30), now conglomerations of hundreds, thousands and tens of thousands of employees are common. The US Wal-Mart Corporation and the UK National Health Service both have more than a million employees. Most employees in developed economies now work in organizations that far exceed those we have learned to work in during the last 200,000 years. Managers and scholars alike underestimate the challenges of teamwork in these large organizations. We do not yet understand nearly enough about how to build successful teams in modern organizations.

This book contributes to that understanding by offering new perspectives from leading scholars in the United Kingdom, Australia, the Netherlands, Hong Kong China, and the United States of America. They reveal both the complexity of teamwork and offer empirically based guidance for how teamwork can be effectively developed in modern organizations. The chapters are grouped into five themes.

The first theme weaves together issues of cooperation, conflict, trust and attachment in teams. Morton Deutsch reviews the progress we have made in understanding conflict resolution. He argues that conflict resolution is vital to effective teamwork, since how conflict is managed will determine whether the conflict contributes to team cooperation and productivity or to its dissolution. Deutsch urges us to redouble our efforts to understand constructive conflict resolution in a world where conflict is both pervasive and intense. M. Audrey Korsgaard, Susan Brodt, and Harry Sapienza explore how individuals' trust in their team is key to cooperation by enabling psychological identification (individuals define themselves in part by their membership of the team) and group attachment style (the extent to which they seek and feel secure in groups). Carsten De Dreu and Laurie Weingart challenge prevailing views about task conflict and problem solving in groups, suggesting that we have to understand group performance as being dependent on the interaction between the type of task the team is performing, the types of task conflict team members experience, and the conflict management strategies they adopt. They reject the idea that conflict is always harmful and destructive to team cooperation, offering new insights into how we can manage these processes in teams.

The second theme explores the cognitions of the team, not so much the individual thoughts about teamwork of members, but team member schemas and team mental models. This theme takes the study of teamwork into a new area and suggests that the intuitive, synchronous and spontaneous dance of effective teams confronted with crises, can be understood. Joan Rentsch and Jacqueline Zelno describe team member schemas in relation to what constitutes effective teamwork (cooperative goal interdependence and openness) and in relation to their fellow team members' expertise and viewpoints. The more congruent and accurate these are across the whole team, they suggest, the higher the level of productive task conflict and the lower the level of interpersonal (or socio-emotional conflict). Janice Langan-Fox explores this same theme by identifying the concept of a team mental model—the shared view of their task world and their processes that team members develop. Team mental models, she suggests, can and should be developed by ensuring common focus, clearly defined roles, support for diversity, resolving conflict effectively, using feedback and managing time successfully.

The third theme identifies critical issues for organizations intent on developing team working. David Johnson and Roger Johnson insist that effective teamwork requires competencies in teamwork. Organizations should therefore invest in team member training in competencies in positive interdependence, individual and group accountability, promoting each other's efforts to complete tasks, social skills, aiding group processes, establishing and maintaining trust, and resolving conflicts constructively. Cheryl Harris and Michael Beyerlein shift attention from teams to their context and integration. They challenge existing organization structures that too often hamper effective teamwork. Instead they say that teams require team-based organizations in which managers also work in teams, the rest of the organization is structured to support teams, and support functions are aligned with team needs. This is a radical change from traditional organizations and Harris and Beyerlein describe in detail the investment, structures and effort required.

The fourth theme runs all through the music of teamwork—team processes. This includes team member decision making, the distribution of effort and reward, the use and abuse of power, team learning, and creativity and innovation in teams. Mary Ann Glynn and Pamela Barr depart from traditional views of decision making in teams to explore team cognition or the "collective mind". This collective mind may arise from the aggregation of individual cognitions, through processes of mutual influence, or through the careful interrelating that enables the collective mind to emerge from the sea of separated team member cognitions. They argue that teams only mature in their decision making when they achieve an understanding of the team as a collective entity. Christel Rutte directly addresses the uncomfortable fact that some team members may work harder than others, producing resentment and withdrawal. She explains how these problems can be overcome through (for example) rewarding individuals and teams appropriately, making individual contributions indispensable and unique, making the team task motivating, increasing team cohesiveness and giving positive feedback on team members' performance. Peter Coleman and Maxim Voronov address another issue that is ignored by most advocates of teamwork. They alert the reader to the hidden assumptions about the legitimacy of power relations between team members higher and lower in the hierarchy. They advocate a process of questioning in all teams and organizations of "taken-for-granted" assumptions, especially those concerned with power, in order that a climate can be created within which all voices are heard and valued, and in which diversity can properly flourish (both ideals of effective teamwork). Amy Edmondson also alerts us to a hidden assumption, that our work in modern organizations requires us to take risks—the outcomes of which may be uncertain and potentially harmful to our image. Power, trust and safety in teams will profoundly affect our choices she argues. The challenge for team leaders is to create a climate of psychological safety that ensures risk taking, while maintaining tough challenges and targets that prevent complacency. Finally Michael West (one of the editors) and Giles Hirst explore how creativity and innovation can be encouraged in teams. Teams, they suggest, are potentially rich sources of creativity and innovation but they have to be established, supported and led with that in mind. They describe how the team task must be structured, the organizational context adapted, and team processes developed to ensure high levels of team creativity and innovation. The role of leaders, they suggest, is crucial.

The final theme is addressed by Kwok Leung, Lin Lu and Xiangfen Liang and is perhaps the most urgent for scholars to address in an era of globalization, international travel and migration: how to work effectively in teams across cultures. China and India are likely to be the economic powerhouses of the next 50 years and more companies will span East and West in response to this global economic change. A holistic view of East–West collaboration is essential for progress in building effective teams they suggest. We tend to focus on one aspect in these relationships, such as the importance of face in interactions or the conflict resulting from technology transfer. But, say the authors, we must focus on all aspects—cultural, technological, socioeconomic, behavioural and structural—to build effective teamwork across cultures.

All the chapters in this book offer the reader new, challenging perspectives on teamwork. They confront some of the assumptions we have long held about teamwork in a way that we believe is stimulating and thought provoking. Most chapters also offer practical guidelines for how the authors' prescriptions for effective teamwork can be implemented in organizations. If this book spurs you to new research or new practice, we will feel it has achieved its aims.

MAW
DT
KGS
January, 2005

1

COOPERATION AND CONFLICT
A PERSONAL PERSPECTIVE ON THE HISTORY OF THE SOCIAL PSYCHOLOGICAL STUDY OF CONFLICT RESOLUTION

Morton Deutsch

INTRODUCTION

Conflict is an inevitable and pervasive aspect of organizational life. It occurs within and between individuals, within and between teams and groups, within and between different levels of an organization, within and between organizations. Conflict has been given a bad name by its association with psychopathology, disruption, violence, civil disorder, and war. These are some of the harmful potentials of conflict when it takes a destructive course. When it takes a constructive course, conflict is potentially of considerable personal and social value. It prevents stagnation, it stimulates interest and curiosity, it is the medium through which problems can be aired and creative solutions developed, it is the motor of personal and social change.

It is sometimes assumed that conflicts within teams in organizations should be suppressed, that conflict impairs cooperation and productivity among the members of a team. This may be true when conflict takes a destructive course as in a bitter quarrel. However, it is apt to strengthen the relations among team members and to enhance productivity when it takes the form of a lively controversy.

In this chapter, I present an overview of the major research questions addressed in the literature related to conflict resolution, as well as a historical perspective to see what progress has been made in this area. My premise is that anyone interested in understanding teamwork and cooperative working should be familiar with the field of conflict resolution. As I stated above, conflict is inevitable in teamwork; how the conflict is managed can lead either to the enhancement or disruption of cooperation and team productivity.

The Essentials *of Teamworking: International Perspectives.*
Edited by M. A. West, D. Tjosvold, and K. G. Smith. © 2005 John Wiley & Sons, Ltd.

Some Definitions

Throughout my many years of empirical and theoretical work in the field of conflict studies, I have thought of conflict in the context of competition and cooperation. I have viewed these latter as idealized psychological processes which are rarely found in their "pure" form in nature, but, instead, are found more typically mixed together. I have also thought that most forms of conflict could be viewed as mixtures of competitive and cooperative processes and, further, that the course of a conflict and its consequences would be heavily dependent upon the nature of the cooperative–competitive mix. These views of conflict lead me to emphasize the link between the social psychological studies of cooperation and competition and the studies of conflict in my assessment of this latter area.

I have defined conflict in the following way (Deutsch, 1973, p. 10): "A *conflict* occurs whenever incompatible activities occur.... An action that is incompatible with another action prevents, obstructs, interferes, injures, or in some way makes the latter less likely or less effective." Conflicts may arise between two or more parties from their opposing interests, goals, values, beliefs, preferences, or their misunderstandings about any of the foregoing. These are *potential* sources of conflict which may give rise to actions by the parties which are incompatible with one another; if they do not give rise to incompatible actions, a conflict does not exist: it is only potential.

The terms "competition" and "conflict" are often used synonymously or interchangeably. This reflects a basic confusion. Although competition produces conflict, not all instances of conflict reflect competition. Competition implies an opposition in the goals of the interdependent parties such that the probability of goal attainment for one decreases as the probability for the other increases. In conflict that is derived from competition, the incompatible action reflects incompatible goals. However, conflict may occur even when there is no perceived or actual incompatibility of goals. Thus if two team members of a sales group are in conflict about the best way to increase sales or if a husband and wife are in conflict about how to treat their son's mosquito bites, it is not necessarily because they have mutually exclusive goals; here, their goals may be concordant. My distinction between conflict and competition is not made merely to split hairs. It is important and basic to a theme that underlies much of my work. Namely, conflict can occur in a cooperative or a competitive context, and the processes of conflict resolution that are likely to be displayed will be strongly influenced by the context within which the conflict occurs.

AT THE BEGINNING...

The writings of three intellectual giants—Darwin, Marx, and Freud—dominated the intellectual atmosphere during social psychology's infancy. Each of these major theorists significantly influenced the writings of the early social psychologists on conflict as well as in many other areas. All three theorists appeared—on a *superficial* reading—to emphasize the competitive, destructive aspects of conflict. Darwin stressed "the competitive struggle for existence" and "the survival of the fittest." He wrote (quoted in Hyman, 1966, p. 29): "...all nature is at war, one organism with another, or with external nature. Seeing the contented face of nature, this may at first be well doubted; but reflection will inevitably prove it is too true." Marx emphasized "class struggle," and as the struggle proceeds, "the whole society breaks up more and more into two great hostile camps, two great, directly antagonistic classes: bourgeoisie and proletariat." He ends *The Communist Manifesto* with a ringing call to class struggle: "The proletarians have nothing to lose but their chains. They have a world to win. Working men of all countries, unite." Freud's view of psychosexual development was largely that of constant struggle between the biologically rooted infantile id and the socially determined, internalized parental surrogate, the superego. As Schachtel (1959, p. 10) has noted:

> The concepts and language used by Freud to describe the great metamorphosis from life in the womb to life in the world abound with images of war, coercion, reluctant compromise, unwelcome necessity, imposed sacrifices, uneasy truce under pressure, enforced detours and roundabout ways to return to the original peaceful state of absence of consciousness and stimulation....

Thus, the intellectual atmosphere prevalent during the period when social psychology began to emerge contributed to viewing conflict from the perspective of "competitive struggle." Social conditions too—the intense competition among businesses and among nations, the devastation of World War I, the economic depression of the 1920s and 1930s, the rise of Nazism and other totalitarian systems—reinforced this perspective.

The vulgarization of Darwin's ideas in the form of "social Darwinism" provided an intellectual rationale for racism, sexism, class superiority, and war. Such ideas as "survival of the fittest," "hereditary determinism," and "stages of evolution" were eagerly *mis*applied to the relations between different human social groups—classes and nations as well as social races—to rationalize imperialist policies. The influence of evolutionary thinking was so strong that, as a critic suggested, it gave rise to a new imperialist beatitude: "Blessed are the strong, for they shall prey upon the weak" (Banton, 1967, p. 48). The rich and powerful were biologically superior; they had achieved their positions as a result of natural selection. It would be against nature to interfere with the inequality and suffering of the poor and weak.

Social Darwinism and the mode of explaining behavior in terms of innate, evolutionary derived instincts were in retreat by the mid-1920s. The prestige of the empirical methods in the physical sciences, the point of view of social determinism advanced by Karl Marx and various sociological theorists, and the findings of cultural anthropologists all contributed to their decline.[1] Since the decline of the instinctual mode of explaining such conflict phenomena as war, intergroup hostility, and human exploitation, two others have been dominant: the "psychological" and the "socio-political–economic." The "psychological" mode attempts to explain such phenomena in terms of "what goes on in the minds of men" (Klineberg, 1964) or "tensions that cause war" (Cantril, 1950); in other words, in terms of the perceptions, beliefs, values, ideology, motivations, and other psychological states and characteristics that individual men and women have acquired as a result of their experiences and as these characteristics are activated by the particular situation and role in which people are located. The "socio-political–economic" mode, in contrast, seeks an explanation in terms of such social, economic, and political factors as levels of armaments, objective conflicts in economic and political interests, and the like. Although these modes of explanation are not mutually exclusive, there is a tendency for partisans of the psychological mode to consider that the causal arrow points from psychological conditions to socio-political–economic

---

[1] This is a decline, not a disappearance. The explanation of social phenomena in terms of innate factors justifies the status quo by arguing for its immutability; such justification will always be sought by those who fear change.

conditions and for partisans of the latter to believe the reverse is true. In any case, much of the social psychological writing in the 1930s, 1940s, and early 1950s on the topics of war, intergroup conflict, and industrial strife was largely nonempirical, and in one vein or the other. The psychologically trained social psychologist tended to favor the psychological mode; the Marxist-oriented or sociologically trained social psychologist more often favored the other mode.

The decline of social Darwinism and the instinctivist doctrines was hastened by the development and employment of empirical methods in social psychology. This early empirical orientation to social psychology focused on the socialization of the individual; this focus was, in part, a reaction to the instinctivist doctrine. It led to a great variety of studies, including a number investigating cooperation and competition. These latter studies are, in my view, the precursors to the empirical, social psychological study of conflict.

EARLY STUDIES OF COOPERATION AND COMPETITION

Two outstanding summaries of the then existing research on cooperation and competition were published in 1937. One was in the volume of Murphy, Murphy, and Newcomb, *Experimental Social Psychology*; the other was in the monograph *Competition and Cooperation*, by May and Doob. It is not my intention here to repeat these summaries but rather to give you my sense of the state of the research and theorizing on cooperation–competition in the 1920s and 1930s.

My impression is that practically none of the earlier research on cooperation and competition would be acceptable in current social psychological journals because of methodological flaws in the studies. Almost all of them suffer from serious deficiencies in their research designs. In addition, there is little conceptual clarity about some of the basic concepts—"competition," "cooperation," "self-orientation"—that are used in the studies. As a result, the operational definitions used to create the differing experimental conditions have no consistency from one study to another or even within a given study.

Further, the early studies of cooperation and competition suffered from a narrowness of scope. They focused almost exclusively on the effects of "competition" versus "cooperation" on individual task output. There was no investigation of social interaction, communication processes, problem-solving methods, interpersonal attitudes, attitudes toward self, attitudes toward work, attitudes toward the group, or the like in these early investigations of cooperation–competition. The focus was narrowly limited to work output. The simplistic assumption was made that output would be an uncomplicated function of the degree of motivation induced by competition as compared with cooperation. The purposes of most of these early investigations appeared to be to support or reject a thesis inherent in the American ideology; namely, that competition fosters greater motivation to be productive than other forms of social organization.

FIELD THEORY, CONFLICT, AND COOPERATION–COMPETITION

During the 1920s, 1930s, and 1940s, quite independently of the work being conducted in the United States on cooperation–competition, Kurt Lewin and his students were theorizing and conducting research which profoundly affected later work in many areas of social psychology. Lewin's field theory—with its dynamic concepts of tension systems, "driving" and "restraining" forces, "own" and "induced" forces, valences, level of aspiration, power fields, interdependence, overlapping situations, and so on—created a new vocabulary for thinking about conflict and cooperation–competition.

As early as 1931, employing his analysis of force fields, Lewin (1931, 1935) presented a penetrating theoretical discussion of three basic types of psychological conflict: *approach–approach*—the individual stands between two positive valences of approximately equal strength; *avoidance–avoidance*—the individual stands between two negative valences of approximately equal strength; and *approach–avoidance*—the individual is exposed to opposing forces deriving from a positive and a negative valence. Hull (1938) translated Lewin's analysis into the terminology of the goal gradient, and Miller (1937, 1944) elaborated and did research upon it. Numerous experimental studies supported the theoretical analysis.

My own initial theorizing on cooperation–competition (Deutsch, 1949a) was influenced by the Lewinian thinking on tension systems which was reflected in a series of brilliant experiments on the recall of interrupted activities (Zeigarnik, 1927), the resumption of interrupted activities (Ovsiankina, 1928), substitutability (Mahler, 1933), and the role of ego in cooperative work (Lewis & Franklin, 1944). But even more of my thinking was indebted to the ideas which were "in the air" at the MIT Research Center for Group Dynamics. Ways of characterizing and explaining group processes and group functioning, employing the language of Lewinian theorizing, were under constant discussion among the students and faculty at the MIT Center. Thus, it was quite natural that when I settled on cooperation–competition as the topic of my doctoral dissertation, I should employ the Lewinian dynamic emphasis on goals and how they are interrelated as my key theoretical wedge into this topic. Even more importantly, the preoccupation with understanding group processes at the Center pressed me to formulate my ideas about cooperation and competition so that they would be relevant to the psychological and interpersonal processes occurring within and between groups. This pressure forced my theory and research (Deutsch, 1949a, b) to go considerably beyond the prior social psychological work on cooperation–competition. My theorizing and research were concerned not only with the individual and group outcomes of cooperation and competition but also with the social psychological processes which would give rise to these outcomes.

My theorizing and research have been published and widely referred to, so there is little need here for more than a brief summary of some of the theory's predictions, which have been validated by extensive research. Assuming that the individual actions in a group are more frequently effective than bungling, among the predictions that follow from the theory are that *cooperative relations* (those in which the goals of the parties involved are predominantly positively interdependent), as compared with competitive ones, show more of these positive characteristics:

1. *Effective communication* is exhibited. Ideas are verbalized, and group members are attentive to one another, accepting of the ideas of other members, and influenced by them. They have fewer difficulties in communicating with or understanding others.
2. *Friendliness, helpfulness, and less obstructiveness* are expressed in the discussions. Members are more satisfied with the group and its solutions and favorably impressed by

the contributions of the other group members. In addition, members of the cooperative groups rate themselves high in desire to win the respect of their colleagues and in obligation to the other members.
3. *Coordination of effort, divisions of labor, orientation to task achievement, orderliness in discussion, and high productivity* are manifested in the cooperative groups (if the group task requires effective communication, coordination of effort, division of labor, or sharing of resources).
4. *Feeling of agreement with the ideas of others and a sense of basic similarity in beliefs and values, as well as confidence in one's own ideas and in the value that other members attach to those ideas*, are obtained in the cooperative groups.
5. *Willingness to enhance the other's power* (for example, the other's knowledge, skills, resources) to accomplish the other's goals increases. As the other's capabilities are strengthened, you are strengthened, they are of value to you as well as to the other. Similarly, the other is enhanced from your enhancement and benefits from your growing capabilities and power.
6. *Defining conflicting interests as a mutual problem to be solved by collaborative effort* facilitates recognizing the legitimacy of each other's interests and the necessity to search for a solution responsive to the needs of all. It tends to limit rather than expand the scope of conflicting interests. Attempts to influence the other tend to be confined to processes of persuasion.

In contrast, a competitive *process* has the opposite effects:

1. Communication is impaired as the conflicting parties seek to gain advantage by misleading the other through use of false promises, ingratiation tactics, and disinformation. It is reduced and seen as futile as they recognize that they cannot trust one another's communications to be honest or informative.
2. Obstructiveness and lack of helpfulness lead to mutual negative attitudes and suspicion of one another's intentions. One's perceptions of the other tend to focus on the person's negative qualities and ignore the positive.
3. The parties to the process are unable to divide their work, duplicating one another's efforts such that they become mirror images; if they do divide the work, they feel the need to check what the other is doing continuously.
4. The repeated experience of disagreement and critical rejection of ideas reduces confidence in oneself as well as the other.
5. The conflicting parties seek to enhance their own power and to reduce the power of the other. Any increase in the power of the other is seen as threatening to oneself.

The competitive process stimulates the view that the solution of a conflict can only be imposed by one side on the other, which in turn leads to using coercive tactics such as psychological as well as physical threats and violence. It tends to expand the scope of the issues in conflict as each side seeks superiority in power and legitimacy. The conflict becomes a power struggle or a matter of moral principle and is no longer confined to a specific issue at a given time and place. Escalating the conflict increases its motivational significance to the participants and may make a limited defeat less acceptable and more humiliating than a mutual disaster.

As Johnson and Johnson (1989) have detailed, these ideas have given rise to a large number of research studies indicating that a cooperative process (as compared to a competitive one) leads to greater productivity, more favorable interpersonal and intergroup relations, better psychological health and higher self-esteem as well as more constructive resolution of conflict.

GAME THEORY AND GAMES

In 1944, von Neumann and Morgenstern published their now classic work, *Theory of Games and Economic Behavior*. Game theory has made a major contribution to social scientists by formulating in mathematical terms the problem of conflict of interest. However, it has not been either its mathematics or its normative prescriptions for minimizing losses when facing an intelligent adversary that has made game theory of considerable value to social psychologists. Rather, it has been its core emphasis that the parties in conflict have interdependent interests, that their fates are woven together. Although the mathematical and normative development of game theory has been most successful in connection with pure competitive conflict ("zero-sum" games), game theory has also recognized that cooperative as well as competitive interests may be intertwined in conflict (as in "coalition" games or "non-zero-sum" games).

The game theory recognition of the intertwining of cooperative and competitive interests in situations of conflict (or in Schelling's (1960) useful term, the "mixed-motive" nature of conflict) has had a productive impact on the social psychological study of conflict, theoretically as well as methodologically. Theoretically, at least for me, it helped buttress a viewpoint that I had developed prior to my acquaintance with game theory—namely, that conflicts were typically mixtures of cooperative and competitive processes and that the course of conflict would be determined by the nature of the mixture. This emphasis on the cooperative elements involved in conflict ran counter to the then dominant view of conflict as a competitive struggle. Methodologically, game theory had an impact on an even larger group of psychologists. The mathematical formulations of game theory had the indirect but extremely valuable consequence of laying bare some fascinating paradoxical situations in such a way that they were highly suggestive of experimental work.

Game matrices as an experimental device are popular because they facilitate a precise definition of the reward structure encountered by the subjects, and hence of the way they are dependent upon one another. Partly stimulated by and partly in reaction to the research using game matrices, other research games for the study of conflict have been developed. Siegel and Fouraker (1960) developed a bilateral monopoly, "buyer–seller" negotiation game; Vinacke and Arkoff (1957) invented a three-person coalition game; Deutsch and Krauss (1960) constructed a "trucking game"; Deutsch (1973) employed an "allocation" game; and many other investigators have developed variants of these games or new ones. Pruitt and Kimmel in 1977 estimated that well over 1000 studies had been published based on experimental games. Much of this research, as is true in other areas of science, was mindless—being done because a convenient experimental format was readily available. Some of it, however, has, I believe, helped to develop more systematic understanding of conflict processes and conflict resolution. Fortunately, in recent years, experimental gaming has been supplemented by other experimental procedures and by field studies which have overcome some of the inherent limitations of experimental gaming.

THEMES IN CONTEMPORARY SOCIAL PSYCHOLOGICAL RESEARCH ON CONFLICT

Social psychological research on conflict, during the past 35 years or so, has primarily addressed the following major questions:

(1) *What are the conditions which give rise to a constructive or destructive process of conflict resolution?* In terms of bargaining and negotiation, the emphasis here is on determining the circumstances which enable the conflicting parties to arrive at a mutually satisfactory agreement which maximizes their joint outcomes. In a sense, this first question arises from a focus on the cooperative potential inherent in conflict.

(2) *What are the circumstances, strategies, and tactics which lead one party to do better than another in a conflict situation?* The stress here is on how one can wage conflict, or bargain, so as to win or at least do better than one's adversary. This second question emerges from a focus on the competitive features of a conflict situation.

(3) *What determines the nature of the agreement between conflicting parties, if they are able to reach an agreement?* Here the concern is with the cognitive and normative factors that lead people to conceive a possible agreement and to perceive it as a salient possibility for reaching a stable agreement: an agreement which each of the conflicting parties will see as "just" under the circumstances. This third question is a more recent one and has been addressed under the heading of research on the social psychology of equity and justice.

(4) *How can third parties be used to prevent conflicts from becoming destructive or to help deadlocked or embittered negotiators move toward a more constructive management of their conflicts?* This fourth question has been reflected in studies of mediation and in strategies of de-escalating conflicts.

(5) *How can people be educated to manage their conflicts more constructively?* This has been a concern of consultants working with leaders in industry and government and also with those who have responsibility for educating the children in our schools.

(6) *How and when to intervene in prolonged, intractable conflicts?* Much of the literature in conflict resolution has been preventive rather than remedial in its emphasis. It is concerned with understanding the conditions that foster productive rather than destructive conflict (as in question (1)) or developing knowledge about the circumstances that lead to intractable, destructive conflict, in the hope of preventing such conflict. More recently, the reality that many protracted, destructive conflicts exist in the world has induced some scholars to focus their attention on this problem.

(7) *How are we to understand why ethnic, religious, and identity conflicts frequently take an intractable, destructive course?* With the end of the Cold War, there appears to be a proliferation of such conflicts. In the past 10 years, interest in such conflicts has been renewed. Attention has been addressed to what causes such conflict but also what can be done after the typical atrocities of such conflict to bring about reconciliation and reconstruction.

(8) *How applicable in other cultural contexts are the theories related to conflict that have largely been developed in the United States and Western Europe?* In recent years, there has been much discussion in the literature of the differences that exist in how people from varying cultural backgrounds deal with negotiations and, more generally, manage conflict.

In the next section, I shall attempt to describe tentative answers which social psychological research has given the foregoing questions.

What Are the Conditions which Give Rise to a Constructive or Destructive Process of Conflict Resolution?

In social psychology this question has been most directly addressed in the work of my students and myself and summarized in my book, *The Resolution of Conflict: Constructive and Destructive Processes* (1973). Our research started off with the assumption that if the parties involved in a conflict situation had a cooperative rather than competitive orientation toward one another, they would be more likely to engage in a constructive process of conflict resolution. In my earlier research on the effects of cooperation and competition upon group process, I had demonstrated that a cooperative process was more productive in dealing with a problem that a group faces than a competitive process. I reasoned that the same would be true in a mixed-motive situation of conflict: a conflict could be viewed as a mutual problem facing the conflicting parties. Our initial research on trust and suspicion employing the prisoners' dilemma game strongly supported my reasoning, as did subsequent research employing other experimental formats. I believe that this is a very important result which has considerable theoretical and practical significance.

At a theoretical level, it enabled me to link my prior characterization of cooperation and competitive social processes to the nature of the processes of conflict resolution which would typically give rise to constructive or destructive outcomes. That is, I had found a way to characterize the central features of constructive and destructive *processes* of conflict resolution; doing so represented a major advance beyond the characterization of *outcomes* as constructive or destructive. This was not only important in itself but it also opened up a new possibility. At both the theoretical and practical level, the characterization of constructive and destructive processes of conflict created the very significant possibility that we would be able to develop insight into the conditions which initiated or stimulated the development of cooperative–constructive versus competitive–destructive processes of conflict. Much of the research of my students and myself has been addressed to developing this insight.

Much of our early research on the conditions affecting the course of conflict was done on an ad hoc basis. We selected independent variables to manipulate based on our intuitive sense of what would give rise to a cooperative or competitive process. We did experiments with quite a number of variables: motivational orientation, communication facilities, perceived similarity of opinions and beliefs, size of conflict, availability of threats and weapons, power differences, third-party interventions, strategies and tactics of game playing by experimental stooges, the payoff structure of the game, personality characteristics, and so on. The results of these studies fell into a pattern which I slowly began to grasp.

All of these studies seemed explainable by the assumption, which I have labeled "Deutsch's crude law of social relations," that *the characteristic processes and effects elicited by a given type of social relationship (cooperative or competitive) also tend to elicit that type of social relationship*. Thus, cooperation induces and is induced by a perceived similarity in beliefs and attitudes; a readiness to be helpful; openness in communication; trusting and friendly attitudes; sensitivity to common interests and de-emphasis of opposed interests; an orientation toward enhancing mutual power rather than power differences; and so on. Similarly, competition induces and is induced by the use of tactics of coercion, threat, or deception; attempts to enhance the power differences between oneself and the other; poor communication; minimization of the awareness of similarities in values and increased sensitivity to opposed interests; suspicious and hostile attitudes; the importance, rigidity, and size of the issues in conflict; and so on.

In other words, if one has systematic knowledge of the effects of cooperative and competitive processes, one will have systematic knowledge of the conditions which typically give rise to such processes and, by extension, to the conditions which affect whether a conflict will take a constructive or destructive course. My early theory of cooperation and competition is a theory of the *effects* of cooperative and competitive processes (see earlier section "Field theory, conflict, and cooperation–competition" (p. 12) and Deutsch & Coleman, 2000, Chapter 1 for a summary). Hence, from the crude law of social relations stated earlier, it follows that this theory provides insight into the conditions which give rise to cooperative and competitive processes.

The crude law is *crude*. It expresses surface similarities between "effects" and "causes"; the basic relationships are genotypical rather than phenotypical. The crude law is crude, but it can be improved. Its improvement requires a linkage with other areas in social psychology, particularly social cognition and social perception. Such a linkage would enable us to view phenotypes in their social environments in such a way as to lead us to perceive correctly the underlying genotypes. We would then be able to know under what conditions "perceived similarity" or "threat" will be experienced as having an underlying genotype different from the one that is usually associated with its phenotype.

What Are the Circumstances, Strategies, and Tactics which Lead One Party to Do Better than Another in a Conflict Situation?

Most of the important theoretical work by social scientists in relation to this question has been done not by social psychologists but by economists, political scientists, and those concerned with collective bargaining. Some of the most notable contributions have been made by Chamberlain (1951), Schelling (1960, 1966), Stevens (1963), Walton and McKersie (1965), Kahn (1965), Jervis (1970, 1976), and Snyder and Diesing (1977). Machiavelli (1950) earlier had described useful strategies and tactics for winning conflicts: Machiavelli's emphasis was on how to use one's power most effectively so as to intimidate or overwhelm one's adversary; Potter's (1965) on how to play upon the good will, cooperativeness, and politeness of one's opponent so as to upset him and make him lose his "cool." More recently, Alinsky (1971) has described a "jujitsu" strategy that the "have-nots" can employ against the "haves" and described various tactics of harassing and ensnaring the "haves" in their own red tape by pressuring them to live up to their own formally stated rules and procedures.

Social psychologists have just barely begun to tap and test the rich array of ideas about strategies and tactics for winning conflicts or for increasing one's bargaining power and effectiveness that exist in the common folklore as well as in the social and political science literature. This research has provided some support and qualification of preexisting ideas about bargaining strategy and tactics. I shall briefly discuss research relating to "being ignorant," "being tough," "being belligerent," and "bargaining power."

"BEING IGNORANT"

Common sense suggests that one is better off if one is informed rather than ignorant. Schelling (1960) has, however, advanced the interesting idea that in bargaining it is sometimes advantageous to be in a position where you are or appear to be ignorant of your opponent's preferences; similarly, it may give you an edge to be in a situation where you could inform your opponent of your preferences but the other hand could not so inform you. Research (Cummings & Harnett, 1969; Harnett & Cummings, 1968; Harnett, Cummings, & Hughes, 1968) provides experimental support for Schelling's idea. In several different bargaining situations it was demonstrated that a bargainer who did not have complete information about the bargaining schedule of his opponent began bargaining with higher initial bids, made fewer concessions, and earned higher profits than bargainers with complete information. Being ignorant of what the other wants, or appearing so, may justify to oneself and to the other a relative neglect of the other's interests in one's proposals; neglecting the other's interests when they are known is a more obvious and flagrant affront.

The bargaining tactic of "ignorance," as well as other tactics such as "brinkmanship" and "appearing to be irrational," can be characterized in terms of the bargaining doctrine of "the last clear chance." The basic notion here is that a bargainer will gain an advantage if he can appear to commit himself irrevocably so that the last clear chance of avoiding mutual disaster rests with his opponent. A child who works himself up to the point that he will have a temper tantrum if his parents refuse to let him sit where he wants in the restaurant is employing this doctrine. So is the driver who cuts in front of someone on a highway while appearing to be deaf to the insistent blasts of the other's horn. Such tactics do not always work. They seem most apt to do so when the situation is asymmetrical (you can use the tactic but your opponent cannot) and when your opponent does not have a strong need to improve or uphold his reputation for "resolve" or "toughness."

"BEING TOUGH"

"Bargaining toughness" has been defined experimentally in terms of setting a high level of aspiration, making high demands, and offering fewer concessions or smaller concessions than one's opponent. It is a widely held view, to quote the late Leo Durocher, that "nice guys finish last." The results of many experiments (see Magenau & Pruitt, 1978) support a more complex conclusion, stated by Bartos (1970, p. 62): "Toughness plays a dual role and has contradictory consequences. On the one hand, toughness *decreases* the likelihood of an agreement, while on the other hand, it increases the payoffs of those who survive this possibility of a failure." A relentlessly tough approach throughout bargaining appears to result in worse outcomes than a more conciliatory approach (Hamner & Baird, 1978; Harnett & Vincelette, 1978). There is, however, some evidence to suggest that initial toughness in terms of high opening demands, combined with a readiness to reciprocate concessions, may facilitate a fuller exploration of the alternative possibilities of agreement and lead to the discovery of an agreement which maximizes payoffs to the bargainers (Kelley & Schenitzki, 1972); premature tendencies to reach an agreement without full exploration of the possibilities may be prevented by tough, initial positions (Deutsch, 1973).

"BEING BELLIGERENT"

Since the initial research of Deutsch and Krauss (1960) demonstrated the deleterious effects of threat upon bargaining, there has been a deluge of bargaining experiments bearing upon the use of weapons, threats, fines, punishments, rewards, promises, and the like. Tedeschi, Schlenker, and Bonoma (1973, p. 141) have summarized the results of this research as follows: "Threats seldom improve and almost always decrease a bargainer's outcomes if his adversary is similarly armed and the values are important to both parties. Yet when threats are available, bargainers are tempted to use them." Research (see Deutsch, 1973) also demonstrates that threats have considerable reputational costs: a "threatener" as compared to a "promiser" is viewed much more negatively and is much less likely to get compliance.

Although belligerent, coercive tactics usually impair negotiation, it is evident that one is apt to yield to an adversary when there is a gun pressed against one's head. Coercion can be successful, especially when the power of the conflicting parties is unequal. Although coercion can be successful, its success is usually limited to immediate compliance; the long-term consequences of the use of such tactics are usually counterproductive.

"BARGAINING POWER"

Common sense would suggest that a bargainer is likely to be better off if he has more power than the adversary. The results of social psychological research indicate that the situation is more complex than it first seems. Experimentally, bargaining power is sometimes defined as the relative power of each of the bargainers to inflict harm upon one another; the relative desirability of the alternatives to bargaining that are available to each of the bargainers; the relative time pressure on each bargainer to reach an agreement; and so forth. The research evidence (Magenau & Pruitt, 1978; Rubin & Brown, 1975) indicates that when bargaining power is equal, agreement is relatively easy to reach and the outcomes to the parties are high. When bargaining power is somewhat unequal, a power struggle often ensues as the bargainer with more power tries to assert superior claims and as these are resisted by the bargainer with lesser power; the result of this struggle is that the agreement is difficult to reach and the bargainers have low outcomes. When bargaining power is markedly unequal, the differences in power are more likely to be accepted as legitimate and lead to quick agreement, with the advantage going to the more powerful bargainer. However, if the differences in power are not viewed as providing a legitimization of relatively low outcomes to the low-power bargainer, he will resist what he considers to be greed and exploitation; agreement here also will be difficult, and outcomes will be low. Differences in bargaining power may lead the bargainer with greater power to make claims which he feels are legitimate but which he cannot force the other to accept; the bargainer with lesser power may resist the claims as being exploitative and illegitimate and as a way of asserting his equal status as a person. His resistance causes the low-power bargainer to suffer relatively more than the high-power bargainer, but the high-power bargainer also suffers. In essence, the bargaining research demonstrates that having higher power than one's bargaining opponent may be less advantageous than having equal power if your fellow bargainer is apt to resist any greater claims that you might make as a result of your greater power.

From this brief and very incomplete survey of some of the experimental research bearing on the strategy and tactics of waging conflict, it is evident that social psychological research has given some support for surprising tactics ("being ignorant") and has raised some doubts about common assumptions relating to the advantages to be obtained from "toughness" as a strategy, from "coercive tactics," and from "superior bargaining power."

The extensive research literature on negotiation (summarized in such books as Bazerman & Neal, 1992; Breslin & Rubin, 1991; Deutsch, 1973; Deutsch & Coleman, 2000; Kritter, 1994; Lewicki & Letterer, 1985a, b; Lewiki, Sanders, & Minton, 1999; Pruitt, 1981; Pruitt & Carnevale, 1993; Rubin, Pruitt, & Kim, 1994; Thompson, 1998) has investigated many of the strategies and tactics that relate to both "integrative" or "win–win" bargaining (those related to the first listed question above) and "distributive" bargaining (those related to the second listed question): only some of which have been discussed here. For a fuller discussion of such topics as "concession making," "the use of time pressure," "promises and threats," "establishing credibility," "enhancing bargaining power," "building rapport," etc., the books listed above should be consulted.

What Determines the Nature of the Agreement between Conflicting Parties if they Are Able to Reach an Agreement?

A bargain is defined in *Webster's Unabridged Dictionary* as "an agreement between parties settling what each shall give and receive in a transaction between them." The definition of "bargain" fits under common social science definitions of the term "social norm." What determines the agreement or social norm for settling the issues in conflict? Two compatible ideas have been advanced in answer to this question, one related to "perceptual prominence" and the other to "distributive justice."

Schelling (1960) has suggested that perceptually prominent alternatives serve a key function in permitting bargainers to come to an agreement. Research has provided some support for Schelling's idea (see Magenau & Pruitt, 1978, for a summary).

Homans (1961, 1974) has suggested that the principle of distributive justice would play a role in determining how people would decide to allocate the awards and costs to be distributed between them. Although Homans was not primarily concerned with conflict or bargaining, it is evident that his conception of distributive justice does not exclude them. In his discussion, Homans has emphasized one particular canon or rule of distributive justice, that of "proportionality" or "equity": in a just distribution, rewards will be distributed among individuals in proportion to their contributions. "Equity theorists" such as Adams (1963, 1965), Adams and Freedman (1976), and Walster, Walster, and Berscheid (1978) have continued Homans' emphasis on the rule of proportionality and have elaborated a theory and stimulated much research to support the view that psychological resistance and emotional distress will be encountered if the rule of proportionality is violated. In recent years, other social psychologists—Lerner (1975), Leventhal (1976), Sampson (1969), and myself (Deutsch, 1974, 1975)—have stressed that proportionality is only one of many common canons of distributive justice. We know very little about what makes a given rule of justice stand out as saliently appropriate in a given situation of conflict. However, a number of us (Deutsch, 1975; Lamm & Kayser, 1978a, b; Lerner, 1975; Leventhal, 1976; Mikula & Schwinger, 1978; Sampson, 1975) have articulated hypotheses about factors favoring the selection of one or another rule and done related experiments. It seems evident that if a conflict is experienced as having been resolved unjustly, it is not likely that the conflict has been adequately resolved; similarly, a bargaining agreement that is viewed as unjust is not apt to be a stable one. "Justice" and "conflict" are intimately intertwined; the sense of injustice can give rise to conflict, and conflict can produce injustice.

Social psychological research on justice and conflict is too new to have led to definitive results. However, let me note the direction of my thinking in this area. I have applied and elaborated my crude hypothesis of social relations (the typical consequences of a given type of social relation tends to elicit that relation) so as to be relevant to the question of what rule of justice will predominate in a group or social system. I (Deutsch, 1975, 1985) have developed rationales to explain the tendency for economically oriented groups to use the principle of equity; for solidarity-oriented groups to use the principle of equality; and for caring-oriented groups to use the principle of need. I have then characterized typical effects of economically oriented relations, solidarity-oriented relations, and caring relations and have hypothesized that these different kinds of typical effects will elicit different principles of distributive justice.

Thus, among the typical consequences of an economic orientation (Diesing, 1962) are:

(1) the development of a set of values which includes maximization, a means–end schema, neutrality or impartiality with regard to means, and competition;
(2) the turning of man and everything associated with him into commodities—including labor, time, land, capital, personality, social relations, ideas, art, and enjoyment;
(3) the development of measurement procedures which enable the value of different amounts and types of commodities to be compared; and
(4) the tendency for economic activities to expand in scope and size.

The crude hypothesis advanced above would imply that an economic orientation and the principle of equity are likely to be dominant in a group or social system if its situation is characterized by impersonality, competition, maximization, an emphasis on comparability rather than uniqueness, largeness in size or scope, and so on. Specific experimental hypotheses could readily be elaborated: the more competitive the people are in a group, the more likely they are to use equity rather than equality or need as the principle of distributive justice; the more impersonal the relations of the members of a group are, the more likely they are to use equity; and so forth.

Results in my laboratory, as well as in the laboratories of other investigators, are consistent with my crude hypothesis. It seems likely that the reason "equity" has been the central principle of distributive justice to social psychologists is that there has been an unwitting acceptance of the view that the dominant orientation of American society, a competitive–economic orientation, is a universally valid orientation. This is too parochial a perspective. Equity is only one of many principles of distributive justice. It is evident that questions of justice may arise in noneconomic social relations and may be decided in terms that are unrelated to input–output ratios. For a fuller discussion of "justice and conflict," see Deutsch and Coleman (2000, Chapter 2) and for a comprehensive discussion of the social psychology of justice see Tyler et al. (1997).

How Can Third Parties Be Used to Prevent Conflicts from Becoming Destructive or to Help Deadlocked or Embittered Negotiators Move toward a More Constructive Management of their Conflicts?

Kenneth Kressel and Dean Pruitt have edited an issue of the *Journal of Social Issues* (1985) and published a book (1989) on mediation research which provide a definitive review of the work being done in this area. As they point out, informal mediation is one of the oldest forms of conflict resolution, and formal mediation has been practiced in international and labor–management conflicts for many years. More recently, formal mediation has been increasingly applied to an ever-widening array of disputes in such areas as divorcing, small-claims cases, neighborhood feuds, landlord–tenant relations, environmental and public-resource controversies, industrial disputes, school conflicts, and civil cases. Following in the wake of the explosion of the practice of mediation (and of the proliferation of textbooks and "how-to-do-it" books on mediation), there has been important but modest growth in research and theorizing on this topic. Most of the research and theorizing has occurred in the past two decades.

Here, I shall highlight some of the main points which emerge from the cogent summary by Kressel and Pruitt of the work in this area.

There is considerable evidence of user satisfaction with mediation and some evidence that the agreements reached through mediation are both less costly to the conflicting parties and more robust than traditional adjudication (Kressel, 2000). However, there is strong evidence to suggest that mediation has dim prospects of being successful under adverse circumstances. As Kressel and Pruitt (1989, p. 405) have succinctly expressed it: "Intensely conflicted disputes involving parties of widely disparate power, with low motivation to settle, fighting about matters of principle, suffering from discord or ambivalence within their own camps, and negotiating over scarce resources are likely to defeat even the most adroit mediators."

Kressel and Pruitt, in characterizing the research describing what mediators do, indicate that their diverse actions can be grouped under four major headings: (1) establishing a working alliance with the parties; (2) improving the climate between them; (3) addressing the issues; and (4) applying pressure for settlement. As Kressel (2000, pp. 525–526) points out:

> Mediation should be helpful in any conflict in which the basic framework for negotiation is present (Moore, 1996). The framework includes these elements:
> - The parties can be identified.
> - They are interdependent.
> - They have the basic cognitive, interpersonal, and emotional capabilities to represent themselves.
> - They have interests that are not entirely incompatible.
> - They face alternatives to consensual agreement that are undesirable (for example, a costly trial).
>
> Mediation is especially likely to prove useful whenever there are additional obstacles that would make unassisted negotiations likely to fail:
> - Interpersonal barriers (intense negative feelings, a dysfunctional pattern of communicating).

- Substantive barriers (strong disagreement over the issues, perceived incompatibility of interests, serious differences about the "facts" or circumstances).
- Procedural barriers (existence of impasse, absence of forum for negotiating).

Although many disputes meet these formal criteria, getting mediation started turns out to be something of a challenge. In interpersonal disputes of all kinds, one-third to two-thirds of those given the opportunity to use formal mediation decline it. It is also apparent that in work settings where informal mediation could be used (as by a manager), the would-be mediator declines to intervene, looks the other way, or chooses to employ power and authority rather than the skills of facilitation. Characteristics of the social environment, the disputing parties, and the potential mediator are among the variables that determine whether or not mediation occurs.

I have, from my theoretical perspective, expressed similar ideas, somewhat differently in answer to the question: *What framework can guide a third person who seeks to intervene therapeutically if negotiations are deadlocked or unproductive because of misunderstandings, faulty communications, the development of hostile attitudes, or the inability to discover a mutually satisfying solution?* I suggest that such a framework is implicit in the ideas that I have described earlier. The third party seeks to produce a cooperative problem-solving orientation to the conflict by creating the conditions which characterize an effective cooperative problem-solving process: these conditions are the typical effects of a successful cooperative process. Helping the conflicting parties to develop a cooperative, problem-solving orientation to their conflict may be sufficient when the conflicting parties have reasonably well-developed group problem-solving and decision-making skills. Often they do not, and, hence, they need tutelage in these skills if they are to deal with their problem successfully. And, often, conflicting parties do not have sufficient substantive knowledge concerning the issues in conflict to manage them constructively. Here, too, they may need tutelage by a third party if their conflict is to be resolved sensibly.

Third parties (mediators, conciliators, process consultants, therapists, counselors, etc.) who are called upon to provide assistance in a conflict require four kinds of skills if they are to have the flexibility required to deal with the diverse situations mediators face. The *first* set of skills are those related to the third party's establishing an effective working relationship with each of the conflicting parties so that they will trust the third party, communicate freely with her, and be responsive to her suggestions regarding an orderly process for negotiations. The *second* are those related to establishing a cooperative problem-solving attitude among the conflicting parties toward their conflict. Much of the earlier discussion of my theoretical work on conflict resolution focuses on this area. *Third* are the skills involved in developing a creative group process and group decision making. Such a process clarifies the nature of the problems that the conflicting parties are confronting (reframing their conflicting positions into a joint problem to be solved), helps to expand the range of alternatives that are perceived to be available, facilitates realistic assessment of their feasibility as well as desirability, and facilitates the implementation of agreed-upon solutions. And, *fourth*, it is often helpful for the third party to have considerable substantive knowledge about the issues around which the conflict centers. Substantive knowledge could enable the mediator to see possible solutions that might not occur to the conflicting parties and it would permit her to help them assess proposed solutions more realistically.

It seems reasonable to assume that the diverse situations facing mediators will emphasize one or another of the four skills just described. When the conflicting parties have suspicions about mediation, the skills involved in establishing a good working relationship with the conflicting parties are especially important; when the relationship between the conflicting parties is a poor one, the skills involved in establishing a cooperative problem-solving attitude between the parties is crucial; when the conflicting parties have inadequate techniques for solving problems and making effective joint decisions, then the mediator needs skills related to facilitating creative group decision making; and when the conflicting parties have little knowledge of the substantive issues they are describing, the knowledgeable mediator can be a very helpful resource person on such issues.

It seems reasonable to assume that mediators will differ in the kinds of skills they have mastered and, thus, one can expect that the effectiveness of mediation will be considerably dependent upon how well matched the mediator's skills are with the needs of the case being mediated. There are undoubtedly some "universally competent" mediators who can be successful across a wide variety of cases, but it is safe to say that they are probably rare. Research has indicated that mediators differ in their styles and skills and also in their effectiveness in particular settings. However, not enough research has been done to make definitive statements about the conditions under which different styles and approaches to mediation are most effective.

Kressel (2000) classifies mediator style into two major types, each of which has two subtypes: *task-oriented* and *social–emotional*. The first subtype of the task-oriented style is the *settlement-oriented* mediator who is primarily interested in reaching agreements on any terms acceptable to the conflicting parties. By contrast, the *problem-solving* subtype attaches greater importance to sound problem solving than to settlement per se. Both subtypes, Kressel indicates, are able to resolve low-level conflicts, but the problem-solving style is more effective in providing durable settlements when there is a high conflict.

Mediators with social–emotional styles focus less on the issues and more on opening lines of communication and clarifying underlying feelings and emotions, with the view that once this is accomplished, the conflicting parties should and will be able to work through the issues to their own solution.

Transformational mediation (elaborated by Bush & Folger, 1994; Folger & Bush, 1996) is considered to be a social–emotional subtype. It focuses not only on the relationship between the conflicting parties through emphasizing *recognition* (which refers to improving the capacity of the disputants to become responsive to the needs and perspectives of the other), but also on *empowerment* (which refers to strengthening each party's ability to analyze its respective needs in the conflict and to make effective decisions). The optimistic hope of the advocates of transformative mediation is that the conflicting parties who are subjected to such mediation will be personally transformed whether or not they are able to reach a settlement. Its advocates are critical of settlement or problem-solving orientations to mediation. They believe that such orientations narrow the parties' opportunity to become self-reflective and autonomous as well as aware of the other's separate reflective and distinctive reality.[2]

As Kressel states (2000, p. 536): "Polemical claims not withstanding, there is no empirical evidence for preferring one mediation style over another." And, I add, it seems likely that

---

[2] See Robert Kegan (1994) for his theory of development of different orders of consciousness which suggests that the transformation that Bush and Folger seek is a desirable movement from the third stage of development where one is socially determined by one's loyalties, group membership, and cultural assumptions, to a fourth stage of development where one is self-knowledgeable, self-reflecting, and self-determining in relation to others and is able to recognize this potential in others. Kegan's research indicates that such a transformation is often difficult and slow to achieve.

the different mediation styles are apt to be differently suitable for different types of issues, parties, circumstances, and social contexts.

To sum up, research on mediation is in its early stages. The research has already demonstrated a high level of user satisfaction in a number of different contexts and it has also suggested that the robustness of agreements and the economy of the process are greater than in traditional methods. But there is as yet insufficient understanding of how to mediate difficult conflicts in adverse circumstances or how to make the most effective match between mediator characteristics and the characteristics of the case to be mediated.

How Can People Be Educated to Manage their Conflicts More Constructively?

During the past two decades, there has been a rapid proliferation of training in conflict resolution—for industry, for government, for families, and for schools—and the publication of many textbooks and how-to-do-it manuals in this area. Unfortunately, there has been very little research to assess the effectiveness and consequences of such training. Most of the existing research has been immediate "consumer satisfaction" studies in which the participants in the training program evaluate their training and indicate how useful the training has been for them. The good news is that these studies indicate a high level of immediate consumer satisfaction; the bad news is that there have been only a few studies which have examined the more enduring consequences of such training. "More enduring" in these instances refers to effects that last for six months or a year (see Bodine & Crawford, 1998; Deutsch & Coleman, 2000, Chapter 27; Johnson & Johnson, 2000, and Jones & Kmitter, 2000, for reviews of the existing research).

There are many different conflict resolution programs which vary as a function of the age, occupation, and types of conflicts on which they focus. I have examined many of them and believe that there are some common elements running through them. These common elements, I believe, derive from the recognition that a constructive process of conflict resolution is similar to an effective, cooperative problem-solving process (where the conflict is perceived as the mutual problem to be solved), while a destructive process is similar to a win–lose, competitive struggle (Deutsch, 1973). In effect, most conflict resolution training programs seek to instill the attitudes, knowledge, and skills which are conducive to effective, cooperative problem solving and to discourage the attitudes and habitual responses which give rise to win–lose struggles. Below I list the central elements which are included in many training programs, but I do not have the space to describe the ingenious techniques that are employed in teaching them. The sequence in which they are taught varies as a function of the nature of the group being taught. Below, I describe what my students have labeled as "Deutsch's Twelve Commandments of Conflict Resolution."

1. *Know what type of conflict you are involved in.* There are three major types: the zero-sum conflict (a pure win–lose conflict), the mixed-motive (both can win, both can lose, one can win and the other can lose), and the pure cooperative (both can win or both can lose). It is important to know what kind of conflict you are in because the different types require different types of strategies and tactics. The common tendency is for inexperienced parties to define their conflict as "win–lose" even though it is a mixed-motive conflict.

In a zero-sum conflict one seeks to amass, mobilize, and utilize the various resources of power in such a way that one can bring to bear in the conflict more effective, relevant power than one's adversary; or if this is not possible in the initial area of conflict, one seeks to transform the arena of conflict into one in which one's effective power is greater than one's adversary. Thus, if a bully challenges you to a fight because you will not "lend" him money and he is stronger than you, you might arrange to change the conflict from a physical to a legal confrontation by involving the police or other legal authority. Other strategies and tactics in win–lose conflicts involve outwitting, misleading, seducing, blackmailing, and the various forms of the black arts which have been discussed by Machiavelli, Potter, Schelling, and Alinsky, among others. The strategy and tactics of the resolution of cooperative conflicts involve primarily cooperative fact-finding and research as well as rational persuasion. The strategy and tactics involved in mixed-motive conflicts are mainly what are discussed below.

2. *Become aware of the causes and consequences of violence and of the alternatives to violence, even when one is very angry.* Become aware of what makes you very angry; learn the healthy and unhealthy ways you have of expressing anger. Learn how to actively channel your anger in ways that are not violent and are not likely to provoke violence from the other. Understand that violence begets violence and that if you "win" an argument by violence, the other will try to get even in some other way. Learn alternatives to violence in dealing with conflict.

3. *Face conflict rather than avoid it.* Recognize that conflict may make you anxious and that you may try to avoid it. Learn the typical defenses you employ to evade conflict, e.g. denial, suppression, becoming overly agreeable, rationalization, postponement, premature conflict resolution. Become aware of the negative consequences of evading a conflict—irritability, tension, persistence of the problem, etc. Learn what kinds of conflicts are best avoided rather than confronted, e.g. conflicts that will evaporate shortly, those that are inherently unresolvable, win–lose conflicts which you are unlikely to win.

4. *Respect yourself and your interests, respect the other and his or her interests.* Personal insecurity and the sense of vulnerability often lead people to define conflicts as "life and death," win–lose struggles even when they are relatively minor, mixed-motive conflicts, and this definition may lead to "conflict avoidance," "premature conflict resolution," or "obsessive involvement in the conflict." Helping people to develop a respect for themselves and their interests enables them to see their conflicts in reasonable proportion and facilitates their constructive confrontation. Helping people to learn to respect the other and the other's interests inhibits the use of competitive tactics of power, coercion, deprecation, and deception which commonly escalate the issues in conflict and often lead to violence.

5. *Distinguish clearly between "interests" and "positions."* Positions may be opposed but interests may not be. Often when conflicting parties reveal the interests underlying their positions, it is possible to find a solution which suits them both.

6. *Explore your interests and the other's interests to identify the common and compatible interests that you both share.* Identifying shared interests makes it easier to deal constructively with the interests that you perceive as being opposed. A full exploration of one another's interests increases empathy and facilitates subsequent problem solving.

7. *Define the conflicting interests between oneself and the other as a mutual problem to be solved cooperatively.* Define the conflict in the smallest terms possible, as a "here-now-this" conflict rather than as a conflict between personalities or general principles, e.g. as a conflict about a specific behavior rather than about who is a better person. Diagnose the problem clearly and then creatively seek new options for dealing with the conflict that lead to mutual gain. If no option for mutual gain can be discovered, seek to agree upon a fair rule or procedure for deciding how the conflict will be resolved.

8. *In communicating with the other, listen attentively and speak so as to be understood: this requires the active attempt to take the perspective of the other and to check continually one's success in doing so.* One should listen to the other's meaning and emotion in such a way that the other *feels* understood as well as is understood. Similarly, you want to communicate to the other one's thoughts and feelings in such a way that you have good evidence that he or she understands the way you think and feel. The feeling of being understood, as well as effective communication, enormously facilitates constructive resolution.

Skills in taking the perspective of others and in obtaining feedback about the effectiveness of one's communications are important. Role reversal seems to be helpful in developing an understanding of the perspective of the other and in providing checks on how effective the communication process has been.

9. *Be alert to the natural tendencies to bias, misperceptions, misjudgments, and stereotyped thinking that commonly occur in oneself as well as the other during heated conflict.* These errors in perception and thought interfere with communication, make empathy difficult, and impair problem solving. Psychologists can provide a checklist of the common forms of misperception and misjudgment occurring during intense conflict. These include black–white thinking, demonizing the other, shortening of one's time perspective, narrowing of one's range of perceived options, and the fundamental attribution error. The fundamental attribution error is illustrated in the tendency to attribute the aggressive actions of the other to the other's personality while attributing one's own aggressive actions to external circumstances (such as the other's hostile actions). The ability to recognize and admit one's misperceptions and misjudgments clears the air and facilitates similar acknowledgment by the other.

10. *Develop skills for dealing with difficult conflicts so that one is not helpless nor hopeless when confronting those who are more powerful, those who do not want to engage in constructive conflict resolution, or those who use dirty tricks.* It is important to recognize that one becomes less vulnerable to intimidation by a more powerful other, to someone who refuses to cooperate except on his or her terms, or to someone who plays dirty tricks (deceives, welches on an agreement, personally attacks you, etc.) if you realize that you usually have a choice: you do not have to stay in the relationship with the other. The alternative may not be great but it may be better than staying in the relationship. The freedom to choose prevents the other, if he or she benefits from the relationship, from making the relationship unacceptable to you. Second, it is useful to be open and explicit to the other about what he or she is doing that is upsetting you and to indicate the effects that these actions are having on you. Third, it is wise to avoid reciprocating the other's noxious behavior and to avoid attacking the other personally for his behavior (i.e. criticize the behavior and not the person); doing so often leads to an escalating vicious spiral.

A phrase that I have found useful in characterizing the stance one should take in difficult (as well as easy) conflicts is to be "firm, fair, and friendly." *Firm* in resisting intimidation, exploitation, and dirty tricks; *fair* in holding to one's moral principles and not reciprocating the other's immoral behavior despite his or her provocations; and *friendly* in the sense that one is willing to initiate and reciprocate cooperation.

11. *Know oneself and how one typically responds in different sorts of conflict situations.* As I have suggested earlier, conflict frequently evokes anxiety. In clinical work, I have found that the anxiety is often based upon unconscious fantasies of being overwhelmed and helpless in the face of the other's aggression or of being so angry and aggressive oneself that one will destroy the other. Different people deal with their anxieties about conflict

in different ways. I have found it useful to emphasize six different dimensions of dealing with conflict which can be used to characterize a person's predispositions to respond to conflict. Being aware of one's predispositions may allow one to modify them when they are inappropriate in a given conflict.

(a) *Conflict avoidance–excessive involvement in conflict.* Conflict avoidance is expressed in denial, repression, suppression, avoidance, and continuing postponement of facing the conflict. Excessive involvement in conflict is sometimes expressed in a preoccupation with conflict, a chip on one's shoulder, a tendency to seek out conflict to demonstrate that one is not afraid of conflict.

(b) *Hard–soft.* Some people are prone to take a tough, aggressive, dominating, unyielding response to conflict, fearing that otherwise they will be taken advantage of and be considered soft. Others are afraid that they will be considered to be mean, hostile, or presumptuous, and as a consequence, they are excessively gentle and unassertive. They often expect the other to "read their minds" and know what they want even though they are not open in expressing their interests.

(c) *Rigid–loose.* Some people immediately seek to organize and to control the situation by setting the agenda, defining the rules, etc. They feel anxious if things threaten to get out of control and feel threatened by the unexpected. As a consequence, they are apt to push for rigid arrangements and rules and get upset by even minor deviations. At the other extreme, there are some people who are aversive to anything that seems formal, limiting, controlling, or constricting.

(d) *Intellectual–emotional.* At one extreme, emotion is repressed, controlled, or isolated so that no relevant emotion is felt or expressed as one communicates one's thoughts. The lack of appropriate emotional expressiveness may seriously impair communication: the other may take your lack of emotion as an indicator that you have no real commitment to your interests and that you lack genuine concern for the other's interests. At the other extreme, there are some people who believe that only feelings are real and that words and ideas are not to be taken seriously unless they are thoroughly soaked in emotion. Their emotional extravagance impairs the ability to mutually explore ideas and to develop creative solutions to impasses; it also makes it difficult to differentiate the significant from the insignificant, if even the trivial is accompanied with intense emotion.

(e) *Escalating versus minimizing.* At one extreme, there are some people who tend to experience any given conflict in the largest possible terms. The issues are cast so that what is at stake involves one's self, one's family, one's ethnic group, precedence for all time, or the like. The specifics of the conflict get lost as it escalates along the various dimensions of conflict: the size and number of the immediate issues involved; the number of motives and participants implicated on each side of the issue; the size and number of the principles and precedents that are perceived to be at stake; the cost that the participants are willing to bear in relation to the conflict; the number of norms of moral conduct from which behavior toward the other side is exempted; and the intensity of negative attitudes toward the other side. Escalation of the conflict makes the conflict more difficult to resolve constructively except when the escalation proceeds so rapidly that its absurdity even becomes self-apparent. At the other extreme, there are people who tend to minimize their conflicts. They are similar to the conflict avoiders but, unlike the avoiders, they do recognize the existence of the conflict. However, by minimizing the seriousness of the differences between self and other, by not recognizing how important the matter is to self and to other, one can produce serious misunderstandings. One may also restrict the effort and work that one may need to devote to the conflict in order to resolve it constructively.

(f) *Compulsively revealing versus compulsively concealing.* At one extreme there are people who feel a compulsion to reveal whatever they think and feel about the other and their suspicions, hostilities, and fears—in the most blunt, unrationalized, and unmodulated manner. Or they may feel they have to communicate every doubt, sense of inadequacy, or weakness they have about themselves. At the other extreme, there are people who feel that they cannot reveal any of their feelings or thoughts without seriously damaging their relationship to the other. Either extreme can impair the development of a constructive relationship. One, in effect, should be open and honest in communication but, appropriately so, taking into account realistically the consequences of what one says or does not say and the current state of the relationship.

12. *Finally, throughout conflict, one should remain a moral person, i.e. a person who is caring and just, and should consider the other as a member of one's moral community, i.e. as someone who is entitled to care and justice.* In the heat of conflict, there is often the tendency to shrink one's moral community and to exclude the other from it: this permits behavior toward the other which one would otherwise consider morally reprehensible. Such behavior escalates conflict and turns it in the direction of violence and destruction.

How and When to Intervene in Protracted, Intractable Conflicts?

Coleman (2000, p. 429) has characterized an intractable conflict as "one that is recalcitrant, intense, deadlocked, and extremely difficult to resolve." Such conflicts persist over time, they usually escalate (Fisher, 2000), and tend to take on a life of their own. I have termed the social process involved in such conflicts, a malignant social process (Deutsch, 1983).

Perfectly sane and intelligent people, groups, and nations—once caught up in such a malignant process—enmesh themselves in a web of interactions and aggressive–defensive maneuvers which instead of improving their situation, make both sides feel less secure and more burdened. They trap themselves in a vicious process that leads to outcomes of mutual loss and harm. In such a social process both sides come to be right in believing that the other side is hostile, malevolent, and intent on inflicting harm. Their interactions provide ample justification for such beliefs. Typically, in such a conflict, the participants see no way of extricating themselves without becoming vulnerable to an unacceptable loss in a value central to their self-identities, self-esteems, or security.

A number of key elements contribute to the development and perpetuation of such a process. They include:

1. *An anarchic social situation*, which provides no basis for mutual trust, in which an attempt by one party to increase its own security or welfare—without regard to the security or welfare of others—is experienced as a threat by the others.
2. *A win–lose or competitive orientation* to the conflict.
3. *Inner conflict* within each of the parties, that are displaced, suppressed, or channeled into the external conflict.
4. *Cognitive rigidity*, which limits the ability to search out or create mutually satisfactory agreements.
5. *Misjudgments and misperceptions* which enhance negativity toward the other and toward possible solutions.

6. *The development and investment* in the skills, attitudes, and institutions involved in waging and perpetuating the conflict.
7. *Self-fulfilling prophecies*, in which one's hostile behavior toward the other elicits a negative response from the other which confirms one's negative view of the other.
8. *Vicious escalating spirals*, which often result from the biased tendency of each side to see their own aggressive–defensive behaviors as justified and the other side's as unjustified.
9. *A gamesmanship orientation* which turns the conflict away from issues of what in real life is being won or lost to an abstract conflict over images of power.

In the social science literature, there has been extended discussion of the question of when an intractable conflict is "ripe" for resolution. Zartman (Touval & Zartman, 1985; Zartman & Berman, 1982; Zartman, 1985), Pruitt and Olzack (1995), and Coleman (1997) have provided important discussions of the concept of ripeness and how it can be fostered. Zartman's (2000, pp. 228–229) definition of the concept is widely used: "If the (two) parties to a conflict (a) perceive themselves to be in a hurting stalemate and (b) perceive the possibility of a negotiated solution (a way out), the conflict is ripe for resolution (i.e., for negotiations toward resolution to begin)." However, as Zartman himself points out; increased pain may, under certain conditions, strengthen the determination to achieve one's objectives. Or to paraphrase one of Festinger's (1957, 1961) quotes illustrating his theory of cognitive dissonance, rats and men come to love and be committed to the things (and to the principles) for which they have suffered.

I shall not summarize here the valuable discussion of Zartman, Pruitt and Olzack, and Coleman (referred to above) about the conditions which foster ripeness. Here, I wish to consider the therapeutic principles involved in helping a married couple who were involved in a bitter stalemate conflict over issues which they considered nonnegotiable to negotiate these issues constructively (Deutsch, 1988). The couple, who were in a "mutually hurting stalemate," sought help for several reasons. On the one hand, their conflicts were becoming physically violent: this frightened them and it also ran counter to their strong constraints making it difficult for them to separate. They felt they would be considerably worse off economically, their child would suffer, and they had mutually congenial intellectual, esthetic, sexual, and recreational interests which would be difficult for them to engage in together if separated.

Let me briefly discuss the steps involved in getting the couple to the point where they were ready to negotiate. There were two major interrelated steps, each of which involved many substeps. The first entailed helping each spouse to recognize that the present situation of a bitter, stalemated conflict no longer served his or her real interests. The second step involved aiding the couple to become aware of the possibility that each of them could be better off than they currently were if they recognized their conflict as a joint problem, which required creative, joint effort in order to improve their individual situations. The two steps do not follow one another in neat order: progress in either step facilitates progress in the other.

It should be recognized that, in many instances, the external conflicts between two parties may be generated or sustained by internal conflicts within each party, e.g. as a way of blaming the other for one's own inadequacies, difficulties, and problems so that one can avoid confronting the necessity of changing oneself. Thus, in the couple I treated, the wife perceived herself to be a victim, and felt that her failure to achieve her professional goals was due to her husband's unfair treatment of her as exemplified by his unwillingness to share responsibilities for the household and child care. Blaming her husband provided her with a means of avoiding her own apprehensions about whether she personally had the abilities and courage to fulfill her aspirations. Similarly, the husband who provoked continuous criticism from his wife for his domineering, imperial behavior employed her criticism to justify his emotional withdrawal, thus enabling him to avoid dealing with his anxieties about personal intimacy and emotional closeness. Even though the wife's accusations concerning her husband's behavior were largely correct, as were the husband's toward her, each had an investment in maintaining the other's noxious behavior because of the defensive self-justifications such behavior provided.

How does a therapist help the conflicting parties overcome such internal deterrents to recognizing that their bitter, stalemated conflict no longer serves their real interests? The general answer, which is quite often difficult to implement in practice, is to help each of the conflicting parties change in such a way that the conflict no longer is maintained by conditions in the parties that are extrinsic to the conflict. In essence, this entails helping each of the conflicting parties to achieve the self-esteem and self-image that would make them no longer need the destructive conflict process as a defense against their sense of personal inadequacy, their fear of taking on new and unfamiliar roles, their feeling of purposelessness and boredom, and their fears of rejection and attack if they act independently of others.

What are the conditions that are likely to help conflicting parties become aware of the possibility that each of them could be better off than they currently are if they recognize that their conflict is a joint problem that requires creative, joint efforts in order to improve the individual situations? A number of such conditions are listed below:

1. Critical to this awareness is the recognition that one cannot impose a solution which may be acceptable or satisfactory to oneself upon the other. In other words, there is recognition that a satisfactory solution for oneself requires the other's agreement, and this is unlikely unless the other is also satisfied with the solution. Such recognition implies an awareness that a mutually acceptable agreement will require at least a minimal degree of cooperation.
2. To believe that the other is ready to engage in a joint problem-solving effort, one must believe that the other has also recognized that he or she cannot impose a solution—that is, the other has also recognized that a solution has to be mutually acceptable.
3. The conflicting parties must have some hope that a mutually acceptable agreement can be found. This hope may rest upon their own perception of the outlines of a possible fair settlement or it may be based on their confidence in the expertise of third parties, or even on a generalized optimism.
4. The conflicting parties must have confidence that if a mutually acceptable agreement is concluded, both will abide by it or that violations will be detected before the losses to the self and the gains to the other become intolerable. If the other is viewed as unstable, lacking self-control, or untrustworthy, it will be difficult to have confidence in the viability of an agreement unless one has confidence in third parties who are willing and able to guarantee the integrity of the agreement.

Issues that seem vitally important to a person, such as one's identity, security, self-esteem, or reputation, often are experienced as nonnegotiable. Thus, consider the husband and wife who viewed themselves in a conflict over a nonnegotiable issue. The wife who worked (and wanted to do so) wanted the husband to share equally in the household and child-care responsibilities: she considered equality between the genders to be one of her core personal values. The husband wanted a traditional marriage with a traditional division of responsibilities, in which he would have primary responsibility for income-producing work outside the home while his wife would have primary responsibility for the work related to the household and child care. The husband considered household work and child care as inconsistent with his deeply rooted image of adult masculinity. The conflict seemed nonnegotiable to the couple—for the wife it would be a betrayal of her feminist values to accept her husband's terms; for the husband, it would be a violation of his sense of adult masculinity to become deeply involved in housework or child care.

However, this nonnegotiable conflict became negotiable when, with the help of the therapist, the husband and wife were able to listen and really understand each other's feelings and the ways in which their respective life experiences had led them to the views they each held. Understanding the other's position fully and the feeling and experiences which were behind them made them each feel less hurt and humiliated by the other's position and more ready to seek solutions that would accommodate the interests of both. They realized that with their joint incomes they could afford to pay for household and child-care help, which would enable the wife to be considerably less burdened by these responsibilities without increasing the husband's chores in these areas: of course, doing so lessened the amount of money they had available for other purposes.

This solution was not a perfect one for either party. The wife and husband each would have preferred that the other share their own view of what a marriage should be like. However, their deeper understanding of the other's position made them feel less humiliated and threatened by it and less defensive toward the other. It also enabled them to negotiate a mutually acceptable agreement that lessened the tensions between them despite their continuing differences in basic perspectives.

The general conclusions that I draw from this and other experiences with a "nonnegotiable" issue is that most such issues are negotiable even though the underlying basic differences between the conflicting parties are not resolved when they learn to listen, understand, and empathize with the other party's position, interests, and feelings, providing they are also able to communicate to the other their understanding and empathy. Even though understanding and empathy do not imply agreement with the other's views, they indicate an openness and responsiveness which reduce hostility and defensiveness and which also allow the other to be more open and responsive. Such understanding and empathy help the conflicting parties to reduce their feelings that their self-esteem, security, or identity will be threatened and endangered by recognizing that the other's feelings and interests, as well as one's own, deserve consideration in dealing with the issues in conflict.

The positions of the conflicting parties may be irreconcilable, but their interests may be concordant. Helping parties in conflict to be fully in touch with their long-term interests may enable them to see beyond their nonnegotiable positions to their congruent interests. An atmosphere of mutual understanding and empathy fosters the conditions that permit conflicting parties to get beyond their initial rigid, nonnegotiable position to their underlying interests (for a comprehensive discussion of various methods of "interactive conflict resolution" that have been employed in intractable intergroup conflicts, see Fisher, 1997).

How Are we to Understand Why Ethnic, Religious, and Identity Conflicts Frequently Take an Intractable, Destructive Course?

It is not uncommon for scholars concerned with intergroup or interethnic relations to assume, implicitly, that all or most intergroup relations are characterized by destructive conflict. However, as Ronald Fisher (2000, p. 166) points out: "In most ongoing intergroup relations in countless settings, cooperative relations exist and conflict is handled more or less constructively, to the satisfaction of the parties involved." Similarly, Gurr (1993, pp. 290–291), in his global survey of ethnopolitical conflicts, writes:

> Some observers have concluded that ethnopolitical conflicts are intractable. The evidence suggests otherwise.... Our images of intractable communal conflicts are largely shaped by ethnonationalist wars in the Middle East, Asia, and Africa. Yet for each example of protracted communal conflict in these regions, one can point to neighboring states where similar conflicts have been managed more effectively.... In central and West Africa more than a dozen states straddle the cultural and religious divide between the Muslim, Arab-influenced peoples of the savannah and the Christian, European-influenced peoples of the forest and coastal regions. Only in Sudan and Chad have protracted civil wars been fought across this divide.

In light of the foregoing, the question above should be reformulated into several questions:

1. What are the factors which lead to a constructive rather than a destructive resolution of communal or ethnic conflict?
2. Is there anything distinctive about ethnic conflict which may predispose it to a destructive resolution?
3. If such a conflict takes a destructive course, how can reconciliation be fostered after each side has inflicted indignities and grievous harm on the other?

Gurr (1993), in his global study of ehtnopolitical conflicts, provides research on 233 ethnic groups involved in communal conflicts of one sort or another which bears upon (1) above. He concludes (p. 213):

> there are two keys to the constructive management of ethnopolitical conflict. One is to search out politically and socially creative policies that bridge the gaps between the interests of minorities and states. All parties, including outside observers, can contribute to this process. The second is to begin the process of creative conflict management in the early stages of open conflict.... States and their leaders... should be able to respond creatively to political mobilization and protest by communal groups before the groups cross the threshold of sustained violence.

Gurr (1993, p. 313) discusses four types of state policies that are used to accommodate the interests of ethnopolitical minorities: regional autonomy, assimilation, pluralism, and power sharing:

> The conclusion for states is one of caution: public efforts to manage ethnopolitical conflicts have risks as well as potential gains. If policies of accommodation are to be effective they must be pursued cautiously but persistently over the long term, slowly enough not to stimulate a crippling reaction from other groups, persistently enough so that minorities do not defect or rebel. The conclusion for communal groups is that persistence in the nonviolent pursuit of group interests is a strategic virtue, and so is a willingness to compromise about the specifics of accommodation.... Violent means in the pursuit of communal interests usually are politically more effective as threats than in actuality.

The answer to the second question (what is distinctive about ethnic conflicts which may predispose them to a destructive resolution?) lies in *the importance of one's membership in an ethnic group to one's self-identity* (see Tajfel, 1978, 1981, and Turner, 1987, who have developed "Social Identity Theory" which articulates in detail the links among group membership, social identity, and self-concept). Among the strongest membership bonds are those arising out of certain ascribed statuses such as family, sex, racial, and national group membership, all of which one acquires by birth rather than by choice. Such statuses can rarely be changed. It is the combination of their unalterability and their social significance that gives these ascribed statuses their personal importance. One's handedness, left or right, may be as difficult to alter as one's race, but it is by no means as socially significant. Membership in a family, racial, sexual, ethnic, or national group affects one's thoughts and actions in many situations; these effects are pervasive. In addition, by common definition, membership in such groups typically excludes membership in other groups of a similar type. That is, if you are black, you are not also white; if you are male, you are not also female; if you are Jewish, you are not also Christian. Thus being a member is thought to be more or less distinctive, and since membership is linked to experiences from early on in one's life, it is not unusual for one to get emotionally attached to such groups, with the result that these memberships play an important positive role in determining one's sense of identity.

Suppose that one is emotionally attached to one's identity as a Jew, woman, or black, but that it results in systematic oppression and discrimination and places one at a distinct disadvantage in obtaining many kinds of opportunities and rewards. How one copes with this situation will be largely determined by whether one views the disadvantages to be just or unjust. If those who are disadvantaged by their group identity accept their disadvantages as being warranted, they are unlikely to challenge and conflict with those who are profiting from their relatively advantaged positions. The sense of being treated unjustly because of one's membership in a group to which one is strongly attached and bound is the energizer for much intergroup conflict. The sense of injustice is felt particularly intensely in interracial, interethnic, and intersex conflicts because of the centrality of these group identities to the individual's self-esteem. When women or blacks or Jews are devalued as a group, those who are identified and identify with the groups also are personally devalued.

There is considerable evidence from the anthropological literature (see LeVine & Campbell, 1972, for a summary and references) that the pyramidal–segmentary social structure is more conducive to destructive intergroup strife within a society than the cross-cutting type. The reason for this is easy to see. If, for example, in a society which has a pyramidal–segmentary social structure a conflict arises between two ethnic groups in the society (e.g. about which group's language shall be paramount in the total society), then the individual's membership in all the groups that are nested within his ethnic group (his neighborhood, his recreation group, his kinship group, etc.) will strengthen his loyalty to his ethnic group's position. But this will happen on both sides, making it more difficult to resolve the differences between the two groups. On the other hand, in a cross-cutting social structure, members of the conflicting ethnic groups are likely to be members of common work groups, common neighborhood groups, and so on. Their common membership will make it difficult to polarize individual attitudes about the ethnic conflict. Doing so would place the individual in the dilemma of choosing between loyalty to his ethnic group and loyalty to his other groups that cut across ethnic lines. Thus cross-cutting membership and loyalties tend to function as a moderating influence in resolving any particular intergroup conflict within a society. However, if the ethnic conflict becomes sufficiently intense even cross-cutting ties may be torn, resulting in an even greater bitterness and violence as one experiences a sense of betrayal of trust.[3]

---

[3] There are excellent discussions of relevant theory and of specific ethnic and other intergroup conflicts in Staub (1989), Gurr (1993), Ross and Rothman (1999), and Christie, Wagner, and Winter (2001). For a recent, excellent symposium on the concept of "Social Identity," see *Political Psychology, 22*(1), 2001, 111–198.

The third question, which focuses on how to achieve forgiveness and reconciliation after bitter conflict, has been of increasing interest to students of conflict. There have been outstanding discussions in Lederach (1997), Shriver (1995), Minow (1998), and in various chapters in Christie, Wagner, and Winter (2001). I have also discussed these matters in Deutsch and Coleman (2000, Chapter 2).

Wessels and Monteiro (2001, p. 263) have articulated very well the scope of the task and challenges involved in reconstruction of civil society after bitter, destructive, dehumanizing ethnic conflict. It involves interrelated tasks of economic, political, and social reconstruction as well as psychosocial intervention. As they point out, "In all of these tasks, a high priority is the establishment of *social justice*, transforming patterns of exclusion, inequity, and oppression that fuel tension and fighting."

In my discussion of reconciliation (Deutsch & Coleman, 2000, pp. 58–62), I have articulated some basic principles for establishing cooperative relations after a bitter conflict. They are:

1. *Mutual security.* After a bitter conflict, each side tends to be concerned with its own security, without adequate recognition that neither side can attain security unless the other side also feels secure. Real security requires that both sides have as their goal *mutual* security. If weapons have been involved in the prior conflict, mutually verifiable disarmament and arms control are important components of mutual security.

2. *Mutual respect.* Just as true security from physical danger requires mutual cooperation, so does security from psychological harm and humiliation. Each side must treat the other side with the respect, courtesy, politeness, and consideration normatively expected in civil society. Insult, humiliation, and inconsiderateness by one side usually leads to reciprocation by the other and decreased physical and psychological security.

3. *Humanization of the other.* During bitter conflict, each side tends to dehumanize the other and develop images of the other as an evil enemy. There is much need for both sides to experience one another in everyday contexts as parents, homemakers, schoolchildren, teachers, and merchants, which enables them to see one another as human beings who are more like themselves than not. Problem-solving workshops, along the lines developed by Burton (1969, 1987) and Kelman (1972), are also valuable in overcoming dehumanization of one another.

4. *Fair rules for managing conflict.* Even if a tentative reconciliation has begun, new conflicts inevitably occur—over the distribution of scarce resources, procedures, values, etc. It is important to anticipate that conflicts will occur and to develop beforehand the fair rules, experts, institutions, and other resources for managing such conflicts constructively and justly.

5. *Curbing the extremists on both sides.* During a protracted and bitter conflict, each side tends to produce extremists committed to the processes of the destructive conflict as well as to its continuation. Attaining some of their initial goals may be less satisfying than continuing to inflict damage on the other. It is well to recognize that extremists stimulate extremism on both sides. The parties need to cooperate in curbing extremism on their own side and restraining actions that stimulate and justify extremist elements on the other side.

6. *Gradual development of mutual trust and cooperation.* It takes repeated experience of successful, varied, mutually beneficial cooperation to develop a solid basis for mutual trust between former enemies. In the early stages of reconciliation, when trust is required for cooperation, the former enemies may be willing to trust a third party (who agrees to serve as a monitor, inspector, or guarantor of any cooperative arrangement) but not yet willing

to trust one another if there is a risk of the other failing to reciprocate cooperation. Also in the early stages, it is especially important that cooperative endeavors be successful. This requires careful selection of the opportunities and tasks for cooperation so that they are clearly achievable as well as meaningful and significant.

How Applicable in Other Cultures Are the Theories Related to Conflict that Have Largely Been Developed in the United States and Western Europe?

I believe there is considerable confusion about this question. It would be presumptuous indeed to think that there exists, at this stage of the development of the field of conflict resolution, a theory which is universally valid across the various cultures, across historic time, and across different types of social actors (individuals, groups, organizations, and nations). There are some of us who hope such theory can ultimately be developed and some of us are even brash enough to think that some of the existing theoretical ideas (e.g. about cooperation–competition) may have considerable generality. However, even if we had a universally valid *theory* at the level of constructs, the operational definition of constructs (i.e. how they are defined empirically or in terms of phenomena) would inevitably differ in different cultures and even, within a given culture, from situation to situation. In Lewinian terminology, constructs are like *genotypes*, and the observational data are similar to *phenotypes*. A given genotype can be expressed in many different types of phenotypes (e.g. the color of two genotypically identical hydrangeas will differ as a function of the acidity of the soil in which they are planted). Similarly, a given construct, such as aggression, can be manifested in many ways depending on the culture and other characteristics of the specific situation in which the parties are involved.

Thus, whether or not we had a universally valid theory (which we don't),[4] we would still need to have detailed, specific knowledge of the culture in which we are employing whatever theoretical ideas or framework we use to orient ourselves to conflict and to cultural differences. A self-reflective practitioner will seek to be aware of his/her own framework and be open to its change in light of challenging, new experiences. S/he will also be sensitive to his/her own cultural assumptions about the power relations between him/herself and the people with whom s/he is working and their appropriateness in the culture within which s/he is working. In addition, s/he will be aware of his/her need to develop knowledge about the culture and background of the people with whom s/he is working by using existing knowledge, informants, coworkers from the culture, and by what Lederach (1995) has termed an "elicitive approach" as s/he works with people from a different culture. While the issue of "cultural" differences is obvious when comparing such differences across societies, it should be recognized that there are also "cultural" differences within societies—among the different socioeconomic classes, between the sexes, among occupations, etc. It is a common mistake to assume that cultures are homogeneous.

There are a number of excellent books which discuss specific differences among cultures as they deal with conflict and negotiation. They include Triandis (1972), Hofstede (1980),

---

[4] I believe that a number of psychological theories (e.g. equity theory) implicitly assume a culture that is individualistic and market-oriented. Sampson (1983) has an excellent critique of psychological theories from this perspective. In Deutsch and Coleman (2000, Chapter 1), I describe the values and social norms underlying our practice of conflict resolution.

Kimmel (1989), Hall and Hall (1990), Cohen (1991), Fisher (1998), Faure and Rubin (1993), Ross (1993), Rahim and Blum (1994), and Leung and Tjosvold (1998).

EVALUATION OF PROGRESS IN THE SOCIAL PSYCHOLOGICAL STUDY OF CONFLICT

I now turn to the important question: what progress, if any, has occurred during the past 70 years or so in the social psychological study of conflict? I am a biased observer, but, even taking my bias into account, I am strongly inclined to believe that significant scientific progress has been made and that important contributions to society are being derived from the scientific study of conflict. Let me briefly characterize the nature of the progress in the methodological, conceptual, empirical, and technological domains.

Methodological

There have been major methodological advances during the past 60 years in the study of cooperation–competition, conflict, bargaining, and negotiation. New and better techniques for studying these phenomena in the laboratory and also in the field have emerged.

Conceptual

In the course of this chapter, I have outlined some of the conceptual developments that have taken place in work on cooperation and competition; on understanding the nature and determinants of constructive and destructive processes of conflict resolution; and on understanding some of the determinants and consequences of different systems of distributive justice. We are beginning to have some understanding of the conditions and processes involved in intractable conflict. Some of the psychological issues involved in ethnic conflict have been highlighted by social identity theory. The functions of such third parties as mediators, the determinants of the effectiveness of mediation, and the nature of the processes involved in mediation are being clarified. This represents significant theoretical progress and a more systematic integration of our knowledge of the social psychological aspects of conflict and distributive justice.

Empirical

We know a great deal more, with considerably more certainty, about the empirical regularities associated with conflict. Thus, we know how such psychological processes as "autistic hostility," "self-fulfilling prophecies," "unwitting commitments," and "biased perceptions" operate to produce an escalation of conflict. We know the social psychological correlates of intensifying conflict and of de-escalating conflict. Thus, as conflict escalates there is an increased reliance upon a strategy of power and upon the tactics of threat, coercion, and deception. Also, there is increased pressure for uniformity of opinion and for leadership and control to be taken over by those elements organized for waging conflict. De-escalation of conflict is characterized by graduated reciprocation in tension reduction;

tactics of conciliation; accentuation of similarities; and enhancement of mutual understanding and goodwill. We are increasingly aware of the social psychological regularities associated with benign and malevolent conflict. We are reasonably sure of the typical effects of certain forms of bargaining strategies and tactics and can reliably conclude that many commonsense beliefs about bargaining are much too simple part-truths.

Technological

There have been many significant social consequences of the scientific study of conflict; not all of these can be attributed to the work of social psychologists. Social psychologists have been important contributors to some changes in thinking about conflict at the national level—as exemplified in Kennedy's American University speech and in the Kerner Commission reports. Also, in recent years, many of the ideas generated in the social psychological study of conflict have been employed in training administrators and negotiators, in schools, labor unions, industry, government, and community organizations, how to deal with conflict more effectively. "Conflict," "negotiation skills," and "mediation skills" workshops are now common features of training for work in organizations in the United States, Europe, and Japan. Osgood's (1962) strategy for de-escalating conflict—"graduated and reciprocated initiatives in tension reduction" (GRIT)—has received considerable experimental support, has been widely discussed in international and national meetings, and appears to have been the basis for the "Kennedy experiment" to end the Cold War. Key participants in the round-table negotiations in Poland between the Communist government and Solidarity have told me that our work on conflict resolution was consciously employed to facilitate successful negotiations. Problem-solving workshops, developed by such people as John Burton, Herbert Kelman, Leonard Doob, and Edward Azar, have been widely used in international and intercommunal conflict (Fisher, 1998).

Let me conclude by stating that although there has been significant progress in the study of conflict, the progress does not yet begin to match the social need for understanding conflict. We live in a period of history when the pervasiveness and intensity of competitive conflict over natural resources are likely to increase markedly. And currently ethnic and national conflicts pose a great danger to peace in many areas of the world. We also live in a period when hydrogen bombs and other weapons of mass destruction can destroy civilized life. The social need for better ways of managing conflict is urgent. In relation to this need, it is my view that too few of us are working on the scientific issues which are likely to provide the knowledge that will lead to more constructive conflict resolution of the many intensive conflicts which await us all.

REFERENCES

Adams, J. S. (1963). Toward an understanding of inequity. *Journal of Abnormal and Social Psychology, 67,* 422–436.

Adams, J. S. (1965). Inequity in social exchange. In L. Berkowitz (ed.), *Advances in Experimental Social Psychology* (Vol. 2). New York: Academic.

Adams, J. S. & Freedman, S. (1976). Equity theory revisited: comments and annotated bibliography. In L. Berkowitz & E. Walster (eds), *Advances in Experimental Social Psychology* (Vol. 9). New York: Academic.

Alinsky, S. D. (1971). *Rules for Radicals: A Practical Primer for Realistic Radicals.* New York: Random House.
Banton, M. (1967). *Race Relations.* New York: Basic Books.
Bartos, O. J. (1970). Determinants and consequences of toughness. In P. Swingle (ed.), *The Structure of Conflict.* New York: Academic.
Bazerman, M. H. & Neal, M. A. (1992). *Negotiating Rationally.* New York: Free Press.
Bodine, R. J. & Crawford, D. K. (1998). *The Handbook of Conflict Resolution Education.* San Francisco: Jossey-Bass.
Breslin, J. W. & Rubin, J. Z. (1991). *Negotiation Theory and Practice.* Cambridge, Mass.: Harvard Program in Negotiation.
Burton, J. W. (1969). *Conflict and Communication: The Use of Controlled Communication in International Relations.* London: Macmillan.
Burton, J. W. (1987). *Resolving Deep-rooted Conflict: A Handbook.* Lanham, Md: University Press of America.
Bush, R. A. B. & Folger, J. P. (1994). *The Promise of Mediation: Responding to Conflict through Empowerment and Recognition.* San Francisco: Jossey-Bass.
Cantril, H. (ed.) (1950). *Tensions that Cause Wars.* Urbana: University of Illinois Press.
Chamberlain, N. (1951). *Collective Bargaining.* New York: McGraw-Hill.
Christie, D. J., Wagner, R. V., & Winter, D. D. (eds) (2001). *Peace, Conflict, and Violence: Peace Psychology for the 21st Century.* Upper Saddle River, NJ: Prentice-Hall.
Cohen, R. (1991). *Negotiations across Cultures.* Washington, DC: United States Institute of Peace.
Coleman, P. T. (1997). Redefining ripeness: a social psychological perspective. *Peace and Conflict: Journal of Peace Psychology, 3,* 81–89.
Coleman, P. T. (2000). Intractable conflict. In M. Deutsch & P. T. Coleman (eds), *Handbook of Conflict Resolution: Theory and Practice.* San Francisco: Jossey-Bass.
Cummings, L. L. & Harnett, D. L. (1969). Bargaining behavior in a symmetric bargaining triad. *The Review of Economic Studies, 36,* 485–501.
Deutsch, M. (1949a). A theory of cooperation and competition. *Human Relations, 2,* 129–152.
Deutsch, M. (1949b). An experimental study of the effects of cooperation and competition upon group process. *Human Relations, 2,* 199–232.
Deutsch, M. (1973). *The Resolution of Conflict: Constructive and Destructive Processes.* New Haven: Yale University Press.
Deutsch, M. (1974). Awakening the sense of injustice. In M. Lerner & M. Ross (eds), *The Quest for Justice.* Toronto: Holt, Rinehart & Winston of Canada.
Deutsch, M. (1975). Equity, equality and need: what determines which value will be used as the basis of distributive justice? *The Journal of Social Issues, 31,* 137–150.
Deutsch, M. (1983). Preventing World War III: a psychological perspective. *Political Psychology, 3*(1), 3–31.
Deutsch, M. (1985). *Distributive Justice: A Social-psychological Perspective.* New Haven: Yale University Press.
Deutsch, M. (1988). On negotiating the non-negotiable. In B. Kellerman & J. Rubin (eds), *Leadership and Negotiation in the Middle East.* New York: Praeger.
Deutsch, M. & Coleman, P. T. (2000). *The Handbook of Conflict Resolution: Theory and Practice.* San Francisco: Jossey-Bass.
Deutsch, M. & Krauss, R. M. (1960). The effect of threat upon interpersonal bargaining. *Journal of Abnormal and Social Psychology, 61,* 181–189.
Diesing, P. (1962). *Reason in Society.* Urbana: University of Illinois Press.
Faure, G. I. & Rubin, J. Z. (1993). *Culture and Negotiation.* Newbury Park, Calif.: Sage.
Festinger, L. (1957). *A Theory of Cognitive Dissonance.* Evanston, Ill.: Row, Peterson.
Festinger, L. (1961). The psychological effect of insufficient reward. *American Psychologist, 16,* 1–11.
Fisher, G. (1988). *Mindsets.* Yarmouth, Me: Intercultural Press.
Fisher, R. J. (1997). *Interactive Conflict Resolution.* Syracuse, NY: Syracuse University Press.
Fisher, R. J. (1998). *Interactive Problem Solving.* Syracuse, NY: Syracuse University Press.
Fisher, R. J. (2000). Intergroup conflict. In M. Deutsch & P. T. Coleman (eds), *Handbook of Conflict Resolution: Theory and Practice.* San Francisco: Jossey-Bass.

Folger, J. B. & Bush, R. A. B. (1996). Transformative mediation and third-party intervention. Ten hallmarks of a transformative approach to practice. *Mediation Quarterly, 13*, 263–278.

Gurr, T. R. (1993). *Minorities at Risk: A Global View of Ethnopolitical Conflicts*. Washington, DC: US Institute of Peace Press.

Hall, E. T. & Hall, M. R. (1990). *Understanding Cultural Differences: Germans, French, and Americans*. Yarmouth, Me: Intercultural Press.

Hamner, W. C. & Baird, L. S. (1978). The effect of strategy, pressure to reach agreement and relative power on bargaining behavior. In H. Sauermann (ed.), *Contributions to Experimental Economics* (Vol. 7). Tübingen: Mohr.

Harnett, D. L. & Cummings, L. L. (1968). Bargaining behavior in an asymmetric triad: the role of information, communication, and risk-taking propensity. Mimeographed manuscript, University of Indiana.

Harnett, D. L., Cummings, L. L., & Hughes, C. D. (1968). The influence of risk-taking propensity on bargaining behavior. *Behavioral Science, 13*, 91–101.

Harnett, D. L. & Vincelette, J. P. (1978). Strategic influences on bargaining effectiveness. In H. Sauermann (ed.), *Contributions to Experimental Economics* (Vol. 7). Tübingen: Mohr.

Hofstede, G. (1980). *Culture's Consequences: International Differences in Work-related Value*. Thousand Oaks, Calif.: Sage.

Homans, G. C. (1961). *Social Behavior: Its Elementary Forms*. New York: Harcourt, Brace, Jovanovich.

Homans, G. C. (1974). *Social Behavior: Its Elementary Forms* (rev. edn). New York: Harcourt, Brace, Jovanovich.

Hull, C. L. (1938). The goal-gradient hypothesis applied to some "field-force" problems in the behavior of young children. *Psychological Review, 45*, 271–299.

Hyman, S. E. (1966). *The Tangled Bank*. New York: Grosset and Dunlap, University Library Edition.

Jervis, A. S. (1970). *The Logic of Images in International Relations*. Princeton: Princeton University Press.

Jervis, A. S. (1976). *Perception and Misperception in International Politics*. Princeton: Princeton University Press.

Johnson, D. W. & Johnson, R. T. (1989). *Cooperation and Competition: Theory and Research*. Edina, Minn.: Interaction.

Johnson, D. W. & Johnson, R. T. (2000). Teaching students to be peacemakers: results of twelve years of research. Unpublished paper, University of Minnesota.

Jones, T. S. & Kmitter, D. (eds) (2000). *Does it Work? The Case for Conflict Resolution Education in Our Nation's Schools*. Washington, DC: Conflict Resolution Education Network.

Kahn, N. (1965). *On Escalation: Metaphors and Scenarios*. New York: Praeger.

Kegan, R. (1994). *In over Our Heads: The Mental Demands of Modern Life*. Cambridge, Mass.: Harvard University Press.

Kelley, H. H. & Schenitzki, D. P. (1972). Bargaining. In C. G. McClintock (ed.), *Experimental Social Psychology*. New York: Holt, Rinehart & Winston.

Kelman, H. C. (1972). The problem-solving workshop in conflict resolution. In R. L. Merritt (ed.), *Communication in International Politics*. Urbana, Ill.: University of Illinois Press.

Kimmel, P. R. (1989). *International Negotiation and Intercultural Exploration: Toward Culture Understanding*. Washington, DC: US Institute of Peace Press.

Klineberg, O. (1964). *The Human Dimensions in International Relations*. New York: Holt, Rinehart & Winston.

Kressel, K. (2000). Mediation behavior. In M. Deutsch & P. T. Coleman (eds), *The Handbook of Conflict Resolution: Theory and Practice*. San Francisco: Jossey-Bass.

Kressel, K. & Pruitt, D. (1985). The mediation of social conflict. A special issue of the *Journal of Social Issues, 41*.

Kressel, K. & Pruitt, D. (1989). *Mediation Research*. San Francisco: Jossey-Bass.

Kritter, P. B. (1994). *Negotiating at an Uneven Table*. San Francisco: Jossey-Bass.

Lamm, H. & Kayser, E. (1978a). The allocation of monetary gain and loss following dyadic performance. *European Journal of Social Psychology, 8*, 275–278.

Lamm, H. & Kayser, E. (1978b). An analysis of negotiation concerning the allocation of jointly produced profit or loss. *International Journal of Group Tensions, 8*, 64–80.

Lederach, J. P. (1995). *Preparing for Peace: Conflict Transformation across Cultures*. Syracuse, NY: Syracuse University Press.
Lederach, J. P. (1997). *Building Peace: Sustainable Reconciliation in Divided Societies*. Washington, DC: US Institute of Peace Press.
Lerner, M. J. (1975). The Justice Motive in Social Behavior: Introduction. *Journal of Social Issues, 31*, 1–20.
LeVine, R. A. & Campbell, D. T. (1972). *Ethnocentrism: Theories of Conflict, Ethnic Attitudes, and Goup Behavior*. New York: Wiley.
Leung, H. & Tjosvold, D. (1998). *Conflict Management in the Asia Pacific*. New York: John Wiley & Sons.
Leventhal, G. S. (1976). *Fairness in Social Relationships*. Morristown, NJ: General Learning Press.
Lewicki, R. J. & Litterer, J. A. (1985a). *Negotiation: Readings, Exercises, and Cases*. Homewood, Ill.: Irwin.
Lewicki, R. J. & Litterer, J. A. (1985b). *Negotiation*. Homewood, Ill.: Irwin.
Lewicki, R. J., Saunders, D. M., & Minton, J. W. (1999). *Negotiation* (3rd edn). New York: McGraw-Hill.
Lewin, K. (1931). Environmental forces in child behavior and development. In C. Murchison (ed.), *A Handbook of Child Psychology*. Worcester, Mass.: Clark University Press.
Lewin, K. (1935). *A Dynamic Theory of Personality*. New York: McGraw-Hill.
Lewis, H. B. & Franklin, M. (1944). An experimental study of the role of the ego in work: II. The significance of task-orientation in work. *Journal of Experimental Psychology, 34*, 195–215.
Machiavelli, N. (1950). *The Prince and the Discourses*. New York: Modern Library.
Magenau, J. M. & Pruitt, D. G. (1978). The social psychology of bargaining: a theoretical synthesis. In G. M. Stephenson & C. J. Brotherton (eds), *Industrial Relations: A Social Psychological Approach*. London: Wiley.
Mahler, W. (1933). Ersatzhandlungen verschiedenen Realitätsgrades. *Psychologische Forschung, 18*, 27–89.
May, M. A. & Doob, L. W. (1937). *Competition and Cooperation*. Social Science Research Bulletin, No. 25. New York.
Mikula, G. & Schwinger, T. (1978). Intermember relations and reward allocation: theoretical considerations of affects. In H. Brandstatter, J. H. Davis, & H. Schuler (eds), *Dynamics of Group Decisions*. Beverly Hills: Sage Publications.
Miller, N. E. (1937). Analysis of the form of conflict reactions. *Psychological Bulletin, 34*, 720.
Miller, N. E. (1944). Experimental studies of conflict. In J. McV. Hunt (ed.), *Personality and the Behavior Disorders* (Vol. 1). New York: Ronald.
Minow, M. (1998). Between vengeance and forgiveness: South Africa's truth and reconciliation commission. *Negotiation Journal, 14*, 319–356.
Moore, C. W. (1996). *The Mediation Process: Practical Strategies for Resolving Conflict* (2nd edn). San Francisco: Jossey-Bass.
Murphy, G., Murphy, L. B., & Newcomb, T. M. (1937). *Experimental Social Psychology* (rev. edn). New York: Harper and Brothers.
Osgood, C. E. (1962). *An Alternative to War or Surrender*. Urbana, Ill.: University of Illinois Press.
Ovsiankina, M. (1928). Die Wiederaufnahme Unterbrochener Handlungen. *Psychologische Forschung, 11*, 302–379.
Potter, S. (1965). *The Theory and Practice of Gamesmanship*. New York: Bantam Books.
Pruitt, D. G. (1981). *Negotiation Behavior*. New York: Academic Press.
Pruitt, D. G. & Carnevale, P. J. (1993). *Negotiation in Social Conflict*. Pacific Grove, Calif.: Brooks/Col.
Pruitt, D. G. & Kimmel, M. J. (1977). Twenty years of experimental gaming: critique, synthesis, and suggestions for the future. *Annual Review of Psychology, 28*, 363–392.
Pruitt, D. G. & Olzack, P. V. (1995). Resolving seemingly intractable conflict. In B. B. Bunkey & J. Z. Rubin (eds), *Conflict, Cooperation, and Justice: Essays Inspired by the Work of Morton Deutsch*, pp. 39–58. San Francisco: Jossey-Bass.
Rahim, A. & Blum, A. A. (1994). *Global Perspectives on Organizational Conflict*. New York: Praeger.
Ross, M. H. (1993). *The Culture of Conflict*. New Haven: Yale University Press.
Ross, M. H. & Rothman, J. (1999). *Theory and Practice in Ethnic Conflict Management: Theorizing Success and Failure*. New York: St Martin's Press.

Rubin, J. Z. & Brown, B. R. (1975). *The Social Psychology of Bargaining and Negotiation*. New York: Academic.
Rubin, J. Z., Pruitt, D. G., & Kim, S. H. (1994). *Social Conflict: Escalation, Stalemate, and Settlement*. New York: McGraw-Hill.
Sampson, E. E. (1969). Studies of status congruence. In L. Berkowitz (ed.), *Advances in Experimental Social Psychology* (Vol. 4). New York: Academic.
Sampson, E. E. (1975). On justice as equality. *The Journal of Social Issues, 31*, 45–64.
Sampson, E. E. (1983). *Justice and the Critique of Peace Psychology*. New York: Plenum.
Schachtel, E. G. (1959). *Metamorphosis: On the Development of Affect, Perception, Attention, and Memory*. New York: Basic Books.
Schelling, T. C. (1960). *The Strategy of Conflict*. Cambridge: Harvard University Press.
Schelling, T. C. (1966). *Arms and Influence*. New Haven: Yale University Press.
Shriver, D. W., Jr (1995). *An Ethic for Enemies: Forgiveness in Politics*. New York: Oxford University Press.
Siegel, S. & Fouraker, L. E. (1960). *Bargaining and Group Decision Making: Experiments in Bilateral Monopoly*. New York: McGraw-Hill.
Snyder, G. H. & Diesing, P. (1977). *Conflict among Nations*. Princeton: Princeton University Press.
Staub, E. (1989). *The Roots of Evil: The Origins of Genocide and Other Group Violence*. New York: Cambridge University Press.
Stevens, C. M. (1963). *Strategy and Collective Bargaining Negotiation*. New York: McGraw-Hill.
Tajfel, H. (1978). *Differentiation between Social Groups: Studies in the Social Psychology of Intergroup Relations*. London: Academic Press.
Tajfel, H. (1981). *Human Groups and Social Categories: Studies in Social Psychology*. Cambridge: Cambridge University Press.
Tedeschi, J. T., Schlenker, B. R., & Bonoma, T. V. (1973). *Conflict Power and Games*. Chicago: Aldine.
Thompson, L. H. (1998). *The Mind and Heart of the Negotiation*. Upper Saddle River, NJ: Prentice-Hall.
Touval, S. & Zartman, I. W. (eds) (1985). *International Mediation in Theory and Practice*. Boulder, Colo.: Westview Press.
Triandis, H. (1972). *An Analysis of Subjective Culture*. New York: John Wiley & Sons.
Turner, J. C. (1987). *Rediscovering the Social Group: A Self-categorization Theory*. New York: Basil Blackwell.
Tyler, T. R., Boeckman, R. J., Smith, H. J., & Huo, Y. J. (1997). *Social Justice in a Diverse Society*. Boulder, Colo.: Westview Press.
Vinacke, W. E. & Arkoff, A. (1957). An experimental study of coalitions in the triad. *American Sociological Review, 22*, 406–414.
Von Neumann, J. & Morgenstern, O. (1944). *Theory of Games and Economic Behavior*. New York: Wiley.
Walster, E., Walster, G. W., & Berscheid, E. (1978). *Equity Theory and Research*. Boston: Allyn and Bacon.
Walton, R. E. & McKersie, R. B. (1965). *A Behavioral Theory of Labor Negotiations: An Analysis of a Social Interaction System*. New York: McGraw-Hill.
Wessels, M. & Monteiro, C. (2001). Psychosocial intervention and post-war reconstruction in Angola: interweaving traditional and Western approaches. In D. J. Christie, R. V. Wagner, & D. N. W. Winter (eds), *Peace, Conflict, and Violence: Peace Psychology for the 21st Century* (pp. 262–276). Upper Saddle River, NJ: Prentice-Hall.
Zartman, I. W. (1985). *Ripe for Resolution*. New York: Oxford University Press.
Zartman, I. W. (2000). Ripeness: the hurting stalemate and beyond. In *International Conflict Resolution after the Cold War*. Washington, DC: The National Academy of Science.
Zartman, I. W. & Berman, M. (1982). *The Practical Negotiator*. New Haven, Conn.: Yale University Press.
Zeigarnik, B. (1927). Uber das Behalten von erledigten und unerledigten Handlungen. *Psychologische Forschung, 9*, 1–85.

2

TRUST, IDENTITY, AND ATTACHMENT
PROMOTING INDIVIDUALS' COOPERATION IN GROUPS

M. Audrey Korsgaard, Susan E. Brodt, and Harry J. Sapienza

This chapter sets out to take a new look at trust and cooperation in work groups by focusing on individuals' attitudes toward the group as a whole, rather than simply assuming that interpersonal relationships within the group "add up" to trust (or distrust) and cooperativeness (or uncooperativeness). We approach the issue of trust in groups with the assumption that an individual's trust in the group is an attitude that is quite distinct from interpersonal trust. Trust in the group is not simply the aggregate or average of a member's interpersonal relationships with other group members. Instead, it is an attitude the individual holds toward the group as a collective. Furthermore, we reinvigorate the discussion by looking beyond presumptive and structural factors to the group processes and individual differences that shape trust and cooperation over the long term.

We believe that the dynamics within the group are important determinants of an individual's trust in the group as a whole. We identify two critical conditions that are necessary for trust in and sustained cooperation with the group: group identity and psychological attachment to the group. Identification, which refers to the extent to which individuals define themselves in terms of their membership in a particular group, is influenced by a wide array of contextual and process factors. We focus on intragroup processes that affect identification, using the lens of procedural justice to identify key processes and behaviors within the group that determine the degree to which individuals identify with the group. Second, drawing on the literature on attachment styles, we introduce the concept of group attachment style, an attribute that reflects a person's propensity to seek and feel secure in group situations. We argue that group attachment styles influence both the propensity to become identified with a group and the relationship between group identification and the individual's trust in the group.

This chapter is laid out as follows. First, we briefly examine the meaning, importance, and challenge of strong forms of cooperation in work groups. Next, we review research on the nature and consequences of trust to argue that trust in the group is a critical and immediate determinant of cooperation in groups. We then review the social identity literature and argue that the extent to which individuals define themselves in terms of group identities promotes

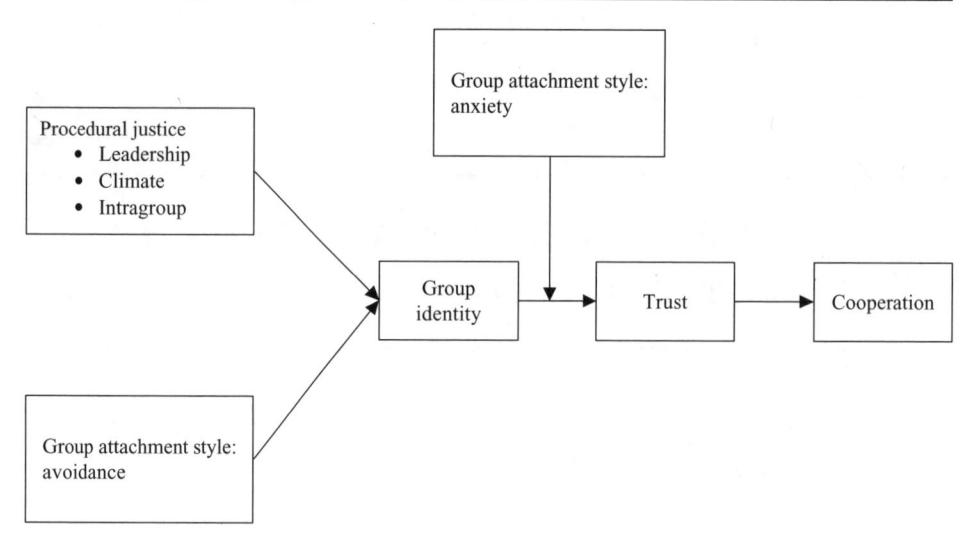

Figure 2.1 A model of the relationships between identity, attachment, trust, and cooperation in groups

trust and cooperation. In establishing the link between identity and trust, we rely on the procedural justice literature to identify antecedents of identification and trust. Drawing on emerging theory and research on group attachment styles, we then illustrate how the nature of attachment in previous group relationships and the formation of interpersonal relationships within the group influence identity and trust in the group. We conclude with a discussion of implications and directions for future research.

The analysis presented in this chapter explicates our model of individuals' trust in and cooperation with groups (see Figure 2.1). Briefly, at the center of this model is group identity, which we view as critical to fostering individuals' trust in and cooperation with their work groups. In essence, individuals form part of their self-concept based on membership in groups, and this identification with the group promotes cooperation. The mechanism by which such cooperation occurs is trust, i.e. identity engenders trust, and trust promotes cooperation. The model identifies two important factors in the development of group identity, namely procedural justice and individual differences in group attachment styles. We argue that fair treatment within the group and individual differences in group attachment styles have a direct effect on group identification. Further, the model suggests that group attachment styles moderate the effect of identification on trust. A particular innovation in our model is our emphasis on a new construct, psychological attachment to the group.

THE CHALLENGE OF COOPERATION IN WORK GROUPS

We define an individual's cooperation with the group as the active and persistent pursuit of the goals of the work group, regardless of personal or interpersonal interests. In its purest form, this definition of cooperation implies an intuitive and/or conscious awareness of what the group wants and a willingness to make one's own interests secondary to those of the group. The type of cooperation we intend implies much more than mere compliance or conformity. Compliance and conformity may be passive and may even thwart group goals when initiative is required. The active component we stress here is analogous to the dichotomy identified by Tyler and Blader (2000, 2001) who distinguish cooperation based on mandatory behavior (i.e. behaviors specifically required by the organization) versus discretionary behavior (i.e. behavior that is voluntary and outside organizational guidelines). Tyler and Blader (2000, 2001) argue that the latter type of cooperation, i.e. that based on discretionary behaviors, is key to the success of groups because groups cannot specify in advance what its members should do in all circumstances.

Besides proactivity, the other key dimension of our definition is the emphasis on proactivity on behalf of the group rather than oneself or favored individuals within the group. Thus, for the purposes of our theorizing we further qualify Tyler and Blader's (2000, 2001) concept of voluntary cooperative behavior to be that which is in reference to the group as a whole. Full cooperation requires a vigilance in raising issues that move the group toward shared goals, not just those of a subset or "lead" set of individuals; it means that self- or friendship interests must sometimes be willingly suppressed. Cooperation may result in challenging others in order to ensure that the group remains on track.

Importance of Cooperation for Work Group Effectiveness

There are numerous reasons why cooperation is essential to long-term group effectiveness. First, cooperation among group members ensures that group efforts will be coordinated toward a common goal, thus enabling the group to perform more effectively (Gladstein, 1984). Moreover, Podsakoff, Ahearn, and MacKenzie (1997) argue that cooperative behavior such as organizational citizenship behavior can directly enhance the productivity of group members. Further, cooperation may promote the efficient use of group resources. Pursuit of individual or subgroup goals can undermine group success either directly by diverting resources or indirectly by weakening the resolve of other group members to continue voluntarily to provide effort on behalf of the group (Korsgaard, Sapienza, & Schweiger, 2001). Cooperation reduces the need to devote the group's resources to group maintenance functions, thereby freeing up resources for more productive purposes (Podsakoff, Ahearn, & MacKenzie, 1997; Podsakoff et al., 2000).

Research on groups and teams in organizations supports a direct relationship between cooperation among group members and group effectiveness. For example, organizational citizenship behavior directed at group members has a positive effect on both the quality and the quantity of performance, as well as customer service (Podsakoff, Ahearn, & MacKenzie, 1997; Podsakoff et al., 2000). The level of cooperation in teams is also positively related to group member satisfaction, effort, and performance evaluations (Campion, Medsker, & Higgs, 1993; Campion, Papper, & Medsker, 1996; Lester, Meglino, & Korsgaard, 2002). Moreover, cooperation in groups indirectly affects performance by enhancing the group's sense of efficacy in its ability to resolve conflicts and perform effectively (Alper, Tjosvold, & Law, 2000; Lester, Meglino, & Korsgaard, 2002).

Despite the positive effect of cooperation on group member attitudes, cooperation in groups need not imply an absence of conflict. Conflict is an inevitable and often desirable fact of work group life (Alper, Tjosvold, & Law, 2000). Indeed, open and productive confrontation of task-based conflict is likely to enhance decision making (Johnson, Johnson, & Tjosvold, 2000), but the process of resolving conflicts has the potential to undermine the group itself (Amason & Sapienza, 1997; Korsgaard, Sapienza, & Schweiger, 2001; Korsgaard, Schweiger, & Sapienza, 1995; Simons & Peterson, 2000). Effective group functioning depends on high-quality decisions, commitment to and understanding of the decisions reached, and group continuity (Korsgaard, Sapienza, & Schweiger, 2001). Research suggests that a cooperative orientation to confronting and resolving conflicts with the group can both enhance the quality of decision making and group members' attitudes and motivation as well (Alper, Tjosvold, & Law, 1998, 2000; Korsgaard, Sapienza, & Schweiger, 2001). For example, Amason and Sapienza (1997) showed that norms of mutuality within top management groups encouraged team continuity without limiting the cognitive or task conflict necessary for reaching effective group decisions.

We have argued that if a work group is to be effective over time, its members must fully cooperate. Mere compliance or conformity is inadequate to meet changing requirements. Further, we have argued that the effectiveness of the group will depend to some extent on the willingness of individuals to take actions that preserve the integrity of the group, regardless of their own interests. Consider, as an example, faculty within a department of a university. These groups face a myriad of tasks such as selecting doctoral candidates for admission, screening job candidates, determining course and class scheduling, and allocating merit raises. Time demands preclude the full involvement of everyone in every task, even if such involvement were desirable. Our foregoing discussion suggests that for the good of the department as a whole, individual faculty must cooperate by supplying adequate effort, sharing information freely and honestly, and suppressing the pursuit of personal or subgroup outcomes. We describe in the next section why we consider trust in the group the essential attitude that enables such strong cooperation to exist in work groups.

The Nature of Trust and its Importance to Work Group Cooperation

Although many different attitudes may be associated with cooperation, trust has emerged as the attitude most critical to the formation of cooperation within groups and organizations (Smith, Carroll, & Ashford, 1995). In a special issue of the *Academy of Management Journal* on cooperation in organizations, Smith, Carroll, and Ashford (1995, p. 10) argued that a difficulty in making sense of organizational research on cooperation is attributable in part to the diversity of definitions of the cooperation construct. Nonetheless, they concluded (pp. 10–11) that "virtually all scholars have agreed that one especially immediate antecedent [of cooperation] is trust." Consistent with definitions of interpersonal trust (e.g. Rousseau et al., 1998; Whitener et al., 1998; Williams, 2001), we define trust in the work group as an individual's intention to accept vulnerability to the group based on the expectation but not the guarantee that the group will act in a considerate and benevolent manner toward the individual. We will argue that this *attitude* is based in large part on the individual's identification with and attachment to the group and on the quality of group processes.

Empirical research supports a relationship between interpersonal trust and cooperation in the workplace. In a meta-analysis of research on interpersonal trust in work organizations, Dirks and Ferrin (2002) found that trust was positively related to organizational citizenship behavior. This relationship holds for both trust in peers (McAllister, 1995) and trust in managers (Korsgaard, Brodt, and Whitener, 2002). Research on procedural justice and contract violations also indicates that trust is an immediate determinant of cooperative behavior (Konovsky & Pugh, 1994; Robinson & Morrison, 1995). Indirect evidence of this relationship is also seen in studies demonstrating a positive relationship between managers' trust-building behavior and employee cooperative behavior (Deluga, 1994; Korsgaard, Brodt, & Whitener, 2002). Although much of the empirical and theoretical work in this area has concerned interpersonal trust, there are reasons to expect a similar relationship between trust in the work group and cooperation.

A consideration of our definition of cooperation and its challenges provides insight into why trust in the group is essential to cooperation. First, individuals who do not believe in the benevolence of the group and who are not willing to be vulnerable to the group are very unlikely to engage in proactive, voluntary behavior because such behavior requires, at minimum, exposure to the threat of censure. Further, cooperation often exposes one to uncertain payoff, lack of reciprocation, and distributive inequity. In short, trust is important because as Kramer, Brewer, and Hanna frame it (1996, p. 358), "In the absence of some basis for thinking that others will reciprocate, therefore, individuals may find it hard to justify the decision to cooperate themselves."

Trust in the work group is especially important because it also enables cooperative behavior that nonetheless challenges the group or individuals in it. Trust in the group frees individuals to respond rapidly to emerging circumstances without waiting for signals of approval (Lind, 2001) and to interpret ambiguous group actions as benign and to respond in kind (Amason & Sapienza, 1997). Simons and Peterson (2000) provided empirical support for the potential beneficial effects of trust in the work group on cooperation by showing that trust in the group attenuates the tendency of individuals to interpret task conflict as relationship conflict. This finding is significant in relation to our definition of cooperation because task conflict involves challenging the group to reach optimal performance, but relationship conflict tends to lead to uncooperativeness and group dissolution (Amason & Sapienza, 1997; Korsgaard, Sapienza, & Schweiger, 2001; Simons & Peterson, 2000).

Although the arguments regarding the effects of cooperation on trust in the work group are intuitively appealing, direct theoretical argumentation and empirical evidence are somewhat scant. Moreover, the antecedents of trust in the work group have rarely been examined explicitly in the literature. Insight into the causes and consequences of trust in the work group can be gleaned from recent theoretical work on the formation of trust and trust in social dilemmas. Theory and research on swift trust highlight the role of group identity in facilitating the formation of trust (McKnight, Cummings, & Chervany, 1998; Meyerson, Weick, & Kramer, 1996). This perspective suggests that group membership confers trust in the collective, for the group is a type or symbol of the individual him/herself. That is, groups formed to complete some special task may engage in a categorization process whereby they see the group as being select or special and therefore will adopt positive expectations of the group.

The limited empirical research on trust in groups or collectives also provides strong arguments for the validity of viewing trust in the collective as a legitimate and important construct. For example, Dirks (1999) examined the effect of trust on group process, although he examined the aggregate of interpersonal trust rather than trust in the group. Simons and Peterson (2000) demonstrated the impact of trust in the group on limiting counterproductive group conflict. Similarly, research on the role of trust in social dilemmas (Kramer, Brewer, & Hanna, 1996) not only provides support for the positive effects of collective trust on cooperation (Kramer, 1999), it also suggests that identification with the group is an important determinant of trust in the collective (Kramer, Brewer, & Hanna, 1996). Given the importance of identity to trust, we next examine the concept of social identity and the intragroup processes related to identification.

SOCIAL IDENTITY

Psychologists have long acknowledged the notion of the self or self-concept and its role in regulating thought and action (e.g. James, 1948). An individual's self-concept contains many facets or aspects that serve to define the self. Social identity is that aspect of a person's self-concept that is determined by her/his membership in a particular group. That is, individuals to a greater or lesser extent define themselves in terms of their membership in various groups. These groups may include demographic, political, religious, social, and work groups. This aspect of the self is at the center of theoretical perspectives on group identity such as social identity theory (Tajfel & Turner, 1979; Brown, 2000), self-categorization theory (Hogg, 2001; Turner et al., 1987), and organizational identity (Ashforth & Mael, 1989; Dutton, Dukerich, & Harquail, 1994). These theories concern the processes by which individuals form identities with groups and the effects such identities have on judgment and action.

The impetus for early work on social identity was to understand intergroup relations, and, today, the emphasis on intergroup issues remains in much of the theory and research on identity. The main thrust of this research is the impact of group identity on ingroup bias. Generally, this literature shows that social identity leads to more favorable evaluations and treatment of ingroup members (i.e. the set of people in the focal individual's group) compared to the evaluation and treatment of outgroup members (i.e. those in groups other than the focal individual's group) (Brown, 2000).

Despite the prevailing interest in intergroup relations, social identity has strong implications for intragroup relations as well. In fact, organizational identity, a particular form of identity associated with a work organization (Ashforth & Mael, 1989), specifically focuses on how identity influences the dynamics within the organization. Consistent with this view, we examine the impact of social identity on relations within the group. Unique to our analysis, however, is a focus on the work group rather than the organization as a whole and especially on the impact of intragroup processes on work group identity.

Importance of Social Identity to Intragroup Cooperation and Trust

Research suggests that identity generally fosters prosocial or cooperative relations within the group. Social dilemma studies have demonstrated the impact of group identity on prosocial or altruistic behavior toward the group (Dawes, van de Kragt, & Orbell 1988; De Cremer & van Vugt, 1999; Kramer, 1993). These studies involved social dilemma-type tasks in which participants decide how to allocate resources within the group. Results consistently showed that participants were more self-sacrificing and cooperative in their allocations when they had formed even a minimal group identity. Similarly, in their study of alumni's identification with their alma mater, Mael and Ashforth (1992) found that identification was related to the altruistic behavior of donating to the organization. A similar relationship between identity and prosocial behavior in the form of organizational citizenship behavior has been observed in work organizations (Bergami & Bagozzi, 2000; O'Reilly & Chatman, 1986).

Some scholars have argued that the effect of social identity on cooperation is largely due to the effect of identity on trust (Kramer, 1993; Kramer, Brewer, & Hanna, 1996; Meyerson, Weick, & Kramer, 1996; Williams, 2001). This interpretation is consistent with research on the ingroup bias effects of social identification (Brewer, 1979) wherein group members tend to ascribe positive attributes such as trustworthiness and cooperativeness to other ingroup members. These inferences are thought to result from the effect identification has on categorization processes (Kramer, Brewer, & Hanna, 1996). Specifically, inferences regarding group members are based on beliefs regarding the group or category rather than on current specific information about the members (Brodt & Ross, 1998; Williams, 2001). It is noteworthy that this form of trust does not require any direct experience with particular individuals within the group and is, in effect, "presumptive" (Kramer, 1993, p. 252).

There is little direct empirical evidence of the effect of identity on trust, and the findings are not fully consistent with theory. For example, a recent study examined the effect of school affiliation (used as a proxy for social identity) on negotiations and found that dyads who shared an affiliation were significantly more cooperative and outperformed mixed dyads but were no higher on trust (Moore et al., 1999). However, another study, one involving permanent versus temporary employees, provided limited support for the relationship between identity and trust (Chattopadhyay & George, 2001). In this study, identity was operationalized in terms of the diversity of permanent versus temporary employees in a work group. The findings indicated a significant relationship between shared identity and trust, but only in groups that were composed predominantly of temporary employees.

In summary, research indicates that group identification has a positive impact on intragroup cooperation. Theory also suggests that this relationship is explained, at least in part, by the impact of group identification on trust in the group. Thus, an exploration of group processes leading to group identification should provide understanding of how to foster trust in group and intragroup cooperation.

Most of the antecedents examined in theories of social identity do not involve intragroup processes. Rather, because of the emphasis on intergroup relations, the social identity literature has focused on the impact of the group's broader social and task environment on identity. For example, attractiveness and distinctiveness are thought to increase identity because they enhance the collective esteem of the group relative to other groups in the social environment. That is, individuals are apt to identify more strongly with groups that possess some relatively attractive or unique attribute (Ashforth & Mael, 1989; Mael & Ashforth, 1992). Another antecedent that is related to the social context of the group is salience, which heightens awareness of the ingroup and outgroups and leads individuals to identify more strongly with the group (Ashforth & Mael, 1989; Haslam et al., 1999). Other antecedents are associated with the uncertainty in the social or task environment. For example, factors such as the lack of clear feedback and task ambiguity (Grieve & Hogg, 1999; Mullin & Hogg, 1998, 1999) have a positive impact on group identity.

The emphasis on the broader social or task environment among these antecedents is consistent with the emphasis on intergroup relations that predominates theories of social identity. However, these antecedents provide limited insight into how dynamics *within* the group influence identity. In consequence, our interest in the internal workings of the group points us in the direction of antecedents suggested by related theory and research on procedural justice.

Social Identity and Procedural Justice

Procedural justice provides a useful framework for examining how group process influences identity. This perspective suggests a distinct motivational function of group identity, namely enhancing or maintaining the individual self-esteem of group members. In contrast to collective esteem enhancement, which involves the group's standing relative to other groups in the social context, individual self-esteem concerns members' status within the group and how it is affected by members' treatment within the group. That is, procedural justice theory suggests that an individual will identify more strongly with a group in which his/her individual worth and status as a member are validated by fair treatment. Theories of procedural justice, in particular the relational model (Tyler & Blader, 2000) and fairness heuristic theory (Lind, 2001), suggest that group members have two main concerns in their social exchanges within the group or organization. First, they are concerned with the prospect that their contributions to the group will not be reciprocated (i.e. they will not be fairly compensated for their efforts). Second, individuals are concerned that, if they link their identity to the group, they are in danger of rejection by the group. This latter concern is thought to be the more powerful motive (Lind, 2001) and to lead to individuals being sensitive to cues regarding their status and value to the group. In consequence, this theory suggests that group identity is central to fostering cooperation (Tyler & Blader, 2001).

Intragroup interactions, viewed through the lens of procedural justice, provide important information to the individual regarding his or her status within the group. That is, being treated in a procedurally just fashion signifies that the individual is a member in good standing within the group or organization. The self-esteem enhancing effect of having their status in the group affirmed leads members to identify strongly with the group. Consequently, procedurally fair treatment is positively associated with favorable attitudes toward the group (Korsgaard, Schweiger, & Sapienza, 1995; Phillips, Douthitt, & Hyland, 2001). In contrast, when an individual's standing in the group is threatened, as is the case when the individual is treated unfairly, and he/she is less likely to use the group as a basis for identity (Mussweiler, Gabriel, & Bodenhausen, 2000).

Procedural justice concerns the fairness of procedures used to make decisions and the fairness of the treatment of individuals when enacting those procedures. Numerous aspects of procedures and treatment result in the perception of procedural justice. The most extensively documented factor is the opportunity for input or voice in the process of making the decision (Lind & Tyler, 1988). Based on the work of Leventhal (1980), several additional procedural criteria have been investigated, including judgment based on evidence, correctability or refutability of the decision, and consistent application of procedures (Folger, Konovsky, & Cropanzano, 1992; Kim & Mauborgne, 1993). Researchers have drawn the distinction between determinants of procedural justice that pertain to formal procedures and those that pertain to the decision maker's conduct, the latter being referred to as interactional justice (Tyler & Bies, 1990). Interactional justice is determined by two sets of factors, interpersonal sensitivity factors—the extent to which individuals are treated with respect and dignity—and informational factors—the extent to which individuals are given adequate and timely information regarding the decision procedure and outcome. Both procedural and interactional factors give rise to judgments of procedural justice, although the relevance or importance of particular factors may vary somewhat depending on the decision context (Greenberg, 1993). Generally, however, to the extent that decisions are made in a fair manner, individuals are likely to be more trusting and behave more cooperatively within the group (Colquitt et al., 2001; Korsgaard, Schweiger, & Sapienza, 1995; Korsgaard & Roberson, 1995; Sapienza & Korsgaard, 1996).

Theory and research on procedural justice have focused primarily on the impact of a group leader or decision-making authority's (e.g. manager's) treatment of individuals. However, there is increasing evidence that procedural justice may also be a collective phenomenon. Recent research has demonstrated the existence of a procedural justice climate or context, a shared perception of procedural justice in work groups (Colquitt, Noe, & Jackson, 2002; Mossholder, Bennett, & Martin, 1998; Naumann & Bennett, 2000). The data suggest that a justice climate has a positive impact on organizational commitment (Johnson, Korsgaard, & Sapienza, 2002), a concept closely related to organizational identification, as well as cooperative behavior (Naumann & Bennett, 2000), performance (Colquitt, Noe, & Jackson, 2002), and satisfaction (Mossholder, Bennett, & Martin, 1998).

To summarize, theory and research in social identity suggest that group identity is important to fostering cooperation within the group. Theory would also suggest that identity directly influences trust, which functions as a mediator of the identity–cooperation relationship. These relationships underscore the importance of identity to fostering cooperative relationships within a group. The centrality of group identity leads us to an examination of the causes and mechanisms underlying group identification. Many of these antecedents involve the broader social context and therefore are beyond the scope of our examination of intragroup processes. However, procedural justice theory provides a useful framework for understanding the effect of group process on group identification. Specifically, it suggests that the degree of fairness of decision-making procedures employed by the group or the group leader influences group members' perceptions of their status and worth to the group and, hence, identification with the group. These relationships are summarized in Figure 2.1.

Two important questions regarding the formation and impact of group identity on trust and cooperation in the group remain unanswered: why have the empirical results regarding the relationship between group identification and trust been inconsistent? And, what role might individual differences play in the formation and effects of group identification? First, although theory suggests that trust mediates the impact of identity on cooperation, evidence of the effect of group identification on trust in the group is mixed. Such inconsistency in findings may result from unidentified moderators in the relationship between identity and trust. Second, evidence suggests that individual differences in propensity to form attachments may play a role in identification and its consequences. For example, Mael and Ashforth (1995) demonstrated that one dimension of past experience (i.e. biodata) influenced individuals' propensity to become identified with a given organization. The authors speculated that this dimension, which they identified as "group orientation," may reflect a generalized tendency toward organizational identification. This view is consistent with research by Smith and colleagues (Smith, Coats, & Murphy, 2001; Smith, Murphy, & Coats, 1999) indicating that individual differences in attachment styles influence group identification. To date, however, the role of individual differences in shaping social identity and in influencing the impact of identity on trust and cooperation in groups is unclear.

We posit that insight into the answers to these questions lies in research and theory on psychological attachment to the group. In the next section, we review this perspective, discuss its implications for trust and cooperation, and integrate it into our model.

PSYCHOLOGICAL ATTACHMENT TO THE GROUP

Psychological attachment to the group, in addition to identification, is necessary for trust and sustained cooperation. Attachment style, with its roots in research on psychological attachment, was a concept initially used in child development (Bowlby, 1982) to describe the affective bonds between a child and caregiver. Psychological attachment styles are presumed to organize the development of personality and guide social behavior not only in infancy but also throughout adult life (Hazan & Shaver, 1987; Main, Kaplan, & Cassidy, 1985). Researchers subsequently applied this concept to adult relationships and found adult attachment styles related to such topics as fear of personal death (i.e. the ultimate separation; Mikulincer, Florian, & Tolmacz, 1990), support seeking and caregiving in romantic relationships (Feeney & Collins, 2001), the suppression of unwanted thoughts (Fraley & Shaver, 1997), affect regulation (Mikulincer, Orbach, & Iavnieli, 1998), intergroup bias (Mikulincer & Shaver, 2001), and even the issues of love and work and the balance of work and family (Hazan & Shaver, 1990).

Extending this work, researchers have recently developed the concept of group attachment style, which describes a group member's propensity to seek and feel secure in group situations (Brodt, forthcoming; Brodt & Korsgaard, 2002; Smith, Coats, & Murphy, 2001; Smith, Murphy, & Coats, 1999). For anyone who has managed work groups or project teams, the concept has intuitive appeal. When a project deadline approaches, the range of reactions can be dramatic: some individuals turn quickly to their groups bringing everyone together whereas others hole up alone and work to complete the task themselves. Yet others, those who work exclusively within their groups, pull even closer together to their "secure base" (Brodt, forthcoming) to get the job done. These behavioral differences are believed to reflect different mental representations or "working models" of the self-as-group-member that develop from the group's availability and responsiveness to the individual. The securely attached group member feels safe and comfortable in his/her organizational environment and knows that his/her group will be available and respond to his/her needs (Brodt, forthcoming). As a consequence, s/he will work independently and freely share information among group members, but also keep in touch with his/her group as deadlines and other urgent group needs arise (Brodt, forthcoming; Brodt & Korsgaard, 2002). As this description suggests, the concept underscores the adaptive significance of group attachment and individuals' strong bonds to a group; it is based on the premise that group attachment styles (including closeness and security) both affect group identification and alter the impact of that identification on intragroup cooperation and performance.

Research on group attachment is in its infancy. However, recent work shows promise on both conceptual and empirical fronts. Smith and colleagues (Smith, Coats, & Murphy, 2001; Smith, Murphy, & Coats, 1999) paved the way for researchers by defining the concept and developing a measure of group attachment. On the conceptual front, they analyzed the relationship between group attachment and identification, proposing that these two psychological processes are complementary. Specifically, they pointed out that social identity theory and research typically focus on identification with the group as an entity and on a single dimension, namely an individual's evaluation of the group (i.e. favorable, unfavorable). Attachment theory underscores individual variation in the type of relationships individuals have to a group and its members. That is, among group members, there are multiple mental models of the self as group member corresponding to differences in attachment styles. Brodt (forthcoming) further developed the concept, emphasizing the role of the group as a secure base from which group members may venture, take risks, and work independently but on behalf of the group. Her analysis includes both group attachment and interpersonal attachment (e.g. attachment to a boss or superior).

On the empirical front, Smith and colleagues developed a measure of group attachment (Smith, Murphy, & Coats, 1999). Borrowing from research on adult attachment (Bartholomew & Horowitz, 1991; Brennan & Shaver, 1995; Fraley & Waller, 1998), they proposed two dimensions—avoidance and anxiety—and developed a scale to measure the attitudes, feelings, and behaviors of individuals. The two dimensions are nearly orthogonal so that individuals can be high on both or low on both as well as high on one or the other. Other researchers have used their attachment measure (Brodt, forthcoming; Brodt & Korsgaard, 2002), creating an emerging literature on group attachment styles.

In the next section, we describe these two components or dimensions of the attachment relationship, and we describe how group attachment styles influence facets of cooperation. We conclude with a discussion of the relationship between group attachment styles and our model.

Group Attachment Avoidance

One aspect of an individual's relationship to a group is typically defined in terms of the extent to which the individual desires to be distant from or independent of the group. This dimension of group attachment is called avoidance and is measured by items such as "I prefer not to depend on my group or to have my group depend on me" and "I want to feel completely at one with my group" (reverse coded) (Smith, Murphy, & Coats, 1999, p. 110). Individuals who report low attachment avoidance accept and value closeness or dependence on groups and attempt to maintain that type of relationship. Part of a secure group attachment style is scoring *low* on this avoidance dimension, implying a desire to be part of a group and an expectation that groups are valuable (Smith, Murphy, & Coats, 1999). In their research, Smith, Murphy, and Coats (1999) found that avoidance was strongly negatively related to group identification and commitment, and positively related to plans to leave the group. Furthermore, Brodt (forthcoming) found that avoidance was strongly positively correlated with behavior aimed at fulfilling self-interest rather than group or organization interest.

Group Attachment Anxiety

The other aspect of group attachment reflects a worry or anxiety about being accepted by one's group. This dimension is measured by items such as "I often worry my group will not always want me as a member," and "I sometimes worry that my group doesn't value me as much as I value my group" (Smith, Murphy, & Coats, 1999, p. 110). Individuals with high group attachment anxiety report a sense of being "unworthy as a group member and feelings of worry and concern regarding acceptance by valued groups" (Smith, Murphy, & Coats, 1999, p. 96). Behaviorally, these individuals are believed to seek to conform in order to "fit in" and be accepted by their groups. Hence, individuals high in group attachment anxiety are unlikely to question the group or to engage in positive group conflict to ensure that the group remains on track. In contrast, individuals who report low attachment anxiety expect to be accepted by the group and are less concerned about group approval. Smith, Murphy, and Coats (1999) found that individuals higher in attachment anxiety perceived fewer and less satisfying social supports within the group and exhibited greater negative affect.

Group Attachment Styles and Cooperation in Groups

Our discussion about psychological attachment and its implications for our analysis of identification, trust, and cooperation within groups are reflected in our model shown in

Figure 2.1. In general, the attachment research has implications for both the development of group identity and for the link between identity and trust in groups. Specifically, the reliable individual differences in group attachment avoidance regarding preference for working alone or with others suggest a direct effect of attachment avoidance on group identification. Persons high in group attachment avoidance will be less likely to identify with a group because they see the self as autonomous and place a low value on closeness. These individuals have a lower need for group identity.

Group attachment anxiety, however, should moderate the relationship between identity and trust. Persons who are high in group attachment anxiety will develop less trust even if they strongly identify with a group because they tend to view others as inconsistent and untrustworthy. That is, even though these individuals may show strong identification with a group, they will not show the expected positive relationship between identification and trust. For these individuals, group identification and attachment stem from a desire for closeness but are tempered by a fear of rejection. By including attachment style as an individual difference in our model, we should increase its predictive power in these specific ways.

CONCLUSIONS

We set out in this chapter to develop an understanding of the factors contributing to trust and cooperation in work groups. The cooperation of individual group members is essential to the collective performance of the group, and trust is a powerful motivator of cooperation. In contrast to interpersonal trust, we focused on individuals' trust in the group. Viewing trust in the group in this way, we sought to explore the role of the intragroup context and of the group's broader social context in this unique form of trust. The preceding review and synthesis of a variety of literatures, principally trust and cooperation, social identity, procedural justice, and psychological attachment, point to three key factors in building individuals' trust in the group, and hence, cooperation: fair treatment in the group, identification with the group, and group attachment styles. We hope that this focus will stimulate research that takes a new approach to intragroup cooperation and effective group processes. To that end we highlight some implications and potentially rewarding avenues for further research.

One important implication of our model is the extension of procedural justice effects to trust in the group. Although the impact of procedural justice on identity and trust is well documented, such research has mainly focused on the dyadic relationship between the decision-making authority (i.e. the manager) and the person affected by the decision. Although researchers have recently begun to investigate the collective experiences and perceptions of groups (Colquitt et al., 2001; Johnson, Korsgaard, & Sapienza, 2002; Mossholder, Bennett, & Martin, 1998; Naumann & Bennett, 2000), these approaches still focus on the impact of a decision-making authority or manager on the groups' perceptions. What has not been examined is the team itself as a decision-making body. That is, little is known about the dynamics of fairness in the exchanges among peers. Given the prevalence of self-managed teams, group members' perceptions of fair treatment in dealings with the group and its members—rather than the supervisor's fairness—may be a more critical determinant of group identity.

Another implication of our model is the specification of the role of individual differences in group attachment styles in the development and effects of identity on trust and cooperation. To date, most of the research on identity, cooperation, and trust has ignored or minimized the role of individual differences. Preliminary research suggests, however, that there is substantial individual variation in the propensity to form attachments to groups (i.e. group attachment avoidance), which may also influence the propensity to identify with a group and, consequently, to trust the group and be truly cooperative. Our model also proposes a moderating effect of the other main dimension of group attachment styles, anxiety. Specifically, research suggests that group attachment anxiety may exert an independent influence on trust in the group. We therefore propose that this dimension of group attachment may work against the positive effects of identity on trust and, hence, cooperation.

The proposed interaction of identity and group attachment has implications for clarifying the centrality of trust to cooperation. As noted earlier, direct empirical evidence of the impact of identity on trust is weak and limited, whereas the documented impact of identity on cooperation is substantial. This inconsistency suggests that perhaps trust is not essential to fostering cooperation and that identity has a direct impact on cooperation or an indirect one through some other mechanisms. Indeed, some researchers using the social dilemma paradigm have suggested that identity effects on cooperation do not require any positive expectations of reciprocation or cooperation on the part of other group members (Dawes, van de Kragt, & Orbell, 1988). Further, some studies have failed to demonstrate a direct impact of trust on cooperation, finding rather that trust interacts with other variables to influence group process and outcomes (Dirks, 1999; Dirks & Ferrin, 2001). We, on the other hand, assert that trust is indeed essential to cooperation, as is evidenced by the strong link between trust and cooperation, and we assert that trust is central to the effect of identity. However, our model suggests that the lack of empirical evidence for the effect of identity on trust may be attributable to past researchers overlooking the moderating role of group attachment anxiety. This implication awaits empirical validation.

Although group attachment styles are considered an individual difference, it is worth noting that it is not necessarily a stable trait (Smith, Murphy, & Coats, 1999). Thus, it is possible that, over time, an individual's experience with various work groups over his or her career may shape that person's attachment style in groups. For example, individuals who have several successful experiences with temporary work teams early in their career may develop a secure attachment style toward teams and quickly identify and cooperate with newly formed teams in the future. Indeed group attachment style may be a latent factor—what managers commonly refer to as "being a good team player." Furthermore, a relationship unexplored in our model, but not inconsistent with thinking in procedural justice, is the possibility that the procedural justice in groups may have some impact on group attachment styles. For example, given that group attachment styles are posited to be affected by group experience, it is possible that over time, an individual's level of group attachment anxiety may change as a result of consistently fair or unfair treatment in a group.

Our model does not define an exhaustive set of the causes and consequences of trust; rather, it explores the role of group and interpersonal factors in engendering trust in the group. Although not specified in our model, it is equally possible that variations in avoidant group attachment style may moderate the antecedents of identity as well. For example, group attachment avoidance may influence reactions to procedural justice within the group. Recall that the procedural justice perspective suggests that procedurally fair treatment provides information about an individual's standing in the group and should therefore reinforce their identification with the group. Persons who are prone to identify with a group (i.e. low in avoidance) may be particularly sensitive to justice cues about their standing, whereas avoidant persons may be relatively indifferent to such cues.

Another possible extension of the model concerns the potential direct effect of procedural justice on trust and cooperation. Identity is only one of several mechanisms underlying the effects of procedural justice. For example, the fairness heuristic theory (Lind, 2001) suggests that individuals respond favorably to fair procedures because they provide diagnostic information about the trustworthiness of authorities and future outcomes in the exchange relationship. Similarly, the self-interest model of procedural justice (Lind & Tyler, 1988) indicates that individuals care about fair procedures because they help assure that over time, their self-interests will be protected. Fairness accountability theory (Folger & Cropanzano, 2001) suggests that fair procedures provide information about the accountability and intent of decision makers. These alternative models, which share a common emphasis on protection of self-interests, suggest that procedural justice may directly contribute to trust in the group as well as indirectly through building identity. However, it is not yet clear whether satisfaction of self-interest concerns described in these models of justice will motivate the level of cooperation that is emphasized in our model.

Another issue worthy of further investigation is the possibility of reciprocal causality or feedback loops. Specifically, research suggests that, in addition to the effect of trust on cooperation, cooperation has a causal impact on trust in the other party (Ferrin, Bligh, & Kohles, 2002). Further, trust in the group may have important consequences for group processes and outcomes beyond those specified by our model. For example, trusting one's manager or co-worker and being trusted by co-workers has a positive impact on in-role performance (Dirks & Ferrin, 2002; Dirks & Skarlicki, 2002). Research also suggests that trust has a negative impact on monitoring (Ferrin, Bligh, & Kohles, 2002). These consequences of interpersonal trust may well extend to the group's overall functioning.

Our purpose in this chapter was to bring recognition to the issues of the causes of an individual's trust and cooperation in work groups. As prior work had largely focused on the development of interpersonal trust, one of our objectives was to clarify how and why formation of trust in the group differs from interpersonal trust. We posited group identity as the immediate determinant of trust and considered two basic antecedents to group identity, including the procedural justice of group processes and individual differences in the avoidance dimension of group attachment style. Finally, we posited a moderating role for the anxiety dimension of group attachment style on the relationship between group identity and trust in the group. We believe that these ideas help to clarify a previously under-recognized distinction between interpersonal trust and trust in groups.

REFERENCES

Alper, S., Tjosvold, D., & Law, K. S. (1998). Interdependence and controversy in group decision making: antecedents to effective self-managing teams. *Organizational Behavior and Human Decision Processes, 74*, 33–52.

Alper, S., Tjosvold, D., & Law, K. S. (2000). Conflict management, efficacy, and performance in organizational teams. *Personnel Psychology, 53*, 625–642.

Amason, A. C. & Sapienza, H. J. (1997). Effects of top management team size and interaction norms on cognitive and affective conflict. *Journal of Management, 23*, 495–516.

Ashforth, B. E. & Mael, F. (1989). Social identity theory and the organization. *Academy of Management Review, 14*, 20–39.

Bartholomew, K. & Horowitz, L. (1991). Attachment styles among young adults: a test of a four-category model. *Journal of Personality and Social Psychology, 61*, 226–244.

Bergami, M. & Bagozzi, R. P. (2000). Self-categorization, affective commitment and group self-esteem as distinct aspects of social identity in the organization. *British Journal of Social Psychology, 39*, 555–577.

Bowlby, J. (1982). *Attachment and Loss*: Vol 1. *Attachment* (2nd edn). New York: Basic Books.

Brennan, K. & Shaver, P. (1995). Dimensions of adult attachment, affect regulation, and romantic relationship functioning. *Personality and Social Psychology Bulletin, 21*, 267–283.

Brewer, M. B. (1979). Ingroup bias in the minimal intergroup situation: a cognitive–motivational analysis. *Psychological Bulletin, 86*, 307–324.

Brodt, S. (forthcoming). Trust is at the heart of negotiating. In R. Kramer & K. Cook (eds), *Trust and Distrust in Organizational Contexts: Enduring Questions, Emerging Perspectives*. Sage.

Brodt, S. & Korsgaard, M. A. (2002). The role of group attachment and trust in group problem solving by newly formed and existing groups. Manuscript in preparation.

Brodt, S. & Ross, L. (1998). The role of stereotypes in overconfident social prediction. *Social Cognition, 16*, 225–252.

Brown, R. (2000). Social identity theory: past achievements, current problems and future challenges. *European Journal of Social Psychology, 30*, 745–778.

Campion, M. A., Medsker, G. J., & Higgs, A. C. (1993). Relations between work group characteristics and effectiveness: implications for designing effective work groups. *Personnel Psychology, 46*, 823–850.

Campion, M. A., Papper, E. M., & Medsker, G. J. (1996). Relations between work team characteristics and effectiveness: a replication and extension. *Personnel Psychology, 49*, 429–452.

Chattopadhyay, P. & George, E. (2001). Examining the effects of work externalization through the lens of social identity theory. *Journal of Applied Psychology, 86*, 781–788.

Colquitt, J. A., Conlon, D. E., Wesson, M. J., Porter, C. O. L. H., & Ng, K. Y. (2001). Justice at the millennium: a meta-analytic review of 25 years of organizational justice research. *Journal of Applied Psychology, 86*, 425–445.

Colquitt, J. A., Noe, R. A., & Jackson, C. L. (2002). Justice in teams: antecedents and consequences of procedural justice climate. *Personnel Psychology. 55*, 83–109.

Dawes, van de Kragt, A. J. C., & Orbell, J. M. (1988). Not me or thee but we: the importance of group identity in eliciting cooperation in dilemma situations: experimental manipulations. *Acta Psychologica, 68*, 83–97.

De Cremer, D. & van Vugt, M. (1999). Social identification effects in social dilemmas: a transformation of motives. *European Journal of Social Psychology, 29*, 871–893.

Deluga, R. J. (1994). Supervisor trust building, leader–member exchange and organizational citizenship behaviour. *Journal of Occupational and Organizational Psychology, 67*, 315–326.

Dirks, K. T. (1999). The effects of interpersonal trust on work group performance. *Journal of Applied Psychology, 84*, 445–455.

Dirks, K. T. & Ferrin, D. L. (2001). The role of trust in organizational settings. *Organization Science, 12*, 450–467.

Dirks, K. T. & Ferrin, D. L. (2002). Trust in leadership: meta-analytic findings and implications for research and practice. *Journal of Applied Psychology, 87*, 611–628.

Dirks, K. T. & Skarlicki, D. P. (April, 2002). *The relationship between coworker trust and performance*. Paper presented at the annual meeting of the Society for Industrial and Organizational Psychology, Toronto, Ontario, Canada.

Dutton, J. E., Dukerich, J. M., & Harquail, C. V. (1994). Organizational images and member identification. *Administrative Science Quarterly, 39*, 239–263.

Feeney, B. & Collins, N. (2001). Predictors of caregiving in adult intimate relationships: an attachment theoretical perspective. *Journal of Personality and Social Psychology, 80*, 972–994.

Ferrin, D. L., Bligh, M. C., & Kohles, J. C. (April, 2002). *Trust, monitoring and cooperation in mixed-motive negotiations: a causal examination of competing theories and a comparison across levels*. Paper presented at the annual meeting of the Society for Industrial and Organizational Psychology, Toronto, Ontario, Canada.

Folger, R. & Cropanzano, R. (2001). Fairness theory: justice as accountability. In J. Greenberg & R. Cropanzano (eds), *Advances in Organizational Justice* (pp. 1–55). Stanford, Calif.: Stanford University Press.

Folger, R., Konovsky, M. A., & Cropanzano, R. (1992). A due process metaphor for performance appraisal. In B. M. Staw & L. L. Cummings (eds), *Research in Organizational Behavior* (Vol. 14, pp. 129–177). Greenwich, Conn.: JAI Press.

Fraley, R. & Shaver, P. (1997). Adult attachment and the suppression of unwanted thoughts. *Journal of Personality and Social Psychology, 73*, 1080–1091.

Fraley, R. C. & Waller, N. G. (1998). Adult attachment patterns: a test of the typological model. In J. Simpson & W. Rholes (eds), *Attachment Theory and Close Relationships* (pp. 78–114). New York: Guilford Press.

Gladstein, D. (1984). A model of task group effectiveness. *Administrative Science Quarterly, 29*, 499–517.

Greenberg, J. (1993). The social side of fairness: interpersonal and informational classes of organizational justice. In R. Cropanzano (ed.), *Justice in the Workplace: Approaching Justice in Human Resource Management* (pp. 79–103). Hillsdale, NJ: Lawrence Erlbaum Associates.

Grieve, P. G. & Hogg, M. A. (1999). Subjective uncertainty and intergroup discrimination in the minimal group situation. *Personality and Social Psychology Bulletin, 25*, 926–940.

Haslam, S. A., Oakes, P. J., Reynolds, K. J., & Turner, J. C. (1999). Social identity salience and the emergence of stereotype consensus. *Personality and Social Psychology Bulletin, 25*, 809–818.

Hazan, C. & Shaver, P. (1987). Romantic love conceptualized as an attachment process. *Journal of Personality and Social Psychology, 52*, 511–524.

Hazan, C. & Shaver, P. (1990). Love and work: an attachment–theoretical perspective. *Journal of Personality and Social Psychology, 59*, 270–280.

Hogg, M. A. (2001). Social identity and the sovereignty of the group: a psychology of belonging. In C. Sedikides & M. B. Brewer (eds), *Individual Self, Relational Self, Collective Self* (pp. 125–142). Philadelphia, Pa: Psychology Press.

James, W. (1948). *Psychology*. New York: World Publishing Company.

Johnson, D. W., Johnson, R. T., & Tjosvold, D. (2000). Constructive controversy: the value of intellectual opposition. In M. Deutsch & P. T. Coleman (eds), *The Handbook of Conflict Resolution: Theory and Practice* (pp. 65–85). San Francisco, Calif.: Jossey-Bass, Inc.

Johnson, J. P., Korsgaard, M. A., & Sapienza, H. J. (2002). Perceived fairness, decision control, and commitment in international joint venture management teams. *Strategic Management Journal, 23*, 1141–1160.

Kim, W. C. & Mauborgne, R. A. (1993). Procedural justice, attitudes, and subsidiary top management compliance with multinationals' corporate strategic decisions. *Academy of Management Journal, 26*, 502–506.

Konovsky, M. A. & Pugh, S. D. (1994). Citizenship behavior and social exchange. *Academy of Management Journal, 37*, 656–669.

Korsgaard, M. A., Brodt, S. E., & Whitener, E. M. (2002). Trust in the face of conflict: the role of managerial trustworthy behavior and organizational context. *Journal of Applied Psychology, 87*, 312–319.

Korsgaard, M. A. & Roberson, L. (1995). Procedural justice in performance evaluation. *Journal of Management, 21*, 657–699.

Korsgaard, M. A., Sapienza, H. J., & Schweiger, D. M. (2001). Organizational justice in strategic decision making. In R. Cropanzano (ed.), *Justice in the Workplace* (Vol. 2, pp. 209–226). Hillsdale, NJ: Lawrence Erlbaum Associates.

Korsgaard, M. A., Schweiger, D. M., & Sapienza, H. J. (1995). The role of procedural justice in building commitment, attachment, and trust in strategic decision-making teams. *Academy of Management Journal, 38*, 60–84.

Kramer, K. M. (1999). Trust and distrust in organizations: emerging perspectives, enduring questions. *Annual Review of Psychology, 50*, 569–598.

Kramer, R. M. (1993). Cooperation and organizational identification. In J. K. Murninghan (ed.), *Social Psychology in Organizations* (pp. 244–267). Englewood Cliffs, NJ: Prentice-Hall.

Kramer, R. M., Brewer, H. B., & Hanna, B. A. (1996). Collective trust and collective action: the decision to trust as a social dilemma. In R. M. Kramer & T. R. Tyler (eds), *Trust in Organizations* (pp. 357–389). Thousand Oaks, Calif.: Sage.

Lester, S., Meglino, B. M., & Korsgaard, M. A. (2002). The antecedents and consequences of group potency: a longitudinal investigation of newly formed groups. *Academy of Management Journal, 45*, 352–369.

Leventhal, G. S. (1980). What should be done with equity theory? In K. J. Gergen, M. S. Greenberg, & H. R. Willis (eds), *Social Exchange: Advances in Theory and Research* (pp. 27–55). New York: Plenum Press.

Lind, E. A. (2001). Fairness heuristic theory: justice judgments as pivotal cognitions in organizational relations. In J. Greenberg & R. Cropanzano (eds), *Advances in Organizational Justice* (pp. 56–88). Stanford, Calif.: Stanford University Press.

Lind, E. A. & Tyler, T. R. (1988). *The Social Psychology of Procedural Justice*. New York: Plenum.

McAllister, D. J. (1995). Affect- and cognition-based trust as foundations for interpersonal cooperation in organizations. *Academy of Management Journal, 38*, 24–59.

McKnight, D. H., Cummings, L. L., & Chervany, N. L. (1998). Initial trust formation in new organizational relationships. *Academy of Management Review, 23*, 473–490.

Mael, F. & Ashforth, B. E. (1992). Alumni and their alma mater: a partial test of the reformulated model of organizational identification. *Journal of Organizational Behavior, 13*, 103–123.

Mael, F. A. & Ashforth, B. E. (1995). Loyal from day one: biodata, organizational identification, and turnover among newcomers. *Personnel Psychology, 48*, 309–333.

Main, M., Kaplan, N., & Cassidy, J. (1985). Security in infancy, childhood, and adulthood: a move to the level of representation. In I. Bretherton & E. Waters (eds), *Growing Points of Attachment Theory and Research. Monographs of the Society for Research in Child Development, 50*(1–2, Serial No. 209), 66–104.

Meyerson, D., Weick, K. E., & Kramer, R. M. (1996). Swift trust and temporary groups. In R. M. Kramer & T. R. Tyler (eds), *Trust in Organizations* (pp. 166–195). Thousand Oaks, Calif.: Sage.

Mikulincer, M., Florian, V., & Tolmacz, R. (1990). Attachment styles and fear of personal death: a case study of affect regulation. *Journal of Personality and Social Psychology, 58*, 273–280.

Mikulincer, M., Orbach, I., & Iavnieli, D. (1998). Adult attachment style and affect regulation: strategic variations in subjective self–other similarity. *Journal of Personality and Social Psychology, 75*, 436–448.

Mikulincer, M. & Shaver, P. (2001). Attachment theory and intergroup bias: evidence that priming the secure base schema attenuates negative reactions to out-groups. *Journal of Personality and Social Psychology, 81*, 97–115.

Moore, D. A., Kurtzberg, T. R., Thompson, L. L., & Morris, M. W. (1999). Long and short routes to electronically mediated negotiations: group affiliations and good vibrations. *Organizational Behavior and Human Decision Processes, 77*, 22–43.

Mossholder, K. W., Bennett, N., & Martin, C. L. (1998). A multilevel analysis of procedural justice context. *Journal of Organizational Behavior, 19*, 131–141.

Mullin, B. A. & Hogg, M. A. (1998). Dimensions of subjective uncertainty in social identification and minimal intergroup discrimination. *British Journal of Social Psychology, 37*, 345–365.

Mullin, B. A. & Hogg, M. A. (1999). Motivations for group membership: the role of subjective important and uncertainty reduction. *Basic and Applied Social Psychology, 21*, 91–102.

Mussweiler, T., Gabriel, S., & Bodenhausen, G. V. (2000). Shifting social identities as a strategy for deflecting threatening social comparisons. *Journal of Personality and Social Psychology, 79*, 398–409.

Naumann, S. E. & Bennett, N. (2000). A case for procedural justice climate: development and test of a multilevel model. *Academy of Management Journal, 43*, 881–889.

O'Reilly, C., III & Chatman, J. (1986). Organizational commitment and psychological attachment: the effects of compliance, identification, and internalization on prosocial behavior. *Journal of Applied Psychology, 71*, 492–499.

Phillips, J. M., Douthitt, E. A., & Hyland, M. M. (2001). The role of justice in team member satisfaction with the leader and attachment to the team. *Journal of Applied Psychology, 86*, 316–325.

Podsakoff, P. M., Aherne, M., & MacKenzie, S. B. (1997). Organizational citizenship behavior and the quantity and quality of work group performance. *Journal of Applied Psychology, 82*, 262–270.

Podsakoff, P. M., MacKenzie, S. B., Paine, J. B., & Bachrach, D. G. (2000). Organizational citizenship behaviors: a critical review of the theoretical and empirical literature and suggestions for future research. *Journal of Management, 26*, 513–563.

Robinson, S. L. & Morrison, E. W. (1995). Psychological contracts and OCB: the effect of unfulfilled obligations on civic virtue behavior. *Journal of Organizational Behavior, 16*, 289–298.

Rousseau, D. M., Sitkin, S. B., Burt, R. S., & Camerer, C. (1998). Not so different after all: a cross-discipline view of trust. *Academy of Management Review, 23*, 405–421.

Sapienza, H. J. & Korsgaard, M. A. (1996). The role of procedural justice in entrepreneur–investor relations. *Academy of Management Journal, 39*, 544–574.

Simons, T. L. & Peterson, R. S. (2000). Task conflict and relationship conflict in top management teams: the pivotal role of intragroup trust. *Journal of Applied Psychology, 85*, 102–112.

Smith, E. R., Coats, S., & Murphy, J. (2001). The self and attachment to relationship partners and groups: theoretical parallels and new insights. In C. Sedikides & M. B. Brewer (eds), *Individual Self, Relational Self, Collective Self* (pp. 109–124). Philadelphia, Pa: Psychology Press.

Smith, E. R., Murphy, J., & Coats, S. (1999). Attachment to groups: theory and measurement. *Journal of Personality and Social Psychology, 77*, 94–110.

Smith, K. G., Carroll, S. J., & Ashford, S. J. (1995). Intra- and interorganizational cooperation: toward a research agenda. *Academy of Management Journal, 38*, 7–23.

Tajfel, H. & Turner, J. C. (1979). An integrative theory of intergroup conflict. In W. G. Austin & S. Worchell (eds), *The Social Psychology of Intergroup Relations* (pp. 33–47). Monterey, Calif.: Brooks/Cole.

Turner, J. C., Hogg, M. A., Oakes, P. J., Reicher, S. D., & Wetherell, M. S. (1987). *Rediscovering the Social Group: A Self-categorization Theory*. Oxford, UK: Blackwell.

Tyler, T. R. & Bies, R. J. (1990). Beyond formal procedures: the interpersonal context of procedural justice. In J. Carroll (ed.), *Applied Social Psychology and Organizational Settings* (pp. 77–98). Hillsdale, NJ: Lawrence Erlbaum Associates.

Tyler, T. R. & Blader, S. L. (2000). *Cooperation in Groups*. Philadelphia, Pa: Taylor & Francis.

Tyler, T. R. & Blader, S. L. (2001). Innovations in organizational justice. Paper presented at the International Round Table on Innovations in Organizational Justice. Vancouver.

Whitener, E., Brodt, S., Korsgaard, M. A., & Werner, J. (1998). Managers as initiators of trust: an exchange relationship framework for understanding managerial trustworthy behavior. *Academy of Management Review, 23*, 513–530.

Williams, M. (2001). In whom we trust: group membership as an effective context for trust development. *Academy of Management Review, 26*, 377–396.

3

A CONTINGENCY THEORY OF TASK CONFLICT AND PERFORMANCE IN GROUPS AND ORGANIZATIONAL TEAMS

Carsten K. W. De Dreu and Laurie R. Weingart

INTRODUCTION

Where people come together to work, there is a need to coordinate their knowledge, skills, abilities, and activities. Coordination is critical to organizations and the quest for optimal coordination is perhaps the oldest and most enduring problem organizational leaders and management scientists face (Jaffee, 2000). For instance, in their classical work on the social psychology of organizations, Katz and Kahn (1978) observe that "... every aspect of organizational life that creates order and coordination of effort must overcome tendencies to action, and in that fact lies the potentiality for conflict" (p. 617).

To many organizational leaders and managers, conflict is a threat to coordination and effective functioning and thus should be avoided and prevented. This traditional view is reflected in the large number of academic and practitioner-oriented writings that have appeared in recent years, bearing such titles as "barriers to dispute resolution" (Arrow et al., 1995), "controlling the cost of conflict" (Slaikeu & Hasson, 1998), and "difficult conversations" (Stone, Patton, & Heen, 1999). Furthermore, there is a tendency in both the academic and the practitioner-oriented literature to denote collaboration and problem solving as the single best solution to emerging conflict in groups (for discussions, see Blake & Mouton, 1964; Pruitt & Rubin, 1986; van de Vliert, 1997; Weingart & Jehn, 2000). In this chapter, we will argue that the traditional view that task conflict is bad is one-sided, and that the suggestion that problem solving is the one-best-way approach to solving task conflict is erroneous. We review research that suggests that conflict can be functional to teamwork at times and detrimental at others. We develop a contingency perspective that views group performance as a function of the interaction between type of task conflict, conflict management strategy, and group tasks.

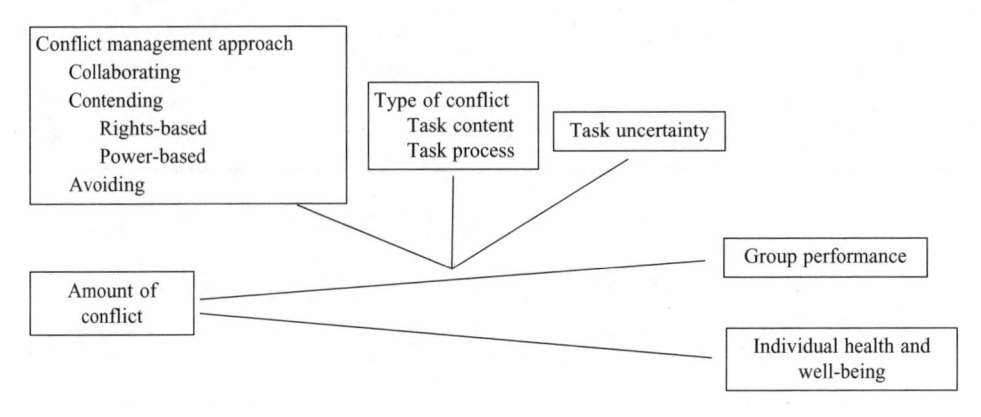

Figure 3.1

Overview of the Contingency Perspective

Figure 3.1 gives an overview of the contingency perspective we will develop in this chapter. A fundamental assumption underlying the model is that conflict affects individuals and the social system in which they function in different ways. Accordingly, we cannot focus exclusively on one outcome variable, such as group performance, and expect to obtain a thorough understanding of conflict at work. Instead, a multifaceted approach that includes multiple outcome variables is necessary. In this chapter, we consider both group performance and individual health and well-being as key outcome variables. We choose these two outcome variables because they represent two levels of aggregation (individual and group) that are the most proximal to many conflict episodes. The impact of task conflict on group performance and individual well-being is considered to depend on (a) the type of conflict (task content or task process); (b) the level of task uncertainty (the extent to which the group tasks are routine versus complex and ill-defined); and (c) whether the group approaches the conflict through collaborating, contending, or avoiding.

In the remainder of this first section we introduce the building blocks of our contingency model. Consecutively, we discuss group performance and individual well-being, the role of task uncertainty, the differences between task-content and task-process conflicts, and conflict management strategies groups may use. In the second section, we review evidence pointing toward the efficacy of a contingency perspective and we develop a set of propositions pertaining to the more novel aspects of the model. We conclude this chapter with some general conclusions and we highlight several fundamental questions awaiting research.

Group Performance and Individual Well-being

In this chapter the terms "group" and "team" are used interchangeably and refer to ongoing (semi)-autonomous sets of interdependent individuals who have a joint responsibility for accomplishing a set of tasks (West, Borrill, & Unsworth, 1998). While the tasks groups perform may vary widely (for discussions and taxonomies, see McGrath, 1984, and Steiner, 1972), a particularly useful distinction when it comes to understanding the effects of conflict relates to the level of task uncertainty (van de Ven, Delbecq, & Koenig, 1976). Task uncertainty refers to the variability (i.e. routineness) and difficulty (i.e. complexity) experienced when performing the task. Variability has been operationalized as the number of work exceptions encountered by a work unit (Perrow, 1967) and the variety of methods used in task processes (Hall, 1972). Difficulty relates to predictability of work methods. Thus the task uncertainty distinction is largely between simple, routine tasks on the one hand, and complex, ill-defined tasks on the other. Examples of more certain (i.e. simple, routine) tasks include signal detection tasks, routine planning and design in logistics, and routine execution tasks in production and manufacturing. Examples of more uncertain tasks include group decision making, creative tasks, or nonroutine production tasks. The task uncertainty dimension is one of three factors important to group performance in our contingency model of conflict (see Figure 3.1).

Researchers have used a variety of indicators of group performance, including productivity, innovativeness, and adherence to constraints. Examples include the team's average productivity (Jehn, 1995), self-assessments of the quality of group decisions (Amason, 1996), the number of innovations (De Dreu & West, 2001), or adherence to time and budget constraints (Lovelace, Shapiro, & Weingart, 2001). To some extent, however, these different indicators all tap into the general construct of *group effectiveness*—the extent to which a group reaches its goals (Hackman, 1983). As we will see below, many studies on conflict and group performance indeed used a global measure of team effectiveness.

The use of a wide range of group performance measures is due to at least two factors. First, relevant indices of group performance can only be identified based on an understanding of the specific group task (Steiner, 1972), thus different group tasks necessitate different performance measures. For example, innovation is a more relevant performance indicator to new product development teams than to production teams. As a result, multiple measures of group performance are necessary to compare conflict effects across multiple studies. Second, in field research one often has to settle for those indicators that are or can be made available.

Individual well-being reflects an individual's evaluation of his/her work environment. The experiences at work may affect an individual in several ways, ranging from depression and despair to elation and work satisfaction. Although frameworks and definitions of well-being exist (e.g. Warr, 1987), a generally accepted conceptualization of well-being is lacking. In studies that explore the impact of conflicts on individual well-being, the emphasis lies on stress and burnout. *Stress* is an ambiguous word that is used as an overarching rubric encompassing, among other things, the (failing) adaptation of individuals to their environment, and feelings of distress resulting in various physiological, behavioral, and psychological consequences (Quick et al., 1997). In the stress literature one may differentiate between the stressor, the stress response, and distress. Within organizations, an example of stressors are the demands in the workplace. These demands bring about the stress response: a generalized, patterned unconscious mobilization of the body's natural energy. We may feel an elevated heart rate, increased respiration, a dry mouth, and an increased alertness. This mobilization becomes detrimental for an individual's well-being if the demands tax or exceed his or her adaptive resources over longer periods of time. Such distress can manifest itself in various ways, including behavioral consequences (e.g. absenteeism, accident proneness, drug abuse), psychological consequences (e.g. depression, psychosomatic complaints, burnout), and medical consequences (e.g. heart disease) (Quick et al., 1997).

Burnout can be considered as a long-term stress reaction that is caused by the prolonged exposure to job stress. The term "burnout" is a metaphor that refers to the draining of energy, that is more energy is lost than replenished, comparable to a car battery which will run empty if not enough energy is generated from the dynamo (Schaufeli & Enzmann, 1998). Burnout is nowadays defined as a syndrome consisting of three dimensions: exhaustion, cynicism, and ineffectiveness (or reduced personal accomplishment) (Maslach & Leiter, 1997).

Conflict in Groups

In everyday speech, conflict is seen as a fight, a struggle, or the clashing of opposed principles (e.g. *Concise Oxford Dictionary*, 1983). As a result, conflict is often avoided, and when confronted, is difficult to reconcile given this negative and active view of conflict (Kolb & Bartunek, 1992; O'Connor, Gruenfeld & McGrath, 1993). Students of conflict, however, have noted that such a definition is problematic because it confounds what the conflict is about, how the conflict is experienced, and how the conflict is managed (Deutsch, 1973; Pondy, 1967). An alternative is to define conflict as a process that begins when one individual or group perceives differences between oneself and another individual or group over something that is important (Thomas, 1992). Perceived differences about issues that matter produce psychological states, including feelings and motivational goals, that in turn drive behaviors intended to intensify, reduce, or solve the tension (De Dreu, Harinck, & van Vianen, 1999; Pruitt, 1998; Thomas, 1992; Wall & Callister, 1995).

CONFLICT TYPE

Critical in the contingency model we outlined in Figure 3.1 is the content of the problem producing the tension. Given that task performance-related activities include those that have to do with the actual task and others that have to do with the process of performing the task or delegating resources and duties, conflicts in work teams can be differentiated into task-content and task-process conflict.[1] *Task-content conflicts* are disagreements among group members' ideas and opinions about the task being performed, such as disagreement regarding an organization's current hiring strategies or determining the information to include in an annual report. Task-content conflicts include debates over facts (driven by data, evidence) or opinions (De Dreu, Harinck, & van Vianen, 1999) and are sometimes referred to as information conflicts (Levine & Thompson, 1996), or cognitive conflicts (Brehmer, 1976; Jehn, 1997). *Task-process conflicts* are about logistical and delegation issues such as how task accomplishment should proceed in the work unit, who is responsible for what, and how things should be delegated (Jehn, 1997). Since task-process conflicts often involve the distribution of scarce resources, whether tangible or intangible, task-process conflict is sometimes equated with resource conflict, a conflict of interest (e.g. De Dreu, Harinck, & van Vianen, 1999; Harinck, De Dreu, & van Vianen, 2000). For example, a cross-functional

---

[1] In some studies, task-content and task-process conflicts have been differentiated from relationship conflicts. Relationship conflicts are personal in nature, including interpersonal conflicts, personality clashes, and disagreements about extracurricular issues. Relationship conflict is generally dysfunctional to team performance. Research suggests that effective teams manage relationship conflicts through avoiding and ignoring the issues, whereas ineffective teams with relationship conflict manage these conflicts in a more active way, through forcing or problem solving (De Dreu & van Vianen, 2001; Jehn, 1997; Murnighan & Conlon, 1991). Avoiding and ignoring personality differences and relationship conflict may prevent the conflict intensifying and translating into nonproductive task conflict.

product development team might disagree about the optimal design for a new product—a task-content conflict. Or they might have a conflict over the timing of completion of an aspect of the aesthetic design—a task-process conflict.

CONFLICT MANAGEMENT

Conflict management refers to the behavior oriented toward the intensification, reduction, and resolution of the conflict. Although an infinite number of conflict management strategies may be conceived of, conflict research and theory tend to converge on a four-way typology distinguishing between (a) collaborating, (b) contending, (c) conceding, and (d) avoiding (Blake & Mouton, 1964; De Dreu et al., 2001; Pruitt & Rubin, 1986; Thomas, 1992). *Collaborating* is oriented toward an agreement that satisfies both own and other's aspirations as much as possible. It involves an exchange of information about priorities and preferences, showing insights, and making trade-offs between important and unimportant issues. Collaboration is related to "constructive controversy" (Tjosvold, 1998), which is defined as the open-minded discussion between parties with opposing points of view but compatible goals. *Avoiding* involves reducing the importance of the issues, and attempts to suppress thinking about the issues. *Contending* involves threats and bluffs, persuasive arguments, and positional commitments. *Conceding*, which can be seen as the flip side of contending, is oriented toward accepting and incorporating the other's will. It involves unilateral concessions, unconditional promises, and offering help. When both parties use a contending strategy, the conflict tends to escalate. Alternatively, a party can concede in response to contention from the other party, resulting in progress toward potential resolution of the conflict.

Ury, Brett, and Goldberg (1993) further differentiated contending strategies into two subcategories, rights and power, in their taxonomy of approaches to dispute resolution. We adopt this distinction because while rights and power are both contending strategies, they are differentially effective. When using a rights-based approach, the parties attempt to resolve the dispute by applying some standard of fairness, precedent, contract, or law. A focus on rights is likely to lead to a distributive agreement in which each party has to give something up to reach an agreement, with the possibility of one party giving much more than receiving. A power-based approach results in the dispute being resolved by determining who is able to force their desired outcome—who is stronger, has higher status, is able to coerce the other, or can force a concession from the other party. A power-based approach usually leads to distributive agreements that have the potential to escalate due to feelings of resentment and a desire for revenge (Brett, Shapiro, & Lytle, 1998; Lytle, Brett, & Shapiro, 1999; Tinsley, 1998, 2001). While either a rights-based or power-based approach can lead to concessions from the other party, rights-based concessions are usually evidenced when there is agreement about a standard, whereas power-based concessions reflect submission to a greater force.

In this model we use four categories of conflict management strategies: collaborating, avoiding, contending rights, and contending power. We do not consider conceding as a separate category because it is a reactive rather than proactive strategy that is often paired with contending. In the next section we explore the role that these conflict management strategies play, along with type of conflict and task uncertainty in our contingency model of conflict on group performance.

A CONTINGENCY PERSPECTIVE OF GROUP CONFLICT

This section develops the contingency model further. We begin by discussing the relationship between conflict at work and individual health and well-being because this relationship is the most straightforward within our model (cf. Figure 3.1). Subsequently, we discuss the relationship between task-related conflict and group effectiveness. We review research and summarize results using meta-analytic techniques. This review provides the input for the third and final part of this section, in which we advance hypotheses about the moderating role of conflict management strategies in high and in low complexity group tasks.

Conflict and Individual Well-being

Conflict is an emotional situation and elicits anger, disgust, and fear. Being in conflict threatens one's self-esteem and requires cognitive resources to cope with the situation. Negative emotions, threatened self-esteem, and heightened cognitive effort impact the physiological system in a multitude of ways: adrenaline levels go up, heartbeat accelerates, and muscle tension increases (Quick et al., 1997). Quite obviously, in the short run conflict and conflict interaction have rather negative consequences for individual health and well-being. When conflict is not resolved but persists over longer periods of time, serious health threats may result. Research suggests that enduring high levels of stress hormones deplete the physiological system and result in psychosomatic complaints including enduring headaches, upset stomach, and the like (Pennebaker, 1982). In addition, enduring conflict at work may increase alcohol intake, and trouble sleeping, which in turn affects the physical and psychic well-being of the individuals involved (Dana & Griffin, 1999).

The notion that enduring conflict at work may have serious consequences for individual health and well-being is supported by various studies. Spector and Jex (1998) summarize the findings of 13 samples involving over 3000 employees and find a positive and significant correlation between conflict at work and physical health complaints. A similar finding was reported in a more recent study by Spector, Chen, and O'Connell (2000). These authors measured conflict at work, anxiety, frustration, and physical complaints. Analyses revealed positive and moderate correlations between conflict at work and anxiety and frustration, and a small but significant correlation between conflict at work and physical complaints. This general pattern is substantiated in various other studies. For instance, Shirom and Mayer (1993) found a small but significant correlation between conflict and burnout among Israeli high-school teachers. Several other studies reported moderately positive correlations between conflict at work and the exhaustion dimension of burnout (e.g. Taylor et al., 1990; van Dierendonck, Schaufeli, & Buunk, 2001; van Dierendonck, Schaufeli, & Sixma, 1994).

Conflict at work not only affects overall stress levels, but translates into psychosomatic complaints. For instance, research has established positive relationships between conflict and psychosomatic complaints, including gastrointestinal symptoms (e.g. nausea, stomach cramps), respiratory symptoms (e.g. pressure on chest, hyperventilation), cardiac symptoms (e.g. rapid heart rate, pounding of heart), dizziness and fainting, headaches, and tingling sensations in the limbs (for reviews, see De Dreu, van Dierendonck, & De Best Waldhober, 2002; Spector & Jex, 1998). Finally, the relationship between conflict at work and stress appears to hold up also when task-related conflict is considered. In a study of 82 hospital staff members, Friedman et al. (2000) found that stress was positively related to task-related conflict. De Dreu, van Dierendonck, and De Best Waldhober (2002) reviewed some of their own (unpublished) research findings showing them to be consistent with Friedman et al., indicating the negative relationship between task-related conflict and stress is robust and generalizes to other organizations, including manufacturing organizations.

The work on conflict and individual health and well-being did not consider the distinction between task-content and task-process conflicts and this is an important area for future research. Task-process conflicts are associated with distribution and fairness to a greater extent than task-content conflicts (Harinck, De Dreu, & van Vianen, 2000), and injustice and violations of basic principles of fairness constitute major threats to individual health and well-being (van Dierendonck, Schaufeli, & Buunk, 1998). In other words, future research could test the hypothesis that task-process conflicts impact individual health and well-being more than task-content conflicts.

While the relationship between individual well-being and conflict management strategies has not been the focus of systematic research, several empirical studies exist. De Dreu, van Dierendonck, and De Best-Waldhober (2002) reviewed these studies, and concluded that a passive and obliging way of dealing with conflict has more negative consequences for health and individual well-being than a more proactive and collaborating approach to conflict. This conclusion is consistent with the idea that collaborating in conflict strengthens interpersonal relationships, and increases self-esteem, feelings of self-efficacy, and satisfaction (De Dreu, Weingart, & Kwon, 2000; Rubin, Pruitt, & Kim, 1994).

Before moving to a discussion about the relationships between conflict and group effectiveness, a word of caution is needed. Without exception, the work on conflict and individual health and well-being is cross-sectional and based on self-report. Although valid scales were used and results were consistent across studies, it cannot be excluded that reduced well-being produces conflict rather than the reverse. We need research using experimental or longitudinal designs to increase our confidence in these results. Also, we would benefit from going beyond self-reports as sole indicators of (deteriorated) health and well-being, and instead incorporate in future studies more objective measures of stress (e.g. hormone levels) and psychosomatic complaints (e.g. number of doctor visits and number of sick days). Finally, future research should focus on teasing apart task-content from task-process conflict.

Conflict and Group Effectiveness

As mentioned at the outset, conflict is inherent to groups and organizations and many see it as inherently bad. It has been argued, however, that there exists a curvilinear relationship between individual and group effectiveness and the level of conflict between individuals or within that group (Robbins, 1974; Walton, 1969). That is, it has been argued that some conflict is better than no conflict at all, and that some conflict is better than intense conflict. Consistent with this, research has shown that when conflict escalates and becomes very intense the social system shuts down and performance suffers badly (Jehn, 1995; Walton, 1969). On the other hand, research on groupthink (Janis, 1972) as well as studies on the role of devil's advocacy in group decision making (Schwenk, 1990) have shown that extreme concurrence seeking in groups (i.e. the avoidance of conflict) may lead to ineffective decision making with sometimes disastrous consequences. Defective decision making is, however, reduced when conflict is stimulated rather than suppressed (Nemeth, 1986; Turner & Pratkanis, 1997).

Table 3.1 Average correlations between task conflict and group performance

Amason & Mooney (2000)	−0.25
De Dreu & West (2001)	−0.21
Janssen, van de Vliert, & Veenstra (2000)	−0.27
Jehn (1994)	+0.38
Jehn & Mannix (2001)	−0.16
Friedman et al. (2000)	−0.39
Amason (1996)	−0.09
Jehn (1995)	−0.29
Jehn et al. (1999)	−0.11
Pelled, Eisenhardt, & Xin (1999)	+0.05
Porter & Lilly (1996)	−0.35
Effect size (Cohen's d)	−0.43
95% Confidence interval	−0.51/−0.35
Average r	−0.21***
Homogeneity Q_w	92.04***

Note: *** $p < 0.001$.

Table 3.1 uses meta-analytic techniques (Johnson, 1989) to summarize the findings from research published between 1994 and 2000 that considered task conflict as the independent variable and group effectiveness as the dependent variable. Most studies measured task conflict with a scale developed by Jehn (1995), but studies varied considerably in how group performance was assessed. Some studies used supervisor ratings of team effectiveness (e.g. Amason, 1996; Jehn, 1994), while others included objective performance measures such as average production per day (e.g. Jehn, 1995). Some studies reported multiple measures of group performance, in which case we took the correlation with the least objectionable performance measure (e.g. we preferred external source data to self-reports, and objective data to subjective assessments of performance).

As can be seen in Table 3.1, there is little evidence for the idea that task conflict has positive consequences for group performance. In fact, the average effect size (i.e. the average correlation, allowing for different sample sizes across the studies) between task conflict and group performance across all studies is negative, significantly different from zero, and moderate in size. Thus, when looking at the average effect sizes across published studies, we have to conclude that task conflict is detrimental to group performance. Interestingly, the variance in correlations between task conflict and group performance is large and significant (as indicated by the homogeneity measure, Q_w).

The large variation in effect size noted in Table 3.1 indicates that moderators of the relationship between task-related conflict and group effectiveness exist. One important moderator may be the way in which task conflict is managed. Weingart and Jehn (2000) have argued that the key to team effectiveness is collaboration. Open-minded debates may be particularly useful in task-content conflict where creativity and novel solutions are key to resolving a dispute. Collaboration is also related to integrative negotiation (Pruitt, 1998), which involves a problem-solving approach to settle divergent interests through substantial information exchange and logrolling (trading unimportant issues for important ones). Integrative negotiation may be particularly useful in task-process conflict where group members have opposing interests.

Some first evidence for the idea that collaboration is a prerequisite for task-related conflict to become productive (or at least not unproductive) comes from a study by Lovelace, Shapiro, and Weingart (2001). In a study of cross-functional new product development teams, they examined the effects of both collaborative (i.e. more objective and problem-focused) and contentious (i.e. emotional and personal) conflict communication on team performance. In general, task conflict was negatively related to team performance in terms of product innovation as well as budget and time constraint adherence. Results showed that teams that used collaborative communication did not suffer from the deleterious effect of conflict on innovation and constraint adherence. However, these collaborative teams did not enjoy any positive effects of conflict. They merely avoided the potential negative effects. Interestingly, contentious communication played a pivotal role in determining constraint adherence. Contentious communication greatly exacerbated the negative effect of task conflict on constraint adherence, to an even greater degree than collaborative communication eliminated the effect.

Additional evidence for the importance of collaboration in task-content conflict comes from a study by De Dreu and West (2001) on innovation in self-managed teams. They assessed, through questionnaires, the extent to which self-managed teams were characterized by task-content conflict (operationalized as minority dissent), as well as the extent to which the team members participated in the decision-making process—a proxy to collaboration. Results showed more innovations when minority dissent was high *and* teams had high levels of participation in decision making. This suggests, indeed, that task-content conflict may be beneficial provided that group members collaborate and participate in the decision-making process.

The results of these two studies are consistent with the results from an extensive program of research by Tjosvold and colleagues on constructive controversy (e.g. Tjosvold, 1991, 1997, 1998). This work reveals that when individuals with task conflict perceive their own and their conflict opponent's goals as cooperative and compatible, they are more likely to engage in "constructive controversy" and debate in an open-minded way about their opposing views, beliefs, and opinions. When, in contrast, they perceive their own and their opponent's goals as competitive and incompatible, they are unlikely to engage in constructive controversy and instead work hard to win from the other. Constructive controversy has been shown to result in stronger interpersonal relations, better and richer understanding of the issues under debate, and more effective employees and work teams.

Conflict Type and Task Uncertainty

Our review so far suggests that task-related conflict appears to require mutual problem solving and collaborating for groups to become effective. While incorporating conflict management strategies into the analysis may account for some of the variation in the relationship between conflict and group performance, additional moderators may exist. We suggest that in addition to conflict management strategies, task uncertainty and conflict type determine the effect of conflict on group performance.

The nature of the task at hand will partly determine whether conflict will be productive rather than dysfunctional. Research suggests that task uncertainty may play an important role. Provided that the group performs uncertain tasks in which standard solutions do not suffice, task conflict may be beneficial (Amason, 1996; De Dreu, 1997; Jehn, 1994,

1995, 1997; Turner & Pratkanis, 1997). The basic premise is that task conflict increases group members' tendency to scrutinize task issues and to engage in deep and deliberate processing of task-relevant information. This fosters learning and the development of new and sometimes highly creative insights, leading the group to become more effective and innovative (De Dreu & West, 2001).

Evidence of the moderating role of task uncertainty comes from a study of intensive care units, which suggests that diagnostic diversity (the array of medical and surgical cases admitted to the same ICU) moderates the effect of conflict management approach (conflict avoidance vs problem solving) on unit performance (Pearce et al., 2001). Pearce et al. (2001) found that in units facing lower diagnostic diversity, more conflict avoidance was associated with better performance (i.e. lower mortality rates, controlling for expected mortality rates), while more active problem solving was associated with worse performance. The performance of the units with high diagnostic diversity was not affected by the conflict management approach taken. It appears that conflict avoidance in units facing more homogeneous, but still complex, tasks may allow team members to focus on standard operating procedures (e.g. use of patient care protocols), thereby improving team performance (i.e. decreasing mortality rates).

It thus appears that task uncertainty matters in determining the effects of conflict management approaches on different types of conflict. High uncertainty tasks require the integration of large amounts of information, multiple perspectives, and many potential actions. These tasks require an active approach to both task-content and task-process conflict as a way to manage potentially contradictory desires and information, and therefore this conflict should not be avoided. Collaboration can be an ideal approach for resolving conflicts that occur when working on uncertain tasks.

In contrast, low uncertainty tasks involve more routine behavior and allow reliance on a set of well-learned, a priori established principles and working assumptions. Collaborating to resolve conflict on low uncertainty, clearly defined tasks only seems appropriate when the group has relied on erroneous assumptions and used the wrong heuristics in making judgements and decisions. Otherwise, intensive collaboration may lead the group to rediscover that their original assumptions and heuristics worked best. Indeed, research on the added value to group decision making of a devil's advocate has shown that task conflict induced by a devil's advocate is counterproductive when the group performs a routine task *and* proceeded on the basis of correct assumptions (Schwenk, 1990). In other words, approaching task-content conflicts with collaborating and creative problem solving is expected to be variable in its consequences for group effectiveness because it risks solving the wrong problem based on incorrect assumptions. Often, dealing with conflict about clearly defined tasks may be best settled through rights-based forms of contending. A rights-based approach shifts the focus to determining the appropriate standard, assumptions, or approach to the problem.

The efficacy of the different conflict management approaches also depends on whether the conflict is driven by scarce resources (a conflict of interest) or by differing opinions about optimal solutions with adequate resources available (a conflict of understanding). Task-process conflict often involves the allocation and distribution of scarce resources like time, money, or people. In this context, rights-based forms of contending may help the group deal with opposing interests regarding allocation in a fair and efficient way. In contrast, task-content conflict is often about verifiable issues, about a matter of taste, or about sacred values, and in such conflicts normative standards cannot be used and fairness principles do not apply (Druckman, 1994; Harinck, De Dreu, & van Vianen, 2000). Instead, parties need either a creative solution that bridges both sides, or one party needs to be truly and profoundly convinced of the superiority of the other party's position. In these task-content conflicts collaborating and creative problem solving may be key, and rights-based (or power-based) forms of contending are considered less optimal.

So far we have proposed independent effects of conflict type, conflict management approach, and task complexity on group performance. But some interesting joint effects occur when the moderators are considered simultaneously. For example, a collaborative approach, while ideal for *task*-content conflicts that are *complex*, might be less so when the conflict is about the *process* or the task is *simple* (where rights-based contention might be more appropriate). In contrast, the use of power, at one extreme, or avoidance, at the other, would be dysfunctional for any high complexity task (task or process conflict) and potentially of mixed effectiveness for low complexity tasks. Table 3.2 provides a look at the possible predictions that could be made when task uncertainty, task conflict type, and conflict management approach are considered together.

CONCLUSIONS AND AVENUES FOR FUTURE RESEARCH

The contingency perspective proposed in this chapter and summarized in Figure 3.1 is consistent with past research on conflict and group performance, yet also contains new elements and predictions that require empirical testing. In this section we summarize the main conclusions that derive from our review and theorizing, and we highlight some important areas for further research.

One first area for future work is to study the interactions between conflict type, conflict management, and individual health and well-being. While an increasing number of studies attests to the negative relationship between conflict at work and health parameters such as stress, psychosomatic complaints, and burnout, research is needed to examine the moderating role of conflict management and conflict type. Some initial evidence suggests that an active approach to conflict, including collaborating and contending, is more positive (or less negative) than a more passive strategy that involves conceding and avoiding. However, the cause–effect sequences need examination, and we need to know whether it matters whether the conflict is about content or process issues.

A second area for future research is to examine the moderating role of conflict management in task-content and task-process conflicts. We have argued that in highly complex tasks, collaborating and creative problem solving are highly effective in task-content conflicts, but that in task-process conflicts a rights-based form of contending may often settle the issue in an effective *and* efficient way. We based this speculation on indirect evidence, and research testing these hypotheses is needed.

At least in some instances, a focus on health rather than group performance leads to rather different prescriptions. For example, with regard to health it appears that collaborating is to be preferred regardless of the type of conflict, while with regard to group effectiveness rights-based forms of contending may be more effective than collaborating and creative problem solving, especially in task-process conflicts. This points to a potentially paradoxical situation group managers and team leaders may find themselves in—the need to stimulate group effectiveness requires a different approach to conflict than the need to safeguard individual health and well-being.

Table 3.2 Joint influence of type of conflict and conflict management approach on group performance when group tasks have high or low levels of uncertainty

		Collaborating	Contending		Avoiding
			Rights	Power	
Examples		Interests-based, problem solving, logrolling, informational influence	Rules, precedent, normative standards	Formal authority, status, coercion	
Task uncertainty	Conflict type				
High uncertainty	Task content	Ideal	Variable	Dysfunctional	Dysfunctional
	Task process	Variable	Ideal	Dysfunctional	Dysfunctional
Low uncertainty	Task content	Variable	Ideal	Variable	Variable
	Task process	Variable	Ideal	Variable	Variable

Despite the limitations noted, we believe the contingency approach provides a fruitful avenue for future research. We need to test the basic propositions that task type, type of conflict, and bases for dispute resolution interact to predict group performance. Such tests can be conducted in the laboratory as well as in the field with ongoing work teams. For instance, in the laboratory one can manipulate task type and prime different ways of dispute resolution. In ongoing work teams, long-term effects can be studied and nontask conflicts are more likely to emerge. In addition to testing the core relationships predicted by the contingency theory, research is needed to examine whether the type of group matters. That is, the question is whether the contingency perspective is equally valid in ongoing teams as in temporary, ad hoc teams that exist only to perform one specific task once.

The contingency perspective is in its infancy. However, it connects better with the general notion in the social sciences that human behavior is a function of the interaction between several key variables than the one-best-way approach to conflict and conflict management we often encounter in organizations, and sometimes in the academic literature. While much more research is needed, we can confidently reject the idea that collaborating is always good, and that conflict in work teams is always bad. The contingency perspective advanced here reveals that group conflict is a multifaceted phenomenon that requires tailor-made interventions that recognize that different types of conflict require different modes of dispute resolution.

ACKNOWLEDGEMENTS

This work was facilitated by a grant from the Carnegie Bosch Institute awarded to Laurie R. Weingart and Carsten K. W. De Dreu, and grant 490-22-173 of the Netherlands Foundation for Scientific Research awarded to Carsten K. W. De Dreu. We thank Dean Tjosvold and Michael A. West for providing us with comments on an earlier version of this chapter.

REFERENCES

Amason, A. C. (1996). Distinguishing the effects of functional and dysfunctional conflict on strategic decision making: resolving a paradox for top management groups. *Academy of Management Journal, 39*, 123–148.

Amason, A. C. & Mooney, A. C. (2000). Past performance as an antecedent of top management team conflict: the effects of financial condition on strategic decision making. *International Journal of Conflict Management, 10*, 340–359.

Arrow, K., Mnookin, R. H., Ross, L., Tversky, A., & Wilson, R. (1995). *Barriers to Dispute Resolution*. New York: Norton.

Blake, R. & Mouton, J. S. (1964). *The Managerial Grid*. Houston, Tex.: Gulf.

Brehmer, B. (1976). Social judgement theory and the analysis of interpersonal conflict. *Psychological Bulletin, 83*, 985–1003.

Brett, J. M., Shapiro, D. L., & Lytle, A. L. (1998). Breaking the bonds of reciprocity in negotiations. *Academy of Management Journal, 41*(4), 410–424.

Concise Oxford Dictionary (1983). Oxford, UK: Oxford University Press.

Dana, K. & Griffin, R. W. (1999). Health and well-being in the workplace: a review and synthesis of the literature. *Journal of Management, 25*, 357–384.

De Dreu, C. K. W. (1997). Productive conflict: the importance of conflict issue and conflict management. In C. K. W. De Dreu & E. van de Vliert (eds), *Using Conflict in Organizations* (pp. 9–22). London: Sage.

De Dreu, C. K. W., Evers, A., Beersma, B., Kluwer, E. S., & Nauta, A. (2001). Toward a theory-based measure of conflict behavior in the work place. *Journal of Organizational Behavior, 22*, 645–668.

De Dreu, C. K. W., Harinck, F., & van Vianen, A. E. M. (1999). Conflict and performance in groups and organizations. In C. L. Cooper & I. T. Robertson (eds), *International Review of Industrial and Organizational Psychology* (Vol. 14, pp. 376–405). Chichester: Wiley.

De Dreu, C. K. W., van Dierendonck, D., & De Best-Waldhober, M. (2002). Conflict at work and individual well-being. In M. J. Schabracq, Jac. Winnubst, & C. L. Cooper (eds), *International Handbook of Occupational and Health Psychology* (2nd edn). Chichester, UK: Wiley.

De Dreu, C. K. W. & van Vianen, A. E. M. (2001). Responses to relationship conflict and team effectiveness. *Journal of Organizational Behavior, 22*, 309–328.

De Dreu, C. K. W., Weingart, L. R., & Kwon, S. (2000). Influence of social motives in integrative negotiation: a meta-analytic review and test of two theories. *Journal of Personality and Social Psychology, 78*, 889–905.

De Dreu, C. K. W. & West, M. A. (2001). Minority dissent and team innovation: the importance of participation in decision making. *Journal of Applied Psychology, 86*, 1191–1201.

Deutsch, M. (1973). *The Resolution of Conflict: Constructive and Destructive Processes*. New Haven, Conn.: Yale University Press.

Druckman, D. (1994). Determinants of compromising behavior in negotiation. *Journal of Conflict Resolution, 38*, 507–556.

Friedman, R. A., Tidd, S. T., Currall, S. C., & Tsai, J. C. (2000). What goes around comes around: the impact of personal conflict style on work group conflict and stress. *International Journal of Conflict Management, 10*, 577–589.

Hackman, R. (1983). The design of effective work groups. In J. W. Lorsch (ed.), *Handbook of Organizational Behavior* (pp. 315–342). Englewood Cliffs, NJ: Prentice-Hall.

Hall, R. (1972). *Organizations, Structures, Processes, and Outcomes*. Englewood Cliffs, NJ: Prentice-Hall.

Harinck, F., De Dreu, C. K. W., & van Vianen, A. E. M. (2000). The impact of conflict issue on fixed-pie perceptions, problem solving, and integrative outcomes in negotiation. *Organizational Behavior and Human Decision Processes, 81*, 329–358.

Jaffee, D. (2000). *Organization Theory: Tension and Change*. New York: McGraw-Hill.

Janis, I. L. (1972). *Victims of Groupthink: A Psychological Study of Foreign-policy Decisions and Fiascos*. Boston: Houghton-Mifflin.

Janssen, O., van de Vliert, E., & Veenstra, C. (2000). How task and person conflict shape the role of positive interdependence in management groups. *Journal of Management, 25*, 117–141.

Jehn, K. (1994). Enhancing effectiveness: an investigation of advantages and disadvantages of value-based intragroup conflict. *International Journal of Conflict Management, 5*, 223–238.

Jehn, K. (1995). A multimethod examination of the benefits and detriments of intragroup conflict. *Administrative Science Quarterly, 40*, 256–282.

Jehn, K. (1997). A qualitative analysis of conflict types and dimensions in organizational groups. *Administrative Science Quarterly, 42*, 530–557.

Jehn, K. & Mannix, E. (2001). The dynamic nature of conflict: a longitudinal study of intragroup conflict and group performance. *Academy of Management Journal, 44*, 238–251.

Jehn, K., Chadwick, C., & Thatcher, S. M. B. (1997). To agree or not to agree: the effects of value congruence, individual demographic dissimilarity, and conflict on work group outcomes. *International Journal of Conflict Management, 8*, 287–305.

Johnson, B. T. (1989). *DSTAT: Software for the Meta-analytic Review of Research Literatures*. Hillsdale, NJ: Lawrence Erlbaum.

Katz, D. & Kahn, D. (1978). *The Social Psychology of Organizing*. New York: McGraw-Hill.

Kolb, D.M. & Bartunek, J. M. (eds) (1992). *Hidden Conflict in Organizations: Uncovering Behind-the-scenes Disputes*. London: Sage.

Levine, J. M. & Thompson, L. L. (1996). Conflict in groups. In E. T. Higgins & A. W. Kruglanski (eds), *Social Psychology: Handbook of Basic Principles* (pp. 745–776). New York: Guilford.

Lovelace, K., Shapiro, D. L., & Weingart, L. R. (2001). Maximizing cross-functional new product teams' innovativeness and constraint adherence: a conflict communications perspective. *Academy of Management Journal, 44*, 779–783.

Lytle, A. L., Brett, J. M., & Shapiro, D. L. (1999). The strategic use of interests, rights, and power to resolve disputes. *Negotiation Journal, 15*(1), 31–49.

McGrath, J. E. (1984). *Groups, Interaction and Performance.* Englewood Cliffs, NJ: Prentice-Hall.

Maslach, C. & Leiter, M. P. (1997). *The Truth about Burnout. How Organizations Cause Personal Stress and What to Do about it.* San Francisco: Jossey-Bass.

Murnighan, J. K. & Conlon, D. E. (1991). The dynamics of intense work groups: a study of British string quartets. *Administrative Science Quarterly, 36*, 165–186.

Nemeth, C. (1986). Differential contributions of majority and minority influence processes. *Psychological Review, 93*, 10–20.

O'Connor, K. M., Gruenfeld, D. H., & McGrath, J. E. (1993). The experience and effects of conflict in continuing work groups. *Small Group Research, 24*, 362–382.

Pearce, B. M., Rousseau, D. M., Shortell, S. M., & Gillies, R. R. (2001). Conflict management and group performance: how context alters the effects of problem solving and avoidance. Working paper, Heinz School of Public Policy and Management, Carnegie Mellon University.

Pelled, L. H., Eisenhardt, K. M., & Xin, K. R. (1999). Exploring the black box: an analysis of work group diversity, conflict, and performance. *Administrative Science Quarterly, 44*, 1–28.

Pennebaker, J. W. (1982). *The Psychology of Physical Symptoms.* New York: Springer-Verlag.

Perrow, C. (1967). A framework for the comparative analysis of organizations. *American Sociological Review, 32*, 194–208.

Pondy, L. (1967). Organizational conflict: concepts and models. *Administrative Science Quarterly, 17*, 296–320.

Porter, T. & Lilly, B. (1996). The effects of conflict, trust, and task commitment on project team performance. *International Journal of Conflict Management, 1*(4), 361–376.

Pruitt, D. G. (1998). Social conflict. In D. Gilbert, S. T. Fiske, & G. Lindzey (eds), *Handbook of Social Psychology* (4th edn, Vol. 2, pp. 89–150). New York: McGraw-Hill.

Pruitt, D. G. & Rubin, J. Z. (1986). *Social Conflict: Escalation, Stalemate, and Settlement.* New York: Random House.

Quick, J. C., Quick, J. D., Nelson, D. L., & Hurrel, J. J. (1997). *Preventive Stress Management in Organizations.* Washington, DC: American Psychological Association.

Robbins, S. P. (1974). *Managing Organizational Conflict: A Nontraditional Approach.* Englewood Cliffs, NJ: Prentice-Hall.

Rubin, J., Pruitt, D. G., & Kim, S. (1994). *Social Conflict: Escalation: Stalemate and Settlement.* New York: McGraw-Hill.

Schwenk, C. R. (1990). Effects of devil's advocacy and dialectical inquiry on decision making: a meta-analysis. *Organizational Behavior and Human Decision Processes, 47*, 161–176.

Shirom, A. & Mayer, A. (1993). Stress and strain among union lay officials and rank-and-file members. *Journal of Organizational Behavior, 14*, 401–413.

Slaikeu, K. A. & Hasson, R. H. (1998). *Controlling the Cost of Conflict.* San Francisco: Jossey-Bass.

Spector, P. E., Chen, P. Y., & O'Connell, B. J. (2000). A longitudinal study of relations between job stressors and job strains while controlling for prior negative affectivity and strains. *Journal of Applied Psychology, 85*, 211–218.

Spector, P. E. & Jex, S. M. (1998). Development of four self-report measures of job stressors and strain: Interpersonal Conflict at Work Scale, Organizational Constraints Scale, Quantitative Workload Inventory, and Physical Symptoms Inventory. *Journal of Occupational Health Psychology, 3*, 356–367.

Steiner, I. D. (1972). *Group Processes and Productivity.* New York: Academic Press.

Stone, D., Patton, B., & Heen, S. (1999). *Difficult Conversations.* New York: Viking.

Taylor, A., Daniel, J. V., Leith, L., & Burke, R. J. (1990). Perceived stress, psychological burnout and paths to turnover intentions among sport officials. *Applied Sport Psychology, 2*, 84–97.

Thomas, K. W. (1992). Conflict and negotiation processes in organizations. In M. D. Dunnette & L. M. Hough (eds), *Handbook of Industrial and Organizational Psychology* (2nd edn, pp. 651–717). Palo Alto, Calif.: Consulting Psychologists Press.

Tinsley, C. H. (1998). Models of conflict resolution in Japanese, German, and American cultures. *Journal of Applied Psychology, 83*, 316–323.

Tinsley, C. H. (2001). How negotiators get to yes: predicting the constellation of strategies used across cultures to negotiate conflict. *Journal of Applied Psychology, 86*, 583–593.

Tjosvold, D. (1991). *The Conflict-positive Organization*. Reading, Mass.: Addison-Wesley.
Tjosvold, D. (1997). Conflict within interdependence: its value for productivity and individuality. In C. K. W. De Dreu and E. van de Vliert (eds), *Using Conflict in Organisations* (pp. 23–37). London: Sage.
Tjosvold, D. (1998). Cooperative and competitive goal approaches to conflict: accomplishments and challenges. *Applied Psychology: An International Review, 47*, 285–342.
Turner, M. E. & Pratkanis, A. (1997). Mitigating groupthink by stimulating constructive conflict. In C. K. W. De Dreu and E. van de Vliert (eds), *Using Conflict in Organizations* (pp. 53–71). London: Sage.
Ury, W. L., Brett, J. M., & Goldberg, S. B. (1993). *Getting Disputes Resolved: Designing Systems to Cut the Costs of Conflict*. Cambridge, Mass.: PON.
Van de Ven, A. H., Delbecq, A. L., & Koenig, R. (1976). Determinants of coordination modes within organizations. *American Sociological Review, 41*(2), 322–338.
Van de Vliert, E. (1997). *Complex Interpersonal Conflict Behaviour*. Hove, UK: Psychology Press.
Van Dierendonck, D., Schaufeli, W., & Buunk, B. (1998). The evaluation of an individual burnout intervention program: the role of inequity and social support. *Journal of Applied Psychology, 83*, 392–407.
Van Dierendonck, D., Schaufeli, W. B., & Buunk, B. P. (2001). Toward a process model of burnout. Results from a secondary analysis. *European Journal of Work and Organizational Psychology, 10*, 41–52.
Van Dierendonck, D., Schaufeli, W. B., & Sixma, H. (1994). Burnout among general practitioners: a perspective from equity theory. *Journal of Social and Clinical Psychology, 13*, 86–100.
Wall, J. & Callister, R. (1995). Conflict and its management. *Journal of Management, 21*, 515–558.
Walton, R. E. (1969). *Interpersonal Peacemaking: Confrontations and Third Party Consultation*. Reading, Mass.: Addison-Wesley.
Warr, P. (1987). *Work, Unemployment and Mental Health*. Oxford, UK: Clarendon.
Weingart, L. R. & Jehn, K. A. (2000). Manage intra-team conflict through collaboration. In E. A. Locke (ed.), *The Blackwell Handbook of Principles of Organizational Behavior* (pp. 226–238). Oxford, UK: Blackwell Publishers.
West, M. A., Borrill, C. S., & Unsworth, K. (1998). Team effectiveness in organizations. In C. L. Cooper & I. T. Robertson (eds), *International Review of Industrial and Organizational Psychology* (Vol. 13, pp. 1–48). Chichester: Wiley.

4

THE ROLE OF COGNITION IN MANAGING CONFLICT TO MAXIMIZE TEAM EFFECTIVENESS

A TEAM MEMBER SCHEMA SIMILARITY APPROACH*

Joan R. Rentsch and Jacqueline A. Zelno

Researchers in organizational behavior, industrial/organizational psychology, social psychology, sociology, political science, and strategic management have long had an interest in intrateam conflict. Early conflict researchers' ideas that conflict is inevitable and that it can be productive remain highly influential today (e.g. Bales, 1955; Boulding, 1962; Coser, 1956; Deutsch, 1969; Mack & Snyder, 1957). Productive conflict, in particular, remains a focus of many contemporary team conflict researchers (e.g. De Dreu & van de Vliert, 1997; Tjosvold, 1991). The purpose of this chapter is to continue to explore productive conflict within teams and to suggest that a cognitive perspective may provide another vantage point from which to approach this area of research. We examine the role of cognition among team members, specifically the role of team member schema similarity, in the development of productive conflict and high team effectiveness.

We placed several boundaries on our presentation. First, we focused our research on work teams. We defined a work team as: two or more individuals interacting interdependently and cooperatively to achieve a common objective (Cannon-Bowers, Salas, & Converse, 1993; Ilgen, 1999). Second, we concentrated exclusively on the dynamics existing within a team and among team members rather than on relationships between teams and external entities. Third, we centered our work on research, conducted in the field and in the laboratory, involving work teams that engage in complex ill-defined tasks such as strategic decision making (e.g. Amason, 1996; Tjosvold, 1991), case resolution (e.g. Sessa, 1996), and problem solving (e.g. Rentsch et al., 1999). Furthermore, we did not include the extensive research literatures on negotiation, sports teams, and team/group competition.

---

* The authors wish to thank Michael A. West and Scott Hutchison for their comments on an earlier version of the chapter.

The Essentials *of Teamworking: International Perspectives.*
Edited by M. A. West, D. Tjosvold, and K. G. Smith. © 2005 John Wiley & Sons, Ltd.

We begin by presenting a focused overview of conceptualizations of conflict and the research that is relevant to productive conflict in teams. Then, we describe team member schema similarity as an approach to the study of cognition in teams, and we integrate this approach with conflict research in an effort to enrich both literatures. Finally, we discuss several mechanisms that promote team member schema similarity.

PRODUCTIVE CONFLICT IN TEAMS

Competition, or a win–lose mentality, typically evidenced by goal incompatibility, is the core of many concepts of conflict (e.g. Baron, 1997; Mack & Snyder, 1957). Conflict has been generally defined as occurring when individuals perceive incompatibilities in interests, goals, or behaviors (Deutsch, 1973; Rubin, Pruitt, & Kim, 1994; Tjosvold, 1997). Perceived incompatibilities may have many sources including power differentials, competition over resources, tendencies to differentiate rather than to converge in decision making, ambiguities, denial of self-concepts or values, and anything else perceived to be annoying (De Dreu & van de Vliert, 1997).

Conflict within teams appears to have a complex relationship with team effectiveness. Research has produced evidence that conflict is negatively associated with such indicators of team effectiveness as productivity, satisfaction, and decision-making quality (e.g. Gladstein, 1984; Guetzkow & Gyr, 1954; Schwenk & Cosier, 1993). In contrast, evidence exists showing conflict to be positively associated with such team effectiveness indicators as flexibility, adaptability, growth, stability (Putnam, 1997), decision quality, performance (e.g. Amason, 1996; Jehn, 1994, 1995), mutual understanding, creativity, integration of diverse ideas (De Dreu, 1997; Tjosvold, 1991), establishment of boundaries, cohesion, establishment of group norms, clarification of goals, and the exploration of common aims (Mack & Snyder, 1957). These latter findings support the long-held view that conflict is potentially productive and even essential for effective team performance (e.g. Coser, 1956; Deutsch, 1969).

Early researchers' distinction between different types of conflict (Mack & Snyder, 1957) offers an explanation for the conflicting research results and serves as a basis of current conceptualizations of conflict. One such distinction was between realistic and nonrealistic conflict (e.g. Coser, 1956; Mack & Snyder, 1957). Realistic conflict referred to interactionally based conflict stemming from incompatibility of means, ends, values, or interests typically exacerbated by resource scarcity. Nonrealistic conflict referred to interpersonally based conflict that occurred between individuals and tended to be related to the need for tension release (Mack & Snyder, 1957).

More recently, researchers attempting to exploit the advantages of conflict have yielded a similar two-dimensional model. This model has its roots in the works of such scholars as Bales (1955), Guetzkow and Gyr (1954), Torrance (1957), and others (Mack & Snyder, 1957), who observed that conflict could be categorized as centering on either task or socioemotional issues. Task conflict (sometimes referred to as cognitive conflict) is similar to realistic conflict and involves disagreements among team members about task issues (e.g. allocation of resources, policies, procedures, roles). Task conflict tends to be associated with constructive conflict management strategies and with positive team outcomes (Tjosvold, 1997). It is through task conflict that team members are thought to identify, extract, and combine their diverse perspectives to maximize performance (Amason & Schweiger, 1994). Task conflict is expected to increase team members' commitment to the team and to its decisions by providing them with an elaborated and common understanding of the rationale underlying the team's decisions and behaviors. In addition, by engaging in task-related debate and thereby gaining a common understanding of decisions, team members are likely to perceive a just process in which members experience a sense of voice and believe that teammates are considering their opinions (Tjosvold, 1991).

Socio-emotional conflict (sometimes referred to as affective conflict) is similar to nonrealistic conflict and involves interpersonal incompatibilities among team members (e.g. issues related to norms, values, identity; Amason & Sapienza, 1997; De Dreu, 1997). Socio-emotional conflict usually yields nonproductive conflict management strategies (De Dreu, 1997) and is associated negatively with team effectiveness variables. Socio-emotional conflict tends to be more threatening to individuals than task conflict because it involves negative emotions and may implicate deep psychological factors such as one's identity (De Dreu, 1997). It is personalized and individually oriented disagreements that are characterized by friction, frustration, and personality clashes. Socio-emotional conflict can obstruct the exchange of information between team members and erode their commitment to the team and to its decisions (Amason & Sapienza, 1997). It detracts from performance because it causes team members to focus on reducing threats, increasing power, and attempting to build cohesion rather than on completing the team's task (Evan, 1965; Jehn, 1997). Furthermore, research results indicate that socio-emotional conflict tends to hinder individuals' processing of complex information, thus further inhibiting task performance (Baron, 1997).

The two-dimensional approach to the study of conflict seems to simplify a complex conflict–team effectiveness relationship. However, this approach has its own complexity. Although there are clear theoretical and empirical distinctions between task and socio-emotional conflict, they are frequently found to co-vary positively (Amason & Sapienza, 1997; Jehn, 1994; Pelled, Eisenhardt, & Xin, 1999).

Several explanations for this covariance exist. The most probable explanation is that team members may take task-related conflicts personally thereby generating socio-emotional conflict. Task conflict involves such behaviors as scrutinizing and challenging others' ideas and opinions that can easily be misinterpreted as personal criticism. For example, Bales (1955) observed that giving suggestions, which is a required process for problem solving, usually elicits more negative reactions than giving information or opinions. Furthermore, people tend to view disagreements or criticisms of their ideas as personal rejection (Torrance, 1957).

A key to achieving productive conflict seems to be to minimize socio-emotional conflict while concurrently increasing task conflict. As Torrance (1957) wrote, "...what we are looking for is a group which can tolerate disagreements without becoming emotionally involved" (p. 318). This is likely to be accomplished when team members perceive their teammates' behaviors as well-intended (i.e. task-oriented and constructive) rather than as personal attacks. In other words, the perception of conflict in a team is based on team members' interpretations of the intentions underlying their teammates' actions.

The recent research on cognition in teams offers a perspective from which to examine how interpretations of team members' behaviors may be associated with intrateam conflict. A cognition in teams perspective also offers mechanisms that influence team members' cognitions through which intrateam conflict can be managed.

A COGNITION IN TEAMS PERSPECTIVE ON PRODUCTIVE INTRATEAM CONFLICT

Cognition in teams has been shown to be related to team processes. However, the major variables, team cognition and team processes, have been conceptualized and operationalized at rather general levels (e.g. Mathieu et al., 2000). The application of a cognitive approach to the study of intrateam conflict will likely be most effective when these variables are conceptualized and operationalized with specificity. Therefore, we propose specific forms and contents of team member cognitions that may be related to intrateam conflict. We propose that members who understand functional teamwork behaviors similarly will not perceive intrateam conflict, but instead they will perceive a productive teamwork process.

Teamwork is a process aimed at facilitating team member interactions through effective communication, coordination, and cooperation in an effort to promote successful task completion and to develop high-quality relationships among team members (Cannon-Bowers, Salas, & Converse, 1993; Salas et al., 1988). The research on team cognition has focused primarily on congruence among team members' cognitions (e.g. Cannon-Bowers, Salas, & Converse, 1993; Rentsch & Hall, 1994). According to most models of team cognition, team members possessing high cognitive congruence will experience efficient and effective interactions, because they will be able to compensate for, anticipate, facilitate, and understand one another's actions (e.g. Nieva, Fleishman, & Reick, 1985); to communicate effectively (Dyer, 1984); to coordinate their behaviors (Klimoski & Mohammed, 1994); and to minimize process losses (Steiner, 1972).

Forms of Team Member Cognition

Schemas regarding teamwork and other team-relevant information are the mechanisms by which team members interpret each other's behavior. Schemas serve to organize knowledge and thereby represent ways of thinking about, interpreting, predicting, and remembering events (Lord & Maher, 1991). Any team-relevant domain may constitute the content of team members' schemas (Cannon-Bowers, Salas, & Converse, 1993). Team members possess similar teamwork schemas when their schemas contain compatible knowledge structures for organizing and understanding teamwork-related phenomena (Rentsch & Hall, 1994). Team member schema similarity (TMSS) may take the form of *schema congruence*,[1] which exists when team members' schemas are comparable in content and/or structure. In Figure 4.1, team member schema congruence is represented by the overlap of Donna's and Mitch's schemas of teamwork (i.e. both schemas contain "trust" and "supporting others").

TMSS may also take the form of *schema accuracy*. A team member's schema is accurate if it is similar to a "true score" or to a target. For example, training effectiveness can be evaluated by examining the degree to which trainees' schemas match the instructor's schema at the conclusion of training (Smith-Jentsch et al., 2001). Schema accuracy also exists to the degree that a team member's schema of a target matches the target's schema. Of primary interest here is the degree to which team members form accurate schemas of their teammates' schemas of teamwork. As illustrated in Figure 4.1, Donna's schema of Mitch's teamwork schema is accurate to the extent that she thinks that for Mitch "getting along"

---

[1] We use the term "schema congruence" to refer to what Rentsch and Hall (1994) referred to as schema agreement.

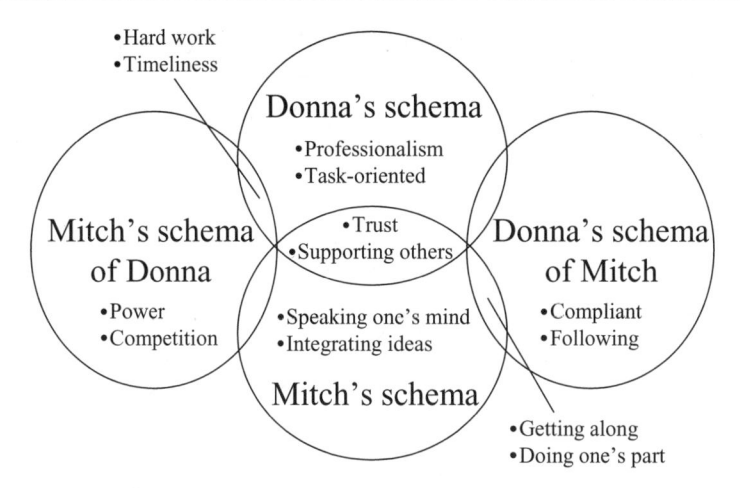

Figure 4.1 Illustration of schema congruence and schema accuracy

and "doing one's part" are important components of teamwork, and Mitch actually believes that "getting along" and "doing one's part" are important parts of teamwork. However, as shown in Figure 4.1, Donna's schema of Mitch is deficient because she does not realize that "speaking one's mind" and "integrating ideas" are parts of Mitch's schema. In addition, her schema of Mitch's schema is contaminated because she thinks that for Mitch "being compliant" and "following" are components of teamwork, but these components are not parts of Mitch's teamwork schema. Because Donna's schema of Mitch is inaccurate, when she observes Mitch adapting his ideas to accommodate other teammates' ideas, she interprets this behavior as compliant and believes that Mitch is a follower. Mitch, on the other hand, believes that he is speaking his mind in an effort to integrate his ideas with his teammates' ideas. Thus, schema accuracy can play a role in team members' interpretations of one another's behaviors.

Accumulating empirical research evidence supports team member schema congruence and team member schema accuracy as correlates of team effectiveness (e.g. Mathieu et al., 2000; Rentsch et al., 1999; Rentsch & Klimoski, 2001). With regard to conflict in teams, teams in which members interpret teammates' behaviors differently or inaccurately will likely experience nonproductive conflict (cf. Baron, 1997; Ensley & Pearce, 2001; Pinkley & Northcraft, 1994). For example, team members may interpret the behaviors of pointing out the weaknesses of arguments (Tjosvold, 1991) and offering dissenting opinions (Amason & Sapienza, 1997) quite differently. Some members may interpret these behaviors, intended as efforts to collaborate, as personal attacks. Team members who interpret their teammates' behavior as personal attacks may begin to believe that their goals and those of their teammates are incompatible. Misinterpretation of behaviors intended to support task conflict as threats or as indicators of goal incompatibility is a potential source of emotional responses that may promote nonproductive conflict (Baron, 1988; Ensley & Pearce, 2001).

Torrance (1957) provides an excellent example of how misinterpretations can result in ineffective team performance, due to nonproductive conflict. He reported an incident in which, following a blizzard, trainees and their instructors crossed an unfrozen creek and continued onward for several hours before pitching camp and drying out. The delay in drying out resulted in a number of the men experiencing severe frostbite. In post-training interviews, trainees and instructors reported that they believed the group should have stopped to dry out earlier than it did. The trainees also reported that they did not express their desire to stop because they believed the instructors to be "unusually intolerant of expressions of disagreement" (p. 315; particularly with regard to a trainee who was perceived to be the trainees' natural leader). The instructors stated that they did not stop the group because they believed the trainees to be apathetic due to the trainees' silence. Misinterpretations, due to low schema congruence and schema accuracy, led to ineffective team performance. Most likely instructors had misinterpreted earlier disagreements with trainees (particularly disagreements with powerful trainees) as threats (i.e. socio-emotional conflict evolved within the group). Therefore, they expressed intolerance for disagreements, which caused trainees to be unwilling to express their desires following the blizzard (i.e. task conflict was squelched within the group).

Influences of Schema Congruence and Schema Accuracy on Productive Conflict

Team member schema congruence and schema accuracy may be related differentially to elements of productive conflict. When teamwork schema congruence is low among team members, then the team members are not thinking similarly with respect to the process of teamwork, and this may produce differential interpretations of teammates' behaviors. For example, some team members may think that effective teamwork involves heated debates in which each team member fights for his or her viewpoint. Other team members may believe that considering the strengths and weaknesses of all perspectives in turn is essential for effective teamwork. In such a situation of low congruence, team members may quickly withdraw from task conflict either by fighting opposing perspectives or by withholding opinions and analyses. Conversely, if team members possess functional and highly congruent schemas regarding the process of teamwork, then they will be likely to interpret behaviors intended to be collaborative as such. This common interpretation will result in members actively engaging in appropriate teamwork behaviors that stimulate and support task conflict. See Figure 4.2.

Low team member schema accuracy is expected to be related to high socio-emotional conflict, because low schema accuracy is likely to produce misattributions (Baron, 1997). As illustrated in Figure 4.1, if Mitch thinks that for Donna "hard work" and "timeliness" are important components of teamwork, and Donna actually believes that "hard work" and "timeliness" are important parts of teamwork, then Mitch's schema of Donna's teamwork schema is accurate. However, as shown in Figure 4.1, Mitch's schema of Donna is deficient because he does not realize that "professionalism" and "being task-oriented" are parts of Donna's schema. Mitch's schema of Donna's schema is also contaminated, because he believes that she thinks "power" and "competition" are components of teamwork, but these components are not in her schema of teamwork. Because Mitch's schema of Donna is inaccurate, when he observes Donna cut off teammates' tangential conversations, he interprets this behavior as power hungry and competitive. Mitch then feels threatened and begins to subtly undercut Donna's suggestions. Donna, on the other hand, believes that she is simply being task-oriented and professional. Therefore, she perceives Mitch's reaction

Cognition in Managing Conflict for Team Effectiveness

		Low task conflict
Low		A
Team member schema congruence		
		B
High		High task conflict

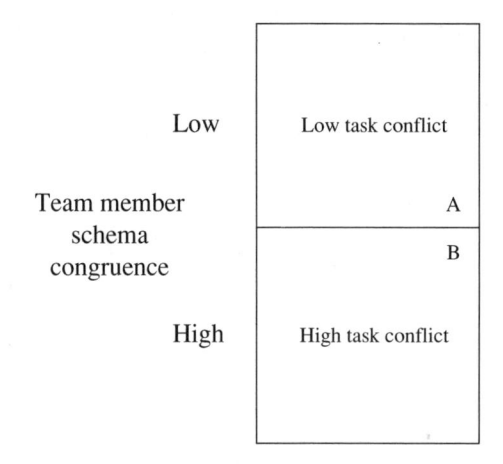

Figure 4.2 Proposed effects of team member schema congruence on task conflict

Team member schema accuracy

Low	High
High socio-emotional conflict	Low socio-emotional conflict
1	2

Figure 4.3 Proposed effects of team member schema accuracy on socio-emotional conflict

as irritating and distracting, so she begins to disregard his comments. Mitch may react with additional negative emotions and the socio-emotional conflict between Donna and Mitch continues to escalate.

When schema accuracy is high, then team members understand how their teammates think about teamwork and therefore are less likely to interpret potentially offensive behavior (e.g. critiquing an idea) as a personal attack. They will have accurate explanations for their teammates' behavior and will be able to understand and predict their teammates' reactions. They will be able to modulate their own emotional responses to their teammates' behavior. See Figure 4.3.

Schema congruence and schema accuracy may offer an explanation for the positive and significant correlations between task conflict and socio-emotional conflict obtained in the empirical research (e.g. Ensley & Pearce, 2001; Pelled, Eisenhardt, & Xin, 1999; Simons & Peterson, 2000). A positive relationship between the two types of conflict may occur

	Team member schema accuracy	
	Low	High
Team member schema congruence — Low	Low task conflict High socio-emotional conflict *Noxious nonproductive conflict* A1	Low task conflict Low socio-emotional conflict *Innocuous nonproductive conflict* A2
Team member schema congruence — High	B1 High task conflict High socio-emotional conflict *Costly productive conflict*	B2 High task conflict Low socio-emotional conflict *Optimal productive conflict*

Figure 4.4 Proposed effects of team member schema accuracy and team member schema congruence on task and socio-emotional conflict

when team members have either low schema congruence and high schema accuracy or high schema congruence and low schema accuracy. These cases are represented in Cells A2 and B1 of Figure 4.4. Cell A2 represents innocuous nonproductive conflict in which the team experiences little task conflict (therefore little task-related activity), but team members are not experiencing negative emotional reactions to the team. Cell B1 represents a costly productive conflict in which the team engages in task conflict (and therefore is actively working on its task), but there is an associated emotional cost. For example, techniques designed to promote critical evaluation of alternatives (i.e. increase task conflict), such as dialectical inquiry and devil's advocacy, can also produce bitterness and lingering resentment (Amason & Sapienza, 1997; Schweiger, Sandberg, & Rechner, 1989).

The cases shown in Cells A1 and B2, representing a negative relationship between the two types of conflict, appear to be rare. Cell A1 represents perhaps the most undesirable case, noxious nonproductive conflict, in which task conflict is low and socio-emotional conflict is high. The team is not engaging in task conflict (or in task-related behaviors) and the team members are feeling negatively about each other and/or the team's processes.

The case that represents optimal productive conflict is Cell B2. High congruence and high accuracy represent a state of consensus (Poole & McPhee, 1983) and is a form of schema similarity that is likely to be related to high levels of team effectiveness (Rentsch & Hall, 1994). In this case, task conflict is high and socio-emotional conflict is low, because team members will have congruent conceptualizations about teamwork and will accurately interpret teammates' team-related behaviors.

We have assumed in the cases of high schema congruence and high schema accuracy that the content of the schema is functional. Although research evidence indicates that high TMSS is related to team effectiveness, it is similarity of functional schemas that is likely to be most strongly related to team effectiveness (Rentsch & Hall, 1994). Achieving productive conflict through TMSS requires addressing the specific content of teamwork schemas. Below, we describe elements of functional schemas that are likely to be related to productive conflict.

Content of Team Member Schemas: Schema Congruence and Task Conflict

Team member schema congruence is expected to be related positively and strongly to task conflict when the schema content is functional. Teamwork schemas conducive to productive conflict include organized knowledge regarding many functional aspects of teamwork. Two examples are those related to supporting cooperative goal interdependence and to encouraging constructive normative behavior.

Cooperative goal interdependence exists when team members believe there is a positive relationship between the attainment of their own goals and the attainment of their teammates' goals. With such beliefs, they are likely to engage in behaviors related to task conflict. These behaviors include actively participating in discussions, attending to others, being influenced by teammates, encouraging and assisting teammates, correcting errors, pooling information, and integrating perspectives (cf. Deutsch, 1949; Tjosvold, 1984).

Team members' perceptions of the degree and type of goal interdependence existing within the team are based, in part, on their interpretations of behaviors occurring within the team (Tjosvold, 1984, 1997). These interpretations are driven by their teamwork schemas. Team members whose teamwork schemas enable them to interpret their teammates' potentially personally offensive behaviors (e.g. correcting errors) as consistent with cooperative goal interdependence are likely to engage in behaviors supportive of task conflict (Alper, Tjosvold, & Law, 1998; Deutsch, 1949). However, if team members misinterpret such behaviors they may avoid these types of behaviors, which would result in minimal task conflict.

When team members possess congruent schemas regarding cooperative goal interdependence, they will develop a high performance spiral. For example, if Mitch and Donna have congruent schemas regarding cooperative goal interdependence, then Mitch will interpret Donna's critique of his ideas as consistent with cooperative goal interdependence. Therefore, he will feel free to respond by disagreeing with her critique. Donna would understand that he intended his response to support cooperative goal interdependence and would listen carefully to his remarks. This cycle of behavior and interpretation would strengthen their congruent schemas of cooperative goal interdependence.

This example illustrates how team members possessing functional and congruent teamwork schemas that enable them to interpret behaviors, such as discussing dissenting views, as indicative of cooperative goal interdependence will be likely to engage in task conflict (Alper, Tjosvold, & Law, 1998; Tjosvold, 1991). They will be prone to believe that they can promote their own welfare by promoting the interests of their teammates (Tjosvold, 1991; Tjosvold & Tjosvold, 1995). They will also expect their teammates to want them to be effective and that their teammates will reciprocate effort and risk-taking (Tjosvold & Tjosvold, 1995).

Congruent teamwork schemas should also include an understanding of constructive normative behaviors. Although many constructive normative behaviors may contribute to task conflict, openness behaviors, such as sharing information, expressing opinions, raising doubts, airing objections, challenging ideas, and evaluating ideas of others, have been shown to be of particular significance (Amason & Sapienza, 1997; Janis, 1982). Many openness behaviors, although conducive to task conflict, may cause team members discomfort if they do not interpret them as well-intended. In order to avoid or minimize uncomfortable or anxiety-arousing situations within the team, members of newly formed teams are not likely to develop behavioral patterns that support task conflict (Cosier & Schwenk, 1990; Hackman & Morris, 1975; Mitchell & Mitchell, 1984). However, behavioral patterns that support openness result in high-quality, innovative solutions, and consensual agreements (Tjosvold, 1991), and are positively related to reported levels of task conflict (Amason & Sapienza, 1997).

Thus, team members who have congruent schemas regarding openness behaviors are likely to engage in task conflict. For example, if team members' teamwork schemas include openness behaviors, then when one team member presents a suggestion for approaching the team's task, another member may immediately begin to articulate the weaknesses of the idea. The first team member will understand that this behavior is an attempt to evaluate the quality of the suggested idea. Schema congruence will enable team members to engage in openness behaviors that their teammates will interpret as supportive of task conflict.

Content of Team Member Schemas: Schema Accuracy and Socio-emotional Conflict

As shown in Figure 4.3, team member schema accuracy is hypothesized to be negatively related to socio-emotional conflict. Although this is likely to be true for teamwork schemas containing cooperative goal interdependence and openness, a stronger relationship may exist for schemas containing accurate information about other team members. Specifically, socio-emotional conflict may be negatively associated with the degree to which team members possess schema accuracy with respect to the other team members' characteristics. Three team member characteristics that may be highly relevant are expertise, internal frames of reference, and task-related constraints.

Team members who have accurate schemas of each other will be able to interpret each other's behaviors nonemotionally. Accurate schemas about teammates are likely to reduce cognitive biases, such as stereotyping and attribution biases, typically used to understand others' behavior. Stereotypes are schemas about specific social groups that influence information processing, and upon activation, may not only affect cognition, but may also elicit strong emotional reactions (Baron, 1997). Therefore, rather than activating stereotypic schemas to interpret teammates' behavior, teams are likely to be more effective, and minimize emotional reactions, if members invoke schemas containing information unique to each teammate (cf. Baron, 1997). If team members have accurate schemas about individual team members then stereotyping and its associated problems may be diminished.

With respect to attributions, if team members perceive the behavior exhibited by another member as undesirable and they have accurate schemas of the "offending" person, then they may be able to correctly attribute the behavior to external forces, such as the individual's personal constraints, rather than to internal forces. If team members do not have accurate schemas of team members' characteristics, then they may find it difficult to interpret evocative behaviors exhibited by teammates. In particular, the hostile attribution bias, associated with aggressive behavior, is likely to be triggered in ambiguous situations. An accurate schema may enable team members to avoid the hostile attribution bias and, thus, enable them to attribute any potentially confrontational action to unintentional causes (Zillmann, 1993). Moreover, making an appropriate external attribution will minimize negative emotional reactions.

In our example above, Donna and Mitch are members of a construction team. Donna is very knowledgeable about the client's financial resources, and Mitch is very knowledgeable about the engineering aspects of construction. If Donna's schema of Mitch contains information that he is an engineering expert, then her schema of Mitch is accurate with respect to his expertise. Mitch's frame of reference as an engineer leads him to suggest the use of high-quality materials without regard for their associated cost. In this case, if Donna has an accurate schema regarding Mitch's frame of reference, she will be able to understand why he focuses on quality materials and tends to disregard cost. Having the knowledge to make an external attribution will assuage the possibility of creating emotional conflict (Baron, 1997).

In addition, members in teams characterized by highly accurate schemas for team members' characteristics will likely justify their own perspectives to their teammates. To continue with our example, Donna responds to Mitch's suggestion by arguing strongly for adhering to a tight budget. Because she has an accurate schema of Mitch's perspective as an engineer, in making her argument she also reveals that she has a task-related constraint due to pressure from the client to work within a budget. As Mitch's schema of Donna becomes increasingly accurate regarding her task-related constraint, he will be able to understand that she has no choice in making her argument. He is therefore likely to accept these justifications rather than misattributing them and exacerbating socio-emotional conflict.

Summary Model of Team Member Schema Similarity and Productive Conflict

Teams with members who have highly accurate schemas and highly congruent schemas are proposed to experience optimal productive conflict (Cell B2 in Figure 4.4). Specifically, congruent schemas regarding functional teamwork processes (e.g. cooperative goal interdependence and openness) are proposed to be related positively to task conflict, and accurate schemas regarding team members' characteristics (e.g. expertise, task-related constraints, internal frames of reference) are proposed to be negatively related to socio-emotional conflict.

Figure 4.4 illustrates the integration of the effects of schema congruence and schema accuracy on intrateam conflict that are shown in Figures 4.2 and 4.3. The specific relationships depicted in Figures 4.2–4.4 are likely to be less distinct than presented. We propose that high schema congruence will be strongly associated with high task conflict, but it may also have a weaker relationship with socio-emotional conflict. For example, if team members achieve the high performance spiral of behavior and interpretations of behavior that support cooperative goal interdependence, then their experience of socio-emotional conflict may be minimized. The same may be true for accurate schemas. We suggest that increased schema accuracy will be strongly associated with decreased socio-emotional conflict, but it may also have some, albeit weaker, relationship with task conflict. For example, if team members understand a teammate's areas of expertise, they may be open to or even probe for that teammate's expert opinions, which will contribute to increased task conflict.

The benefit of this model is that it offers an approach for eliminating, reducing, or reversing the positive correlation typically found between task conflict and socio-emotional conflict, because forces are exerting differential pressure on each type of conflict. Consistent with previous research findings, the resulting productive conflict is expected to be related to team effectiveness variables such as team viability, member growth, client satisfaction, creativity/innovation, and commitment to the teams' decision or product. Members of teams experiencing productive conflict are less likely to be distracted by concerns about each other's underlying assumptions and goals, and they are less likely to undermine task conflict by engaging in opportunistic and self-serving behaviors (Ensley & Pearce, 2001). Essentially, they will be able to focus on task work and to engage in it without undue negative emotional reactions.

DEVELOPMENT OF APPROPRIATE SCHEMA FORMS AND CONTENTS

Several mechanisms may facilitate the development of these specific forms (i.e. schema congruence and schema accuracy) and contents (e.g. goal interdependence, openness, team member expertise, constraints, and frames of reference) of team members' cognitions. Three such mechanisms are team member characteristics, training, and technology.

Team Member Characteristics

Many team member characteristics may play a role in the development of schema congruence and schema accuracy. We will focus on experience as a major determinant of schema congruence and on individual differences (i.e. trust, perspective taking, and social anxiety) as influencing schema accuracy.

Similar experiences among team members are expected to increase their *schema congruence* (Rentsch & Hall, 1994). Experience takes many forms, including team, functional, organizational, and industry experience, and experiences related to the team's task. Team members' team experience, which refers to the extent of their experience working in teams (this may include experience working with any particular team), has been shown to be related to schema congruence among team members (e.g. Rentsch & Klimoski, 2001). With respect to functional background (e.g. marketing or production), team members from the same functional background were found to attend to information that relates to the goals of their functional area (Dearborn & Simon, 1958). This tendency indicates that members with similar experience related to function may have congruent schemas. Evidence also indicates that team members who have similar organizational and industry experience may possess schema congruence (Smith et al., 1994). Heterogeneity of team members' organizational and industry experience was found to be negatively related to informal communication (Smith et al., 1994). A lack of schema congruence may be what causes the team members to resort to formal channels of communication.

The development of *schema accuracy* among team members will involve person perception processes. Person perception depends extensively on the perceiver observing and processing information and on the target disclosing information and behaving consistently (London, 1995; Mischel, 1983). Several individual difference variables, including trust, perspective taking, and social anxiety, may be related to these tendencies. High levels of trust among team members will increase their willingness to disclose teamwork-related information (e.g. expertise, task constraints, and frames of reference; Morgan & Hunt, 1994; Pistole, 1993). They may also be willing to accept teammates' disclosures (Alper, Tjosvold, & Law, 1998). This free exchange of information may enable them to develop high team member schema accuracy. Perspective taking is also likely to be related to team member schema accuracy, because high perspective-taking targets tend to communicate so that others may understand them easily (i.e. tend to self-disclose; Feffer & Suchotliff, 1966). In addition, high perspective-taking perceivers tend to understand others' messages and perspectives accurately (Johnson, 1971). Burnett, Rentsch, and Zelno (2002) reported evidence supporting the relationship between team members' levels of trust and perspective taking and their ability to accurately report their teammates' schema of teamwork.

Social anxiety is also expected to be related to schema accuracy. Highly anxious individuals tend to be more self-focused than less anxious individuals, and when people are overly self-focused (e.g. concerned about how others will view them) they exert most of their cognitive efforts on behavior management at the expense of person perception (Patterson, 1996). Not only are low anxiety team members likely to have the cognitive resources to devote to developing schema accuracy, but they will also be likely to gaze at teammates, to engage in nonverbal interactions, and to rely minimally on stereotyping and attribution biases (Patterson, 1996). All of these tendencies are likely to increase their ability to form accurate schemas about their teammates.

Team member characteristics are expected to influence the development of schema congruence and schema accuracy. However, they are expected to contribute less to the development of specific schema content than will training and technology.

Training

One purpose of training is to alter cognitive structures. Training focused on specific schema content should result in team members developing congruent schemas that promote productive conflict. Training related to teammates' perspectives and roles (e.g. cross-training) should enhance team member schema accuracy regarding teammates. Another purpose of training is to broaden and deepen behavioral repertoires through skill development. In order for schema congruence and schema accuracy to manifest productive conflict, team members must possess the skills to execute the schema consistent behaviors.

Training designed to increase team member *schema congruence* should include a knowledge component that focuses on the development of declarative knowledge aimed at defining cooperative goal interdependence and openness, and on recognizing behaviors that support these notions. Because knowledge development does not ensure skill development (Smith-Jentsch, Salas, & Baker, 1996; Tjosvold & Tjosvold, 1995), training should also include a practice-based component that complements the knowledge-based component. For example, with respect to openness, trainees could be instructed on giving and receiving communicative signals that are reliable and straightforward and that help to ensure that each party understands the other (Mitchell & Mitchell, 1984). This would include summarizing, clarifying, asking focused questions, and cueing active listening (Tjosvold, 1991). Skill development is important to the application of schema-based knowledge, but the combination of well-developed skills and well-developed teamwork knowledge is essential for perpetuating schema congruence among team members. Training should also include a feedback component by which team members learn to support and teach each other about cooperative goal interdependence and openness as the team engages in its task. These three training components should produce teams capable of functioning as high performance systems that will continually strengthen functional teamwork schema congruence (and, therefore, task conflict).

Training designed to increase *schema accuracy* regarding teammates should include cross-training and opportunities for team members to share frames of reference (Mitchell, 1986). Cross-training, which requires team members to be trained on their teammates' tasks and responsibilities, enables team members to understand their teammates' task constraints and expertise (Volpe et al., 1996). Verbal training and position rotation are two effective methods for cross-training team members with respect to task functions that provide them with their teammates' perspective (Cannon-Bowers et al., 1998; Volpe et al., 1996).

Sharing frames of reference, which typically highlights personal and interpersonal issues, complements the task focus associated with cross-training. Team members will possess an internal frame of reference for aligning their self-interests with their job demands (Mitchell, 1986). When team members share their internal frames of reference they increase their understanding of one another's alignments and increase their schema accuracy.

Technology

Technology designed to facilitate schema-related communications should increase schema congruence and schema accuracy. The use of innovative technologies applies to many types of teams, but it has perhaps the most relevance to virtual teams (i.e. teams in which members are distributed) and to teams working in virtual environments. These types of teams are unable to engage in information-rich face-to-face interactions that can accelerate, strengthen, and enhance the development of schema congruence and accuracy. For example, geographically distributed team members must interact using communications technologies (sometimes equipped with special programs designed to support group processes; Andriessen & van der Velden, 1995). Technologies that promote communications among team members that support a common understanding of teamwork will aid in the development of schema congruence. Technologies designed to provide information about teammates will promote the development of schema accuracy.

Technologies designed to ease frequent and explicit communications among team members promote the development of *schema congruence*. Distributed team members rely on technology to cultivate friendships and working alliances with their teammates. Therefore, the technology should be designed to enable them to engage in many of the social "niceties" that are frequently absent in a virtual world (e.g. a "virtual handshake"; cf. Nunamaker, 1997), as well as to engage in task-related activities.

One challenge is to design technology that supports the development of specific schema content related to productive conflict (e.g. goal interdependence and openness). This challenge may be met by designing technologies using the advanced cognitive engineered intervention technologies approach (ACE-IT; Rentsch & Hutchison, 1999a). The ACE-IT approach involves conducting a collaborative task analysis, which is an analysis of the social and cognitive requirements associated with the team's work (McNeese & Rentsch, 2001). One result of the analysis is the identification of the ideal content for the given team members' schemas with respect to that team's particular task. The ideal content is integrated with the team members' existing schemas to develop functional schema content using team enhanced action mediators (TEAMs; Rentsch & Hutchison, 1999a). TEAMs may consist of combinations of software mediators, intelligent agents, and technological interventions with the purpose of enhancing team member schema congruence. For example, embedded software prompts, designed to encourage openness behaviors and positive interpretations of these behaviors, presented to team members at regular intervals as they work on the team task, will enhance team members' communication of schema-relevant information. Prompts as simple as: "Ask your teammates to point out the strengths and weaknesses of your suggestion" and "Provide assistance to your teammates so the team can meet its goal" are likely to enhance team performance and may increase schema congruence (Rentsch & Hutchison, 1999b).

The ACE-IT approach to the technology design may also increase team member *schema accuracy* about team members. In general, virtual reality technology presents a multitude of opportunities to increase schema accuracy. Three examples are intelligent agents, avatars, and replaying virtual reality experiences.

Intelligent agents that remind team members about each other's constraints can increase schema accuracy regarding team members. To return to our example, Donna and Mitch are now members of a virtual team using a technologically enhanced communication system. As they plan the construction project, Donna mentions that she is constrained by the client's budget. An intelligent agent, which is part of the communication technology, recognizes this type of task constraint information and stores it in memory. In a later meeting, Donna and Mitch are discussing building materials. Mitch is about to suggest using a high-quality but expensive material when the intelligent agent reminds him of Donna's task constraint regarding budget. In response to this reminder, Mitch suggests a material that he believes will provide acceptable quality and will be in line with the client's budget.

Technology can also increase schema accuracy through the careful design of avatars, the multidimensional images that represent team members in a computerized virtual environment. Avatars can affect interactions, because they tend to become associated with the personalities and behaviors of the individuals they represent (Nunamaker, 1997). They can also convey information about expertise. The technology that Donna and Mitch are using could contain avatars representing each of them. Mitch's avatar could be a headshot of him wearing a tie with equations and buildings on it to remind his teammates of his engineering expertise.

Virtual reality technology also provides the opportunity for team members to experience their teammates' frames of reference. For example, while the team completes a task, each team members' sensory experience and behaviors could be recorded. The recordings could be replayed so each team member could experience the activity from their teammates' perspectives.

SUMMARY AND CONCLUSION

In summary, we have explored a possible role of cognition among team members in the development of productive conflict and high team effectiveness. The proposed relationships

Mechanism	Team Member Schema	Conflict	Team Effectiveness
Member characteristics related to similar experiences	Congruent schemas of functional teamwork	Increased task conflict	Commitment Team viability Member growth Client satisfaction Creativity/innovation
Training focused on functional teamwork knowledge and skills			
Technology designed to cultivate friendships and working alliances			
Member characteristics related to person perception	Accurate schemas of team members	Decreased socio-emotional conflict	
Training focused on teammates' roles and perspectives			
Technology designed to provide information about teammates			

Figure 4.5 Proposed model of team member schemas and productive team conflict

are summarized in Figure 4.5. The core relationship is the effect of TMSS on intrateam conflict. A primary contribution of this paper is the identification of specific forms and contents of team members' schemas that we expect to be related to specific types of intrateam conflict. We propose that congruent schemas containing functional teamwork knowledge (e.g. cooperative goal interdependence and openness) will be associated with increased task conflict. We expect that accurate schemas regarding team members (e.g. expertise, task-related constraints, and frames of reference) will be related to decreased socio-emotional conflict. The resulting high task conflict and low socio-emotional conflict define optimal productive conflict, which is expected to be positively related to team effectiveness variables. A second contribution of the chapter is the identification of forces that exert differential pressure on each type of conflict. Management of these forces offers a potential means for eliminating, reducing, or reversing the positive correlation typically found between task and socio-emotional conflict. Another contribution is the specification of the mechanisms by which schema congruence and accuracy may be developed and managed. Schema congruence and accuracy are expected to be affected by different forms of these mechanisms (i.e. training, technology, team member characteristics).

In conclusion, several issues require brief clarification. First, the schema and conflict variables are presented in Figures 4.2–4.4 as dichotomous. This was done to simplify the discussion of the fundamental concepts and their relationships. However, it should be noted that we believe these variables to be continuous. In addition, the two-dimensional model of conflict may be oversimplifying a complex phenomenon. We suggest that researchers might alternate their attention between the two-dimensional model and a more holistic perspective such as that represented by Tjosvold's (1984) long-standing notion of constructive controversy. This type of "figure-ground" approach might yield a richer understanding of the conflict process. Second, we focused on schema congruence and accuracy, but other forms of TMSS may exist. In addition, we identified specific schema contents, but other schema contents relevant to intrateam conflict no doubt exist. In this chapter, we chose to detail schema forms and contents that are most likely to be highly related to conflict. Third, we discussed each mechanism for creating schemas in isolation, but we expect that they may operate most effectively in combination. For example, technology designed to increase schema congruence and accuracy can be used to train teams whose members have been selected based on their characteristics (e.g. experience). Fourth, the conflict process is complex and we presented a simplified account of the relationships between the types of conflict and team outcomes to illustrate the potential role of team member schemas. However, in order to isolate the effects of each type of conflict on team outcomes, it is necessary to account for other influential variables such as team type and task complexity (De Dreu & Weingart, Chapter 3 this volume). Although the model we presented is intended to be applicable to many types of teams, we expect that it will be most applicable to teams performing complex, ill-defined tasks such as problem solving and strategic decision making. Fifth, given that we expect our model to be most applicable to these types of teams, we focused on a specific set of team effectiveness variables that included attitudinal reactions to the team's process and outputs. However, we recognize that many forms of team outcomes (e.g. satisfaction, individual well-being, objective performance; De Dreu & Weingart, Chapter 3 this volume) are appropriate for understanding the effects of conflict on teams.

REFERENCES

Alper, S., Tjosvold, D., & Law, K. S. (1998). Interdependence and controversy in group decision making: antecedents to effective self-managing teams. *Organizational Behavior and Human Decision Processes, 74*(1), 33–52.
Amason, A. C. (1996). Distinguishing the effects of functional and dysfunctional conflict on strategic decision making: resolving a paradox for top management teams. *Academy of Management Journal, 39*, 123–148.
Amason, A. C. & Sapienza, H. J. (1997). The effects of top management team size and interaction norms on cognitive and affective conflict. *Journal of Management, 23*(4), 495–516.
Amason, A. C. & Schweiger, D. M. (1994). Resolving the paradox of conflict, strategic decision making, and organizational performance. *The International Journal of Conflict Management, 5*(3), 239–253.
Andriessen, J. H. E. & van der Velden, J. M. (1995). Teamwork supported by interaction technology: the beginning of an integrated theory. In J. M. Peiro, F. Prieto, J. L. Melia, & O. Luque (eds), *Work and Organizational Psychology: European Contributions of the Nineties* (pp. 155–169). Oxford: Erlbaum (UK) Taylor & Francis.
Bales, R. F. (1955). How people interact in conferences. *Scientific American, 192*(3), 31–35.
Baron, R. A. (1988). Attributions and organizational conflict: the mediating role of apparent sincerity. *Organizational Behavior and Human Decision Processes, 41*, 111–127.
Baron, R. A. (1997). Positive effects of conflict: insights from social cognition. In C. K. W. De Dreu & E. van de Vliert (eds), *Using Conflict in Organizations* (pp. 177–191). London: Sage Publications.
Boulding, K. (1962). *Conflict and Defense*. New York: Harper and Row.
Burnett, D. D., Rentsch, J. R., & Zelno, J. A. (2002). Composing great teams: the role of person perception in building team member schema similarity. In T. Halfhill (Chair), *Work Group Composition and Effectiveness: Personality, Diversity, and Citizenship*. Symposium presented to the 17th Annual Conference of the Society for Industrial and Organizational Psychology, Toronto, Ontario, Canada, April 12–14, 2002.

Cannon-Bowers, J. A., Salas, E., Blickensderfer, E., & Bowers, C. A. (1998). The impact of cross-training and workload on team functioning: a replication and extension of initial findings. *Human Factors, 40*, 92–101.

Cannon-Bowers, J. A., Salas, E., & Converse, S. (1993). Shared mental models in expert team decision making. In N. J. Castellan (ed.), *Individual and Group Decision Making* (pp. 221–246). Hillsdale, NJ: Lawrence Erlbaum Associates.

Coser, L. A. (1956). *The Functions of Social Conflict.* New York: Free Press.

Cosier, R. A. & Schwenk, C. R. (1990). Agreement and thinking alike: ingredients for poor decisions. *Academy of Management Executive, 4*(1), 69–74.

Dearborn, D. C. & Simon, H. A. (1958). Selective perception: a note on the departmental identifications of executives. *Sociometry, 21*, 140–144.

De Dreu, C. K. W. (1997). Productive conflict: the importance of conflict management and conflict issue. In C. K. W. De Dreu & E. van de Vliert (eds), *Using Conflict in Organizations* (pp. 9–22). London: Sage Publications.

De Dreu, C. K. W. & van de Vliert, E. (1997). *Using Conflict in Organizations.* London: Sage Publications.

Deutsch, M. (1949). A theory of co-operation and competition. *Human Relations, 2*(2), 129–152.

Deutsch, M. (1969). Conflicts: productive and destructive. *Journal of Social Issues, 25*(1), 7–41.

Deutsch, M. (1973). *The Resolution of Conflict: Constructive and Destructive Processes.* New Haven, Conn.: Yale University Press.

Dyer, J. L. (1984). Team research and team training: a state-of-the-art review. In F. A. Muckler (ed.), *Human Factors Review: 1984* (pp. 285–323). Santa Monica, Calif.: The Human Factors Society, Inc.

Ensley, M. D. & Pearce, C. L. (2001). Shared cognition in top management teams: implications for new venture performance. *Journal of Organizational Behavior, 22*, 145–160.

Evan, W. M. (1965). Conflict and performance in R&D organizations. *Industrial Management Review, 7*, 37–46.

Feffer, M. & Suchotliff, L. (1966). Decentering implications for social interaction. *Journal of Personality and Social Psychology, 4*, 415–422.

Gladstein, D. L. (1984). Groups in context: a model of task group effectiveness. *Administrative Science Quarterly, 29*, 499–517.

Guetzkow, H. & Gyr, J. (1954). An analysis of conflict in decision making groups. *Human Relations, 7*, 367–381.

Hackman, J. R. & Morris, C. G. (1975). Group tasks, group interaction process, and group performance effectiveness: a review and proposed integration. In L. Berkowitz (ed.), *Advances in Experimental Social Psychology* (pp. 45–99). New York: Academic Press.

Ilgen, D. (1999). Teams embedded in organizations: some implications. *American Psychologist, 54*, 129–139.

Janis, I. L. (1982). *Groupthink: Psychological Studies of Foreign Policy Decisions and Fiascoes* (2nd edn). Boston, Mass.: Houghton-Mifflin.

Jehn, K. A. (1994). Enhancing effectiveness: an investigation of advantages and disadvantages of value-based intragroup conflict. *The International Journal of Conflict Management, 5*(3), 223–238.

Jehn, K. A. (1995). A multimethod examination of the benefits and detriments of intragroup conflict. *Administrative Science Quarterly, 40*, 256–282.

Jehn, K. A. (1997). A qualitative analysis of conflict types and dimensions in organizational groups. *Administrative Science Quarterly, 42*, 530–557.

Johnson, D. W. (1971). Role reversal: a summary and review of the research. *International Journal of Group Tensions, 7*, 318–334.

Klimoski, R. & Mohammed, S. (1994). Team mental model: construct or metaphor? *Journal of Management, 20*(2), 403–437.

London, M. (1995). *Self and Interpersonal Insight.* New York: Oxford University Press.

Lord, R. G. & Maher, K. J. (1991). Cognitive theory in industrial and organizational psychology. In M. D. Dunnette & L. M. Hough (eds), *Handbook of Industrial and Organizational Psychology* (Vol. 2, pp. 1–62). Palo Alto, Calif.: Consulting Psychologists Press.

Mack, R. W. & Snyder, R. C. (1957). The analysis of social conflict: toward an overview and synthesis. *Journal of Conflict Resolution, 1*(2), 212–248.

McNeese, M. D. & Rentsch, J. R. (2001). Social and cognitive considerations of teamwork. In M. D. McNeese, E. Salas, & M. Endsley (eds), *New Trends in Cooperative Activities: Understanding System Dynamics in Complex Environments* (pp. 96–113). Santa Monica, Calif.: Human Factors and Ergonomics Society Press.

Mathieu, J. E., Heffner, T. S., Goodwin, G. F., Salas, E., & Cannon-Bowers, J. A. (2000). The influence of shared mental models on team process and performance. *Journal of Applied Psychology, 85*, 273–282.

Mischel, W. (1983). Alternatives in the pursuit of the predictability and consistency of persons: stable data yield stable interpretations. *Journal of Personality, 51*, 578–604.

Mitchell, R. (1986). Team building by disclosure of internal frames of reference. *The Journal of Applied Behavioral Science, 22*(1), 15–28.

Mitchell, R. C. & Mitchell, R. R. (1984). Constructive management of conflict in groups. *Journal for Specialists in Group Work, 9*(3), 137–144.

Morgan, R. M. & Hunt, S. D. (1994). The commitment–trust theory of relationship marketing. *Journal of Marketing, 58*, 20–38.

Nieva, V. F., Fleishman, E. A., & Reick, A. (1985). *Team Dimensions: Their Identity, Their Measurement, and Their Relationships*. Washington, DC: Advanced Research Resources Organization.

Nunamaker, J. F., Jr (1997). Future research in group support systems: needs, some questions and possible directions. *International Journal of Human–Computer Studies, 47*(3), 357–385.

Patterson, M. L. (1996). Social behavior and social cognition. In J. L. Nye & A. M. Brower (eds), *What's Social about Social Cognition?: Social Cognition Research in Small Groups* (pp. 87–105). London: Sage Publications.

Pelled, L. H., Eisenhardt, K. M., & Xin, K. R. (1999). Exploring the black box: an analysis of work group diversity, conflict, and performance. *Administrative Science Quarterly, 44*, 1–28.

Pinkley, R. L. & Northcraft, G. B. (1994). Conflict frames of reference: implications for dispute processes and outcomes. *Academy of Management Journal, 37*(1), 193–205.

Pistole, M. C. (1993). Attachment relationships: self-disclosure and trust. *Journal of Mental Health Counseling, 15*, 94–106.

Poole, M. S. & McPhee, R. D. (1983). A structurational analysis of organizational climate. In L. L. Putnam & M. E. Pacanowsky (eds), *Communication and Organizations: An Integrative Approach* (pp. 195–219). Beverly Hills, Calif.: Sage Publications.

Putnam, L. L. (1997). Productive conflict: negotiation as implicit coordination. In C. K. W. De Dreu & E. van de Vliert (eds), *Using Conflict in Organizations* (pp. 147–160). London: Sage Publications.

Rentsch, J. R., Burnett, D. D., McNeese, M. D., & Pape, L. J. (1999). Team member interactions, personalities, schemas, and team performance: Where's the connection? Paper presented to the Fourteenth Annual Conference of the Society of Industrial and Organizational Psychology, Atlanta, Georgia, April 30–May 2.

Rentsch, J. R. & Hall, R. J. (1994). Members of great teams think alike: a model of team effectiveness and schema similarity among team members. In M. M. Beyerlein, D. A. Johnson, & S. T. Beyerlein (eds), *Advances in Interdisciplinary Studies of Work Teams: Theories of Self-managing Work Teams* (Vol. 1, pp. 223–261). Greenwich, Conn.: JAI Press, Inc.

Rentsch, J. R. & Hutchison, A. S. (1999a). *Advanced Cognitive Engineered Intervention Technologies (ACE-IT)*. Knoxville, Tenn.: Organizational Research Group.

Rentsch, J. R. & Hutchison, A. S. (1999b). *Assessment and Measurement of Team Member Schema Similarity in BMC3I demonstrations*. Knoxville, Tenn.: Organizational Research Group.

Rentsch, J. R. & Klimoski, R. J. (2001). Why do "great minds" think alike?: antecedents of team member schema agreement. *Journal of Organizational Behavior, 22*, 107–120.

Rubin, J. Z., Pruitt, D. G., & Kim, T. (1994). *Social Conflict: Escalation, Stalemate and Settlement*. New York: McGraw-Hill.

Salas, E., Montero, R. C., Glickman, A. S., & Morgan, B. B. (1988). Group development, teamwork skills, and training. Paper presented at the American Psychological Association Meetings, Atlanta, Georgia, August.

Schweiger, D. M., Sandberg, W. R., & Rechner, P. L. (1989). Experiential effects of dialectical inquiry, devil's advocacy, and consensus approaches to strategic decision making. *Academy of Management Journal, 32*(4), 745–772.

Schwenk, C. & Cosier, R. (1993). Effects of consensus and devil's advocacy on strategic decision making. *Journal of Applied Social Psychology, 23*, 126–139.

Sessa, V. I. (1996). Using perspective taking to manage conflict and affect in teams. *Journal of Applied Behavioral Science, 32*(1), 101–115.

Simons, T. L. & Peterson, R. S. (2000). Task conflict and relationship conflict in top management teams: the pivotal role of intragroup trust. *Journal of Applied Psychology, 85*(1), 102–111.

Smith, K. G., Smith, K. A., Olian, J. D., Sims, H. P., Jr, O'Bannon, D. P., & Scully, J. A. (1994). Top management team demography and process: the role of social integration and communication. *Administrative Science Quarterly, 39*, 412–438.

Smith-Jentsch, K. A., Campbell, G. E., Milanovich, D. M., & Reynolds, A. M. (2001). Measuring teamwork mental models to support training needs assessment, development, and evaluation: two empirical studies. *Journal of Organizational Behavior, 22*, 179–194.

Smith-Jentsch, K. A., Salas, E., & Baker, D. P. (1996). Training team performance-related assertiveness. *Personnel Psychology, 49*, 909–936.

Steiner, I. D. (1972). *Group Process and Productivity*. New York: Academic Press.

Tjosvold, D. (1984). Cooperation theory and organizations. *Human Relations, 37*(9), 743–767.

Tjosvold, D. (1991). Rights and responsibilities of dissent: cooperative conflict. *Employee Responsibilities and Rights Journal, 4*(1), 13–23.

Tjosvold, D. (1997). Conflict within interdependence: its value for productivity and individuality. In C. K. W. De Dreu & E. van de Vliert (eds), *Using Conflict in Organizations* (pp. 23–37). London: Sage Publications.

Tjosvold, D. & Tjosvold, M. M. (1995). Cross-functional teamwork: the challenge of involving professionals. *Advances in Interdisciplinary Studies of Work Teams, 2*, 1–34.

Torrance, E. P. (1957). Group decision-making and disagreement. *Social Forces, 35*, 314–318.

Volpe, C. E., Cannon-Bowers, J. A., Salas, E., & Spector, P. E. (1996). The impact of cross-training on team functioning: an empirical investigation. *Human Factors, 38*, 87–100.

Zillmann, D. (1993). Mental control of angry aggression. In D. M. Wegner & J. W. Pennebaker (eds), *Handbook of Mental Control* (pp. 370–392). Upper Saddle River, NJ: Prentice-Hall.

5

SKILL ACQUISITION AND THE DEVELOPMENT OF A TEAM MENTAL MODEL
AN INTEGRATIVE APPROACH TO ANALYSING ORGANIZATIONAL TEAMS, TASK, AND CONTEXT

Janice Langan-Fox

TEAMWORK AND THE NEEDS OF TEAMS IN ORGANIZATIONS

The Problem with Teams

As commercial environments become increasingly competitive, organizations are searching for new methods to improve workforce productivity. As well as becoming more competitive, workplaces are becoming knowledge-intensive, requiring a wider skill base, and continual training upgrades. In this scenario, workers in knowledge-intensive professions may find it increasingly more difficult to keep up to date. To meet these challenges organizations are employing teams that can pool resources and skills (Coates, 1996; Jacobs & James, 1994; Kozlowski, 1995; Magney, 1995; Marchington et al., 1994), the idea being that, collectively, the team will have more knowledge than any one individual member and that through team member interaction, performance will be greater than any individual part. However, untrained teams often find themselves operating in a new environment of asynchronous communication, new communication technologies, such as email, groupware, and teleconferencing, and new social and increased organizational pressures (Langan-Fox, 2001a, b; Langan-Fox, Code, & Langfield-Smith, 2000). This environment poses new opportunities and challenges that need to be considered in order to maximize a team's efficiency. So-called "high performance teams" have been offered as a central vehicle for achieving innovation (West, 1997). Some of the distinguishing features of "expert" teams are coordinated action, mutual understanding, high commitment, role differentiation, and shared goals (Marchington et al., 1994).

The Essentials *of Teamworking: International Perspectives.*
Edited by M. A. West, D. Tjosvold, and K. G. Smith. © 2005 John Wiley & Sons, Ltd.

There are many instances where teams are not living up to expectations (Kozlowski, 1995; West, 1997). Teams may inadequately coordinate their actions; fail to share key knowledge; be poorly constructed and trained; have a lack of role clarity; or experience disputes over processes and ideas. A greater theoretical understanding needs to be developed of what facilitates high performance teams and how this can be developed and trained in other teams. Unfortunately, little is known about the human resource systems necessary for the management and support of team-based work, and findings from past research are not readily transferable to organizational teams in general (Coates, 1996; Jacobs & James, 1994; Kozlowski, 1995; McClough et al., 1998; Magney, 1995; Marchington et al., 1994).

Unlike laboratory teams, organizational teams have:

(a) ongoing rather than temporary status;
(b) tasks that are complex and evolving, not simple or set;
(c) task allocators who are managers not university staff or students;
(d) team members who typically do not have a university education;
(e) members who bring a history of organizational experience with them to the team;
(f) tasks which can be impacted by a range of factors singly, or together;
(g) outcomes and processes which affect organizational profitability and take-home pay of team members.

NEED FOR AN ANALYTIC FRAMEWORK

To facilitate the analysis of expert teams, a framework is required that facilitates several organizational needs. The design of training programmes could be guided by such a framework in determining team skill shortages. Career coaching could provide feedback to employees on their relative strengths and weaknesses in team-based domains, and suggestions for how skills can be improved. It could inform infrastructure support through providing communication technologies that enable teams to better communicate, or set up incentive schemes that reward team-based responsibility. Selection at the point of recruitment and at the level of allocation of employees to teams could be guided by such a model by making transparent employees' ability to operate in teams and their team-operated style.

If, as is argued, teams are attempting to find solutions to problems in complex environments with a skill shortfall in team training, a conceptual framework for investigating the acquisition and development of all those variables necessary for team efficiency and smooth working would be helpful. In recent times, authors have suggested that a "team mental model" is important for understanding the dynamics and difficulties of teams (see e.g. Langan-Fox, Code, & Langfield-Smith, 2000). A team mental model would be useful for: problem diagnosis; identifying differences in the mental models of team members; team development; analysing team member relationships; and evaluating team success. As people learn about a new system of relationships (a team), or about operating in a team to solve a particular task, their mental models of that system of knowledge and relationships (e.g. team and task) changes, adapts, and develops.

Knowledge about people in a team, a task, and those features of the task which intersect with the organizational environment might always be in a state of growth and development as compared to the mental model of, say, a telecommunications system, which can reach "expert" level: the person "knows" all there is to know about the operation of the system. This is because contemporary organizations are dynamic and changing, as are the people, roles, and environments of that organization (Clegg, 1994; Langan-Fox, 2001a, b; Langan-Fox et al., 2002b). Thus any one individual is constantly in a state of learning as knowledge and experience are incorporated into an existing team mental model, the individual evaluates that knowledge and realigns his/her understanding of the situation, and adjusts his/her behaviour as a consequence of that new information in a cycle commonly found in cybernetic models of self-regulation (see e.g. Carver & Scheier, 1982). The process can also be described as one of skill acquisition. From the point of formation, teams are acquiring skills and as they come to acquire more experience and develop their knowledge, move from being a "novice" team member to an "expert" team member. These concepts will be explored later in this chapter.

The Utility and Definition of the Team Mental Model Construct

In terms of utility, the team mental model construct (hereinafter referred to as TMM) is useful because of its comprehensiveness. It could be described as a "grand landscape" variable. Its potential is as a summary variable: it can consist of the whole picture or snapshot of the situation as it currently stands. In terms of structure or architecture, it can comprise networks or webs of relationships among and between relevant variables consisting of any factors that team members think are vital to ensuring team success. Like organizational culture, the TMM construct is dynamic: it is capable of capturing the more "invisible" or hidden (micro) elements affecting team performance, especially as regards relationships but also general and unique (macro) factors of the organizational environment. Langan-Fox, Code, and Langfield-Smith (2000) list the sort of factors that can be elicited from teams. The construct is more complex than many other organizational variables such as "team performance" (see e.g. Robins, Pattison, & Langan-Fox, 1995), which might consist of some unitary form of output, e.g. solutions found, number of "widgets" produced.

TMM Construct

GENERAL DEFINITIONS

The social cognition literature acknowledges the notion that mental processes can be understood at the group level of analysis (Klimoski & Mohammed, 1994). Advocates of shared cognition suggest that in order to work together successfully, individuals must perceive, encode, store, and retrieve information in a parallel manner (Cannon-Bowers et al., 1995; Converse, Cannon-Bowers, & Salas, 1991; Duffy, 1992). That is, they must hold a "shared mental model" which can be described as the extent to which a group (or dyad) of individuals possess a similar cognitive representation of some situation, phenomenon, or activity (Cannon-Bowers et al., 1995). One aspect of this shared mental model might include, for example, a shared understanding of how the group operates as a system. Another aspect might include a shared understanding of the nature of the problem facing the group (Duffy, 1992). It should be noted, though, that the notion of a "shared mental model" is distinct from the notion of a "team mental model", in that the latter refers to what is shared among the members of a team as a collectivity, not shared cognition among dyads of individuals, which the former phrase allows for (Klimoski & Mohammed, 1994). Shared mental models can roughly be defined as common mental understandings of a particular domain between two or more people, where such understandings are mutually recognized by the other person. Shared mental model theorists imply that common mental models will invariably lead to improved team performance, although this view needs to be substantially qualified to situation and task (Levesque, Wilson, & Wholey, 2001). TMMs are more prescriptive. TMMs are conceptually broader and prescriptively less confined than shared mental models. They describe, define, and measure the individual mental models of members for a team-relevant domain, how these individual mental models interact, and what commonalities, differences, and conflicts exist. The TMM construct allows for a better understanding of a team's shared mental understanding and how the individual mental models of team members interact to effect team efficiency. Alternatively, TMMs prescribe coalitions of TMMs that lead to complementary understandings, which may sometimes be shared, but are at other times reflecting role differentiation.

The relationship of TMMs to shared mental models is similar to the concept of team to group. Teams are about member interdependence, role differentiation, and shared goals, whereas groups may or may not have these characteristics. Teams are in some sense prescriptive (often in terms of roles) of how individuals need to interact to be truly cooperating towards a shared goal. Likewise, TMMs are concerned with what coalition of individual mental models leads to effective team performance which may not involve shared mental models. Related to this understanding of TMMs is the notion of complementarity, which suggests that expert TMMs are dependent on the *right* combination of individual mental models, incorporating specialization and shared understanding. Such a perspective would define expert TMMs pragmatically and view them as context-dependent in regard to the organization, the task, and the team members.

DISTINCTION FROM MENTAL MODELS

TMMs theoretically presume the existence of individual mental models. TMMs by definition are concerned with the interaction of team members' individual mental models, and congruence, complementarity, similarity, and acknowledgement of individual mental models are at the essence of any conception of TMMs. These features explain the TMM in terms of a dynamic emergent property of the interactions and relationships of the team members' individual mental models. Specifically, TMMs relate to individual mental models of team processes, representations of other team members, and the individual tasks completed by team members (Langan-Fox, Code, & Langfield-Smith, 2000). TMMs are concerned with only a portion of an individual's mental model, that which has relevance to the goals and tasks of the team. Thus, there needs to be a clear distinction between team and individual mental models. TMMs are not held by any one individual but are some form of aggregation, abstraction, or team functional capacity. TMMs need to be clearly differentiated from an individual's mental model of a team and from an individual's mental model of how to collaborate and effectively work in a team.

MULTIPLE MENTAL MODELS

Would it be more efficient to attempt to capture the multiple mental models of individuals? For instance, of the team, the task, the environment, and so on? It is debatable whether team members will hold several different mental models for team functioning (see e.g. Cannon-Bowers et al., 1995; Duffy, 1992). However, it is probably not possible nor desirable to construct mental models of all of these, for instance to capture separate mental models for "equipment" and "task". But we do acknowledge that there exist alternative views about the number of mental models held by a single person and whether multiple mental models should be captured (see e.g. Olson & Biolsi, 1991). If we were to attempt to capture separate, multiple mental models from team members, some degree of artificiality may well arise. As described elsewhere (Langan-Fox, Code, & Langfield-Smith, 2000), the semantic features of a mental model are contained in various associative networks in a hierarchical fashion which might be accessed separately, for instance the role functions of individual team members. But, in the mind of the person, such separation may not exist. What gain, then, is secured by accessing sub-mental models? Although there may be some advantage in securing sub-mental models, for instance in the case of diagnosing causal attributes of an industrial accident, for parsimony and efficiency, there is benefit in gleaning a single mental model from an individual because the essential features of the model are crystallized in a coherent way. Perhaps the overriding issue could be to capture accurate mental models on a regular basis from all those individuals involved in the team task.

PAST FRAMEWORKS OF TMMs

For the purpose of constructing a theoretical framework, an important question is the content of the TMM. Several authors have proposed that there may be multiple mental models of team functioning. Glickman et al. (1987) found that two separate tracks of behaviour evolve during team training. The "taskwork" track involves skills that are related to the execution of the task and/or mission (e.g. operating equipment, following procedures) and a second track, the "teamwork" track, involves skills that are related to functioning effectively as a team member. Thus, it could be hypothesized that mental models of both the task and team will be required. Similarly, Converse, Cannon-Bowers, and Salas (1991) proposed a framework of a hierarchical mental model of team functioning. At the highest (and most abstract) level of the framework is a model of the external environment in which the team functions. Clustered within that model is a model of the team environment in which information about team norms is stored. Within the team environment model are team models (e.g. models of teammate behaviour, abilities, and personal characteristics) and task models (e.g. models of the team goal, task structure, teammates' tasks, and the individual's own task). In later publications, Cannon-Bowers and colleagues (Cannon-Bowers, Salas, & Converse, 1993; Orasanu & Salas, 1993; Rouse, Cannon-Bowers, & Salas, 1992) argued that mental models of team functioning are likely to be composed of models of the task, equipment, team, and team interaction. To support this argument, the authors provided an example of the multiple knowledge structures required by team operators in a Navy tactical decision task. In addition, they argued that the exact content of what must be shared/compatible among team members within each of the models (team, task, team interaction, equipment) is most likely to be task dependent. For instance, they suggested that the team model would be less important for relatively proceduralized tasks but more important for dynamic tasks which require a high level of flexibility and adaptability. It could also be argued that equipment models would be more important in highly specific technical tasks (such as air traffic control or nuclear plant monitoring) rather than in organizational team problem-solving tasks.

An examination of the literature reveals that there are a number of taxonomies of teamwork (see e.g. Brannick et al., 1995; Cannon-Bowers et al., 1995; Morgan et al., 1986; Prince & Salas, 1989) but comparatively fewer frameworks or taxonomies of mental models for teamwork. Furthermore, of the TMM frameworks that have been proposed, these have not been geared towards TMMs for teamwork, but rather, TMMs of task procedures in a particular team context (e.g. the cockpit). Much work needs to be done on team mental models in civilian organizational environments where the product of teamwork results not just in better coordination of activities, but, for example, the number of units produced or sold. In other words, the influence of the "customer", absent in laboratory and military team research, has an impact in the real world of organizations. Besides this, TMM research in organizations is scarce.

Problems with the TMM Construct

However, in order to utilize the concept of TMMs fully for the purpose of maximizing expert teams, several theoretical and methodological issues need to be addressed. Several reviews in the area of shared cognition and TMMs in particular have noted the challenges developing the area (Cannon-Bowers & Salas, 2001; Klimoski & Mohammed, 1994). In particular there is the mutually interdependent problem that the theoretical construct of TMMs is dependent on how it is measured, but useful measures cannot be designed until the construct is better defined. There is a risk present that any attempt to develop and improve the concept of TMMs leads to the risk of further fracturing the current understanding that has developed in the field. Another challenge is making theoretical ideas practical enough that translate into productivity and work satisfaction improvements. These issues will be further discussed and the recommendation made that TMMs become more aligned with the applied needs for developing expert teams.

CHAPTER AIMS

In order to meet the challenges mentioned above, this chapter will elaborate on the potential of using the TMM construct in conjunction with a three-phase theory of skill acquisition to better understand team interaction and processes (see e.g. Langan-Fox, Code, & Edlund, 1998; Langan-Fox, Waycott, & Galna, 1997). By incorporating the TMM concept within a skill acquisition framework, a better understanding may be attained of the developmental nature of TMMs; the properties of TMMs will be apparent, and how they may be supported to speed up the developmental process from novice to expert team.

The current work presents a model which describes the factors likely to affect the acquisition and development of TMMs in organizations: the effects of team, task, processes, and context can be utilized in theory-building in the area of teamwork and mental models and as a framework for designing and investigating research, training, and practice in organizational teams. The article focuses on findings which suggest that more work is required to make the TMM concept of value to people in the field attempting to improve team performance. Thus, the current work aims to explicate the concept and show how it can be reconceptualized to be of applied utility. In order to do this, the concept will first be discussed from a historical, comparative, analytic, and pragmatic perspective, drawing out pertinent theoretical and methodological issues. After a working concept has been defined, the literature will be integrated with that of skill acquisition to highlight the developmental nature of TMMs, and allow for cross-fertilization of the already sophisticated theoretical ideas present in the skill acquisition field. Finally, growing out of the developmental perspective of TMMs that is a consequence of the skill acquisition approach, applied considerations will be discussed.

THE DEVELOPMENT OF EFFECTIVE TEAMS

TMM Attributes

TMMs and teamwork in general are developed over time through extensive interaction. High performance teams do not generally form themselves but are developed through a range of factors such as organizational support, communication opportunities, and appropriate role allocation. Teams are in a continuous state of development or learning, as they face new tasks, members change, and understandings grow (see e.g. Langan-Fox et al., 2002b).

Thus the concept of TMM is multifaceted and complex. It is made more complicated by the fact that various researchers have defined, measured, and utilized TMMs in different ways (Klimoski & Mohammed, 1994). In some respects the domain TMMs occupy and the utility it provides is dependent on how broadly it is defined. Thus, it would be beneficial to draw out the different attributes of possible definitions of TMMs in order to decide how best to define the construct.

With appropriate support, fluent teams can emerge where cooperation and coordination of activities occur. These variables are crucial in understanding how expert teams arise.

COOPERATION

Cooperation, the "shared effort by individuals, groups, or political units for common economic, political, or social benefit" (Encarta, 2001), implies goodwill between involved parties but may simply be a function of mutual benefit. Such a concept goes to the essence of teams. As stated in the foregoing, people work in teams because there is a belief by team creators that teams will produce output that is in some way superior than if the individuals were to act alone. This may be in the form of higher creativity, improved efficiency, or increased, higher-quality output. Cooperation and interdependence discriminate teams from groups, which is suggestive of the team's potential to transform organizational effectiveness.

Cooperation is a component of a TMM (Jones & George, 1998). Team members have conceptions of team climate; how much support can be expected from other team members; how coordinated and fluid the team coordination process is; and how cooperation is provided by external stakeholders to aid the team in completion of their goals. Cooperation is the individual difference factor explaining team relations. Chatman and Barsade (1995) found that cooperative individuals in collectivistic cultures were reported to work with the greatest number of people, and had the strongest preferences for evaluating work performance on the basis of contributions to teams rather than individual achievement.

COMMONALITY

The term "team mental model" does not refer to multiple levels or sets of shared knowledge, nor is it simply an aggregate of the mental models of individual team members. Rather, it refers to some inherent degree of similarity or overlap that exists among the mental models of individual team members. This attribute is implied in that it involves a similarity or commonality in mental models. The attribute of congruence is defined specifically in terms of the relationship between the individual mental model and the degree to which they are similar between individuals in a team. Thus, if individual team members have a similar understanding of the task, a similar understanding of their purpose and role within the organization, and a similar understanding of each other's strengths and weaknesses, the overlap between individual mental models could be described as the TMM. Commonality is theorized to improve team performance by improving coordination or activities and making communication more efficient.

Commonality may also be indicative of the fact that the team has a more accurate mental model. Consensus is generally used as an indication that ideas have been communicated and discussed throughout the team and that there is least some form of rationale for holding them, although this may not always be the case. Implications for inaccuracy of the TMM based on low commonality are dependent on whether team members hold contradicting mental models in a particular domain or whether the mental models are merely more developed in some people than others. For example, someone new to a team may not understand team norms and processes and thus does not share a mental model with the team leader who may have a developed mental model of team processes. The implications of this example might be that the new team member requires team training. This is different from when two team members conflict over how work should be done or how team members should interact with one other. Such differences in commonality require conflict resolution.

This immediately raises issues about how similar the individual mental models need to be in order to be considered the same or strongly similar. It also raises the question of how many individuals need to hold the same understanding before it is deemed representative of the team. One problem with this definition, if taken too literally, is that it can result in a lowest common denominator effect. For example, if one team member out of five does not understand something about the task that the other four do, does that mean that that knowledge does not form part of the TMM? Thus, while congruence is important, it would seem that in order for the TMM concept to have utility, congruence needs to be seen in perspective, while acknowledging the other types of relationships between individual members' mental models that can influence team performance. Cannon-Bowers and Salas (2001) summarized the key questions which need to be answered in relation to shared cognitions: What must be shared? What does shared mean? How should shared be measured? What outcomes do we expect shared cognition to affect? (p. 195).

COMPLEMENTARITY

A third attribute of the TMM construct is that of complementariness. Previously, it was an untested assumption that the greater the degree of overlap in TMMs, all things being equal, the higher the performance of the team. However, from empirical studies that have been conducted, investment in achieving congruence in TMMs may result in a redundancy of learning and a loss of specialization. Research into teams of software engineers (Levesque, Wilson, & Wholey, 2001) showed that contrary to predictions, team members' mental models about the group's work and each other's expertise did not become more similar over time. Structural equation modelling revealed that as role differentiation increased in these teams, it led to a decrease in interaction and a corresponding decline in shared mental models. From this study and others (e.g. Cannon-Bowers & Salas, 2001), it has become apparent that there may be something more important than mental model congruence, especially when the task is one involving role differentiation.

The importance of mental model complementariness to the conceptualizing of TMMs includes the following organizational rationales: teams may attempt to combine the expertise of group members so that the total knowledge is greater than any of the individuals; teams provide an ideal environment to develop new staff by positioning experts with new recruits in order to encourage the transfer of knowledge and skills across the organization; what differentiates a team from a group is the team's capacity to be mutually reliant which often involves role differentiation. Through role differentiation, people are able to specialize their skills to maximize group outcomes.

TEAM TASK CONTEXT

When addressing the question of the relative importance of commonality versus complementarity in TMMs, it is important to identify the contexts and domains when one is more important than another. Context refers to what the team does, whether they are software engineers, manufacturing work teams, or operating room teams. Contexts where complementarity is likely to be important would be when teams require specialized knowledge, there is clear role differentiation, division of labour and structure to team processes, and where creativity and diversity of opinions are important. Commonality is likely to be highly important when the context is in many respects the opposite to that stated for complementarity, including when interaction and communication levels are high, processes are implied, and when the task is unstructured. In addition to context, domains of TMMs vary in requirements for complementarity and commonality. Some domains such as team processes, shared vocabulary, and knowledge of team members' strengths and abilities may require greater commonality to improve team performance.

Clearly both factors are important, but it is likely that in some cases putting resources into complementarity may lead to less commonality. This is the case in cross-disciplinary teams. Such teams have the potential to do improved work because the combined pool of knowledge is greater. However, the challenge that results from less commonality may require work to develop a common language between team members. Teams with a transactional style will benefit more from shared mental models.

From the foregoing, it becomes apparent that the teams' potential to function effectively is not only a function of having a congruent understanding, but also a complementary understanding. Complementariness can be defined as the degree to which individual mental models aid and assist the teams' understanding. Similarly, Klimonski and Mohammed (1994) suggested that in order for shared mental models to exist, two team members not only need to have the same understanding of a particular team domain but also need to be aware that the other person has the same understanding. In this sense the concept of shared understanding also involves sharing the workload or what Klimoski and Mohammed

(1994) have referred to as dividing the mental model (see also Mohammed & Dumville, 2001).

DISTRIBUTED COGNITION

Traditionally in psychology the individual is seen as the unit of analysis for understanding cognitive processes and problem solving. Banks and Millward (2000) suggest that theory normally takes the individual as its unit of analysis. However, the interactions of individual members' mental models may form a phenomenon that has an effect on performance beyond the individual alone. Exploring this concept, Banks and Millward found that cognitive processes used in a team-reasoning task were distributed among the team and with the consequent organization of the sharing having an influence on the problem-solving processes.

If it is accepted that the TMM is in some way related to the teams' capacity to function and is not reliant on absolute congruence for an idea to be considered part of the TMM, there arises a need to understand the distribution of knowledge and power within a team. Constructs from social network analysis might be of benefit here (Langan-Fox et al., 2001; Robins, Pattison, & Langan-Fox, 1995). TMMs can be described in terms of density (i.e. the number of members with a shared understanding), intensity of exchange, and as nodes that are outliers and bridges within various team networks such as power, information exchange, and task execution. Such a conceptualization of the TMM construct moves beyond an understanding where a TMM either does or does not exist, to one where the level of complementarity and congruence can be seen as an indicator of the type and sophistication of the TMM, providing greater utility as a diagnostic tool in setting out how teams can improve their coordination of activities and highlight what knowledge or information needs to be exchanged to improve team functioning.

THEORETICAL CHALLENGES

Representations of TMMs

While the TMM construct provides insight into team processes and assists in developing teams' potential, several challenges exist which serve to confuse discussion, stultify theory development, and limit industry applicability (Canon-Bowers & Salas, 2001; Klimoski & Mohammed, 1994; Mohammed & Dumville, 2001). However, some inroads have been made in the area of measurement.

MEASUREMENT

Measurement of TMMs is a major problem for the TMM construct. Current measures are generally time and labour intensive and may fail to tap into the desired construct (see Langan-Fox, Code, & Langfield-Smith, 2000; Mohammed, Klimoski, & Rentsch, 2000, for reviews of methodologies and analytic techniques). One problem is that the measurement tool can define the construct. However, the paradox is that until the construct is defined, it is very difficult to design measures for it. It would appear, also, that some of the measures are quite computationally intensive, suggesting that as the cost decreases and power of computers increases over time, more powerful measures will be available. There is a need for greater comparisons of measures so that the value of the different measures can be ascertained. In addition the predictive and developmental value of the measures needs to be further developed.

MULTIPLE CONSTRUCTS

Klimoski and Mohammed (1994) highlighted the fact that there is a diverse range of constructs related to team and shared mental models with a great deal of commonality between them. Such a multiplicity of constructs can inhibit knowledge exchange across the different disciplines by preventing developments in one construct from filtering through to another. Specific issues that need to be resolved relate to:

(a) whether TMMs should be conceptualized as a single entity or whether a team possesses multiple TMMs;
(b) whether members need to be mutually aware of their shared understanding for that knowledge to contribute to the conception of the team's mental model;
(c) the amount of congruence both in relation to the content of members' understanding and the number of team members, for a set of ideas to be considered part of the TMM;
(d) whether complementariness should form part of the construct of TMMs or whether such an understanding should be considered a separate concept altogether.

Until such theoretical difficulties are resolved, the development of the concept in relation to developing theory, measurement, and a surrounding body of empirical work will be hampered.

MENTAL MODEL OVERLAP

Notwithstanding the benefits of teams developing a TMM, the process of analysing mental model similarity or overlap at the team level has proven to be an obstacle for researchers (Klimoski & Mohammed, 1994). For instance, while a number of techniques have been developed to measure mental model similarity dyadically, the development of techniques to elicit and represent TMMs has been slow (Converse, Cannon-Bowers, & Salas, 1991). Furthermore, the few techniques that have been generated (e.g. Eby et al., 1998; Heffner, Mathieu, & Cannon-Bowers, 1998) are lacking in that they either cannot compare more than two mental models at once, or where more than two mental models can be compared, make assumptions about uniformity or normality which might otherwise be considered inappropriate. The measurement of mental model similarity must be related to some sensible mathematical construct of similarity. It should also be possible to use the measure in some kind of distribution-free statistical analysis that does not rely on random sampling since, particularly in an organizational context, it may be difficult to gain access to participants which would then lead to small, non-random samples (see e.g. Langan-Fox et al., 2001).

DEGREES OF MENTAL MODEL OVERLAP

A problem exists in specifying the optimal degree of overlap among team members. Generally speaking, most researchers agree that a major benefit of teamwork is that team members are able to bring multiple perspectives to bear on the problem at hand. However, a high degree of mental model overlap could be likened to the phenomenon of "groupthink" (Janis, 1972) in which the desire to maintain team cohesion (through unanimity) is awarded priority over the decision-making process, and the evaluation and consideration of divergent viewpoints become neglected. An undesirable degree of overlap could occur if team members refused to abandon inaccurate mental models because the rest of the team held these models to be correct (Cannon-Bowers, Salas, & Converse, 1993). Conversely, too little shared knowledge could lead to poor coordination, thus reducing the team's ability to cope with, and adapt to, changing environmental demands (Cannon-Bowers, Salas, & Converse, 1993). It could be the case that the optimal distribution of knowledge, that is, mental model overlap, varies according to the team task situation (Greene, 1989), or that different kinds of knowledge may be optimally distributed in the team in different ways (Heffner, Mathieu, & Cannon-Bowers, 1998). There is some agreement that broader distributions of knowledge are beneficial to teams that operate in particular environments such as when the jobs of team members are homogeneous rather than divisible and when the status differences between team members are small rather than large (Carley, 1990; Wilkins & Ouchi, 1983). Since poorly coordinated teams would be likely to fail, Cannon-Bowers, Salas, and Converse (1993) have maintained that the simple answer to the question of optimal overlap is that TMMs should be fostered as much as possible. Research is needed into this issue as, unfortunately, little is known about the dynamics of optimally distributed knowledge in teams (Kraiger & Wenzel, 1997).

Thus, there is a certain intangible quality to TMMs which has no doubt led to the multiplicity of construct definitions. Klimoski and Mohammed (1994), when reviewing the literature, examined whether shared mental models were a metaphor or a scientific construct and concluded that it did have the necessary elements and clarity to be a scientific construct. But the very fact that these researchers (Klimoski & Mohammed, 1994) asked this question hints at the abstractness of the construct. Are TMMs something that exist at a social level or are they merely an abstraction from individual mental models? If they do have some tangible quality, how should this be represented and conceptualized?

There is also the issue that TMMs have tended to be used in a prescriptive sense and as synonymous with shared or congruent mental models. But as has previously been discussed, there is some doubt as to whether common understanding is always beneficial to team performance or the best way to conceptualize what occurs in TMMs. In addition TMMs have often been seen as a categorical variable, as either present or not present.

COMPONENTS OF THE TMM

It would seem more beneficial to treat TMMs as something descriptive and occurring on several dimensions. Thus, all teams would be understood to have a TMM, but the nature, quality, and effectiveness of this TMM could be described. Such a description would be explicit to team goals and congruence and mutual awareness would become descriptive dimensions. The concept of complementariness could also be developed further and be defined in prescriptive terms with an explicit applied meaning as the effectiveness to which the interaction of individual member mental models meets team goals.

One important distinction within the TMM construct is between those components pertaining to the team and those to the task. Task mental models are concerned with technical skills and task-relevant knowledge and are closely tied to the individual mental models that team members have that are based on their skills and competencies. At a team level, task mental models represent an aggregation of the task-relevant skills of the team. Team knowledge features suggested by Cooke et al. (2000) include task type and team processes. The aggregation includes lowest common denominator representations, reflecting skills that every member has, and all-encompassing representations reflecting the total amount of knowledge and skills that are present in the team, even if held by only one member. Alternatively, team process mental models are concerned with processes of team interaction, understanding fellow team members' strengths and weaknesses, social and political considerations, and need for certain actions like anticipation of other members' training or information needs. TMMs guide the provision and acceptance of feedback, allocation of roles, and the interactions that occur within the team.

HIERARCHICAL NATURE OF THE TEAM TASK

It is possible to link the concept of TMMs in a hierarchical fashion. In such a system TMMs are an emergent phenomenon that comes about from the interactions of the individual mental models of the team members in relation to team-based activities. The individual mental models are also made of particular individual mental models that operate for sets of domains. Figure 5.1 displays these relationships, highlighting the multiple levels of analysis that can be used when attempting to understand mental models within a team context. When interpreting the model it should be noted that the individual domains of mental models held by team members cover similar domains, and in the sense that there is a shared mental model between members there will be cross-over in perspective and content.

For the purpose of identifying elements of the task in which team interaction occurs, an analysis of the task can be performed. Hierarchical task analysis (HTA) was developed by Annett and Duncan (1967) and has been further elaborated by Shepard (1985) and Patrick (1992). It is a means of analysing and breaking a task down into its constituent component tasks. The four main features of HTA are hierarchical breakdown, operations, criterion for stopping analysis, and plans. Hierarchical breakdown is the process of taking a general task and progressively breaking it down into an exhaustive set of constituent subtasks, which are in turn broken down into finer-grained distinctions. Operations are the unit of analysis and are "any unit of behaviour, no matter how long or short its duration and no matter how simple or complex its structure which can be defined in terms of its objective" (Annett et al., 1971). Criterion for stopping analysis is a heuristic for determining how many levels of subtasks are required for functional purposes and is defined as the combination of the probability that without training inadequate performance will occur and the cost to the system of inadequate performance. Finally, the plan integrates these tasks into a procedure or strategy that guides when and in what order an individual will carry out component tasks.

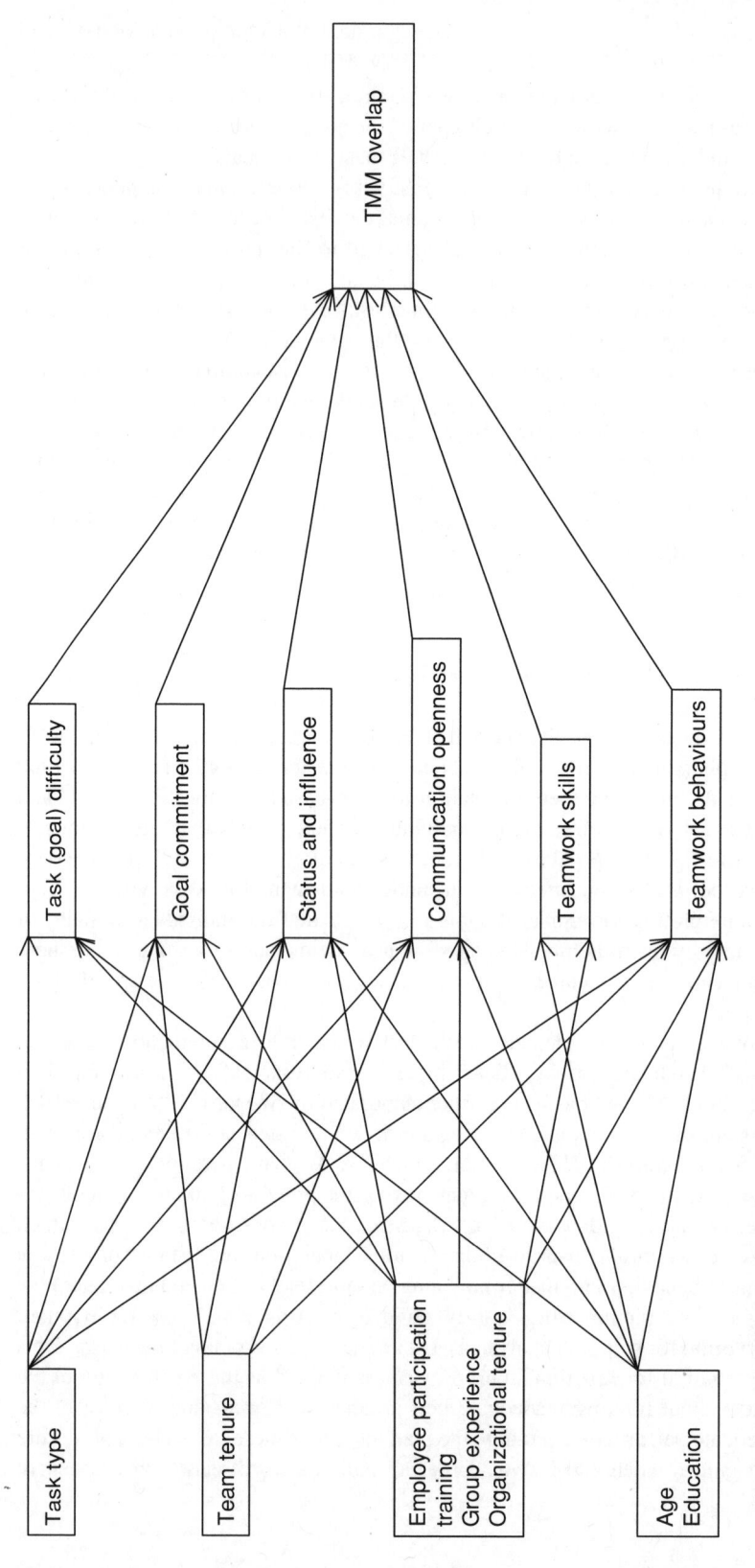

Figure 5.1 Relationship between individual and TMMs

HTA TO TMMs

Benefits of this approach include the fact that it is flexible in analysis requirements, has broad applicability, facilitates translation of tasks into training objectives, and is logically exhaustive. Disadvantages are that it is difficult and is strongly based on the ability of the analyst to exhaust and understand the domain. Other approaches include critical incident technique (Flanagan, 1954) which involves observing and recording either extremely good or poor examples of task behaviour and proceeding through a process of categorization, interpretation, and reporting with the aim of identifying task components and training needs. Task inventories involve getting lists of tasks rated across a range of measures, such as applicability, time spent, difficulty, etc., on a particular job.

Several elements of the task then can be isolated and an attempt made to ascertain those points of the task where there is mental model overlap. It may be useful to distinguish between the concept of shared mental models to describe overlap and the concept of complementary mental model as synonymous with TMMs. The TMM reflects what the team is capable of. The TMM reflects its potential to solve problems, predict outcomes, and perform tasks. Just as individual mental models map closely with the understanding that an individual has of the environment, systems, and task and relates to their performance potential, the TMM should relate to the teams' understanding of environment/system/task. Mohammed and Dumville (2001) suggest that there is a need to qualify the knowledge similarity concept. Overlapping knowledge in teams with distinct roles may be inefficient, create a redundancy of effort, and contribute to a less than optimal use of resources. Therefore, rather than measuring similarity globally and assuming that all team members need to have common knowledge in all domains, future research should work towards specifying the domains and conditions under which distributed and common knowledge will aid or hinder team performance.

The working definition of TMMs used in this chapter involves TMMs being the team level phenomena that are involved in team task completion. TMMs are emergent phenomena that come out of the interactions of the individual mental models. These individual mental models may involve common features or may complement each other through skill differentiation. Mutual recognition is not at the essence of TMMs but merely represents one form of a more cohesive TMM. TMMs cover various domains, including the task itself and the social and interactional team processes.

TMMs AND SKILL ACQUISITION

In the foregoing discussion, the nature of the mental model and TMM concepts, and problems of shared understandings about team tasks and issues of measurement, have been explored. Further, issues of training have been highlighted; how some workers may not have the various skills and abilities necessary for teamwork, and how this issue draws attention to the utility of the TMM concept. We turn now to how a team member might acquire a TMM. Figure 5.2 presents the proposed components of a three-phase theory of TMM acquisition, from the initial novice phase to the high performance or expert team. It also draws out causal factors such as individual differences and accelerators, and performance-related outcome factors.

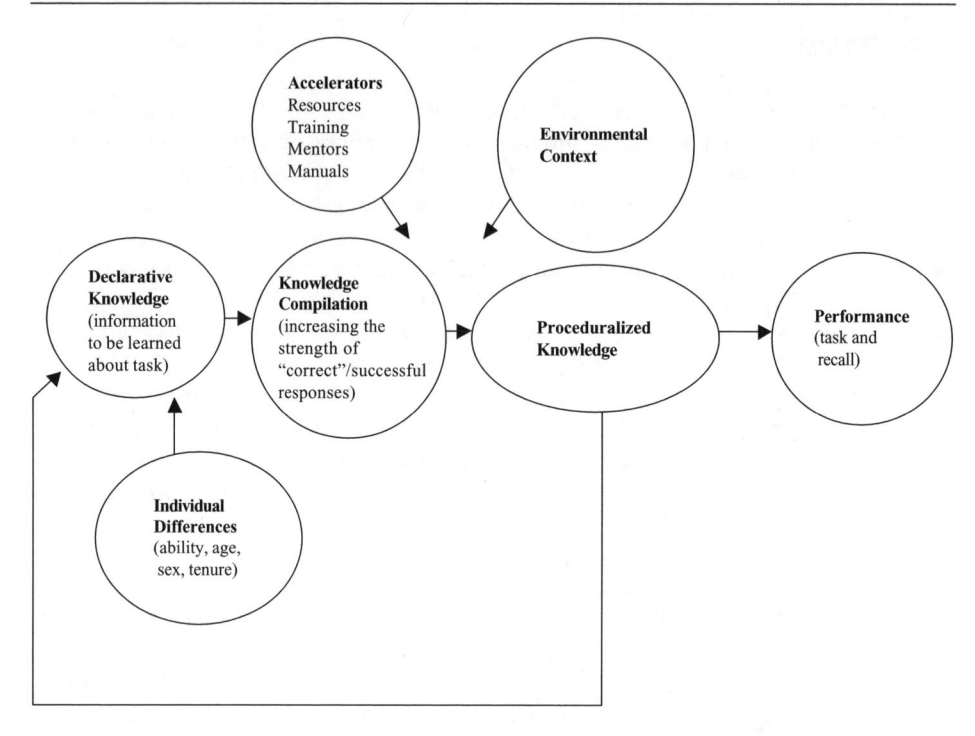

Figure 5.2 Acquisition and development of a mental model of team functioning

It can be concluded that team behaviour in organizations is affected by a combination of individual and team characteristics as well as the conditions of the overall organizational system. Although there are a number of taxonomies in the area of TMMs, progress towards a TMM theory has not been forthcoming (Klein, 1997). To this end, there is theoretical gain to be made in paralleling the acquisition and development of a TMM as comparable to skill acquisition phases. Research into skill acquisition and expert/novice differences illustrate the way in which knowledge is acquired, structured, and represented (Anderson, 1982, 1987; Langan-Fox et al., 2002a; Langan-Fox, Waycott, & Galna, 1997). The new integration called acquisition and development of team mental models (ADTMM) will draw upon the formative work of early theorists in skill acquisition, mental models, and other empirical work in the area of teams and processes.

The acquisition and development of a mental model are ongoing and changing, and cannot be well catered for by lock-step linear models represented by input–process–output research designs. There is no simple "end-product". Our model is therefore a process model that may describe, at one point in time, the shared understanding of the team about the team, task, and the team context. Thus our framework of mental models of team functioning also represents an attempt at identifying the important variables which would influence the ebb and flow of interactions in the organizational context, is strongly ecological, and somewhat phenomenological. At the same time, the model should provide the researcher with features of TMM acquisition and development that can be generalized beyond teams in particular organizations.

The development of TMMs can be described as a process consisting of three learning phases as identified by Anderson's ACT* cognitive skill acquisition model, that is, the declarative, knowledge compilation, and procedural phases (Anderson, 1982, 1987). In organizations, the phases of skill acquisition can be described in terms of team member challenges and experiences and how learners may be affected while completing the team task. Figure 5.2 could loosely be described as one simple example of how the individual and/or team acquires a mental model and the various stages involved in becoming an expert, from an initial stage of acquiring facts about the task, to a final stage when they have successfully completed the task. It is proposed that, secondly, as novices learn about teamwork, they progress through these phases and continue to engage in a learning phase that is typical of the feedback cycles found in cybernetic models. Models of self-regulation are instructive in illustrating the importance of feedback systems which operate through self-monitoring and salient reference values or standards (Carver & Scheier, 1982). Model features are described in more detail below. The Appendix gives some tentative propositions which could be tested by researchers in investigating the dynamics of the acquisition and development of TMMs. First, we describe the acquisition and development of a TMM as it relates to cognitive skill acquisition.

Phase 1: Declarative Phase

THE TEAM MEMBERS

Kay and Black (1990) presented a model of the acquisition of expertise which could be extended to describe the acquisition of any skill. According to this model, the team member builds complex knowledge representations by acquiring knowledge during different learning phases. The first stage is the building of preconceptions—the team member might have preconceptions about the team, the team task, and the organization, based on prior knowledge. Schumacher and Czerwinski's (1992) three-phase description of mental model development reflects cyclic changes in memory retrieval. This framework is based on the assumption that novices initially rely on the superficial features of a domain but with increasing expertise come to rely on the structural or causal features of it. So for novices, first impressions would help to determine initial knowledge of teamwork. These first impressions could be formed on the basis of team composition variables, for instance easily recognizable characteristics of individuals such as their age, sex, education, years of training, tenure, organizational experience, and other variables which we understand to be typically available from organizational records. In the pre-theoretic stage of the model, an individual's understanding is also based on similar instances in memory (analogies), that is, the similarities of the current system or domain, with other more familiar systems. Perhaps experience in groups or other teams might have influence at this stage. Additionally, it may be based on, or interpreted by, analogies with other teams with which the person is familiar. For example, individuals may perceive teamwork in an organization as analogous to playing in a football team. These analogies might be useful for initial understanding of teamwork and teamwork functions. The development of a mental model, then, could rely on collections of experiences that are retrieved from memory based on similarities to prior events.

Also, we know that the first stage of skill acquisition is based on declarative knowledge, that is, knowledge about teamwork which may be provided to learners in the form of instructions. During this stage, interactions that the person has with teamwork may be highly dependent upon rules (Blessing & Anderson, 1996). For example, Blessing and Anderson found that, initially, learners of simple algebra-type problems were heavily reliant upon given rules and examples, but with practice they learned to skip steps and to adapt their behaviour to complete tasks more quickly. Similarly, Norman (1983) observed that people often do extra physical operations rather than the mental planning that would allow them to avoid these actions. This is especially true where the extra actions allow one simplified rule to apply to a variety of situations, thus minimizing the chance of confusion. Presumably, this is how people initially understand a new set of interactions—in terms of broad rules that can be applied with the avoidance of confusion. Thus, learners' initial mental models are composed of declarative, rule-based knowledge that incorporates analogies with other familiar teamwork experiences and organizational systems.

Diversity

In the early stages of acquiring skill about working in teams, easily recognizable characteristics of individuals such as age, sex, education, years of training, tenure, organizational experience and the like, and other team composition variables would affect the new team members' perceptions of each other and also their expectations of each other's future team performance. The issue of diversity of team characteristics is an important early team formation variable, and there have been questions as to whether it is advantageous to have teams that are homogeneous or heterogeneous with respect to team member characteristics (Campion, Medsker, & Higgs, 1993; Guzzo & Dickson, 1996; Jackson, 1992, 1996; Maznevski, 1994; Tziner & Eden, 1985; West, 1997). Diversity can be measured along a number of different dimensions, but most researchers have focused on task-oriented attributes (e.g. specialized knowledge, skills, and abilities), and person-oriented attributes (those inherent to the individual, e.g. age, gender, ethnicity, seniority, personality) (Maznevski, 1994). It is well established at least for tasks that are truly interdependent that it is the level of task-oriented attributes in the team, not homogeneity, that is the crucial factor. For example, high-ability homogeneous teams outperform low-ability homogeneous teams (Tziner & Eden, 1985). However, since heterogeneity automatically implies that each team member will contribute a different set of knowledge and skills to the problem (a necessary ingredient for creative solutions), it should lead to superior performance on complex tasks (see e.g. Campion, Medsker, & Higgs, 1993; Guzzo & Dickson, 1996). In addition, there is some evidence to suggest that teams composed of combinations of person-oriented attributes (e.g. personality traits) perform better on particular tasks (see e.g. Driskell, Hogan, & Salas, 1987). Orpen (1987) refers to "an appropriate" mix of skills and traits and clearly takes the view that homogeneity is not desirable.

On the other hand, diversity can trigger stereotypes and prejudice which in turn (via group conflict) can affect team processes and outcomes (Jackson, 1996; Pfeffer, 1981). The theoretical descriptions that have guided much of the research on diversity in person-oriented attributes include the attraction–selection–attrition model (Schneider, 1987), similarity-attraction theory (Byrne, 1971), and self-categorization theory (Turner et al., 1987). A basic premise of these theories is that we are attracted to those who are similar to ourselves and repelled by those who are dissimilar. Indeed, there is considerable evidence to suggest that demographic characteristics such as age, sex, and education predict conflict, employee turnover, social integration, communication patterns, employee satisfaction, supervisor–subordinate relationships, absenteeism, and organizational commitment (see Mowday &

Sutton, 1993; O'Reilly, Caldwell, & Barnett, 1989; O'Reilly & Flatt, 1989; O'Reilly & Roberts, 1977).

A form of person-oriented diversity that has received particular attention is organizational tenure (Argote & McGrath, 1993). Katz (1982) found that the average group tenure in research and development teams was related to performance in the form of an inverted-U function: increases in group tenure or longevity were associated with increases in performance until about the two- to four-year mark and thereafter were associated with decreases in performance. O'Reilly and Flatt (1989) reported a negative relationship between tenure, diversity, and social integration which was in turn associated with higher turnover rates. The importance of affect and friendship ties, as a product of similarity of values, interests, and the like, has also been emphasized (George, 1989, 1990, 1995; Ibarra, 1992; Robins, Pattison, & Langan-Fox, 1995). George (1990) found that negative affect teams tended to be more rigid in their decision making than positive affect teams, an effect that he attributed to differences in TMM development. It seems, then, that one difficulty in TMM development could be the issue of diversity.

Status characteristics

Besides helping to determine preconceptions about team members, one of the most important aspects of team composition "diversity" is the affect it exerts on status and influence processes. These processes can be captured very well by network and process variables as in the proposed model. The fact that diversity of team member attributes has been linked to attitudes and behaviours in organizational teams (e.g. Pfeffer, 1981) suggests that workers must process and evaluate the characteristics of their workmates in some way. Status characteristics (SC) theoreticians describe how knowledge and attitudes about teammate characteristics are translated into beliefs about the relative status of individuals in the team. Status characteristics theory (SCT) suggests that the order of influence in small groups can be attributed to expectations about performance activated by status characteristics: "... any characteristic that has differentially evaluated states that are associated directly or indirectly with expectation states" (Berger et al., 1977, p. 35). Status characteristics may be external to the team or emerge during the course of interaction (Umberson & Hughes, 1987). The significance of external (or diffuse) status characteristics is defined in the larger social context, prior to and outside the task situation. Examples include gender, education level, seniority in the organization, and whether or not an individual is formally designated as group leader. In contrast, the expectations associated with an internal (or specific) status characteristic are limited to a particular task or situation, e.g. "most valuable team member" or "most helpful technical adviser" (see e.g. Cohen & Zhou, 1991). Since interacting on a collective task requires individuals to estimate the abilities of themselves and others, they will use status characteristics in that estimation, unless there are specific barriers to such use (Cohen & Zhou, 1991). On any given task, the high status affiliates of a status characteristic will automatically be perceived as more competent than the low status affiliates unless there is specific information to suggest otherwise and is typically known as the "burden of proof principle" (see e.g. Cohen & Zhou, 1991). Where individuals possess more than one distinguishing status characteristic, this information will be combined to produce an aggregate status level. The more direct the linkage, or the shorter the path of task relevance between a differentiating status characteristic and a task outcome, the greater the strength of the bond between them and the differentiating effect of the characteristic. This has typically been known as the "path of relevance principle" (see e.g. Berger et al., 1977). As a result of such processes, a schema for the relative influence of each team member is formed in which some degree of consensus and predictability in the team context is granted (Riley & Burke, 1995).

The expectations derived from status characteristics will powerfully determine the prestige order in the team and be manifest in inequalities in interaction. Specifically, distributions of participation level, influence attempts and acceptances, and evaluations, correspond to this power and prestige order (Cohen & Zhou, 1991). Shetzer (1993), while ignoring the importance of task and environment/context models, argued that individuals classify task situations in terms of the relative influence of actors along a "relative equality" to "extreme inequality" continuum and that team interaction can only proceed efficiently when team members share the same action-related knowledge.

THE TEAM TASK

Besides encountering each other as described in the foregoing, the task itself dominates the thinking of individual members. A task is the piece of work to be accomplished and it is possible for the completion of the task to be a goal. In most goal-setting studies, however, the term "goal" refers to attaining a specific standard of proficiency of a given task usually within a specified time limit (Locke & Latham, 1990). A goal is most likely to be achieved when it is in a moderate range of difficulty and there are no constraints to block goal attainment (Locke & Latham, 1990). If a goal is not set within an appropriate range of difficulty for the individual (i.e. if it is perceived as too difficult or too complex) then it will not be attained (Bandura, 1986). Similarly, if goal attainment is blocked by constraints in the environment, the person is less likely to attain the goal (Locke & Latham, 1990). Also tasks that are ill structured or ambiguous may hold an added dimension of difficulty and complexity for team members which may block performance. For instance, teams often develop poor strategies for task completion when faced with difficult goals and tasks of moderate to high complexity particularly when they are unfamiliar with the task (Earley, Lee, & Hanson, 1990). A further complication is a decline in goal commitment. A number of studies have shown that as goal difficulty increases and/or the person's perceived chances of reaching the goal decline, commitment to that goal decreases (see e.g. Erez & Zidon, 1984). These influences presumably take place through the effects of goal difficulty on expectancy and self-efficacy (Locke & Latham, 1990). Poor goal (or task) commitment in a team may present itself as a malaise or illness that begins to grow evident in team processes and performance. Evidence for a positive relationship between goal commitment and performance has been demonstrated in several studies (see e.g. Allscheid & Cellar, 1996; Klein & Kim, 1998; Klein & Wright, 1994; Martin & Manning, 1995; Theodorakis, 1996).

Planning

One tool that can be used to combat difficult and complex tasks is planning. Generally speaking, there are two types of planning: pre-planning which is planning that takes place prior to the onset of task performance, and in-process planning, planning that takes place during task performance (Weingart, 1992). In-process planning reduces uncertainty in unfamiliar task situations because information gained while working on the task can be integrated into the plan as the task progresses. Weingart (1992) found that the quality of the planning process mediated the relationship between the amount of planning and team performance in problem-solving teams. However, only planning about resources and team member roles were important to performance. In-process planning appeared to be central in the planning process and constituted a larger percentage of total planning in the teams than did pre-planning. In addition, there is evidence to suggest setting goals at both the individual and the team level leads to higher goal commitment (see e.g. Bandura, 1986; Brickner & Bukatko, 1987).

Task type difficulty

Although a task can be considered in one sense a goal, we think that the variable of "task type" has substantial implications for the team and its potential success in the sense that more difficult tasks will preoccupy and test the skills of the team than more simple tasks. The influence of task design on team performance has been well documented (Campion, Medsker, & Higgs, 1993; Campion, Papper, & Medsker, 1996; Cohen, Ledford, & Spreitzer, 1994; Drory & Shamir, 1988; Gladstein, 1984; Goodman, 1986; Steiner, 1972). Interest in task design can be traced back to an early study by Kent and McGrath (1969) who found that task characteristics accounted for 87.9 per cent of the variance in group performance. Subsequent research has resulted in a number of task classification schemes. American researchers in the field of task design have tended to classify tasks at a global level such that each task is assigned to one category (West, Borrill, & Unsworth, 1998). For example, Steiner (1972) distinguished between unitary, maximizing, optimizing, conjunctive, disjunctive, and additive tasks. McGrath's (1984) Group Task Circumplex classified task design according to four different performance functions: generating, choosing, resolving, and executing. In contrast, European researchers have tended to classify team tasks in terms of their hierarchical (goals and subgoals), sequential (the order in which different parts of the task are carried out), and cyclical process requirements (e.g. generating goals, planning, decision making, executing behaviour, and reviewing performance for each element of the task) (see West, Borrill, & Unsworth, 1998, for a complete description). One dimension of task design that is highly relevant in the complex setting of an organization is task ambiguity. Grummon (1997) argued that tasks range in their level of ambiguity from well structured to ill structured or ambiguous. The most well-structured tasks are ones with a single "right" answer or solution or a particular performance target (e.g. productivity). Somewhat more ambiguous are tasks requiring teams to generate one or more solutions to problems that have vague boundaries. The most ambiguous or ill-structured tasks are ones where there are numerous solutions and often few criteria for deciding what represents an acceptable solution. Examples of "real world", ill-structured, ambiguous tasks include, for instance, the design and installation of new machinery or setting up a career structure for part-time workers. Complex tasks such as these are tied to the broader organizational context of the team and require deliberation not only within the team itself, but also with key stakeholders in the organizational environment external to the team.

Teams having well-structured tasks may interact in ways that differ from teams with ambiguous tasks (Grummon, 1997). For example, since there are unlikely to be more than a few ways of achieving the goal of well-structured tasks, team members could be likely to simply turn to the team member perceived as the most competent or knowledgeable for the solution. This approach tends to focus team discussion on existing expertise and may result in limited interaction among team members through, say, less contention about what should be done. As a result, status differentials may become particularly salient, with members simply following the dictates of various experts within the team and where perhaps less effort is required of the team (e.g. discussion and problem solving). In contrast, tasks with greater ambiguity may encourage a broader range of team member participation by virtue of the fact that the endpoint of the task has yet to be defined and many subtasks exist for reaching the final goal. Ambiguous problems and difficult–complex tasks, then, could have the effect of reducing status differentials and increase the need for teamwork in completing the team task.

THE ORGANIZATIONAL CONTEXT

Although modest in volume compared to the more traditional areas of team research, the impact of the organizational environment or context on individual and team behaviour has become an important area of investigation (O'Reilly, 1991). Few precise definitions of the organizational context are evident in the literature; however, reviews by Campelli and Sherer (1993) and Cummings (1981) suggest that it encompasses the environment external to the individual and/or team, and phenomena that surround and thus exist within the environment external to the individual and/or team. A person's location within the social context of the organization—the people, jobs, tools, organizational change, and the organization as a whole—influences his/her experience of organizational life.

In the past 20 years, the contextual factors thought to be important to team functioning have grown from a few selected "inputs" to a long list of factors that have been examined both theoretically and empirically, and a number of models of organizational context have been proposed. Sundstrom, DeMuese, and Futrell (1990) argued for an eight-factor model of organizational context: organizational culture, technology, task design, mission clarity, autonomy, rewards, performance feedback, training, consultation, and the physical environment. In contrast, Hackman (1990) suggested reward, educational, and information systems are important features of the organizational context, and there is some support for the effects of reward systems (e.g. Hackman, 1983; Steiner, 1972) and feedback on team effectiveness (e.g. Locke & Latham, 1990). Tannenbaum, Beard, and Salas (1992) proposed that there are eight key aspects of the organizational context: reward systems, resource scarcity, management control, level of organizational stress, organizational climate, competition, inter-group relations within the organization, and environmental uncertainty. However, West, Borrill, and Unsworth (1998) argued that while these factors have high face validity in models of work group functioning there is little evidence of their effects on work group effectiveness. More recently, Cohen and Bailey (1997) pointed to customer expectations and the diffusion of work practices as important features of the organizational context. They described "organizational context design variables", features that can be directly manipulated by managers to create conditions for effective performance and which included rewards, supervision, training, and resources.

Physical context

A large part of the work environment consists of workspace characteristics, such as room darkness, interpersonal distance, and social density (Oldham & Fried, 1987). Steele (1986) provided examples of the effects of physical setting features (furniture arrangements, traffic-ways, aisles, lighting, design of entrances) on organizational behaviour (breaks in concentration, fatigue, stress, stimulation of thought and action). Features such as job differentiation, density of people in the work area, and proximity of other workers have been linked to processes such as communication and attitude formation (Monge, Edwards, & Kirste, 1983; Rice & Ayden, 1991). For instance, Rice and Ayden (1991) reported that employees' attitudes towards a new data processing system were similar to those of their supervisor and others with whom they interacted on a regular basis at work. These effects of "proximal information systems", were found even after controlling for the effects of system usage, occupational characteristics, and attitude levels in employee work teams.

Cultural context

A recent shift in the team processes literature has been to consider the cultural context of teams (West, Borrill, & Unsworth 1998). Hofstede (1980) distinguished four different cultural dimensions across which teams may vary. Smith and Noakes (1996) argued that variation in these dimensions is likely to be related to team processes. Individualistic cultures, for example, may view a team as a set of individuals who are each responsible for a specific part of the task, while a collectivist culture may define a team as a set of individuals who share responsibility for all aspects of the task.

Phase 2: Knowledge Compilation

At the experiential stage of Schumacher and Czerwinski (1992) and Kay and Black's (1990) second stage of skill acquisition, the goal of initial learning is that the team member overcomes the prior knowledge bias and an understanding of causal relationships emerges. In the model being outlined, it is difficult to state when this second phase would occur. Indeed in the skill acquisition literature there is no way of accurately determining when learning passes from one phase to another (see Ackerman, 1988; Langan-Fox, Waycott, & Galna, 1997). But one example might be through the actions of individual members, say a leader, who makes various initiatives, which are then taken up by the team. Once individuals have acquired basic knowledge, they learn the combinations of requirements that are often used together to accomplish goals. The novice is able to increase expertise: users combine simple plans into more compound plans to accomplish major goals and develop rules for selecting the best plan to achieve a given goal in a particular situation. There is also a reorganization of the knowledge that results in the development of new links between the components of the representation.

In this phase as the learner gains some experience and involvement in the team, procedures specific to the task develop that do not require the active maintenance of declarative knowledge about how to be involved in teamwork, and how to do the team task. That is, the learner gradually constructs (compiles) a set of skill-specific productions that directly incorporate the relevant declarative knowledge (Charney & Reder, 1987). As Blessing and Anderson (1996) have shown, for some tasks, learners may be able to skip steps thus performing the team task in less time. They suggest that initially learners are unable to do this because they follow the given rules. However, with practice they pick up short cuts and begin to apply them, for instance, they get to know "how things get done around here", making the problems easier to solve in one step. Kay and Black (1990) also suggested that during their "plan development" stage (which can be likened to the knowledge compilation stage of the ACT model), individuals begin to realize certain mistakes they have made. This realization leads to a reorganization of the knowledge representation to accommodate the command sequences or plans that are used to accomplish goals. That is, team members learn that there are combinations of rules (norms, values of the team and others in the organization), which are often used together to accomplish goals, so they are able to form plans by combining the actions that were previously represented separately. Similarly, Roschelle (1996) found that when students encounter a new system they initially construct knowledge that is sufficient for solving most tasks but bears little similarity to scientific knowledge. With practice, the students encountered problems and in their attempt to resolve these problematic experiences they transformed their mental models dramatically, bringing them closer to an expert's model.

During phase 2 the role of self-correction becomes more refined. Self-correction is a process carried out by effective teams and involves reviewing events, correcting errors, discussing strategies, and planning for future events (Blickensderfer, Cannon-Bowers, & Salas, 1997). Blickensderfer, Cannon-Bowers, and Salas (1997) argue that effective teams have a natural tendency to self-correct their team cognitions, attitudes, and behaviours without an outside intervention. The key requirement for such behaviour to be facilitated is opportunities for communication.

It is proposed that after people have some experience at working as a team, going through a trial-and-error process of discovering inadequacies in their existing knowledge and possible short cuts that they could use, their mental models develop to incorporate production rules which are constructed and compiled. Therefore, knowledge comes to involve greater understanding of the connections among features and functions of the team, teamwork, and the organization, and relies less upon analogies to other familiar groups and teams.

THE TEAM, TASK, AND ENVIRONMENTAL CONTEXT

Internal and external team relations

One of the ways in which learning how to make "short cuts" would highly benefit the team as it makes its progress towards achieving its task is in the way the team negotiates the relations internal to the team and relations external to it. This aspect of teamwork may provide the strongest test of team members' skills.

Traditional models of team processes tend to treat teams as closed systems or settings that shape individual attitudes, attributions, and decisions, with the major focus being on interaction among team members (Ancona, 1990). Such models hypothesize that a team will perform well to the extent that it manages its internal processes. In reality, however, such a view is much too simple. Crucial to the success of an organizational team is its ability to negotiate and navigate its way in and around the sociocultural, organizational environment. Teams need to interact with individuals and groups outside the team in order to acquire resources, gain legitimacy, manipulate systems (including politics), understand and meet their performance requirements, coordinate their activities with other teams (e.g. union), and so forth (Argote & McGrath, 1993; Campelli & Sherer, 1991). Thus, in studying organizational teams, it is important to extend the theoretical lens from the team boundary outwards, such that the focus shifts to a team in its context, which has an existence and purpose beyond the individuals composing it. We use the term "external relations" (Ancona, 1990; Ancona & Caldwell, 1989, 1992) to refer to the collection of strategies the team uses in interacting with the sociocultural environment, including management, co-workers, outside agencies, unions, shift groups, organizational committees, and others who have the potential to affect the team task.

Research interest in external relations can be traced to a study of 100 sales teams in the telecommunications industry (Gladstein, 1984) which found that while internal relations activity predicted team member satisfaction and ratings of team performance, only external relations activity predicted an objective, external measure of performance, sales revenue. Gladstein (1984) concluded that external relations which had been virtually ignored in the literature previously affected organizational team performance in ways that internal relations did not. Ancona and Caldwell (1992) reported that a key difference between teams with high and low levels of external relations was the team task. For example, a higher degree of external relations was found in teams where the team task was of high priority or importance and required innovation, flexibility, and imagination. Ancona and Caldwell (1992) suggested that the high level of external relations exhibited by these teams was possibly due to a greater pressure to obtain input from other parts of the organization. Team-level antecedents of external relations were specialized roles, experience, skills, and personality: team leaders engaged in more external relations in general and more upward relations (as opposed to lateral) than team members; team members with prior team experience were more likely to engage in external relations than team members with no prior team experience; and those who engaged in external relations were often those with the most technical knowledge, although these individuals often lacked the interpersonal skills to promote the team and negotiate with outsiders.

Achieving a balance between internal and external demands may be one of the most difficult tasks faced by organizational teams. In order to perform successfully, the team must satisfy the requirements of the broader organizational system yet at the same time maintain enough independence to perform its own specialized functions. It will be recalled that earlier in this chapter it was argued that there is probably a skill shortfall in team training. It is in managing the demands of internal and external relations where this shortfall may be most apparent. High external relations activity may have long-term costs for the cohesiveness of the team: team members may have the external knowledge they need but lack the cohesion to pool their perspectives due to substantial investments of time being lost to external activity (Ancona, 1990). Therefore, external relations may present the most challenging aspect of the team's overall activity to complete their task.

On the basis of recent research with teams (Langan-Fox, Code, & Langfield-Smith, 2000; Langan-Fox et al., 2001), six forms of external relations are proposed:

1. Obtaining information: identifying outsiders who can supply task-related and political information and ideas;
2. Obtaining resources: obtaining support, materials, and assistance;
3. Threat evaluation: interpreting, signalling, and gauging individuals who may be a threat to the team;
4. Moulding opinion: influencing and persuading those who are important to the team task;
5. Coordination: coordinating the team's activity with other individuals or groups;
6. Performance monitoring: gaining information about the likelihood of meeting performance requirements.

Another factor that has been linked with external relations is the physical proximity of key individuals and groups in the environment external to the team. Ivancevich (1972, 1974) argued for the importance of frequent team–manager interaction. The manager, responsible for the distribution information to suppliers, workers, and customers, provides a key channel through which the team can achieve two-way, upward, downward, horizontal communication throughout the organization. The capacity for external relations activity may also depend on the extent to which informal, face-to-face interaction is fostered by the shop floor and designated meeting places (Miller, 1959; Sundstrom, 1986).

Phase 3: Proceduralized Knowledge

In phase 2, knowledge compilation included the beginnings of a set of skills in that a person knows how to perform. During the third or procedural phase, performance is thought to become relatively automatic but we suggest continues to improve through refinement of the production rules—the "how to" rules. In an organization, this would consist of negotiating the various routes and gates that would apply to knowing "how things get done around here". The so-called "expert" stage is reached when the individual is able to make abstractions across various representations. Novices have superficial understandings of central terms and concepts whereas experts' knowledge is more structured and interconnected (Glaser, 1989). Experts use knowledge more efficiently (Ericsson & Staszewski, 1989), have the ability to see what is relevant when faced with a problem, and can easily access relevant knowledge (Hollnagel, Hoc, & Cacciabue, 1995). At this stage, the individual team member should be able to recognize systemic patterns of behaviour and retrieve old system knowledge and might also be able to make predictions and outcomes of the work of the team. That is, he/she is able to "run" a mental model of the team task (Cannon-Bowers et al., 1995) and visualize the problem, solution, and outcome.

FLUENT OR OVERLAPPING UNDERSTANDING

Team member–supervisor (expert) relations

The level of shared understanding between the team and their supervisor or manager is equally as important as shared understandings between team members. The team's manager represents a resource controller, judge, evaluator, and performance assessor. Thus, it could be hypothesized that in order to work together effectively, managers and teams need to share an understanding of the problem at hand and to develop the capacity to perceive, encode, store, and retrieve team-related information in a parallel manner (Cannon-Bowers & Salas, 1990; Converse, Cannon-Bowers, & Salas, 1991; Kleinman & Serfaty, 1989; Rouse, Cannon-Bowers, & Salas, 1992).

Does the mental model of the manager and the team need to be congruent? This may depend on the particular task or situation, but some diagnosis is going to be helpful in determining whether there is a misconception about the nature of the team task (the goal) or the manager or the team have "inaccurate" task mental models. Alternatively, different understandings by the manager and team could be naturally occurring and appropriate given that such differences of the team task could merely be representative of their different roles and responsibilities. Differing models would provide a complement to the potentially "total" mental model which comprises the task at hand. However, there may be some aspects of the various mental models which must be congruent and these would need to be identified, for instance the method/s techniques to be used by the team to achieve their goal. It must be remembered that the team's activities draw upon the resources of the organization, that they will be accountable for these, and that the adoption of efficient methods and approaches intrinsic to the team's task would need to be reflected in the degree of mental model overlap between manager and team. Thus, team and manager mental models can be used not only to determine distance and similarity in mental model overlap, but as a diagnostic tool to ascertain a "state of affairs", to log progress, and as a monitoring check of procedures which need to be incorporated in the "working mental model" of the team and the manager. "Working mental model" represents perhaps only a momentary picture of the complete current mental model, an abbreviation in other words, and is analogous to Markus and Nurius's notion of a "working self-concept" (Markus & Nurius, 1991).

In many situations in organizations we might want to regard the team's manager and supervisor as the "expert", in which case the expert mental model would be the one from which some sort of gap or audit analysis would be conducted to ascertain the degree of difference between the expert and any novice TMM. The gap would then be identified and rectified through training. This situation could arise where no alternative mental model to the expert mental model would exist, perhaps in cases of nuclear power plants or an oil rig installation.

HIGH PERFORMANCE TEAMS (EXPERT TMMs)

There has been much written about high performance teams and it is one of the aims of this chapter to assist in developing a theory that could facilitate the development of such teams. Some of the features suggested by Blinn (1996) to characterize high performance include having a common focus, clearly defined team member roles, utilizing internal and external resources, being supportive of diversity and having good conflict resolution mechanisms, effectively using feedback, and successfully managing time and meetings.

FLUENT, EXPERT TEAMS

Expert teams should have greater output, higher performance, smooth operation, with team members comfortable in their roles. They should understand each other's strengths, weaknesses, and role within the team; they should waste less resources and be better coordinated with a high degree of complementarity and cross-transfer of knowledge and skills. They may also be able to predict the actions of other team members.

APPLIED CONSIDERATIONS

General Utility of Framework and Bottom-line Improvements

TMMs have the potential to make communication and coordination more efficient by requiring less communication for the same result (i.e. by using a common language). They should make mutual team member learning more rapid, improve the allocation of tasks and decision control through awareness of team member strengths and weaknesses. There is a need to know how dimensions of TMMs and the notion of expert TMMs relate to enhanced performance by elucidating causal pathways.

The concept of TMMs serves as an organizing framework within which successful teamwork can be understood and specific predictions about team performance generated (Cannon-Bowers, Salas, & Converse, 1993; Cannon-Bowers et al., 1995). Given the complex nature of teamwork in organizations, the cognitive structure (the mental model) that team members use to organize information about team functioning is extremely important. TMMs provide team members with a set of organized expectations for team performance from which timely and accurate predictions about team member behaviour can be drawn (Converse, Cannon-Bowers, & Salas, 1991). Such knowledge forms the basis of team functioning by providing an understanding of global teamwork concepts (i.e. the team goal) and specific aspects of team performance (i.e. knowledge of special skills of team members). This suggests that team members must hold knowledge structures about the task and the team that are compatible with those held by fellow team members. Indirect evidence for a positive relationship between TMMs and performance has been reported by several authors (Foushee et al., 1986; Kleinman & Serfaty, 1989; Orasanu, 1990; Orasanu & Salas, 1993). Furthermore, there is evidence from the work of Walsh, Henderson, and Deighton (1988) to suggest that TMMs play an important role in aspects of team decision making and shared information processes, for instance problem definition, speed and flexibility, alternative evaluation, and implementation.

Acquiring and Training an Expert TMM

The process of ensuring the acquisition of a TMM would involve a TMM developmental programme whereby at regular meetings, teams would regularly check the accuracy and timeliness of their joint understandings of their task, of each other, and their working context. This could be done by a facilitator or supervisor, who would also note any shortfalls. The measurement issue in the applied context could be problematic and this issue remains a difficult one, with more research yet to be achieved.

With a better understanding of mental models for team functioning, organizations might be able to develop training programmes to foster an understanding of the core dimensions of teamwork (see e.g. Stevens & Campion, 1994), and help to develop "accurate" or expert mental models which must be shared among the team and other important people related to the team task. The goal of training would be to enable the development of relevant and accurate mental models that allow for greater understanding of the system and effective performance. With respect to teamwork, it is hoped that participants develop elaborate mental models of team functioning that incorporate all of the structures and processes inherent in team functioning, how they are related, and their purposes. Thus, users should develop mental models that integrate declarative and procedural knowledge in such a way as to allow a full understanding of the team and effective teamwork.

Research has shown that the format of instructions presented during learning affects performance and the mental models that learners develop (e.g. Eylon & Reif, 1984; Hegarty & Just, 1993; Hong & O'Neil, 1992; Kieras & Bovair, 1984; Mayer, 1989a; Zeitz & Spoehr, 1989). For instance, it has been shown that breadth-first, hierarchically organized information is a more effective instructional technique than the use of depth-first or linear representations of knowledge (Eylon & Reif, 1984; Zeitz & Spoehr, 1989). Zeitz and Spoehr defined depth-first knowledge as understanding that is built up from explanations of each of the lowest level elements in the domain. Breadth-first knowledge, on the other hand, involves generating an explanation at the highest level of the domain, then recursively decomposing the representation one level at a time. It has been found that experts tend to use top-down breadth-first strategies when faced with a problem-solving task, whereas novices do not (e.g. Jeffries et al., 1981, cited in Anderson, 1993). Based on the idea that experts organize their knowledge hierarchically, Zeitz and Spoehr predicted that hierarchically organized instructional materials would facilitate learning and that it would be possible to accelerate students' acquisition of procedural expertise by manipulating the organization with which the domain knowledge is presented. The results of their study supported this prediction, with subjects who were given breadth-first knowledge displaying superior performance than depth-first subjects at all phases of the experiment. Similarly, in a series of studies, Mayer (1989a) showed that the provision of an overall conceptual model prior to the presentation of normal instructional material had substantial positive learning effects.

Since it is possible that mental models are likely to be influenced by idiosyncratic experience, attitudes, and beliefs, Converse, Cannon-Bowers, and Salas (1991) argued that there are features of team functioning which may only be weakly impacted by idiosyncrasies and that it should be possible to train shared mental models of the team goal, the overall team task, individual tasks, and procedures. Rouse, Cannon-Bowers, and Salas (1992) suggested that "the emphasis (should be) on training that provides the mechanisms...knowledge structures...that enable formation of accurate and useful expectations and explanations" (p. 1303). However, the determination of the types of mental models that it is possible to train should not serve as the only selection criterion in training content. Rather, what is required is an analysis of the types of mental models that will enhance teamwork (Rouse, Cannon-Bowers, and Salas, 1992). Some concerted effort needs to be undertaken to ascertain whether faulty mental models do exist, perhaps through weekly team meetings, but also, diagnosis and analysis of mental models can be facilitated by team discussion and quantitative information obtained through techniques mentioned elsewhere (see e.g. Langan-Fox, Code, & Langfield-Smith, 2000; Langan-Fox et al., 2002b). In cases where individuals hold faulty or inaccurate mental models in important team task areas, it may be necessary to alter the structure and content of some members' models. Thus, the establishment of methods to train or manipulate mental models is essential. Research to date suggests that fostering or changing mental models is not simply a process of providing information about the general principles of a system or task, but rather giving instruction about the various components of teamwork and the relationships between them. Kieras and Bovair (1984) found that the explicit instruction of mental models through training could be used to manipulate the speed and course of TMM development. Much of what we have learned about mental models has come from human factors or aviation research and, consequently, has examined task-specific mental models as opposed to process-oriented (e.g. teamwork) ones. Research to date on this issue is encouraging (Azar, 1997).

Obviously in occupations where mistakes in the task can be expensive and/or highly undesirable, for instance in cockpit crews, ambulance teams, and the like, the risk of having inaccurate mental models needs to be minimized. But one could argue just as strongly that on the shop floor, production runs, placement of equipment on the factory floor, etc., can involve just as much risk and danger when knowledge is not mutually shared among a team. Therefore, training could provide the platform for achieving accuracy and refinement of individual and TMMs to eliminate those instances where it is undesirable to have "faulty" mental models.

Challenges of Teams in 21st Century and TMM Consequences

Technology is enabling new measurement possibilities. IT will influence TMMs through the creation of intranets and groupware. Knowledge management systems are facilitating communication and knowledge sharing. Knowledge sharing, communication, and working together is at the heart of developing TMMs.

The TMM framework varies from past frameworks in a number of crucial ways. First, it not only emphasizes models of internal team interaction or team context/environmental influence, but models the interplay between the team and its context. Such a perspective focuses on the processes that influence and are influenced by people in the environment as opposed to, say, internal processes in isolation. Second, it emphasizes that external team relations may play a crucial role in the development of the TMM. External relations have been neglected in past frameworks, possibly as a result of being developed on the basis of theory or in closed-environment teams (e.g. cockpit crews), rather than in collaboration with actual organizational teams. Third, the framework was developed from experiences of actual organizational teams in industry and has good ecological validity. Fourth, a dynamic multidimensional interactive approach is taken with a number of variables involved: team composition, task type, organizational context, internal and external team relations, task characteristics, and the development of mental models of team functioning incorporating these factors. Unlike past frameworks, the current one imposes no constraints on the relative importance of these variables. The extent to which each set of factors will be present in a given TMM will vary, depending on which set of variables is most salient for that particular team. Fifth, it is theoretically dynamic, being a new integration drawing upon theories in cognitive and social psychology and human factors. Finally, the model is developmental in the sense that it assumes a degree of noviceness associated with being an organizational team member and that this is a skill acquisition process involved in becoming a team member expert. However, further work is needed to establish the predictive validity of the framework across organizational teams. For instance, predictive validity could be determined by testing the relationship between within-team mental model overlap or team member–manager mental model overlap and performance (e.g. productivity).

Depending on how the TMM construct is measured (there is no established measure as such), the degree of generalizability of the framework will be limited because of the different measures that will be used, especially in the case of using elicited constructs of TMMs. TMMs can be a precursor to performance so the model could be adapted as a model of team performance. Thus, it has a number of potentials, not least of which would be identifying the appropriate content of team member training, the skill acquisition phase of that content, and the processes involved in the team member novice–expert transition.

FUTURE RESEARCH/DEVELOPMENT

TMM research is at a formative stage. The extension of cognition (i.e. shared and TMMs) appears to be a useful heuristic for interpreting the complexity of team functioning in the hurly-burly of modern-day organizations (see e.g. Langan-Fox et al., 2002b). However, there is little theoretical or empirical work (Klimoski & Mohammed, 1994), and there is little research on shared cognition in shop floor teams or between shop floor teams and their managers.

Given these issues, crucial research questions are: Do teams and managers hold similar mental models of team functioning? What should be the degree of overlap between members of a team and between a team and their manager? How do team member characteristics, task characteristics, and internal and external team relations influence the development of a TMM? Propositions for research are given in the Appendix. Figure 5.2 shows a graphical illustration of the framework and the factors that may influence the development and content of mental models of team functioning in an organizational setting. The dynamics of this framework have implications for the formation of shared mental models, between a team and their manager, and for the formation of a TMM. The framework developed with a focus on team processes and in particular the variables that predict a "mental model of team functioning" as opposed to team performance, of which it is a precursor. This variable could be added as a further phase in the model by a researcher. It should be noted that the framework does not claim to represent the complete content of a mental model for any particular individual or team but rather a cross-section or "slice" of what are likely to be the most salient aspects. Considering the complex and dynamic nature of cognitive processes, it would be difficult to obtain a "complete" mental model in the true sense. This concurs with descriptions of the nature of mental models given above.

The framework could be used to elicit individual mental models of important aspects of team functioning and how these are interrelated. Individual (team member) mental models could then be compared for their similarity or "overlap" to derive the TMM (for further information on the elicitation and representation of a TMM, see Langan-Fox et al., 2000). Team member mental models could also be compared for their similarity to the manager's or supervisor's mental model.

Research Needs

INTEGRATED APPLICATION SYSTEMS AND FACILITATING TMMs

New tools could aid in the use of the TMM construct. Such a system would incorporate measurement, analysis, and recommendations or would allow for easy interpretation. There is a need for recommendations to be clearly and validly linked to organizational needs. Technological improvements (e.g. software programs such as Groupware) facilitating teams such as expert identification systems could create teams with the ideal set of members.

TMM ideas need to be oriented towards organizational needs. This could be done by relating TMMs more to performance goals and by defining TMMs in relation to complementary individual mental models, and not necessarily absolutely shared individual mental models. TMMs could be seen as a tool for organizations, not an abstract theoretical construct. Thus, there is also a need for a better understanding of what complementariness means, and how it varies across tasks and organizational contexts.

ACKNOWLEDGEMENTS

Grateful thanks are given to Sharon Code and Jeromy Anglim for assistance with literature reviews. Financial support for this chapter from the Australian Research Council is acknowledged.

APPENDIX

Propositions

Proposition 1: Team members' mental models of team functioning will overlap more in teams composed of members with similar person-oriented attributes than in teams composed of members with dissimilar person-oriented attributes.

Proposition 2: Team members' mental models of the team will correspond with the power and prestige order of the team as defined by the status characteristics of individual team members.

Proposition 3: There should be more overlap between team members' mental models of the task in structured task teams than in unstructured task teams, since structured tasks are associated with well-defined role responsibilities and there is less room for confusion about the requirements of the task.

Proposition 4: Mental models of team interaction will be more important for unstructured task teams than for structured task teams as unstructured tasks are likely to require higher levels of team interaction.

Proposition 5: Team member–manager mental model similarity will be greater for structured tasks than for unstructured tasks, since there are less possible courses of action for achieving the goal.

Proposition 6: Proximity facilitates interaction and communication among team members, therefore team members' mental models should overlap more when their work stations are located within close proximity to one another.

Proposition 7: Individualistic team members will develop mental models of team functioning specific to their own role in the team as opposed to a more global, collective, or TMM. Thus, there should be more mental model overlap in teams composed of collectivist team members than in teams composed of individualist team members.

Proposition 8: There will be less overlap between the mental models of team members when commitment to the goal is low due to a decline in active participation in the task by team members.

Proposition 9: Team members who engage in in-process task planning will have more similar mental models than team members who engage in pre-planning, as the nature of the task and team (functioning) is likely to change over time.

Proposition 10: Where team members fail to strike a balance between the amount of time devoted to internal team relations and external team relations, the TMM is likely to be weak as a consequence of poor team cohesiveness and communication.

Proposition 11: Structured task teams yield "one-of-a-kind" outputs (i.e. generate the same or similar outputs over and over), require only "one off" instances of synchronization with support staff or competitors, have longer cycles of independent, within-team work, and have low external relations requirements. Unstructured task teams (e.g. employee participation teams) yield unique inputs which impact on stakeholders in the organizational environment, need to gather task-relevant information and support from outside the team, and have high external relations requirements. Thus, external relations should feature more significantly in the mental models of unstructured task team members than structured task team members.

Proposition 12: Team member–manager mental model overlap will be greater when there is frequent interaction between the team and the manager.

BIBLIOGRAPHY

Ackerman, P. L. (1988). Determinants of individual differences during skill acquisition: cognitive abilities and information processing. *Journal of Experimental Psychology: General, 117,* 288–318.

Allscheid, S. P. & Cellar, D. F. (1996). An interactive approach to work motivation: the effects of competition, rewards and goal difficulty on task performance. *Journal of Business and Psychology, 11*(2), 219–237.

Ancona, D. G. (1990). Outward bound: strategies for team survival in an organization. *Academy of Management Journal, 33,* 334–365.

Ancona, D. G. & Caldwell, D. F. (1989). Beyond task and maintenance: defining external functions in teams. *Team and Organization Studies, 13,* 488–494.

Ancona, D. G. & Caldwell, D. F. (1992). Bridging the boundary: external activity and performance in organizational teams. *Administrative Science Quarterly, 37*(4), 634–665.

Anderson, J. (1982). Acquisition of cognitive skill. *Psychological Review, 89,* 369–406.

Anderson, J. R. (1987). Skill acquisition: compilation of weak-method problem solutions. *Psychological Review, 94,* 192–210.

Anderson, J. R. (1993). Problem solving and learning. *American Psychologist, 48*(1), 35–44.

Annett, J. & Duncan, K. D. (1967). Task analysis and training design. *Occupational Psychology, 41,* 211–221.

Annett, J., Duncan, K. D., Stammers, R. B., & Gray, M. J. (1971). Task analysis. *Training Information No. 6.* London: HMSO.

Arad, S., Hanson, N., & Schneider, R. (1991). Organizational context. In N. G. Peterson & M. D. Mumford (eds), *An Occupational Information System for the 21st Century: The Development of ONET* (pp. 147–174). Washington, DC: American Psychological Association.

Argote, L. & McGrath, J. E. (1993). Team processes in organizations: continuity and change. In C. L. Cooper & I. T. Robertson (eds), *International Review of Industrial and Organizational Psychology 1993* (Vol. 8, pp. 333–389). New York: John Wiley & Sons.

Azar, B. (1997). Team building isn't enough: workers need training too. *APA Monitor,* July, 13–14.

Bandura, A. (1986). Differential engagement of self-reactive influences in cognitive motivation. *Organizational Behavior and Decision Processes, 38,* 92–113.

Banks, A. P. & Millward, L. J. (2000). Running shared mental models as a distributed cognitive process. *British Journal of Psychology, 91*(4), 513–531.

Barrick, M. R., Stewart, G. L., Neubert, M. J., & Mount, M. K. (1998). Relating team member ability to work team processes and team effectiveness. *Journal of Applied Psychology, 83*(3), 377–391.

Berger, J. M., Fisek, H., Norman, R. Z., & Zelditch, M., Jr (1977). *Status Characteristics and Social Interaction: An Expectation-States Approach.* New York: Elsevier.

Blessing, S. B. & Anderson, J. R. (1996). How people learn to skip steps. *Journal of Experimental Psychology: Learning, Memory, & Cognition, 22*(3), 576–598.

Blickensderfer, E., Cannon-Bowers, J. A., & Salas, E. (1997). Theoretical bases for team self-corrections: fostering shared mental models. In M. M. Beyerlein & D. A. Johnson (eds), *Advances in Interdisciplinary Studies of Work Teams* (Vol. 4, pp. 249–279). Stamford, Conn.: JAI Press.

Blinn, C. K. (1996, Nov–Dec). Developing high performance teams. *Online, 20, 6*, p. 56(1). Online: http://www.coachcarla.com/articles.html

Brannick, M. T., Prince, A., Prince, C., & Salas, E. (1995). The measurement of team process. *Human Factors, 37*(3), 641–651.

Brickner, M. A. & Bukatko, P. A. (1987). Locked into performance: goal setting as a moderator of social loafing affect. University of Ackron, unpublished manuscript.

Bruning, N. S. & Liverpool, P. R. (1993). Membership in quality circles and participation in decision making. *The Journal of Applied Behavioral Science, 29*, 76–95.

Byrne, D. (1971). *The Attraction Paradigm.* New York: Academic Press.

Campelli, P. & Sherer, P. D. (1993). The missing role of context in OB: the need for a meso-level approach. *Research in Organizational Behavior, 13*, 55–110.

Campion, M. A., Medsker, G. J., & Higgs, A. C. (1993). Relations between work group characteristics and effectiveness: implications for designing effective work groups. *Personnel Psychology, 46*, 823–850.

Campion, M. A., Papper, E. M., & Medsker, G. J. (1996). Relationships between work team characteristics and effectiveness: a replication and extension. *Personnel Psychology, 49*, 429–452.

Cannon-Bowers, J. A. & Salas, E. (1990). Cognitive psychology and team training: shared mental models in complex systems. *Human Factors Society Bulletin, 33*, 1–4.

Cannon-Bowers, J. A. & Salas, E. (2001). Reflections on shared cognition. *Journal of Organizational Behavior, 22* (Special Issue), 195–202.

Cannon-Bowers, J. A., Salas, E., & Converse, S. (1993). Shared mental models in expert team decision making. In N. J. Castellan, Jr (ed.), *Individual and Team Decision Making* (pp. 221–246). New Jersey: Lawrence Erlbaum Associates.

Cannon-Bowers, J. A. & Tannenbaum, S. I. (1991). Toward an integration of training theory and technique. *Human Factors, 33*(3), 281–292.

Cannon-Bowers, J. A., Tannenbaum, S. I., Salas, E., & Volpe, C. E. (1995). Defining team competencies and establishing training requirements. In R. Guzzo & E. Salas (eds), *Team Effectiveness and Decision Making in Organizations* (pp. 333–380). San Francisco: Jossey-Bass.

Carley, K. M. (1990). Coordinating for success: trading information redundancy for task simplicity. *Proceedings of the 23rd Annual Hawaii International Conference on System Sciences, 3*, 261–270.

Carver, C. S. & Sheier, M. F. (1982). *Attention and Self-regulation: A Control Theory Approach to Human Behavior.* New York: Springer.

Charney, D. A. & Reder, L. M. (1987). Initial skill learning: an analysis of how elaborations facilitate the three components. In P. Morris (ed.), *Modelling Cognition* (pp. 135–165). New York: John Wiley & Sons.

Chatman, J. A. & Barsade, S. G. (1995). Personality, organizational culture, and cooperation: evidence from a business simulation. *Administrative Science Quarterly, 40*(3), 423–443.

Clegg, C. (1994). Psychology and information technology: the study of cognition in organizations. *British Journal of Psychology, 85*(4), 449–477.

Coates, J. (1996). How to improve the quality of our organizations through the use of TQM, continuous improvement strategies. In *The Olympics of Leadership: Overcoming Obstacles, Balancing Skills, and Taking Risks.* Proceedings of the Annual International Conference of the National Community College Chair Academy, Phoenix, Ariz.

Code, S. & Langan-Fox, J. (2001). Motivations, cognitions and traits: predicting occupational health, well being and performance. *Stress and Health, 17*, 159–174.

Cohen, B. P. & Zhou, X. (1991). Status processes in enduring work teams. *American Sociological Review, 56*, 179–188.

Cohen, S. G. & Bailey, D. E. (1997). What makes teams work: group effectiveness research from the shop floor to the executive suite. *Journal of Management, 23*(2), 239–290.

Cohen, S. G., Ledford, G. E., & Spreitzer, G. M. (1994). A predictive model of self-managing work team effectiveness. *Human Relations, 49*(5), 643–676.

Collins, A. M. & Loftus, E. F. (1975). A spreading activation theory of semantic processing. *Psychological Review, 82*, 407–428.

Converse, S. A., Cannon-Bowers, J. A., & Salas, E. (1991). Team member shared mental models: a theory and some methodological issues. *Proceedings of the Human Factors Society 35th Annual Meeting*, 1417–1421.

Cooke, N. J., Salas, E., Cannon-Bowers, J. A., & Stout, R. J. (2000). Measuring team knowledge. *Human Factors, 42*(1), 151–173.

Cummings, L. L. (1981). Organizational behaviour. *Annual Review of Psychology, 33*, 541–579.

Driskell, J. E., Hogan, R., & Salas, E. (1987). Personality and group performance. *Review of Personality and Social Psychology, 9*, 91–112.

Drory, A. & Shamir, B. (1988). Effects of organization and life variables on job satisfaction and burnout. *Group and Organization Studies, 13*(4), 441–455.

Duffy, L. (1992). Team decision making biases: an information processing perspective. In G. A. Klein, J. Orasanu, R. Calderwood, & C. E. Zsambok (eds), *Decision Making in Action: Models and Methods*, (pp. 234–242). Norwood, NJ: Ablex.

Earley, P. C., Lee, C., & Hanson, L. A. (1990). Joint moderating effects of job experience and task component complexity: relations among goal setting, task strategies, and performance. *Journal of Organizational Behavior, 11*, 3–15.

Eby, L. T., Meade, A., Parisi, A. G., Douthitt, S. S., & Midden, P. (1998). Measuring mental models for teamwork at the individual- and team-level. Paper presented at the Annual Meeting of the Society for Industrial and Organizational Psychology, Dallas, Texas.

Encarta (2001). *Cooperation*. Microsoft Corporation. Online: http://encarta.msn.com

Erez, M. & Zidon, I. (1984). Effect of goal acceptance on the relationship of goal difficulty to performance. *Journal of Applied Psychology, 69*, 69–78.

Ericsson, K. A. & Staszewski, J. J. (1989). Skilled memory and expertise: mechanisms of exceptional performance. In D. Klahr & K. Kotovsky (eds), *Complex Information Processing: The Impact of Herbert A. Simon* (pp. 235–267). Hillsdale, NJ: Lawrence Erlbaum Associates.

Eylon, B. & Reif, F. (1984). Effects of knowledge organization on task performance. *Cognition & Instruction, 1*(1), 5–44.

Flanagan, J. C. (1954). The critical incident technique. *Psychological Bulletin, 51*, 327–358.

Foushee, H. C., Lauber, J. K., Baetge, M. M., & Acomb, D. B. (1986). *Crew Factors in Flight Operations III: The Operational Significance of Exposure to Short-haul Air Transport Operations*. Mountain View, Calif.: NASA.

Gentner, D. & Collins, A. (1981). Studies of inference from lack of knowledge. *Memory and Cognition, 9*(4), 434–443.

Gentner, D. & Stevens, D. (1983). *Mental Models*. Hillsdale, NJ: Lawrence Erlbaum Associates.

George, J. M. (1989). Mood and absence. *Journal of Applied Psychology, 74*, 317–324.

George, J. M. (1990). Personality, affect, and behaviour in groups. *Journal of Applied Psychology, 75*, 107–166.

George, J. M. (1995). Leader positive mood and group performance: the case of customer service. *Journal of Applied Social Psychology, 25*, 778–794.

Gladstein, D. (1984). Groups in context: a model of task group effectiveness. *Administrative Science Quarterly, 29*, 210–216.

Glaser, R. (1989). Expertise and learning: how do we think about instructional processes information processing. In D. Klahr & K. Kotovsky (eds), *Complex Information Processing: The Impact of Herbert A. Simon* (pp. 235–267). Hillsdale, NJ: Lawrence Erlbaum Associates.

Glickman, A. S., Zimmer, S., Montero, R. C., Guerette, P. J., Campbell, W. J., Morgan, B. B., & Salas, E. (1987). *The Evolution of Teamwork Skills: An Empirical Assessment with Implications for Training*. Orlando: Naval Training Systems Centre.

Goodman, P. S. (1986). Impact of task and technology and group performance. In P. S. Goodman (ed.), *Designing Effective Work Groups* (pp. 120–167). San Francisco: Jossey-Bass.

Graham, J. W. & Verma, A. (1991). Predictors and moderators of employee responses to employee participation programs. *Human Relations, 44*, 551–568.

Greene, C. N. (1989). Cohesion and productivity in work groups. *Small Group Behavior, 20*(1), 70–86.

Griffin, M. & Mathieu, J. (1997). Modelling organizational processes across hierarchical levels: climate, leadership, and group processes in work groups. *Journal of Organizational Behavior, 18*(6), 731–744.

Grummon, P. T. H. (1997). Assessing teamwork skills for workforce readiness. In H. F. O'Neil (ed.), *Work Readiness: Competencies and Assessment*. Hillsdale, NJ: Lawrence Erlbaum Associates.

Guenther, R. K. (1998). *Human Cognition*. Saddle River, NJ: Prentice-Hall.

Guzzo, R. A. & Dickson, M. W. (1996). Teams in organizations: recent research in performance and effectiveness. *Annual Review of Psychology, 46*, 307–338.

Hackman, J. R. (1983). A normative model of work team effectiveness (Technical Report No. 2). *Research Program on Group Effectiveness*. Yale School of Organization and Management.

Hackman, J. R. (1990). *Groups that Work (and Those that Don't)*. San Francisco: Jossey-Bass.

Heath, C. & Luff, P. (1996). Convergent activities: line control and passenger information on the London underground. In Y. Engestron & D. Middleton (eds), *Cognition and Communication at Work* (pp. 96–129). New York: Cambridge University Press.

Heffner, T. S., Mathieu, J., & Cannon-Bowers, J. A. (1998). The impact of shared mental models on team performance: sharedness, quality or both? Paper presented at the Annual Meeting of the Society for Industrial and Organizational Psychology, Dallas, Texas.

Hegarty, M. & Just, M. A. (1993). Constructing mental models of machines from text and diagrams. *Journal of Memory & Language, 32*(6), 717–742.

Hofstede, G. (1980). *Culture's Consequences: International Differences in Work-related Values*. Beverly Hills, Calif.: Sage.

Hollnagel, E., Hoc, J.-M., & Cacciabue, P. C. (1995). Work with technology: some fundamental issues. In J.-M. Hoc, P. C. Cacciabue, & E. Hollnagel (eds), *Expertise and Technology: Cognition and Human–Computer Cooperation*. New York: Lawrence Erlbaum Associates.

Hong, E. & O'Neil, H. F., Jr (1992). Instructional strategies to help learners build relevant mental models in inferential statistics. *Journal of Educational Psychology, 84*, 150–159.

Hutchins, E. (1991). The social organization of distributed cognition. In L. B. Resnick, J. M. Levine, & S. D. Teasly (eds), *Perspectives on Socially Shared Cognition* (pp. 283–307). Washington, DC: American Psychological Association.

Ibarra, H. (1992). Homophilly and differential returns: sex differences in network structure and access in an advertising firm. *Administrative Science Quarterly, 37*, 422–437.

Ivancevich, J. M. (1972). A longitudinal assessment of management by objectives. *Administrative Science Quarterly, 17*, 126–138.

Ivancevich, J. M. (1974). Changes in performance in a management by objectives program. *Administrative Science Quarterly, 19*, 563–574.

Jackson, S. E. (1992). *Diversity in the Workplace: Human Resources Initiatives*. The Professional Practice series. New York: Guilford Press.

Jackson, S. E. (1996). The consequences of diversity in multidisciplinary work teams. In M. A. West (ed.), *Handbook of Work Group Psychology* (pp. 53–76). Chichester: Wiley.

Jacobs, G. M. & James, J. E. (1994). A comparison of workplace groups with groups in education. *Annual Meeting of Teachers of English to Speakers of Other Languages*, Baltimore, Md.

Janis, I. L. (1972). *Victims of Groupthink*. Boston: Houghton-Mifflin.

Jeffries, R., Turner, A., Polson, P., & Atwood, M. (1981). The processes involved in designing software. In J. R. Anderson (ed.), *Cognitive Skills and Their Acquisition*. Hillsdale, NJ: Lawrence Erlbaum Associates.

Johnson-Laird, P. (1983). *Mental Models*. Cambridge, Mass.: Harvard University Press.

Jones, G. R. & George, J. M. (1998). The experience and evolution of trust: implications for cooperation and teamwork. *Academy of Management Review, 23*(3), 531–546.

Katz, R. (1982). The effects of group longevity on communication and performance. *Administrative Science Quarterly, 27*, 81–104.

Kay, D. S. & Black, J. B. (1990). Knowledge transformations during the acquisition of computer expertise. In S. P. Robertson & W. W. Zachary et al. (eds), *Cognition, Computing, and Cooperation* (pp. 268–303). Norwood, NJ: Ablex.

Kelly, G. A. (1955). *The Psychology of Personal Constructs*. New York: W. W. Norton and Company.

Kent, R. N. & McGrath, J. E. (1969). Task and group characteristics as factors influencing group performance. *Journal of Experimental Social Psychology, 5*, 429–440.

Kieras, D. E. & Bovair, S. (1984). The role of a mental model in learning to operate a device. *Cognitive Science, 8*(3), 255–273.

Klein, G. (1997). An overview of naturalistic decision making applications. In C. E. Zsambok & Gary Klein (eds), *Naturalistic Decision Making. Expertise: Research and Applications* (pp. 49–59). Hillsdale, NJ: Lawrence Erlbaum Associates.

Klein, H. J. & Kim, J. S. (1998). A field study of the influence of situational constraints, leader–member exchange, and goal commitment on performance. *Academy of Management Journal, 41*(1), 88–95.

Klein, H. J. & Wright, P. M. (1994). Antecedents of goal commitment: an empirical examination of personal and situational factors. *Journal of Applied Social Psychology, 24*(2), 95–114.

Kleinman, D. L. & Serfaty, D. (1989). Team performance assessment in distributed decision making. In R. Gibson, J. P. Kincaid, & B. Goldiez (eds), *Proceedings for Interactive Networked Simulation for Training Conference* (pp. 22–27). Orlando: Institute for Simulation and Training.

Klimoski, R. & Mohammed, S. (1994). Team mental model: construct or metaphor? *Journal of Management, 20*, 403–437.

Kozlowski, S. W. (1995). Organizational change, informal learning, and adaptation: emerging trends in training and continuing education. *Journal of Continuing Higher Education, 43*(1), 2–11.

Kraiger, K. & Wenzel, L. H. (1997). Conceptual development and empirical evaluation of measures of shared mental models as indicators of team effectiveness. In M. T. Brannick & E. Salas (eds), *Team Performance Assessment and Measurement: Theory, Methods, and Applications*. Series in applied psychology (pp. 63–84). Mahwah, NJ: Lawrence Erlbaum Associates.

Langan-Fox, J. (2001a). Communication in organizations: speed, diversity, networks and influence on organizational effectiveness, human health and relationships. In N. Anderson, D. S. Ones, H. K. Sinangil, & C. Viswesvaran (eds), *International Handbook of Work and Organizational Psychology* (Vol. 2). London: Sage Publications.

Langan-Fox, J. (2001b). Teamwork in organizations: measurement, methodologies and effectiveness. In M. O'Driscoll, P. Taylor, & T. Kalliath (eds), *Organizational Psychology in Australia and New Zealand*. London: Oxford University Press.

Langan-Fox, J., Armstrong K., Anglim, J., & Balvin, N. (2002a). Process in skill acquisition: motivation, interruptions, memory, affective states and metacognition. *Australian Psychologist, 37*(2), 104–117.

Langan-Fox, J., Code, S., & Edlund, G. (1998). *Team Organizational Mental Models: An Integrative Framework for Research*. Annual Conference of the Ergonomics Society, Cirencester, England, 125 pp. (April). London: Taylor & Francis.

Langan-Fox, J., Code, S., Gray, R., & Langfield-Smith, K. (2002b). Supporting employee participation: attitudes and perceptions in trainees, employees and teams. *Group Processes and Intergroup Relations, 5*(1), 53–82.

Langan-Fox, J., Code, S., & Langfield-Smith, K. (2000). Team mental models: methods, techniques and applications. *Human Factors, 42*(2), 1–30.

Langan-Fox, J. & Grey, R. (1999) Improving shop floor performance through industrial participation training. In J. Langan-Fox & M. Griffin (eds), *Human Performance and the Workplace* (Vol. 1). Melbourne: APS Imprint Books.

Langan-Fox, J., Waycott, J., & Galna, C. (1997). Ability–performance relations during skill acquisition. *Australian Psychologist, 32*(3), 153–158.

Langan-Fox, J., Waycott, J., Morizzi, M., & McDonald, L. (1998). Predictors of participation in performance appraisal: a voluntary system in a blue collar work environment. *International Journal of Selection and Assessment, 6*(4), 249–260.

Langan-Fox, J., Wirth, A., Code, S., Langfield-Smith, K., & Wirth, A. (2000). Analysing mental models of teams, managers and experts. In *Challenges for the New Millenium*. Proceedings of the Human Factors and Ergonomics Annual Conference, San Diego, July, pp. 146–150.

Langan-Fox, J., Wirth, A., Code, S., Langfield-Smith, K., & Wirth, A. (2001). Analyzing shared and team mental models. *International Journal of Industrial Ergonomics, 28*, 99–112.

Levesque, L. L., Wilson, J. M., & Wholey, D. R. (2001). Cognitive divergence and shared mental models in software development project teams. *Journal of Organizational Behavior, 22*(Special Issue), 135–144.

Levine, J. M. & Moreland, R. L. (1991). Culture and socialization in work teams. In L. B. Resnick, J. M. Levine, & S. D. Teasley (eds), *Perspectives on Socially Shared Cognition* (pp. 257–282). Washington, DC: American Psychological Association.

Locke, E. A. & Latham, G. P. (1990). *A Theory of Goal Setting and Task Performance*. Englewood Cliffs, NJ: Prentice-Hall.

McClough, A. C., Rogelberg, S. G., Fisher, G. G., & Bachiochi, P. D. (1998). Cynicism and the quality of an individual's contribution to an organizational diagnostic survey. *Organization Development Journal, 16*(2), 31–41.

McGrath, J. E. (1984). *Groups: Interaction and Performance*. Englewood Cliffs, NJ: Prentice-Hall.

Magney, J. (1995). Teamwork and cooperative learning in technical education. Paper presented at the American Vocational Association Convention, Denver, Colo.

Marchington, M., Wilkinson, A., Ackers, P., & Goodman, J. (1994). Understanding the meaning of participation: views from the workplace. *Human Relations, 47*(8), 867–894.

Markus, H. & Nurius, S. (1991). Possible selves. *American Psychologist, 41*, 249–260.

Martin, B. A. & Manning, D. J. (1995). Combined effects of normative information on task difficulty and the goal commitment–performance relationship. *Journal of Management, 21*(1), 65–80.

Maslow, A. H. (1970). *Motivation and Personality* (2nd edn). New York: Harper and Row.

Mayer, R. E. (1989a). Models for understanding. *Review of Educational Research, 59*(1), 43–64.

Mayer, R. E. (1989b). Teaching for thinking: research on the teachability of thinking skills. In I. S. Cohen (ed.), *The G. Stanley Hall Lecture Series* (Vol. 9, pp. 139–164). Washington, DC: American Psychological Association.

Maznevski, M. L. (1994). Understanding our differences: performance in decision making groups with diverse members. *Human Relations, 47*(5), 531–552.

Miller, E. J. (1959). Technology, territory, and time: the internal differentiation of complex production systems. *Human Relations, 12*, 245–272.

Miller, R. W. & Prichard, F. N. (1992). Factors associated with workers' inclination to participate in an employee involvement program. *Group and Organization Management, 17*(4), 414–430.

Mohammed, S. & Dumville, B. C. (2001). Team mental models in a team knowledge framework: expanding theory and measurement across disciplinary boundaries. *Journal of Organizational Behavior*. Special Issue: *Shared Cognition, 22*, 89–106.

Mohammed, S., Klimoski, R., & Rentsch, J. R. (2000). The measurement of team mental models: we have no shared schema. *Organizational Research Methods, 3*(2), 123–165.

Monge, P. R., Edwards, J. A., & Kirste, K. K. (1983). Determinants of communication network involvement, connectedness, and integration. *Group and Organizational Studies, 8*(1), 83–111.

Morgan, B. B., Glickman, A. S., Woodward, E. A., Blaiwes, A. S., & Salas, E. (1986). *Measurement of Team Behaviours in a Navy Environment* (Tech. Rep. No. TR-86-014). Orlando, Fla: Naval Training Systems Center.

Mowday, R. T. & Sutton, R. I. (1993). Organizational behavior: linking individuals and teams to organizational contexts. *Annual Review of Psychology, 44*, 195–229.

Norman, D. A. (1983). Some observations on mental models. In D. Gentner & L. Stevens (eds), *Mental Models* (pp. 7–14). Hillsdale, NJ: Lawrence Erlbaum Associates.

Oldham, G. R. & Fried, Y. (1987). Employee reactions to workplace characteristics. *Journal of Applied Psychology, 72*(1), 75–80.

Olson, J. R. & Biolsi, K. J. (1991). Techniques for representing expert knowledge. In K. A. Ericsson & J. Smith (eds), *Toward a General Theory of Expertise: Prospects and Limits* (pp. 240–285). New York: Cambridge University Press.

Orasanu, J. (1990). Shared mental models and crew decision making. In *Proceedings of the 12th Annual Conference of the Cognitive Science Society*, Cambridge, Mass.

Orasanu, J. & Salas, E. (1993). Team decision making in complex environments. In G. A. Klein, J. Orasanu, R. Calderwood, & C. E. Zsambok (eds), *Decision Making in Action: Models and Methods* (pp. 327–345). Norwood, NJ: Ablex.

O'Reilly, C. A. (1991). Organizational behaviour: where we've been, where we're going. *Annual Review of Psychology, 42*, 427–458.

O'Reilly, C. A., Caldwell, D. F., & Barnett, W. P. (1989). Work group demography, social integration and turnover. *Administrative Science Quarterly, 34*, 21–37.

O'Reilly, C. A. & Flatt, S. (1989). Executive team demography, organizational innovation, and firm performance (Working Paper). Berkeley, Calif.: University of California.

O'Reilly, C. A. & Roberts, K. H. (1977). Communication and performance in organizations. Paper presented at *Academy of Management annual meeting*, Orlando, Fla.

Orpen, C. (1987). Strategic planning through group decision-making. *Management and Labor Studies, 12*(3), 133–139.
Patrick, J. (1992). *Training: Research and Practice.* London: Academic Press.
Pfeffer, J. (1981). A partial test of the social information model of job attitudes. *Human Relations, 33*, 457–476.
Pfeffer, J. (1986). A resource dependence perspective on inter-corporate relations. In M. S. Mizruchi & M. Schwartz (eds), *Structural Analysis of Business* (pp. 117–132). New York: Academic Press.
Prince, C. & Salas, E. (1989). Air crew performance: coordination and skill development. In D. E. Daniel, E. Salas, & D. M. Kotick (eds), *Independent Research and Independent Exploratory Development Programs: Annual Report for Fiscal Year 1988* (NTSC Tech. Rep. No. 89-009, pp. 45–48). Orlando, Fla: Naval Training Systems Center.
Rice, L. E. & Ayden, C. (1991). Attitudes toward new organizational technology: network proximity as a mechanism for social information processing. *Administrative Science Quarterly, 36*, 219–244.
Riley, A. L. & Burke, P. J. (1995). Identities and self-verification in the small group. *Social Psychology Quarterly, 58*(2), 61–73.
Robins, G., Pattison, P., & Langan-Fox, J. (1995). Group effectiveness: a comparative network analysis of interactional structure and performance in organizational workgroups. *Social Networks Annual Conference*, London, pp. 240–251.
Roschelle, J. (1996). Designing for cognitive communication: epistemic fidelity or mediating collaborative inquiry? In D. L. Day & D. K. Kovacks (eds), *Computers, Communication and Mental Models* (pp. 15–27). Philadelphia, Pa: Taylor & Francis.
Rouse, W. B., Cannon-Bowers, J. A., & Salas, E. (1992). The role of mental models in team performance in complex systems. *IEEE Transactions on Systems, Man, and Cybernetics, 22*(6), 1296–1308.
Rouse, W. B. & Morris, N. M. (1986). On looking into the black box: prospects and limits in the search for mental models. *Psychological Bulletin, 100*, 349–363.
Salomon, G. (1993). *Distributed Cognitions: Psychological and Educational Considerations.* New York: Cambridge University Press.
Schavaneveldt, R. W. (1990). *Pathfinder Associative Networks: Studies in Knowledge Organization.* Norwood, NJ: Albex.
Schneider, B. (1987). The people make the difference. *Personnel Psychology, 40*, 437–453.
Schumacher, R. & Czerwinski, M. (1992). Mental models and the acquisition of expert knowledge. In R. Hoffman (ed.), *The Psychology of Expertise.* New York: Springer-Verlag.
Shepard, A. (1985). An improved tabular format for task analysis. *Journal of Occupational Psychology, 49*, 93–104.
Shetzer, L. (1993). A social information processing model of employee participation. *Organization Science, 4*(2), 252–268.
Smith, E. E., Shoeben, E. J., & Rips, L. J. (1974). Structure and process in semantic memory: a featural model for semantic decisions. *Psychological Review, 81*, 214–241.
Smith, P. B. & Noakes, J. (1996). Cultural differences in group processes. In M. A. West (ed.), *Handbook of Work Group Psychology* (pp. 477–502). Chichester: Wiley.
Steele, F. (1986). *Making and Managing High Quality Workplaces: An Organizational Ecology.* New York: Teachers College Press.
Steiner, I. D. (1972). *Group Processes and Productivity.* New York: Academic Press.
Stevens, M. J. & Campion, M. A. (1994). The knowledge, skill, and ability requirements for teamwork: implications for human resource management. *Journal of Management, 20*, 503–530.
Sundstrom, E. (1986). *Work Places.* New York: Cambridge University Press.
Sundstrom, E., DeMeuse, K. P., & Futrell, D. (1990). Work teams: applications and effectiveness. *American Psychologist, 45*(2), 120–133.
Sweezey, R. W. & Salas, E. (1992). *Teams: Their Training and Performance.* Norwood, NJ: Ablex.
Tang, T. L. P. & Butler, E. A. (1997). Attributions of quality circles' problem-solving failure: differences among managers, supporting staff and quality circle members. *Public Personnel Management, 26*(2), 203–225.
Tannenbaum, S. I., Beard, R. L., & Salas, E. (1992). Team building and its influence on team effectiveness: an examination of conceptual and empirical developments. In K. Kelley (ed.), *Issues, Theory,*

and *Research in Industrial–Organizational Psychology* (pp. 117–153). Amsterdam: Elsevier Science Publishers B. V.

Theodorakis, Y. (1996). The influence of goals, commitment, self-efficacy and self-satisfaction on motor performance. *Journal of Applied Sport Psychology, 8*(2), 171–182.

Turner, J. C., Hogg, M. A., Oakes, P. J., Reicher, S. D., & Wetherell, M. S. (1987). *Rediscovering the Social Group: A Self-categorisation Theory*. New York: Basil Blackwell Inc.

Tziner, A. & Eden, D. (1985). Effects of crew composition on crew performance: does the whole equal the sum of its parts? *Journal of Applied Psychology, 70*(1), 85–93.

Umberson, D. & Hughes, M. (1987). The impact of physical attractiveness on achievement and psychological wellbeing. *Social Psychology Quarterly, 50*(3), 227–236.

Walsh, J. P., Henderson, C. M., & Deighton, J. (1988). Negotiated belief structures and decision performance: an empirical investigation. *Organizational Behavior and Human Decision Processes, 42*(2), 194–216.

Weingart, L. R. (1992). Impact of group goals, task component complexity, effort, and planning on group performance. *Journal of Applied Psychology, 77*(5), 682–693.

West, M. A. (1997). *Developing Creativity in Organizations*. Chichester: Wiley.

West, M. A., Borrill, C. S., & Unsworth, K. L. (1998). Team effectiveness in organizations. *International Review of Industrial and Organizational Psychology, 13*, 1–48.

Wilkins, A. C. & Ouchi, W. G. (1983). Efficient cultures: exploring the relationship between culture and organizational performance. *Administrative Science Quarterly, 28*(3), 468–481.

Zeitz, C. M. & Spoehr, K. T. (1989). Knowledge organization and the acquisition of procedural expertise. *Applied Cognitive Psychology, 3*(4), 313–336.

6

TRAINING FOR COOPERATIVE GROUP WORK

David W. Johnson and Roger T. Johnson

INTRODUCTION

There are few skills more essential for the modern organization than the ability to work effectively in groups. The practical aspects of group work are directly based on both theory and research. In this chapter the nature of social interdependence theory and cooperative group work are defined, a meta-analysis of the research on cooperation among adults is presented, the essential elements of cooperation are discussed, and the factors that enhance the effectiveness of cooperation are presented. Group members must be quite skilled in creating and maintaining cooperation if they are to realize the advantages of collaborative efforts.

COOPERATIVE GROUP WORK

In order to discuss the need to train individuals to work effectively in cooperative groups, it is first necessary to define cooperation. By far the most important theory dealing with co-operation is social interdependence theory. *Social interdependence* exists when individuals share common goals and each individual's outcomes are affected by the actions of the others (Deutsch, 1949, 1962; Johnson & Johnson, 1989; Tjosvold, 1986). It may be differentiated from *social dependence* (i.e. the outcomes of one person are affected by the actions of a second person but not vice versa) and *social independence* (i.e. individuals' outcomes are unaffected by each other's actions). There are two types of social interdependence: cooperative and competitive. The absence of social interdependence and dependence results in individualistic efforts.

Cooperation exists when individuals work together to accomplish shared goals (Deutsch, 1949, 1962; Johnson & Johnson, 1989). When a situation is structured cooperatively, individuals' goal achievements are positively correlated; individuals perceive that they can reach

The Essentials *of Teamworking: International Perspectives.*
Edited by M. A. West, D. Tjosvold, and K. G. Smith. © 2005 John Wiley & Sons, Ltd.

their goals if and only if the others in the group also reach their goals. Thus, individuals seek outcomes that are beneficial to all those with whom they are cooperatively linked. *Competition* exists when individuals work against each other to achieve a goal that only one or a few can attain (Deutsch, 1949, 1962; Johnson & Johnson, 1989). When a situation is structured competitively, individuals' goal achievements are negatively correlated; each individual perceives that when one person achieves his or her goal, all others with whom he or she is competitively linked fail to achieve their goals. Thus, individuals seek an outcome that is personally beneficial but detrimental to all others in the situation. Finally, *individualistic efforts* exist when each individual works by him- or herself to accomplish goals unrelated to the goals of others (Deutsch, 1962; Johnson & Johnson, 1989). When a situation is structured individualistically, there is no correlation among participants' goal attainments. Each individual perceives that he or she can reach his or her goal regardless of whether other individuals attain or do not attain their goals. Thus, individuals seek an outcome that is personally beneficial without concern for the outcomes of others.

The *basic premise* of social interdependence theory is that the type of interdependence structured in a situation determines how individuals interact with each other which, in turn, determines outcomes (Deutsch, 1949, 1962; Johnson & Johnson, 1989). Positive interdependence tends to result in promotive interaction, negative interdependence tends to result in oppositional or contrient interaction, and no interdependence results in an absence of interaction. Depending on whether individuals promote or obstruct each other's goal accomplishments, there is *substitutability* (i.e. the actions of one person substitute for the actions of another), *cathexis* (i.e. the investment of psychological energy in objects and events outside of oneself), and *inducibility* (i.e openness to influence) (Deutsch, 1949). In cooperative situations, the actions of participants substitute for each other, participants positively cathect to each other's effective actions, and there is high inducibility among participants. In competitive situations, the actions of participants do not substitute for each other, participants negatively cathect to each other's effective actions, and inducibility is low. When there is no interaction, there is no substitutability, cathexis, or inducibility. The relationship between the type of social interdependence and the interaction pattern it elicits is bidirectional. Each may cause the other.

OUTCOMES OF COOPERATIVE GROUP WORK

There are hundreds of studies conducted during the last 100 years on the effectiveness of cooperative group work compared with competitive and individualistic efforts (Johnson & Johnson, 1989). The numerous dependent variables studied may be subsumed in three broad and interrelated outcomes (Johnson & Johnson, 1989): effort to achieve, quality of relationships, and psychological health.

Effort to Achieve

Over the past 100 years over 375 studies have been conducted on the relative impact of cooperative, competitive, and individualistic efforts on productivity and achievement (Johnson & Johnson, 1989). Of those studies, 165 measured performance of adults (individuals 18 years and older). The studies on adults focused on two questions:

1. Do groups outperform individuals? In these studies, group performance was compared with the performance of individuals working alone competitively or individualistically (group performance was the dependent measure).
2. Do individuals working in groups outperform individuals working alone? In these studies, the performance of individual group members was compared with the performance of individuals working alone competitively or individualistically (individual performance was the dependent measure).

GROUPS VS INDIVIDUALS

Since 1928 over 57 studies have compared the relative effectiveness of groups and individual efforts (see Table 6.1). The majority of these studies were conducted before 1970. Group efforts resulted in higher group productivity than did individual efforts structured either competitively or individualistically (effect sizes of 0.63 and 0.94 respectively). When only the methodologically high-quality studies were included in the analysis, group efforts were still more effective than competitive or individualistic efforts (effect sizes of 0.96 and 0.66 respectively). Groups tend to perform higher, make better decisions, and solve problems better than do individuals.

The studies used a wide variety of tasks (see Table 6.2). The tasks were classified into those that required verbal skills to complete (such as reading, writing, and orally presenting), mathematical skills to complete, or procedural skills to present (such as sports like swimming, golf, and tennis). When the results were analyzed for type of task, groups outperformed individual efforts structured competitively and individualistically on verbal tasks (effect sizes = 0.73 and 1.47 respectively), on mathematical tasks (effect sizes = 0.26 and 0.86 respectively), and on procedural tasks (effect sizes = 1.37 and 0.95 respectively). From these results it may be concluded that group efforts promoted higher group performance than did individual efforts on all three types of tasks. There is reason to believe, however,

Table 6.1 Achievement

Conditions	Effect size	Standard deviation	Cases
Group performance			
Cooperation vs competition	0.63	0.98	16
Cooperation vs individualistic	0.94	1.34	34
Competitive vs individualistic	−0.66	0.00	1
High-quality studies			
Cooperation vs competition	0.96	0.88	10
Cooperation vs individualistic	0.66	0.68	19
Competitive vs individualistic	−0.66	0.00	1
Individual performance			
Cooperation vs competition	0.54	0.86	29
Cooperation vs individualistic	0.41	0.43	52
Competitive vs individualistic	0.63	0.77	13
High-quality studies			
Cooperation vs competition	0.61	0.99	9
Cooperation vs individualistic	0.35	0.35	31
Competitive vs individualistic	0.34	0.80	7

Table 6.2 Type of task

Conditions	Effect size	Standard deviation	Cases
Group performance			
Cooperative vs competitive			
Verbal	0.73	0.22	3
Math	0.26	0.86	9
Procedural	1.37	1.29	4
Rote/decoding	0.00	0.00	0
Cooperative vs individualistic			
Verbal	1.47	1.37	8
Math	0.86	1.41	21
Procedural	0.95	0.29	2
Rote/decoding	0.00	0.00	0
Individual performance			
Cooperative vs competitive			
Verbal	0.36	0.35	29
Math	0.45	0.52	17
Procedural	0.95	0.29	2
Rote/decoding	0.00	0.00	0
Cooperative vs individualistic			
Verbal	0.66	0.68	19
Math	1.32	1.90	14
Procedural	1.06	0.00	1
Rote/decoding	0.00	0.00	0

that on brainstorming tasks individuals may do just as well as groups (Johnson & Johnson, 2000a).

GROUP MEMBERS VS INDIVIDUALS

Over 120 studies have compared the relative efficacy of group and individual efforts on individual performance. While the first study was conducted in 1924, 70 percent of the studies have been conducted since 1970. In these studies, working in a group resulted in higher individual performance than did working alone competitively or individualistically (effect sizes of 0.54 and 0.51 respectively). When only the methodologically high-quality studies were included, working in a group still promoted greater individual productivity than did competitive or individualistic efforts (effect sizes of 0.61 and 0.35 respectively). These results indicated that there was greater group-to-individual transfer than there was individual-to-individual transfer. Hagman and Hayes (1986) conducted two studies in which they demonstrated that the superiority of group-to-individual transfer over individual-to-individual transfer increased as participants worked toward a group (as opposed to an individual) reward and as the size of the group got smaller. Groups in which members (a) interacted with each other and discussed the material being learned and (b) received a group reward, had the greatest amount of group-to-individual transfer. In a study involving children as participants, learning in a group resulted in greater individual transfer than did learning as an individual for complex higher-level tasks, but not for simple lower-level tasks (Gabbert, Johnson, & Johnson, 1986). In a recent study, Jensen, Johnson, and Johnson (in press) had college students take a series of quizzes and biweekly examinations. Students were randomly assigned to conditions. Students who took the quizzes in small groups achieved higher on the subsequent biweekly examinations taken individually than did students who took the quizzes alone.

When the results were analyzed for type of task, individuals working in groups outperformed individuals working alone competitively or individualistically on verbal tasks (effect sizes = 0.36 and 0.66 respectively), on mathematical tasks (effect sizes = 0.45 and 1.32 respectively), and on procedural tasks (effect sizes = 0.95 and 1.06 respectively). From these results it may be concluded that working in a group promoted higher individual proficiency and knowledge than did working alone competitively or individualistically on all three types of tasks.

Positive Relationships and Social Support

GROUPS VS INDIVIDUALS

Since the 1940s there have been over 22 studies on group performance in which the quality of relationships among individuals was examined. Within groups, there tends to be greater

Table 6.3 Results for interpersonal attraction, social support, and self-esteem

Conditions	Mean	Standard deviation	Cases
Group performance			
Interpersonal attraction			
Cooperation vs competition	0.64	0.51	14
Cooperation vs individualistic	0.39	0.97	7
Competitive vs individualistic	0.70	0.00	1
Social support			
Cooperation vs competition	0.13	0.59	10
Cooperation vs individualistic	0.38	0.37	5
Competitive vs individualistic	−0.30	0.00	1
Self-esteem			
Cooperation vs competition	0.86	1.70	6
Cooperation vs individualistic	0.68	0.00	1
Competitive vs individualistic	0.21	0.00	1
Individual performance			
Interpersonal attraction			
Cooperation vs competition	0.68	0.54	57
Cooperation vs individualistic	0.55	0.62	31
Competitive vs individualistic	−0.04	0.96	7
Social support			
Cooperation vs competition	0.60	0.43	54
Cooperation vs individualistic	0.51	0.39	35
Competitive vs individualistic	−0.29	0.32	11
Self-esteem			
Cooperation vs competition	0.47	0.40	39
Cooperation vs individualistic	0.29	0.41	24
Competitive vs individualistic	−0.35	0.37	14

interpersonal attraction than among individuals working competitively (effect size = 0.64) or individualistically (effect size = 0.39).

In addition to liking, relationships among individuals may be characterized by social support. *Social support* involves the exchange of resources intended to enhance mutual well-being and the existence and availability of people on whom one can rely for emotional, instrumental, informational, and appraisal aid. The studies focusing on group performance found that cooperation promoted greater social support than did individualistic (effect size = 0.38) efforts, but surprisingly, the difference between cooperative and competitive efforts (effect size = 0.13) was lower than one would expect.

GROUP MEMBERS VS INDIVIDUALS

Since the 1940s, there have been 95 studies on the performance of individual group members in which the quality of relationships among individuals was examined. Individual group members liked each other better than did individuals working alone competitively (effect size = 0.68) or individualistically (effect size = 0.55).

In the studies focusing on individual performance of individuals, group efforts promoted greater social support than did individual efforts structured competitively (effect size = 0.60) or individualistically (effect size = 0.51).

Psychological Health and Self-esteem

PSYCHOLOGICAL HEALTH

Several studies have directly measured the relationship between social interdependence and psychological health (Crandall, 1982; Hayes, 1976; James & Johnson, 1983; James & Johnson, 1988; Johnson, Johnson, & Krotee, 1986; Johnson & Norem-Hebeisen, 1977; Norem-Hebeisen et al., 1984). The samples studied included university individuals, older adults, suburban high-school seniors, juvenile and adult prisoners, step-couples, and Olympic hockey players. The results indicate that cooperative attitudes are highly correlated with a wide variety of indices of psychological health, competitiveness was in some cases positively and in some cases negatively related to psychological health, and individualistic attitudes were negatively related to a wide variety of indices of psychological health.

SELF-ESTEEM

In regard to self-esteem, the studies focusing on group productivity found that group efforts promoted higher self-esteem than did competitive (effect size = 0.86) or individualistic (effect size = 0.68) efforts. The studies focusing on individual proficiency found that individuals working in groups had higher self-esteem than did individuals working alone competitively (effect size = 0.47) or individualistically (effect size = 0.29). Not only is the level of self-esteem affected by being part of a group effort, but the process by which individuals make judgments about their self-worth is also. Norem-Hebeisen and Johnson (1981) conducted four studies involving 821 white, middle-class, high-school seniors in a midwestern suburban community. They found that cooperative experiences promoted basic self-acceptance, freedom from conditional acceptance, and seeing oneself positively compared to peers. Competitive experiences were related to conditional self-acceptance and individualistic attitudes were related to basic self-rejection, including anxiety about relating to other people. Cooperative, group-based experiences seem to result in (a) the internalizing perceptions that one is known, accepted, and liked as one is, (b) internalizing mutual success, and (c) developing multidimensional views of self and others that allow for positive self-perceptions (Johnson & Johnson, 1989).

ENSURING GROUP WORK IS COOPERATIVE: THE BASIC ELEMENTS OF COOPERATION

Potential Group Performance

Not all groups are effective (Johnson & Johnson, 2000a). Placing people in the same room, seating them together, telling them they are a group, and advising them to "work together," does not mean they will work together effectively. Project groups, lab groups, committees, task forces, departments, and councils are groups, but they are not necessarily effective. Many groups are ineffective and some are even destructive. Almost everyone has been part of a group that has wasted time, was inefficient, and generally produced poor work. Ineffective and destructive groups are characterized by a number of dynamics (Johnson & Johnson, 2000a), such as social loafing, free-riding, group immaturity, uncritically and quickly accepting members' dominant response, and group-think. Such hindering factors are eliminated by carefully structuring the five essential elements of cooperation. Those elements are positive interdependence, face-to-face promotive interaction, individual and group accountability, appropriate use of social skills, and group processing.

Positive Interdependence: We Instead of Me

The first and most important set of competencies needed for cooperative group work is establishing and strengthening positive interdependence. *Positive interdependence* exists when one perceives that one is linked with others in a way so that one cannot succeed unless they do (and vice versa) and/or that one must coordinate one's efforts with the efforts of others to complete a task (Deutsch, 1962; Johnson & Johnson, 1989). Effective groups begin with structuring positive interdependence. Group members have to know that they "sink or swim together," that is, they have two responsibilities: to maximize their own productivity and to maximize the productivity of all other group members. There are two major categories of interdependence: outcome interdependence and means interdependence (Johnson & Johnson, 1989). When persons are in a cooperative or competitive situation, they are oriented toward a desired outcome, end state, goal, or reward. If there is no outcome interdependence (goal and reward interdependence), there is no cooperation or competition. In addition, the means through which the mutual goals or rewards are to be accomplished specify the actions required on the part of group members. Means interdependence includes resource, role, and task interdependence (which are overlapping and not independent from each other).

Positive interdependence has numerous effects on individuals' motivation and productivity, not the least of which is highlight the fact that the efforts of all group members are needed for group success. When members of a group see their efforts as dispensable for the group's success, they may reduce their efforts (Kerr, 1983; Kerr & Bruun, 1983; Sweeney, 1973). When group members perceive their potential contribution to the group as being unique they increase their efforts (Harkins & Petty, 1982). When goal, task, resource, and role interdependence are clearly understood, individuals realize that their efforts are required in order for the group to succeed (i.e. there can be no "free-riders") and that their contributions are often unique.

A series of research studies were conducted to clarify the impact of positive interdependence on achievement. The results indicate that:

1. Group membership in and of itself does not seem sufficient to produce higher achievement and productivity—positive interdependence is also required (Hwong et al., 1993). Knowing that one's performance affects the success of group mates seems to create "responsibility forces" that increase one's efforts to achieve.
2. Interpersonal interaction is insufficient to increase productivity—positive interdependence is also required (Lew et al., 1986a, b; Mesch, Johnson, & Johnson, 1988; Mesch et al., 1986). Individuals achieved higher under positive goal interdependence than when they worked individualistically but had the opportunity to interact with classmates.
3. Goal and reward interdependence seem to be additive (Lew et al., 1986a, b; Mesch, Johnson, & Johnson, 1988; Mesch et al., 1986). While positive goal interdependence is sufficient to produce higher achievement and productivity than individualistic efforts, the combination of goal and reward interdependence is even more effective.
4. Both working to achieve a reward and working to avoid the loss of a reward produced higher achievement than did individualistic efforts (Frank, 1984). There is no significant difference between the working to achieve a reward and working to avoid a loss.
5. Goal interdependence promotes higher achievement and greater productivity than does resource interdependence (Johnson et al., 1991).
6. Resource interdependence by itself may decrease achievement and productivity compared with individualistic efforts (Johnson et al., 1990; Ortiz, Johnson, & Johnson, 1996).
7. The combination of goal and resource interdependence increased achievement more than goal interdependence alone or individualistic efforts (Johnson et al., 1990; Ortiz, Johnson, & Johnson, 1996).
8. Positive interdependence does more than simply motivate individuals to try harder, it facilitates the development of new insights and discoveries through promotive interaction (Gabbert, Johnson, & Johnson, 1986; Johnson & Johnson, 1981; Johnson, Skon, & Johnson, 1980; Skon, Johnson, & Johnson, 1981). Members of cooperative groups use higher-level reasoning strategies more frequently than do individuals working individualistically or competitively.
9. The more complex the procedures involved in interdependence, the longer it will take group members to reach their full levels of productivity (Ortiz, Johnson, & Johnson, 1996). The more complex the group work procedures, the more members have to attend to group work and the less time they have to attend to task work. Once the group work procedures are mastered, however, members concentrate on task work and outperform individuals working alone.

Individual Accountability/Personal Responsibility

The second set of competencies needed for cooperative group work is establishing and strengthening individual and group accountability. *Group accountability* exists when the overall performance of the group is assessed and the results are given back to all group members to compare against a standard of performance. *Individual accountability* exists when the performance of individual students is assessed, the results are given back to the individual and the group, and the member is held responsible by group mates for contributing his or her fair share to the group's success. It is important that the group knows who needs more assistance, support, and encouragement in completing their share of the work. It is also important that group members know they cannot "hitchhike" on the work of others. Group members tend to reduce their contributions to goal achievement when it is difficult to identify members' contributions, there is an increased likelihood of redundant efforts, there is a lack of group cohesiveness, and there is lessened responsibility for the final outcome (Harkins & Petty, 1982; Ingham et al., 1974; Kerr & Bruun, 1981; Latane, Williams & Harkins, 1979; Moede, 1927; Petty et al., 1977; Williams, 1981; Williams, Harkins, & Latane, 1981). The higher the individual accountability, the clearer the contributions of each member, the less members' efforts are redundant, the more every member is responsible for the final outcome, and the more cohesive the group. Under such conditions, the social loafing effect vanishes. The smaller the size of the group, in addition, the greater the individual accountability may be (Messick & Brewer, 1983).

Archer-Kath, Johnson, and Johnson (1994) investigated whether or not positive interdependence and individual accountability are two separate and independent dimensions. They compared the impact of feedback to the learning group as a whole with the individual feedback to each member on achievement, attitudes, and behavior in cooperative learning groups. Individuals received either individual or group feedback in written graph/chart form only on how frequently members engaged in the targeted behaviors. If individual accountability and positive interdependence are unrelated, no differences should be found in perceived positive interdependence between conditions. If they are related, individuals in the individual feedback condition should perceive more positive interdependence than individuals in the group feedback condition. Individual feedback resulted in greater perceptions of cooperation, goal interdependence, and resource interdependence than did group feedback, indicating that positive interdependence and individual accountability are related, and by increasing individual accountability perceived interdependence among group members may also be increased.

Promotive (Face-to-face) Interaction

The third set of competencies needed for cooperative group work is establishing and strengthening promotive interaction among group members. *Promotive interaction* exists when individuals encourage and facilitate each other's efforts to complete tasks and achieve the group's goals. In order to promote each other's success, group members (a) help and assist each other, (b) exchange needed resources such as information and materials, (c) provide each other with feedback, (d) challenge each other's conclusions and reasoning, (e) advocate working harder to achieve the group's goals, (f) influence each other, and (g) act in trusting and trustworthy ways (Johnson & Johnson, 1989). The amount of research documenting the impact of promotive interaction on achievement is too voluminous to review here. Interested readers are referred to Johnson and Johnson (1989).

Social Skills

The fourth set of competencies needed for cooperative group work is appropriately engaging in small group and interpersonal skills. Placing socially unskilled individuals in a group and telling them to cooperate will obviously not be successful. Individuals must be taught the interpersonal and small group skills needed for high-quality cooperation, and be motivated to use them. To coordinate efforts to achieve mutual goals, individuals must master the interpersonal skills of:

(a) getting to know and trust each other;
(b) communicating accurately and unambiguously;
(c) accepting and supporting each other;
(d) resolving conflicts constructively (Johnson, 2000).

Individuals must also master the group skills:

(a) ensuring each member is committed to clear mutual goals that highlight members' interdependence;
(b) ensuring accurate and complete communication among members;
(c) providing leadership and appropriate influence;
(d) flexibly using decision-making procedures that ensure all alternative courses of action receive a fair and complete hearing and each other's reasoning and conclusions are challenged and critically analyzed;
(e) resolving their conflicts constructively (Johnson & Johnson, 2000a).

Interpersonal and small group skills form the basic nexus among individuals, and if individuals are to work together productively and cope with the stresses and strains of doing so, they must have a modicum of these skills.

In their studies on the long-term implementation of cooperation, Marvin Lew and Debra Mesch (Lew et al., 1986a, b; Mesch, Johnson, & Johnson, 1988; Mesch et al., 1986) investigated the impact of a reward contingency for using social skills as well as positive interdependence and a contingency for individual productivity on performance within cooperative groups. In the cooperative skills conditions, individuals were trained weekly in four social skills and each member of a cooperative group was given two bonus points toward the quiz grade if all group members were observed by the teacher to demonstrate three out of four cooperative skills. The results indicated that the combination of positive goal interdependence, an academic contingency for high performance by all group members, and a social skills contingency, promoted the highest achievement.

Archer-Kath, Johnson, and Johnson (1994) trained individuals in the social skills of praising, supporting, asking for information, giving information, asking for help, and giving help. Individuals received either individual or group feedback in written graph/chart form on how frequently members engaged in the targeted behaviors. The researchers found that giving individuals individual feedback on how frequently they engaged in targeted social skills was more effective in increasing individuals' achievement than was group feedback. The more socially skillful individuals are, the more attention teachers pay to teaching and rewarding the use of social skills, and the more individual feedback individuals receive on their use of the skills, the higher the individual performance that can be expected within cooperative groups.

Not only do social skills promote higher productivity, they contribute to building more positive relationships among group members. Putnam et al. (1989) demonstrated that, when individuals were taught social skills, were observed by their superior, and were given individual feedback as to how frequently they engaged in the skills, their relationships became more positive.

Group Processing

The fifth set of competencies needed for cooperative group work is engaging in group processing. In order to achieve, individuals in cooperative groups have to work together effectively. Effective group work is influenced by whether or not groups periodically reflect on how well they are functioning and how they may improve their work processes. A *process* is an identifiable sequence of events taking place over time, and *process goals* refer to the sequence of events instrumental in achieving outcome goals. *Group processing* may be defined as reflecting on a group session to (a) describe what member actions were helpful and unhelpful in achieving the group's goals and ensuring members work together effectively and (b) make decisions about what actions to continue or change.

Yager, Johnson, and Johnson (1985) examined the impact on productivity of (a) cooperative groups in which members discussed how well their group was functioning and how they could improve its effectiveness, (b) cooperative groups without any group processing, and (c) individualistic efforts. The results indicate that the high-, medium-, and low-achieving individuals in the cooperation with group processing condition performed higher on daily achievement, post-instructional achievement, and retention measures than did the individuals in the other two conditions. Individuals in the cooperation without group processing condition, furthermore, achieved higher on all three measures than did the individuals in the individualistic condition.

Putnam et al. (1989) conducted a study in which there were two conditions: cooperative groups with social skills training and group processing and cooperative groups without social skills training and group processing. Forty-eight fifth-grade individuals (32 nonhandicapped and 16 individuals with IQs ranging from 35 to 52) participated in the study. In the cooperative groups with social skills training condition the teacher gave individuals examples of specific cooperative behaviors to engage in, observed how frequently individuals engaged in the skills, gave individuals feedback as to how well they worked together, and had individuals discuss for five minutes how to use the skills more effectively in the future. In the uninstructed cooperative groups condition individuals were placed in cooperative groups and worked together for the same period of time with the same amount of teacher intervention (aimed at the academic lesson and unrelated to working together skillfully). Both nonhandicapped and handicapped individuals were randomly assigned to each condition. They found more positive relationships developed between handicapped and nonhandicapped individuals in the cooperative skills condition and that these positive relationships carried over to post-instructional free-time situations.

Johnson et al. (1990) conducted a study comparing cooperative groups with no processing, cooperative groups with teacher processing (teacher specified cooperative skills to use, observed, and gave whole class feedback as to how well individuals were using the skills), cooperative groups with teacher and individual processing (teacher specified cooperative skills to use, observed, gave whole class feedback as to how well individuals were using the skills, and had groups discuss how well they interacted as a group), and individualistic efforts. Forty-nine high-ability Black American high-school seniors and entering college freshmen at Xavier University participated in the study. A complex computer-assisted problem-solving assignment was given to all individuals. All three cooperative conditions performed higher than did the individualistic condition. The combination of teacher and individual processing resulted in greater problem-solving success than did the other cooperative conditions.

Archer-Kath, Johnson, and Johnson (1994) provided cooperative groups with either individual or group feedback on how frequently members had engaged in targeted social skills. Each group had five minutes at the beginning of each session to discuss how well the group was functioning and what could be done to improve the group's effectiveness. Group processing with individual feedback was more effective than was group processing with whole group feedback in increasing individuals' (a) achievement motivation, actual achievement, uniformity of achievement among group members, and influence toward higher achievement within cooperative groups, (b) positive relationships among group members and between individuals and the teacher, and (c) self-esteem and positive attitudes toward the subject area.

The results of these studies indicated that engaging in group processing clarifies and improves the effectiveness of the members in contributing to the achievement of the group's goals, especially when specific social skills are targeted and individuals receive individual feedback as to how frequently and how well they engaged in the skills.

ENHANCING VARIABLES: TRUST AND CONFLICT

During the 1950s and 1960s, Deutsch (1962, 1973) researched two aspects of the internal dynamics of cooperative groups that potentially enhanced outcomes: trust and conflict.

Trust

The sixth set of competencies needed for cooperative group work is establishing and maintaining a high level of trust. Trust includes:

(a) the awareness that beneficial or harmful consequences could result from one's actions;
(b) realization that others have the power to determine the consequences of one's actions;
(c) the awareness that the harmful consequences are more serious than are the beneficial consequences;
(d) confidence that the others will behave in ways that ensure beneficial consequences for oneself (Deutsch, 1958, 1960, 1962).

Interpersonal trust is built through placing one's consequences in the control of others and having one's confidence in the others confirmed. Interpersonal trust is destroyed through placing one's consequences in the hands of others and having one's confidence in the others disconfirmed through their behaving in ways that ensure harmful consequences for oneself.

Trust tends to be developed and maintained in cooperative situations and it tends to be absent and destroyed in competitive and individualistic situations (Deutsch, 1958, 1960, 1962; Johnson, 1971, 1974; Johnson & Noonan, 1972).

Trust is composed of two sets of behaviors. *Trusting* behavior is the willingness to risk beneficial or harmful consequences by making oneself vulnerable to another person. *Trustworthy* behavior is the willingness to respond to another person's risk-taking in a way that ensures that the other person will experience beneficial consequences. In order to establish trust, two or more people must be trustworthy and trusting. The greater the trust among group members, the more effective their cooperative efforts tend to be (Deutsch, 1962; Johnson, 2000; Johnson & Noonan, 1972).

Conflict

The seventh set of competencies needed for cooperative group work is resolving conflicts constructively. Conflict within cooperative groups, when managed constructively, enhances the effectiveness of cooperative efforts (Deutsch, 1973; Johnson & Johnson, 1989). There are two types of conflict that occur frequently and regularly within cooperative groups—constructive controversy and conflict of interests (Johnson & Johnson, 1995a, b).

CONSTRUCTIVE CONTROVERSY

Constructive controversy exists when group members have different information, perceptions, opinions, reasoning processes, theories, and conclusions, and they must reach agreement (Johnson & Johnson, 1995b). When the group is faced with a problem to be solved or a decision to be made, even if it is about how to proceed to achieve the group's goals, each alternative course of action is assigned to a subgroup. Members then (a) prepare the best case possible for their assigned position, (b) make a persuasive presentation of their position, (c) engage in an open discussion in which they continue to advocate their position, refute the other alternative courses of action, and rebut attacks on their position, (d) drop all advocacy and view the issue from all perspectives, and (e) achieve consensus as to the course of action to adopt based on the best reasoned judgments of all group members.

When controversies arise, they may be dealt with constructively or destructively, depending on how they are managed and the level of interpersonal and small group skills of the participants. When managed constructively, controversy promotes uncertainty about the correctness of one's views, an active search for more information, a reconceptualization of one's knowledge and conclusions, and, consequently, greater mastery and retention of the material being discussed and a more reasoned judgment on the issue being considered. Individuals working alone in competitive and individualistic situations do not have the opportunity for such a process and, therefore, their productivity, quality of decision making, and achievement suffer (Johnson & Johnson, 1995b).

Compared with concurrence-seeking, debate, and individualistic efforts, controversy results in greater mastery and retention of the subject matter, higher-quality problem solving, greater creativity in thinking, greater motivation to learn more about the topic, more productive exchange of expertise among group members, greater task involvement, more positive relationships among group members, more accurate perspective taking, and higher self-esteem. In addition, individuals enjoy it more (Johnson & Johnson, 1995b).

Controversies tend to be constructive when the situational context is cooperative, group members are heterogeneous, information and expertise is distributed within the group, members have the necessary conflict skills, and the canons of rational argumentation are followed.

INTEGRATIVE NEGOTIATION AND PEER MEDIATION

A *conflict of interests* occurs when the actions of one person striving to achieve his or her goal interfere with and obstruct the actions of another person striving to achieve his or her goal (Johnson & Johnson, 1995a, 2000b). Within the ongoing relationships of a group, conflicts of interests are resolved constructively when group members (a) negotiate integrative agreements and (b) mediate the conflicts among their group mates. Group members negotiate integrative agreements by (a) describing what they want, (b) describing how they feel, (c) describing the reasons for their wants and feelings, (d) taking the perspective of the opposing member, (e) inventing several optional agreements that would maximize joint benefits, and (f) selecting the agreement that seems most effective (Johnson & Johnson, 1995a). When group members use integrative negotiations and peer mediation, group productivity is considerably enhanced.

When group members are unable to negotiate an agreement, other group members may wish to mediate. A *mediator* is a neutral person who helps two or more people resolve their conflict, usually by negotiating an integrative agreement. Mediation consists of four steps (Johnson & Johnson, 1995a): (a) ending hostilities, (b) ensuring disputants are committed to the mediation process, (c) helping disputants successfully negotiate with each other, and (d) formalizing the agreement into a contract.

A meta-analysis of the studies on teaching children and adolescents to use the integrative negotiation and peer mediation procedures has recently been completed (Johnson & Johnson, 2000b). Individuals who received training mastered the integrative negotiation and peer mediation procedures, maintained that mastery months after the training had ended, applied the learned procedures to actual conflicts in classroom, school, and family settings, developed more positive attitudes toward conflict, and generally resolved the conflicts in their lives more constructively.

CONCLUSIONS

The application of social interdependence theory and research to cooperative group work is one of the most successful and widespread applications of social psychology. The theory provides a conceptual framework from which practical procedures that individuals may use to promote cooperative group work may be developed. The power of cooperative group work comes from its foundation on a profound and strategic theory, the substantial research validating its effectiveness, and the practical procedures that have been developed.

Over the past 100 years researchers have focused on such diverse outcomes as productivity, achievement, higher-level reasoning, retention, quality of decision making and problem solving, creativity, achievement motivation, intrinsic motivation, transfer of learning, interpersonal attraction, social support, friendships, valuing differences, self-esteem, social competencies, psychological health, moral reasoning, and many others. These numerous outcomes may be subsumed within three broad categories: effort to achieve, positive interpersonal relationships, and psychological health. Cooperative efforts, compared with competitive and individualistic ones, tend to result in higher levels of these outcomes. This is true when the studies compared group and individual productivity, and it is true when the studies compared individual performance of group members with the performance of individuals working alone competitively or individualistically.

In order to capitalize on the potential effects of cooperation, group members must be skilled in establishing strong positive interdependence, individual accountability, promotive interaction, appropriate use of social skills, and group processing. In addition, group members must be able to establish and maintain a high level of trust and resolve conflicts constructively. Two of the most important types of conflicts inherent in group work are constructive controversy and conflicts of interests.

Finally, the research on social interdependence has an external validity and a generalizability rarely found in the social sciences. The more variations in places, people, and procedures the research can withstand and still yield the same findings, the more externally valid the conclusions. The research has been conducted in 10 different historical decades. Research participants have varied as to age, gender, economic class, nationality, and cultural background. A wide variety of research tasks, ways of structuring the types of social interdependence, and measures of the dependent variables have been used. The research has been conducted by many different researchers with markedly different theoretical and practical orientations working in different settings and even in different countries. The diversity of participants, settings, age levels, and operationalizations of social interdependence and the dependent variables give this work a validity and a generalizability rarely found in the educational literature.

REFERENCES

Archer-Kath, J., Johnson, D. W., & Johnson, R. (1994). Individual versus group feedback in cooperative groups. *Journal of Social Psychology, 134*, 681–694.
Crandall, J. (1982). Social interest, extreme response style, and implications for adjustment. *Journal of Research in Personality, 16*, 82–89.
Deutsch, M. (1949). A theory of cooperation and competition. *Human Relations, 2*, 129–152.
Deutsch, M. (1958). Trust and suspicion. *Journal of Conflict Resolution, 2*, 265–279.
Deutsch, M. (1960). The effects of motivational orientation upon trust and suspicion. *Human Relations, 13*, 123–139.
Deutsch, M. (1962). Cooperation and trust: some theoretical notes. In M. R. Jones (ed.), *Nebraska Symposium on Motivation* (pp. 275–319). Lincoln: University of Nebraska Press.
Deutsch, M. (1973). *The Resolution of Conflict*. New Haven, Conn.: Yale University Press.
Frank, M. (1984). A comparison between an individual and group goal structure contingency that differed in the behavioral contingency and performance–outcome components (Doctoral dissertation, University of Minnesota). *Dissertation Abstracts International, 45*/05, 1341-A.
Gabbert, B., Johnson, D., & Johnson, R. (1986). Cooperative learning, group-to-individual transfer, process gain and the acquisition of cognitive reasoning strategies. *Journal of Psychology, 120*(3), 265–278.
Hagman, J. & Hayes, J. (1986). Cooperative learning: effects of task, reward, and group size on individual achievement (Technical Report 704). Boise, Idaho: Scientific Coordination Office, US Army Research Institute for the Behavioral and Social Sciences (ERIC Document Reproduction Service No. ED 278 720).
Harkins, S. G. & Petty, R. E. (1982). The effects of task difficulty and task uniqueness on social loafing. *Journal of Personality and Social Psychology, 43*, 1214–1229.
Hayes, L. (1976). The use of group contingencies for behavioral control: a review. *Psychological Bulletin, 83*, 628–648.

Hwong, N., Caswell, A., Johnson, D. W., & Johnson, R. (1993). Effects of cooperative and individualistic learning on prospective elementary teachers' music achievement and attitudes. *Journal of Social Psychology, 133*, 53–64.

Ingham, A., Levinger, G., Graves, J., & Peckham, V. (1974). The Ringelmann effect: studies of group size and group performance. *Journal of Personality and Social Psychology, 10*, 371–384.

James, N. & Johnson, D. W. (1983). The relationship between attitudes toward social interdependence and psychological health within three criminal populations. *Journal of Abnormal and Social Psychology, 121*, 131–143.

James, S. & Johnson, D. W. (1988). Social interdependence, psychological adjustment, orientation toward negative life stress, and quality of second marriage. *Journal of Social Psychology, 128*(3), 287–304.

Jensen, M., Johnson, D. W., & Johnson, R. (in press). Impact of positive interdependence during electronic quizzes on discourse and achievement. *Journal of Educational Research*.

Johnson, D. W. (1971). Role reversal: a summary and review of the research. *International Journal of Group Tensions, 1*, 318–334.

Johnson, D. W. (1974). Communication and the inducement of cooperative behavior in conflicts: a critical review. *Speech Monographs, 41*, 64–78.

Johnson, D. W. (2000). *Reaching Out: Interpersonal Effectiveness and Self-actualization* (7th edn). Boston: Allyn & Bacon.

Johnson, D. W. & Johnson, F. (2000a). *Joining Together: Group Theory and Group Skills* (7th edn). Boston: Allyn & Bacon.

Johnson, D. W. & Johnson, R. (1981). Effects of cooperative and individualistic learning experiences on interethnic interaction. *Journal of Educational Psychology, 73*(3), 454–459.

Johnson, D. W. & Johnson, R. (1989). *Cooperation and Competition: Theory and Research*. Edina, Minn.: Interaction Book Company.

Johnson, D. W. & Johnson, R. (1995a). *Teaching Students to be Peacemakers*. Edina, Minn.: Interaction Book Company.

Johnson, D. W. & Johnson, R. (1995b). *Creative Controversy: Intellectual Challenge in the Classroom*. Edina, Minn.: Interaction Book Company.

Johnson, D. W. & Johnson, R. (2000b). Teaching students to be peacemakers: a meta-analysis. Paper presented at the Convention of the Society for the Psychological Study of Social Issues, Minneapolis, June.

Johnson, D. W., Johnson, R., & Krotee, M. (1986). The relationship between social interdependence and psychological health within the 1980 United States Olympic ice hockey team. *Journal of Psychology, 120*, 279–292.

Johnson, D. W., Johnson, R., Ortiz, A., & Stanne, M. (1991). Impact of positive goal and resource interdependence on achievement, interaction, and attitudes. *Journal of General Psychology, 118*(4), 341–347.

Johnson, D. W., Johnson, R., Stanne, M., & Garibaldi, A. (1990). Impact of group processing on achievement in cooperative groups. *Journal of Social Psychology, 130*, 507–516.

Johnson, D. W. & Noonan, P. (1972). Effects of acceptance and reciprocation of self-disclosures on the development of trust. *Journal of Counseling Psychology, 19*(5), 411–416.

Johnson, D. W. & Norem-Hebeisen, A. (1977). Attitudes toward interdependence among persons and psychological health. *Psychological Reports, 40*, 843–850.

Johnson, D. W., Skon, L., & Johnson, R. (1980). Effects of cooperative, competitive, and individualistic conditions on children's problem-solving performance. *American Educational Research Journal, 17*(1), 83–94.

Kerr, N. (1983). The dispensability of member effort and group motivation losses: free-rider effects. *Journal of Personality and Social Psychology, 44*, 78–94.

Kerr, N. & Bruun, S. (1981). Ringelmann revisited: alternative explanations for the social loafing effect. *Personality and Social Psychology Bulletin, 7*, 224–231.

Kerr, N. & Bruun, S. (1983). The dispensability of member effort and group motivation losses: free-rider effects. *Journal of Personality and Social Psychology, 44*, 78–94.

Latane, B., Williams, K., & Harkins, S. (1979). Many hands make light the work: the causes and consequences of social loafing. *Journal of Personality and Social Psychology, 37*, 822–832.

Lew, M., Mesch, D., Johnson, D. W., & Johnson, R. (1986a). Positive interdependence, academic and collaborative-skills group contingencies and isolated students. *American Educational Research Journal, 23*, 476–488.

Lew, M., Mesch, D., Johnson, D. W., & Johnson, R. (1986b). Components of cooperative learning: effects of collaborative skills and academic group contingencies on achievement and mainstreaming. *Contemporary Educational Psychology, 11*, 229–239.

Mesch, D., Johnson, D. W., & Johnson, R. (1988). Impact of positive interdependence and academic group contingencies on achievement. *Journal of Social Psychology, 128*, 345–352.

Mesch, D., Lew, M., Johnson, D. W., & Johnson, R. (1986). Isolated teenagers, cooperative learning and the training of social skills. *Journal of Psychology, 120*, 323–334.

Messick, D. & Brewer, M. (1983). Solving social dilemmas: a review. In L. Wheeler & P. Shaver (eds), *Review of Personality and Social Psychology* (Vol. 4, pp. 11–44). Newbury Park, Calif.: Sage Publications.

Moede, W. (1927). Die Richtlinien der Leistungs-Psychologie. *Industrielle Psychotechnik, 4*, 193–207.

Norem-Hebeisen, A. & Johnson, D. W. (1981). Relationships between cooperative, competitive, and individualistic attitudes and differentiated aspects of self-esteem. *Journal of Personality, 49*, 415–425.

Norem-Hebeisen, A., Johnson, D. W., Anderson, D., & Johnson, R. (1984). Predictors and concomitants of changes in drug use patterns among teenagers. *Journal of Social Psychology, 124*, 43–50.

Ortiz, A., Johnson, D. W., & Johnson, R. (1996). The effect of positive goal and resource interdependence on individual performance. *Journal of Social Psychology, 136*(2), 243–249.

Petty, R., Harkins, S., Williams, K., & Latane, B. (1977). The effects of group size on cognitive effort and evaluation. *Personality and Social Psychology Bulletin, 3*, 575–578.

Putnam, J., Rynders, J., Johnson, R., & Johnson, D. W. (1989). Collaborative skill instruction for promoting positive interactions between mentally handicapped and nonhandicapped children. *Exceptional Children, 55*(6), 550–557.

Skon, L., Johnson, D., & Johnson, R. (1981). Cooperative peer interaction versus individual competition and individualistic efforts: effects on the acquisition of cognitive reasoning strategies. *Journal of Educational Psychology, 73*(1), 83–92.

Sweeney, J. (1973). An experimental investigation of the free-rider problem. *Social Science Research, 2*, 277–292.

Tjosvold, D. (1986). *Working Together to Get Things Done*. Lexington, Mass.: D. C. Heath.

Williams, K. (1981). The effects of group cohesiveness on social loafing. Paper presented at the annual meeting of the Midwestern Psychological Association, Detroit.

Williams, K., Harkins, S., & Latane, B. (1981). Identifiability as a deterrent to social loafing: two cheering experiments. *Journal of Personality and Social Psychology, 40*, 303–311.

Yager, S., Johnson, D., & Johnson, R. (1985). Oral discussion, group-to-individual transfer, and achievement in cooperative learning groups. *Journal of Educational Psychology, 77*(1), 60–66.

7

TEAM-BASED ORGANIZATION
CREATING AN ENVIRONMENT FOR TEAM SUCCESS

Cheryl L. Harris and Michael M. Beyerlein

Team-based organization (TBO) shifts attention from teams to their context and integration. This chapter reviews the essential components of TBOs. Although redesign of a traditional organization to a TBO is an expensive and risky undertaking, attending to the key components ought to increase the probability of success in using teams as a mechanism for achieving strategic goals of the business. The claims below are based on a review of a small literature and projects at the Center for the Study of Work Teams including: 610 interviews with team members and leaders, 28 conferences on teams for 16,000 participants from 350 organizations over 13 years, fieldwork with the steering committees in TBOs, and interviews of 21 recognized experts. The result is thus an integration of findings from the Center's work, the experts, and the several scholars who have published in the area, particularly Susan Mohrman of the Center for Effective Organizations.

A TBO results from a desire to organize work in a way that formally optimizes collaborative capability. There is recognition that teams enable line workers, support workers, and managers to be more effective in their work. However, there is also recognition that the effectiveness is limited unless the environment or context of the organization surrounding those teams is aligned with them. Many teams fail to achieve expected results, because the context contradicts, abandons, or undermines team functioning. The TBO is designed to address that problem.

The last two decades ushered in a much more complex business environment, causing two trends in organizations: a need for speed and flexibility, and increased use of teams to help achieve that. Focusing on creating teams alone provided limited success. Recently, focus shifted to the context around teams. In a study of 25 knowledge work teams in four companies, the "team context appeared to be the overwhelming determinant of whether a team functioned effectively in accomplishing its goals" (Mohrman, Cohen, & Mohrman, 1995, p. 34).

When teams are formed without heed to the organizational context, they tend to become isolated and cut off from the rest of the organization. The isolated team becomes akin to a disease in the body; the larger organization acts as an immune system (Pinchot, 1985) doing

---

The Essentials *of Teamworking: International Perspectives.*
Edited by M. A. West, D. Tjosvold, and K. G. Smith. © 2005 John Wiley & Sons, Ltd.

whatever it can to expel the disease. "When teams are introduced as an isolated practice, they fail. My gut feeling is most are introduced in isolation.... And time and time again teams fall short on their promise because companies don't know how to make them work together with other teams" (Dumaine, 1994, p. 92).

The term "team-based organization" (TBO) was coined to describe the new type of organization theorized to support teams. TBO is an organization that uses teams as the core performing units, and the organization is designed to support teams. The logic of the organization shifts from individual-oriented to team-oriented, and a dual focus on both the team and the larger context of the team is required (Mohrman, Cohen, & Mohrman, 1995). One criticism of the term TBO is that some see it as implying teams as an end, not a means to an end. Another is that TBO implies long-term and static organizations, which simply does not fit the current business environment of increasing complexity and change (Harris & Steed, 2001). Because of these negative connotations, many have shied away from the term TBO. However, the practices associated with TBO remain in place.

We suggest that a fully realized redesign effort ultimately produces a TBO. Achieving TBO is the ideal. However, that term connotes an ending point. Once people perceive (correctly or incorrectly) that the ending point is met, the energy around the initiative often wanes. As energy diminishes, the organization tends to go back to bad habits, saying, "TBO—we've done that, and it didn't work for us." In reality, the journey never ends, and the effort must be sustained indefinitely. Accordingly, the term "team-based organizing" (TBO*ing*) represents continuous improvement and continuous reinvention. The TBO*ing* approach and the historically dominant approach that focuses on the individual as the unit of accountability, leadership, and support are radically different!

The primary goal of this chapter is to explore the answer to the question, "what is TBO*ing*?" Since each organization is unique, there is no step-by-step list to follow. Instead, we will share some of our general findings in an effort to describe TBO*ing*.

WHAT IS TEAM-BASED ORGANIZING?

"Team" is the core building block of the team-based organization (TBO). However, focusing solely on the team is not enough to ensure team effectiveness. The crucial point to be made in team-based organizing (TBO*ing*) is the focus on the organization. The key tenets to our definition of TBO*ing* are:

- Teams are the basic units of accountability and work.
- Only use teams when teams are appropriate.
- Teams lead teams.
- Use an array of teams.
- Recognize that it is a never-ending, continuous process.
- Design in flexibility for adaptability.
- Design organization to support teams.
- Hold it all together with alignment.
- Organization leaders must have TBO-compatible philosophy.
- It requires intentional effort.

Each of these tenets is briefly reviewed below.

Teams are the Basic Units of Accountability and Work

This is the most widely accepted tenet of research on the topic of TBO, and the major element that distinguishes TBOs from other organizations. While TBO*ing* often incorporates elements from other initiatives (e.g. total quality management, business process reengineering, and many others), having teams as the basic work unit sets TBO apart from other initiatives. TBOs and organizations that use teams are very different. In a TBO, the organization must be redesigned to support the work of teams. An organization that simply uses teams for special purposes in parallel to a traditional hierarchical structure is not a TBO (Mohrman, Cohen, & Mohrman, 1995). TBOs use teams to perform the core work of the organization (Mohrman, Cohen, & Mohrman, 1995; Mohrman & Mohrman, 1997; Shonk, 1997). In a TBO, teams are responsible for doing the planning, decision making, and implementation of the work (Shonk, 1997).

Transforming a work group to a team or an organization to a TBO represents decisions that are subject to the criterion of cost/benefit analysis. There is a cost and there is a risk that the transformational effort will fail. Costs include time invested in training, lost production time during reorganization, loss of knowledge sets when supervisors or middle managers are laid off or reassigned, etc. Benefits include increased employee commitment, quick response to customers, reduced error rates, and reduced absenteeism. But the investment and risk are only worthwhile if they fit the nature of the work and the strategic plan of the top management group. The strategic plan dictates the design needed to deliver a given set of products or services to customers in a way that generates a profit.

Smolek, Hoffman, and Moran (1999) argue that the structure of the design must include some essential features for teams to be the right choice. The features include:

1. Clarity of purpose so the team knows "why are we here?";
2. Appropriate measures of performance, both qualitative and quantitative, that are aligned with the organization's goals;
3. Clearly defined boundaries that identify the team's scope, responsibilities, authority, and resources;
4. Work processes that require interdependence of the team's members in performing production tasks, but also in making decisions, getting information, and generating feedback.

We agree that features like this are prerequisite to effective teaming; the features are either in place or are established as early phases of the transformation to a TBO. Smolek, Hoffman, and Moran (1999) offer the example of MotorCo (a pseudonym for a real company) where the top management groups of the nine plants were charged with transforming to work team structures to increase competitiveness in the difficult market of electric motor production. After seven months of design work, the plants were ready to implement the transformation. Initial results were mixed, but outstanding teams exceeded expectations and it became clear that investing in people and organization had a larger potential payoff than investing in equipment.

Teams must not become the new silos in an organization. So, while the core performing unit is the team, attention must be focused on business unit and above levels of performance and on promoting integration among teams.

Only Use Teams when Teams are Appropriate

While the core work unit of the TBO is the team, not every person in the organization necessarily belongs on a team. This is a common myth that must be debunked. Teams should only be used when teams are appropriate. Some tasks simply are not appropriate for a team. In this case, a team should not be launched. In the case that an individual is more appropriate for the task, that individual still must learn how to deal with teams in the organization, as the primary organizing feature is the team. Molecular structure may represent an appropriate analogy: individuals act as atoms which combine into teams at the molecular level which mix as business units in compounds to form the chemistry of organizations. There is value in focusing on any of the three levels, but practical value usually emerges from the mixture of new compounds.

In a TBO, the natural inclination should be to put a team on a task. The goal is to maximize the effectiveness of teams, when a team is appropriate. However, before assuming a team is the best structure for accomplishing the task, the work itself has to be analyzed to see if it is amenable to a team structure. A team is a complex solution inappropriate for simple problems; applying a team to a task that individuals can accomplish wastes resources, particularly time. Teams are only appropriate when the work requires the extra investment. It is important to identify collective work, and create teams around that work. The work has to require interdependent effort by multiple people in order for a team structure to emerge and leverage resources.

Teams Lead Teams

Putting the workforce in teams is not enough for successful TBO*ing*. Teams must cascade down throughout the organization, with teams leading teams leading teams. Having teams at all levels models and reinforces the team concept (Mohrman, Cohen, & Mohrman, 1995). The top management group must become a team for three reasons:

(a) building tacit understanding of teaming, so top management group members can recognize challenges and appreciate value added from teaming;
(b) leading the TBO*ing* change effort by modeling it;
(c) aligning support systems top management group members control.

In many organizations the top management group remains relatively unchanged while pushing the rest of the organization to change—a formula for failure. An effective top management group that can function as a team not only supports TBO*ing*, but also increases market success (Mathews, 1996).

Use an Array of Teams

Some believe that using a TBO implies the use of long-term, permanent work teams. We suggest that, as long as teams are performing the core work of the organization, any type of team may be used. For example, project teams are becoming a prevalent work structure in technologically oriented organizations. We would include these project-team-based organizations under the TBO umbrella.

A TBO uses a variety of team types (e.g. work teams, management teams, task teams, and project teams) to meet the needs of each situation. The type of team varies as the work varies—different types of teams are needed for different types of work. TBO can accommodate both permanent and temporary teams. Finally, as discussed in the previous section, management teams are important as well.

Recognize that it Is a Never-ending, Continuous Process

The question "is your organization a TBO?" is a difficult one to answer. The question presumes a dichotomous relationship between TBO and traditional, individually oriented organizations. In reality, organizations fall on a continuum of progress toward the elusive TBO ideal, so they have degrees of TBO. If we look at TBO as the ideal target, then TBO*ing* is the process of moving toward that target. Reframed as a process instead of an end, TBO*ing* is better understood as the continuous improvement process that it is. Too often organizations chase the TBO goal, and then either decide it is too difficult to achieve, or think they have achieved it, rest on their laurels, and immediately start a decline. TBO*ing* suggests that the journey is never over, and the organization must constantly strive to improve in terms of TBO*ing* and its resulting adaptability in order to succeed.

The catchphrase in the 1980s was "reinvention"; today it must be "continuous invention." The change process must be a continuous one to constantly adapt to environmental demands. A major transformation like TBO must also be viewed as a continuous process. The principles of continuous improvement seem to act at least as metaphors, if not as actual tools for change. The TBO initiative builds collaborative capability through education and redesign of the organization that takes many years. There is periodic renewal based on data from regular assessment of the change initiative, the need to reenergize the initiative at critical points, and the continuous need to provide cost/benefit data to the strategic decision makers who have the power to sustain the initiative or starve it.

One manufacturing plant was designed as a TBO from its conception in 1987. Five years later, the emphasis on TBO*ing* was dropped because workload required such a rapid increase in the number of employees in a short period (from 600 to about 2000 over two years) that the systems in place for teams could not be maintained. For example, the use of existing teams as assessors in assessment center processes for selecting new team members was replaced by traditional HR processes for selection. Five years later in response to union demands and a new corporate emphasis on people, a new steering team was formed to plan transformation back to a TBO. Three years after that when a rapid drop in business demand occurred as a result of the bursting technology bubble and the terrorist attacks on September 11, 2001, top management again abandoned teaming and initiated layoffs of 40 percent of the employees. Nine months later, under significant pressure from a new vice president and after reorganization to a project-based matrix organization, the team initiative was again brought to the top of the priority list.

Design in Flexibility for Adaptability

Flexibility is a key effectiveness factor in TBO*ing*, as flexibility throughout the organization must be designed to meet the needs of the fluid business environment. Flexibility of structures, systems, and individuals is crucial for adaptability. To meet the needs of the work and the environment, the organization must be flexible enough to launch different types of teams quickly. The systems of the organization also need to be flexible to deal with these various types of teams and individual and team structures. If the work of the organization requires different team types, then flexibility of systems would become more crucial than for an organization with fairly homogeneous tasks. Individuals within the TBO must also be flexible. They must be willing to make a change, and willing to adapt to the demands on them at any given time or over the long term. This adaptability enhances the organization's ability to meet the needs of changing external circumstances.

The continuous development of the TBO initiative enables the steering team to base progress on many small steps rather than one grand change. As a result, risk is reduced and the ability to adapt the initiative to changing business conditions is possible. The design remains reconfigurable. As with many management decisions, getting started with a modest plan is more effective than waiting until a perfect plan has been developed. Incremental change allows for adjustments along the path toward the goal state. One example involves the radical change at a national bank.

Devane (in press) described the transformation of the Land Bank of South Africa into a TBO under the dynamic leadership of its new president. The intent was to create an adaptive organization, so "the formal design of the organizational structure was never considered 'done.'" This contrasted with prior change experience for the bank, which was "cast in concrete for eight to 20 years." Through empowerment and education, branches of the bank could be redesigned as their members felt the need.

At Hewlett-Packard and other companies whose industries are subject to rapid technological change and short product life cycles, employees must be closely in touch with customers, so quick decisions can be made to facilitate mass customization. Employees must be both motivated and organized to help with the transformation to an organizational design that can be that responsive (Zell, 1997). At the Roseville plant, the HP design team created self-managing teams with "the necessary power, knowledge, authority, and information to make decisions on their own" (p. 137). They achieved alignment among the teams and the rest of the organization through use of the "Bull's-Eye" diagram, which placed customers and values in the center surrounded by concentric circles for the business system, the structural system, the support system, and finally the people system. The latter had the most room for improvement. At the Roseville plant, the redesign work was fairly straightforward, but at the Santa Clara plant, the "structure had to be completely dismantled before a business strategy could be established."

Design Organization to Support Teams

Team-based organizing is not about teams. It is about the organization. Most publications and most examples focus on individual teams. The leap from team to team-based system of work is as large as the leap from individual work to teamwork. Redesign to a TBO demands redesign of the organization as a whole. The environment the teams work in is critical to their performance level, so redesigning the whole makes effectiveness possible at the lower level (Beyerlein & Harris, in press).

TBO applies to organizations of all sizes. When we say "organization," we mean the site or department level. Preferably, the entire site would be transformed in a TBO*ing* effort.

However, a full redesign at the corporate level is rare, as the size of the organization makes transformative change difficult to manage.

Hold it All Together with Alignment

Alignment is the foundational principle in our definition of TBO. In order to be successful, alignment must occur externally and internally in the organization. Externally, the organization must align with stakeholders, customers, suppliers, competitors, and partners. Internally, alignment must occur across: (a) multiple change initiatives; (b) deployment of strategy, mission, vision, and values; (c) support systems (with each other and with team needs); and (d) teams forming lateral relationships.

As with any organization design, organizational structure, systems, and culture should be aligned with each other. Therefore, if the organization is comprised of teams, the organization context and systems must be congruent with teams. In studies of team failures (Beyerlein et al., 1997; Mohrman & Tenkasi, 1997), the key factor that emerged was alignment of support systems with work teams. Beyerlein et al. suggested that more than 50 percent of the failure of teams to achieve expected gains was due to lack of alignment. Mohrman and Tenkasi suggested 90 percent of the failures were due to context factors and specified support systems as the key. Lack of alignment between support systems creates contextual inconsistencies that send mixed messages to team members (e.g. rewards based exclusively on individual achievement when managers are saying "work as a team") or that undermine performance as an integrated team (e.g. information systems that prevent access to work-relevant material by anyone but the team's formal manager). Mohrman (Mohrman, Cohen, & Mohrman, 1995) suggests that the alignment issue will only become salient with experience in TBO*ing*—manager awareness shifts from surface features to deeper structure as understanding of the new design grows.

One of the most critical forms of alignment is the TBO*ing* effort with business strategy. If the motivation for TBO*ing* does not directly relate to business reasons, then the initiative is doomed to failure. The investment required for successful TBO*ing* is large and long term, and a significant expectation for business improvement must be pursued in order to build and maintain the momentum of the redesign effort.

Strategic decision makers at the top of the organization base many decisions on financial information and financial goals (often short-term goals). Work teams and TBO*ing* provide a number of benefits, but sometimes the mechanisms are not in place for valuing those benefits in financial terms. Kennedy describes a system for using management accounting concepts and team effectives and support system alignment data for providing such data to top management (Kennedy, 2002). Plants for such companies as Shell, Raytheon, and Colgate, and departments at First American Financial have been testing the model. The initial goal was to provide feedback to the top management group about the success of teams, so strategic decision making would sustain the initiative. More recently, the idea of building an innovation culture has been added to the project, since the dollar value of team process improvements is captured and aggregated at several levels.

Jones and Moffett (1999) emphasize the alignment of the team's strategy with the organization's strategy as a way of focusing on business results. They call this "line of sight" and argue that it must be clear; that is, team members need enough knowledge of the business strategy to clearly see how to align their decisions with it. Two examples they present illustrate this alignment. At Xerox, the corporate document called "Vision 2000" shared the corporate goal and the competitive pressures that strategy targeted. When teams needed to upgrade their technical skills because of a product transformation to digital equipment, the teams' goals became clear and the measurement system was adapted to capture the change.

At Electronic Components (a fictional name for a real company), teams worked to solve productivity problems that impacted bottom-line performance. Focusing on the reduction of defects enabled the teams to cut cycle time, reduce overtime, and improve on-time delivery to the customer. This improved team performance measures and the company's profits. The use of theory of constraints (TOC) through total preventive maintenance (TPM) teams at many semiconductor plants, including Harris Semiconductor (Rose, Gilmore, & Odom, 1998), formalizes the process for identifying defects in process that act as bottlenecks to production flow. The general pattern is for the teams to collect and analyze data to identify the point in a complex set of production steps that is acting as the greatest constraint, such as the slowest machine or the point where most breakdowns occur. The teams then fix the problem or get help to do so before moving on to the next slowest step. The result is speeded production and greater efficiency in the process.

Organization Leaders Must Have TBO-Compatible Philosophy

Although leadership represents a support system and is treated in that section of this chapter, it deserves notice here, because it is the only system that is responsible for changing the systems. It is also one of the hardest systems to change. Organization change starts with self-change. If management does not change, it stifles the rest of the initiative. Moran (1996) discovered that 77 percent of team initiatives failed due to lack of management support.

Organization leaders advocate TBO through words and actions, which are indicative of their management philosophy. First, the management philosophy must be one of involvement. The organization is built on the principle that people have a right to be involved in matters that affect them. In return, people will make decisions in the best interest of the organization because of awareness of mutual benefit. Second, management development must be built around the team concept, focusing on a collaborative, facilitative, development role. Part of this includes redefining the ego role to become less controlling. Top management in the business unit (as well as the other levels of management) must have announced and demonstrated commitment to the team concept in order for it to succeed.

Implementation Requires Intentional Effort

Creating an environment where teams can thrive does not happen by chance, but comes through time, effort, and commitment. Teams and the larger organization must give some careful thought to what is needed to support teams. These reflective activities must occur regularly. The most important points must be supported by systems that reinforce their occurrence (Mohrman, Cohen, & Mohrman, 1995).

TBO is a decision, just like personal health is a decision. Unless one makes a decision to establish the practices that generate and maintain health and fitness, a gradual deterioration occurs and achievable performance goals become more and more humble. High performance levels in an organization that relies on teams require that decision makers commit to the transformation effort that is necessary in creating a TBO. It starts with a decision.

The manufacturing plant example earlier in the chapter represented a TBO*ing* effort that has already covered 15 years and may have 15 more to reach a mature state. Literature on teams published in the 1990s suggested the transformation typically took 6–11 years. Most efforts are not so complete; few organizations make the investment to actually create a fully developed TBO. Many organizations prefer to stop part way along the journey. For example, one meat packing company is only interested in having self-directed work teams embedded within an otherwise traditional hierarchy.

COMPONENTS OF TEAM-BASED ORGANIZING

The Organizational "Road Map"

In this section, we will delve further into the details of TBO*ing*. The components are organized using a theoretical "road map" of an organization. This "road map" could be a model for any organization using any type of work. It is an alignment model, with congruent design as the goal. In a TBO, teams would carry out the majority of work, which assumes that the work is amenable to teams. We will use it as a road map for sharing themes related specifically to TBO. How does the organization, including culture, systems, and structure, have to change from the traditional design in order to support teams to maximize effectiveness? We will explore this in the rest of the chapter.

The Work

The work is at the center of the organizational "road map," because the ultimate objective of the organization is to accomplish its task—whether the work is production, service, or new product development. The organizational pieces—culture, structure, and systems—must create a bridge of alignment between the work and the environment. While the characteristics of the work in most situations are fairly set, the task can be reframed through work process redesign (Dalton, 1998). The following points characterize TBO work.

INTERDEPENDENT WORK

In a TBO, teams should be created around tasks that are appropriate to teams. Appropriate team tasks require interdependence (Mohrman, Cohen, & Mohrman, 1995; Saavedra, Earley, & van Dyne, 1993). This interdependence requires the integration of the knowledge and work of different individuals. In other words, simple, single-function tasks, such as turning a screw to complete a roller skate, would be less appropriate for a team than assembly and inspection of an entire roller skate. In a TBO, teams are created based on their interdependencies. In teams, members depend on each other to achieve work goals.

The interdependencies of the work are often identified through process analysis (Dalton, 1998).

WHOLE PIECE OF WORK

In a TBO, the whole organization is designed to create units comprised of the various skills and experiences necessary to do a whole piece of the business (Mohrman, Cohen, & Mohrman, 1995). These units are then given responsibility and accountability for their part of the business. When the overall task is too complex for a single team (e.g. building an airplane), then the work of the team represents a complete piece of the larger project, e.g. the paint team handling the entire exterior of the plane rather than breaking it into tail section, wings, or fuselage for separate work groups, resulting in the work having less segmentation (Goodman, Devadas, & Hughson, 1988; Lawler, 1990). Because teams are organized around whole pieces of work, the organization becomes more process than product focused (Harris & Steed, 2001). An important result of cross-functional teams looking at a whole piece of work is that the individuals begin to see themselves as customers and suppliers, a mentality that cascades throughout the internal and external supply chains.

INCREASE IN LATERAL WORK

In a traditional organization, much of the work is accomplished vertically. If a person has a problem, he or she goes to the boss, who sends it to the next boss, and so on, until the appropriate functional silo is able to answer the question. Instead, since TBO*ing* organizations are organized into teams conducting whole pieces of work, they have many more lateral work opportunities, decreasing the amount of time that decisions have to go up and down the hierarchy and reducing the isolation caused by chimney structures or silos. The teams are empowered to make many decisions themselves. The results are faster and higher-quality decisions. In addition to lateral work within the team, successful TBO*ing* requires integration among teams, causing even more lateral work. The members readily reach out across functional and project boundaries to gather information or coordinate flow of work.

BROADER SKILL SETS

Because of the more holistic nature of work in teams, broader skills are required. Jobs are enlarged to include planning, control, and coordination, instead of just doing the work.

CHANGES IN ROLE DIFFERENTIATION AND COMMUNICATION

It is a myth that all team members must be cross-trained. Instead, specialists in a team must learn enough about the other specialties to be able to communicate with them (Klein, 1993). In fact, a moderate degree of role differentiation is required. If each person has exactly the expertise and experiences, what is the point in putting them together in a team? It is this diversity that makes a team strong. As a result of the improved decisions, individuals learn that it is valuable to see another point of view (Harris & Steed, 2001).

APPROPRIATENESS OF THE WORK FOR TEAMING

The nature of work is not completely a given in each organization. If work is not amenable to teams, then perhaps it should be. Are there opportunities for increased collaboration? How can this occur? Work process redesign facilitates this process. Not all work is teamwork, but some work that looks like individual work can be redesigned to be teamwork, and is better as a result. Not everyone in a TBO has to be in a team, and team members usually spend a significant proportion of their time working individually.

Work teams and TBOs are not appropriate for all situations. First, their success depends on sustained support and investment that are not always available. Second, the work may not always require a team approach or seem to. For example, sales may be handled in the field by individuals working alone, if the products are not complex or dependent on service. When complexity of a product requires input from people with a variety of types of expertise or tailoring by engineering before manufacture or extensive service support, such as enterprise resource planning software, a sales team approach will be far more effective. One microwave antenna manufacturer made this change and found customers were much more satisfied—they worked with a stable group who had the expertise to provide high-quality service, so relationships evolved that facilitated the work. Successful execution of the work must drive the decision to use a team approach.

Even when teams are adopted and a TBO infrastructure surrounds them, not all members of the organization need to work in teams. Also, team members usually spend a significant proportion of their time working individually, moving back and forth between the group interaction and the solo role where concentration may be enhanced.

THE CHANGING NATURE OF WORK

The nature of work has been changing in recent years in a number of ways. For example, the work simplification approach that developed out of the Taylorist tradition has been giving way to job enlargement and enrichment—increasing responsibilities in both vertical and horizontal directions. The design trend has led to a shift from emphasis on the use of job descriptions toward use of job roles. Those new roles include a shift in attention for frontline employees for simple job duties to the welfare of the entire organization. Such changes seem to align with the shift toward a greater emphasis on knowledge work and a more educated body of employees, as well as the increasing dependence of strategic advantage on the optimal use of all the intelligence in an organization. TBO provides a natural fit with these changes and capitalizes on the options they provide.

Automation, cell-based clustering of people and machines, just-in-time procedures, total quality management, product and materials changes, and other influences have contributed to changes in job design. Job design aims at two goals: employee motivation and efficient use of resources, including work flow. There are many ways to design most jobs and clusters of jobs. The choice of design must align with the organization's strategy. Traditional approaches to job design tend to focus on efficiency; psychological approaches focus on motivation. TBO*ing* needs to focus on both within the framework of the mission-based strategy. Intelligent effort by individuals must be leveraged by appropriate collaboration and smooth work flow. Since TBO*ing* attempts to be comprehensive in its examination of work infrastructure, it provides an opportunity for a more complete approach to job design.

The Environment

Trends in today's environment include globalization, a fast pace of change, increased complexity, permeable organizational boundaries, and rapid technology change. A central principle of organizational design is matching the logic of organization to the environment and to the work or task to be accomplished (Dijksterhuis & van den Bosch, 1999). Traditional command-and-control organizations were appropriate for their time, when the environment was simpler and more stable, the work more segmented, and employees less educated. However, command and control is structurally maladaptive, given today's environment. At present, the environment calls for organizations that meet the six Fs—flat, fast, flexible, fun, focused, and "fatherless" (referring to the employment contract that is no longer paternalistic, but rather requires individuals to develop themselves) (cf. Crawford & Brungardt, 1999). To fit this complex environment, organizations must "complexify." The complexity of the environment must be matched by the complexity of the organization's design. TBO*ing* is one method of decentralizing knowing and decision making to promote the six Fs. The old cliché rings true—"all of us are smarter than any of us!"

The current environment demands adaptability. Adaptable organizations are flexible organizations with reorganization ability. Adaptability requires both awareness of the environment and the capability to change internally to meet the challenges of the environment. This need for constant environmental awareness calls for continuous links to the environment. TBO*ing* builds in adaptability by creating a few broad rules (Brown & Eisenhardt, 1998), then facilitating self-design by the teams. Teams are in touch with customers and suppliers and can make rapid adjustments when changes occur in the market place. The bottom level is the most adaptable level within the organization (Baskin, 2001). Stifling the bottom through rigid control reduces adaptability, whereas supporting it increases adaptability. Part of remaining adaptable includes connecting beyond the traditional walls of the organization to multiple organizations. The number, quality, and malleability of those connections add up to the viability of the organization. TBO*ing* enables this to occur.

At Lockheed Martin Electronics and Missiles in Orlando, Florida, integrated product teams (IPTs) bring together multiple disciplines on the production floor. In addition, customers and suppliers participate in these teams (http://www.bmpcoe.org/bestpractices/external/lmem/lmem_39.html). The teams represent one of the ways that Lockheed Martin builds bridges in the supply chain or value chain. Other mechanisms for involving suppliers include strategic alliances, teaming directly with suppliers, design of materials flow, and joint supply purchases. Building mutually advantageous relationships with suppliers is considered a best practice, meaning that it sets a standard of practice with the goal of all participating organizations forming an integrated process partly based on mandatory membership of suppliers on the IPTs.

Organizational Culture

Most scholars view organizational culture as a pattern of shared organizational values, basic underlying assumptions, and informal norms that guide the way work is accomplished in an organization (e.g. Ott, 1989). This approach assumes that a shared cognitive framework creates a social glue that holds people together in an organization. Hofstede and Neuijen (1990) argue that such a view may be more appropriate for thinking about national cultures. They emphasize shared practices as the glue in work organizations that enables coordination of activity. They state that "most authors will probably agree on the following characteristics of the organizational/corporate culture construct: it is (1) holistic, (2) historically determined, (3) related to anthropological concepts, (4) socially constructed, (5) soft, and (6) difficult to change."

The focus on practice was reinforced by the work of Brown and Duguid (2000) in their study of the idiosyncrasies of practice. They found that policy, principles, and engineered processes were generic only because they were propagated at a level above practice. The situational nature of practice requires local adjustments on machines, in relationships, and in interpretation of information. Coordination of activity among employees then depends on the way practice occurs. Hofstede and Neuijen (1990) indicate that practices may be referred to as "conventions," "customs," "habits," "mores," "traditions," or "usages." Since practices are learned at work, the opportunity to change organizational culture seems to improve when education and design of the work environment recognize and support certain practices and sharing of practices. Culture change at the higher level of values, beliefs, and assumptions remains a worthwhile goal that provides the socio-cognitive infrastructure for establishing overall alignment for activities within the organization but one that requires long-term investment through education, reward, modeling, and selection. Tailoring processes to fit the practice level requires some discretion and authority. These are provided through empowerment and self-management. The addition of teaming creates an environment where small clusters of people may work together within an environment that facilitates use of collaboration in problem solving. Subcultures and nested cultures are likely to arise in such settings where sharing is more intense at the local level. The culture in a TBO is very different than in a traditional organization. Some of the assumptions of the TBO culture are explored below.

DECISION MAKING WHERE THE WORK IS DONE

Because the employees actually doing the work have the most expertise about that work, it makes sense to push decision making down to these workers. In a traditional organization, the decision is passed upward to someone who may not have the relevant expertise to make the decision. As a result of decision making being pushed down to lower levels, work is coordinated and controlled at local levels as well. Day-to-day operational decisions are made lower in the organization. Responsibility, authority, and autonomy are pushed to the team level to support decision making (Harris & Steed, 2001).

TEAMS MAKE DECISIONS, WHEN APPROPRIATE

When crucial decisions require multiple types of expertise, the team makes the decisions. However, a delicate balance exists between individual decision making and willingness to involve others. Excess in either direction creates dysfunction. If all decisions become team decisions, then decision making becomes an arduous, frustrating, and time-consuming process. If too many decisions become individual decisions, then the trust and cohesiveness of the team dissipate. Also, sometimes decisions must be escalated to a higher level in the organization. It is important to work with teams to determine which types of decisions are team decisions, and which are not.

ENGAGEMENT OF EMPLOYEES LEADS TO INCREASED COMMITMENT

A foundational principle of effective TBO*ing* is the engagement of all employees in the work process. Employees also must be engaged in the design and change process. People are engaged well beyond traditional workplace norms. Employees are invited into decision making and ownership of outcomes. The increased engagement leads to greater ownership and commitment. It also mitigates the negative impact of stress (Maslach & Leiter, 1997). Because of the increased participation, everyone has a shared stake in the output. The responsibility for the health of the organization is shared much more evenly across the organization. It is not just top management's job to figure it out.

Organizational Structure

In a TBO, work is done collaboratively in a team structure. Teams are the basic performing unit, the formal organizing unit, of the organization. Some of the characteristics of structure in a TBO are explored below.

A VARIETY OF TEAM TYPES SUPPORTS DIFFERENT TYPES OF WORK

Because flexibility and adaptability are so important to meeting the demands of the ever-changing business environment, organizational structure of a TBO must be able to flex and change as well. Because of the different needs, many different types of teams exist.

Teams can be temporary or permanent, single function or multifunctional, inside one organization or across several, and have co-located or distributed membership. Cohen and Bailey (1997) identified four types of teams in their review of empirical team studies published from 1990 to 1996. Work teams are long-term and fairly stable teams that are responsible for producing goods or services. Parallel teams are short-term teams with limited authority (usually with recommendation power only) that exist in parallel to existing organizational structure. Project teams are short-term teams with a specific goal or objective that is completed, and then the team is disbanded. Project teams usually are cross-functional. Finally, management teams are long-term teams of managers that coordinate, integrate, and provide direction to other teams.

In order to avoid making teams the new silos, integration mechanisms among teams are necessary. One way to do this is via boundary workers, where team members are members of more than one team (Harris & Steed, 2001). Integration teams can also be created where representatives from several teams work together (Mohrman, Tenkasi, & Mohrman, 2000). This is especially important when the work between teams is highly interdependent (e.g. building an airplane).

TEAMS VARY IN THEIR LEVEL OF EMPOWERMENT

Just as a TBO contains various types of teams, teams vary in their level of empowerment. Different types of tasks may call for different levels of empowerment. Ray and Bronstein

(1995) describe a continuum of group structures as follows:

- Type I: Leader centered/leader focused
- Type II: Leader centered/function focused
- Type III: Leader centered/integrated-task focused
- Type IV: Self-led/time and task focused
- Type V: Self-led/task focused

As levels of competency and accompanying empowerment increase, the team becomes more able to make decisions and act on its own, without reliance on a manager or supervisor.

TEAMS ORGANIZE AROUND PROCESS OR PRODUCT

In a TBO, teams are organized around processes, products, or customers in order to maximize the use of cross-functional teams that bring diverse experience and expertise together. Because of the process or product focus, the TBO has a more lateral focus to work as opposed to a vertical silo focus (Harris & Steed, 2001).

TEAMS LEADING TEAMS IN A FLAT HIERARCHY

As mentioned previously, an important defining characteristic of TBO is that teams lead teams. In other words, it is not just the workforce that is in teams; the management is organized in teams as well (Mohrman, Tenkasi, & Mohrman, 2000). TBOs represent a flatter organization than the traditional, individually focused organization. Flat reporting relationships mean less hierarchy, and communication goes across the organization instead of exclusively up one chain and down the other, increasing the speed of communication. However, "flat" does not mean an absence of hierarchy. The organizational structure looks like a flat hierarchy of layers of teams leading teams.

NOT EVERYONE HAS TO BE IN A TEAM

Contrary to popular myth, not everyone in a TBO*ing* organization must belong to a formal team. Some tasks exist that may be more appropriate to an individual. In contrast to an individually oriented organization where an individual is immediately put on a task, the immediate reaction in a TBO is to put a team on it. However, that does not mean that everyone necessarily has to be on a team. Often individuals in specialized roles or with rare knowledge become contract workers to the teams rather than official members of lots of teams.

TBO UNIT OFTEN MUST INTERFACE WITH TRADITIONAL CORPORATE ENTITY

Unfortunately, not every part of every organization will be a TBO. Since TBO is a fairly new organizational form, TBO*ing* organizations are rare. A challenge occurs when the TBO unit interfaces with other entities that are more accustomed to dealing with traditional systems.

This dichotomy can occur between the TBO*ing* business unit and suppliers, customers, and even different parts of the broader organization. Enterprise systems built at the corporate level often pose a challenge for business units attempting new ways of working. This reality must be addressed in the organizational change, and mechanisms put in place to deal with the dichotomy.

Organizational Systems

Team-based support systems are enablers of a healthy team environment. The idea of changing the environment (infrastructure and culture) of teams is overwhelming when looked at from a broad perspective. The term "support system" is used to further define the organizational surroundings. A support system is "part of the organizational infrastructure that facilitates carrying out the processes necessary to do the work; to manage, control, coordinate, and improve it; and to manage the people who are doing it" (Mohrman, Cohen, & Mohrman, 1995, p. 302). For optimal success, organizational support systems must be aligned with the organizational design and the type of work being done. Therefore, if a team is chosen as the basis of organizational design, presumably because the work requires a team, then the organizational support systems must be team-based. The whole array of support systems should also be viewed as a system. When individual support systems conflict with each other, quality of support drops, and team performance drops with it.

For TBOs to be effective, they must have a comprehensive and complementary set of support systems that guide teams to meet organizational and business unit goals (Mohrman, Cohen, & Mohrman, 1995). To the degree that the teams lack support systems aligned with their needs, they will fall short of performance possibilities. Leaders and designers need to consider all these parts of the organizational context when making a change to teams. They will be disappointed to the extent that they consider only the within-team aspects.

TRADITIONAL VERSUS TEAM-BASED SUPPORT SYSTEMS

In general, support systems in a traditional organization are focused on individual performance. In a TBO, support systems must be modified and created to facilitate team performance. In a traditional organization, systems are controlled by management, are strongly linked to the chain of command, and promote stability and uniformity. In contrast, TBO support systems promote flexibility, continuous adjustment, and are self-managed (Mohrman, Cohen, & Mohrman, 1995).

FLEXIBILITY OF SUPPORT SYSTEMS

Support systems must be flexible to deal with changes in the external environment. Much attention has been paid lately to the increasing rate of change and complexity in our ever-global world environment. Organizations must be able to deal quickly with, and even think ahead of, changes in the environment. Because changes occur so often, support systems must also be able to flex with the needs of the environment. TBOs are much more flexible organizations than traditional organizations, and better able to meet the needs of the changing environment. In turn, teams must be supported by more flexible systems than the norm.

Support systems must be flexible to deal with various team types, as well as individual and teamwork. Different types of tasks require different kinds of teams (e.g. management team, project team, work team, parallel team, cross-functional team, or integration team). In fact, some tasks may require an individual instead of a team. Since organizational support systems need to be aligned with the organizational design for optimization, support systems need to be flexible to accommodate various team types and individual work. Support systems should create an umbrella so the organization can remain a cohesive whole, yet be flexible to meet the needs of various teams and individuals under the umbrella of support.

LIST OF SUPPORT SYSTEMS

Support systems can be defined in many different ways. The list below comes from five years of research on team-based support systems (Beyerlein & Harris, in press). After the list, some general findings about how some of the support systems look in a TBO are described. For definitions of the support systems and supporting references, see Table 7.1.

- Leadership, including executive leaders, direct supervision, team leaders, and team members/shared leadership.
- Organization and team design.
- Performance management, including goal setting, performance measurement, performance feedback, rewards, and recognition.
- Financial and resource allocation.
- Learning, including communication, information, knowledge management, and training.
- Physical workspace and tools.
- Change and renewal.
- Integration, including between-teams integration, teams and systems integration, and change initiatives integration.
- Creativity and innovation.

In a TBO, teams are organized around deliverables of some kind, and have shared objectives. Teams set and monitor their own team goals, and are appraised as a team, ensuring team accountability for the work. Ideally, teams are able to set up their own goals, ensuring commitment to the goals. Teams measure team performance themselves and have their own measures that align with organizational measures. Importantly, all team members understand how measures relate to daily performance. Finally, while measures can occur at the team level, it is critical that they also take place at the business unit level, to ensure that measurements are aligned to business level results.

In terms of information, communication, and learning, a sign of a successful TBO is greater information sharing all around (including upward and downward communication), where everyone throughout the organization knows what is going on. Because of the flatness and complexity of the organizational structure, TBOs have more complex communication networks and decision-making patterns. Often TBOs have a higher level of technology in order to facilitate greater sharing of information. TBOs place a greater emphasis on training and development, and are better learning organizations, because they design in learning through the sharing of lessons learned and lateral and horizontal interactions among team members and across teams.

Table 7.1 Team-based support systems

Support system category	Support system	Team-based definition	References
Leadership	Executive leaders	Formal and informal processes that top leaders use to create leadership conducive to teamwork	Beyerlein & Harris (in press) Hall (1998) Leader's roles—Sundstrom and associates (1999)
	Direct supervision	Formal and informal processes that direct supervisors use to create leadership conducive to teamwork	Beyerlein & Harris (in press) Hall (1998) Leader's roles—Sundstrom and associates (1999)
	Team leaders	Formal and informal processes that team leaders use to create leadership conducive to teamwork	Beyerlein & Harris (in press) Leader's roles—Sundstrom and associates (1999)
	Team members/shared leadership	Formal and informal processes that team members use to create leadership conducive to teamwork	Beyerlein & Harris (in press)
Design	Organization design	Methods of looking at the organization as a whole and determining appropriate places for teams, and supporting them through support system design and culture work	Beyerlein & Harris (in press) Group design—Hall (1998) Team structure—Sundstrom and associates (1999)
	Team design	At the team level, making sure the team has the inputs it needs to get the work done	Beyerlein & Harris (in press) Team structure—Sundstrom and associates (1999)
Performance management	Goal-setting system	Methods of establishing aligned goals (e.g. goals, priorities, and tasks)	Beyerlein & Harris (in press) Direction setting—Mohrman, Cohen, & Mohrman (1995)
	Performance measurement system	Methods of identifying and measuring appropriate performance	Beyerlein & Harris (in press) Defining performance—Hall (1998) Defining performance—Mohrman, Cohen, & Mohrman (1995) Measurement and feedback—Sundstrom and associates (1999)

	Performance feedback system	Methods (formal and informal) of reviewing and appraising appropriate performance and other desired behaviors associated with performance	Beyerlein & Harris (in press) Performance appraisal—Hall (1998) Reviewing performance—Mohrman, Cohen, & Mohrman (1995) Measurement and feedback—Sundstrom and associates (1999)
	Reward system	Methods of rewarding performance and other desired behaviors (individual, team, business unit levels of performance)	Beyerlein & Harris (in press) Hall (1998) Rewarding performance—Mohrman, Cohen, & Mohrman (1995)
	Recognition system	Methods recognizing, formally and informally, performance and other desired behaviors (individual, team, business unit levels of performance)	Beyerlein & Harris (in press)
Financial	Financial system	Creating financial systems to support teams, including the accounting and reporting systems	Beyerlein & Harris (in press)
	Resource allocation system	Processes for ensuring that teams get the resources they need to get the work done	Beyerlein & Harris (in press)
Learning (formal and informal)	Communication system	Methods for communication throughout the organization	Beyerlein & Harris (in press) Mohrman, Cohen, & Mohrman (1995) Communication technology—Sundstrom and associates (1999)
	Information system	Methods for teams to get the information it needs to perform effectively (access and sharing, e.g. common databases, goals, and priorities)	Beyerlein & Harris (in press) Hall (1998) Information technology—Mohrman, Cohen, & Mohrman (1995) Sundstrom and associates (1999)
	Knowledge management system	Processes for acquiring, organizing, sharing, utilizing knowledge	Beyerlein & Harris (in press)

(continues overleaf)

Table 7.1 (continued)

Support system category	Support system	Team-based definition	References
	Training system	Methods for teams and individuals to identify and get the skills needed to perform (e.g. interpersonal skills training, and business skills training)	Beyerlein & Harris (in press) Hall (1998) Developing performance—Mohrman, Cohen, & Mohrman (1995) Sundstrom and associates (1999)
Selection system	Selection system	Processes for bringing new and transferred employees with the right skills into the right teams	Beyerlein & Harris (in press) Team staffing—Sundstrom and associates (1999)
Physical workspace and tools	Physical workspace and tools	The actual space in which the team works. If it is a virtual team, then the "space" created by technology (e.g. budgets, tools, and computers)	Beyerlein & Harris (in press) Facility—Sundstrom and associates (1999)
Change and renewal	Renewal system	Methods for periodically reevaluating and changing organizational design and systems, when necessary	Beyerlein & Harris (in press)
Integration	Between-teams integration	Methods for ensuring that teams do not become the new silos, and instead are pieces of an integrated whole (e.g. informal integration, formal leadership roles, and policies)	Beyerlein & Harris (in press)
	Change initiatives integration	Methods for ensuring that multiple change initiatives are aligned in terms of complementary content and sequence	Beyerlein & Harris (in press)
Creativity and innovation	Creativity and innovation system	Methods for ensuring that creativity and innovation are built into the system	Beyerlein & Harris (in press)

In a TBO, there is a shift from individual to team-based accountability. This accountability is designed into the organization. This means that any team in the organization can hold any other team accountable for not doing their work or creating problems for them. Because accountability at the team level is designed into the organization, the hierarchy of control and accountabilities becomes clearer, which is contrary to the popular myth that TBOs not only reduce control of the work, but that control and accountability lines become fuzzy. Control increases because of peer pressure—concertive control (Barker, 1995).

In a TBO, formal managers and leaders do not play traditional oversight roles. Instead, they become participative partners with employees—working with and through them, rather than over them—facilitating a philosophy that employees want to do the right thing for the organization, and tapping the expertise of team members in an environment that is too complex for one person to make good decisions. In a TBO, there is a different role definition of who does what kinds of activities—oversight tasks of traditional managers become the responsibility of the team, leaving the manager free to do more strategic work. Managers have responsibility for cultivating an environment of involvement where everyone is engaged or invited to engage in the business, a supportive environment where participation is the rule, and where everyone's voice counts. Because of this environment and the increased communications and interaction it brings, top management becomes more aware of the needs, values, and concerns of employees. Formal leaders have to develop facilitative leadership styles, and become less directive with an emphasis on coaching and facilitation. The role of formal leaders is to enable, inspire, and guide the teams.

CONCLUSION

In this chapter, we shared a descriptive overview of TBO*ing*. In summary, the key tenets of TBO*ing* are reviewed here. The team replaces the individual as the unit of work, of assessment, and to some extent, of reward. There are a variety of team designs and the chosen design should match the work situation. However, multiple designs should be combined into an array of interdependent and intact social/work systems—whether temporary or permanent, co-located or distributed, single function or multifunctional. In most organizations using teams, the structure at the management levels does not change; in a TBO, managers also work in teams. The rest of the organization surrounding the working teams must be organized to support them. That depends on aligning support functions with team needs. This all represents a radical change from traditional design. It requires substantial investment and intentional effort.

A big problem when discussing TBO*ing* is the lack of a common language. In a recent interview study of individuals with knowledge in the area, only 70 percent used the term "TBO" (Harris & Steed, 2001), and of these, many did not use the term consistently. Some similar terms include:

- High-performance work organizations.
- Self-managing work teams.
- Flexible, lateral organization.
- Socio-technical systems.
- New design plants.
- Self-managing organizations.

- Collaborative work systems.
- Project-based organization.

The majority of participants indicated that they tended to use whatever terminology was preferred by the customer organization. The bottom line is that anyone using TBO language must be careful to educate and create a shared meaning among the people using it.

TBO is only one approach to designing organizations to achieve strategic objectives, and it is not the right choice for every organization. TBO*ing* takes more time, effort, and investment than working individually. TBO*ing* is an expensive advanced social technology that requires commitment and resources to succeed, but, when done well, the social and financial benefits are tremendous. We believe that those who are successfully implementing this advanced social technology have a competitive advantage in a complex business environment. Further research will articulate the benefits, as well as the key critical success factors, for TBOs.

ACKNOWLEDGEMENTS

Thanks to the Center for Creative Leadership for supporting the interview study of experts in TBO. Special acknowledgement goes to colleagues Judith Steed and Gina Hernez-Broome for their help conceptualizing the study. Thanks to David Loring for supporting the idea. Special appreciation goes to the interview participants who gave from one to four hours of their busy schedule to share their thoughts on this exciting topic. Thank you!

REFERENCES

Barker, J. R. (1995). Communal–rational authority as the basis of leadership for self-managing teams. In M. Beyerlein, D. Johnson, & S. Beyerlein (eds), *Advances in Interdisciplinary Studies of Work Teams*, Vol. 3, *Team Leadership*. Greenwich, Conn.: JAI Press.

Baskin, K. (2001). What your body would tell you if it could talk. Keynote presentation, *Collaborative Work Systems Symposium*, University of North Texas, May 23–25, Denton, Tex.

Beyerlein, M., Hall, C., Harris, C., & Beyerlein, S. (1997). The failure of transformation to teams. *Proceedings of the International Conference on Work Teams*, Dallas, pp. 57–62.

Beyerlein, M. M. & Harris, C. L. (in press). Critical success factors in team-based organizing: a top ten list. In M. Beyerlein, C. McGee, G. Klein, J. Nemiro, & L. Broedling (eds), *The Collaborative Work Systems Fieldbook: Strategies, Tools & Techniques*. San Francisco: Jossey-Bass.

Brown, J. S. & Duguid, P. (2000). *The Social Life of Information*. Cambridge, Mass.: Harvard Business School Press.

Brown, S. L. & Eisenhardt, K. M. (1998). *Competing on the Edge: Strategy as Structured Chaos*. Cambridge, Mass.: Harvard Business School.

Cohen, S. & Bailey, D. (1997). What makes teams work: group effectiveness research from the shop floor to the executive suite. *Journal of Management, 23*, 239–290.

Crawford, C. B. & Brungardt, C. L. (1999). Building the corporate revolution: real empowerment through risk leadership. *Proceedings of the Annual Meeting of the International Leadership Association*, Atlanta, Ga, http://www.academy.umd.edu/ila/1999proceedings/crawford.htm

Dalton, G. L. (1998). The collective stretch. *Management Review, 87*(11), 54–60.

Devane, T. (in press). Big change fast: a case study in transformation from a traditional organization to a team-based organization. In J. Nemiro, G. Klein, C. McGee, & M. Beyerlein (eds), *The Collaborative Work System Casebook*. San Francisco: Jossey-Bass/Pfeiffer.

Dijksterhuis, M. S. & van den Bosch, F. (1999). Where do new organizational forms come from? Management logics as a source of coevolution. *Organization Science, 10*(5), 569–583.

Dumaine, B. (1994). The trouble with teams. *Fortune*, 5 September, pp. 86–92.

Goodman, P. S., Devadas, S., & Hughson, T. L. (1988). Groups and productivity: analyzing the effectiveness of self-managing teams. In J. P. Campbell, R. J. Campbell, & associates (eds), *Productivity in Organizations* (pp. 295–327). San Francisco: Jossey-Bass.

Harris, C. L. & Steed, J. (2001). *Team-based Organizations: Crafting the Organizational Context for Team Success*. Colloquium presented at the Center for Creative Leadership, Colorado Springs, Colorado.

Hofstede, G. & Neuijen, B. (1990). Measuring organizational cultures: a qualitative and quantitative study across twenty cases. *Administrative Science Quarterly*, 35(2), 286–317.

Jones, S. & Moffett, R. G., III (1999). Measurement and feedback systems for teams. In E. Sundstrom (ed.), *Supporting Work Team Effectiveness: Best Management Practices for Fostering High Performance*. San Francisco: Jossey-Bass.

Kennedy, F. (2002). Managing a team-based organization: a proposed strategic model. In M. M. Beyerlein, D. A. Johnson, & S. T. Beyerlein (eds), *Team-based Organizing*. Oxford: JAI/Elsevier.

Klein, J. A. (1993). Maintaining expertise in multi-skilled teams. In M. Beyerlein, D. Johnson, & S. Beyerlein (eds), *Advances in Interdisciplinary Studies of Work Teams*, Vol. 1, *Theories of Self-Managing Work Teams* (pp. 145–166). Greenwich, Conn.: JAI Press.

Lawler, E. E., III (1990). The new plant revolution revisited. *Organizational Dynamics*, 19(2), 5–14.

Maslach, C. & Leiter, M. P. (1997). *The Truth about Burnout: How Organizations Cause Personal Stress and What to Do about It*. San Francisco: Jossey-Bass.

Mathews, L. L. (1996). Top management groups: the relationships among member characteristics, group processes, business environments, and organizational performance. Dissertation, University of North Texas, Denton.

Mohrman, S. A., Cohen, S. G., & Mohrman, A. M. Jr (1995). *Designing Team-based Organizations: New Forms for Knowledge Work*. San Francisco: Jossey-Bass.

Mohrman, S. A. & Mohrman, A. M. Jr (1997). *Designing and Leading Team-based Organizations: A Workbook for Organizational Self-design*. San Francisco: Jossey-Bass.

Mohrman, S. A. & Tenkasi, R. (1997). Patterns of cross-functional work: behaviors and benefits. Paper presented at the University of North Texas Symposium on Work Teams, Dallas, Tex.

Mohrman, S. A., Tenkasi, R. V., & Mohrman, A. M. Jr (2000). Learning and knowledge management in team-based new product development organizations. In M. M. Beyerlein, D. A. Johnson, & S. T. Beyerlein (eds), *Advances in Interdisciplinary Studies of Work Teams* (Vol. 5, pp. 63–88). Amsterdam: JAI Press.

Moran, L. (1996). *Keeping Teams on Track: What to Do When the Going Gets Rough*. New York: McGraw-Hill.

Ott, S. J. (1989). *The Organizational Culture Perspective*. Florence, Ky: Brooks/Cole.

Pinchot, G., III (1985). *Intrapreneuring: Why You Don't Have to Leave the Corporation to Become an Entrepreneur*. New York: Harper & Row.

Ray, D. & Bronstein, H. (1995). *Teaming up: Making the Transition to a Self-directed, Team-based Organization*. New York: McGraw-Hill.

Rose, E., Gilmore, S., & Odom, R. D. (1998). Organizational transformation for effectively implementing a team-based culture. In S. D. Jones & M. M. Beyerlein (eds), *Developing High-performance Work Teams*. Alexandria, Va: ASTD Publications.

Saavedra, R., Earley, R. C., & van Dyne, L. (1993). Complex interdependence in task-performing groups. *Journal of Applied Psychology*, 78: 61–72.

Shonk, J. H. (1997). *Team-based Organizations: Developing a Successful Team Environment*. Homewood, Ill.: Business One Irwin.

Smolek, J., Hoffman, D., & Moran, L. (1999). Organizing teams for success. In E. Sundstrom (ed.), *Supporting Work Team Effectiveness: Best Management Practices for Fostering High Performance*. San Francisco: Jossey-Bass.

Sundstrom, E. & associates (1999). *Supporting Work Team Effectiveness: Best Management Practices for Fostering High Performance*. San Francisco: Jossey-Bass.

Zell, D. (1997). *Changing by Design: Organizational Innovation at Hewlett-Packard*. Ithaca, NY: ILR Press.

8

TEAM DECISION MAKING IN ORGANIZATIONS

Mary Ann Glynn and Pamela S. Barr

Today, organizations operate in fast-paced, pluralistic, complex, and uncertain environments; to keep pace, they increasingly use teams to make decisions (Hollenbeck et al., 1995). There is good reason for doing so. A robust tradition of research offers ample testimony to the fact that, on average, teams tend to make better quality and more accurate decisions than individuals (e.g. Gruenfeld et al., 1996; Hollenbeck et al., 1995, 1998). As a set of individuals, teams have the potential for incorporating more breadth and depth of expertise, defined as the "allocation of critical information (cues) about the decision to individuals in the team and knowledge of how that information should be used to reach decisions" (Hollenbeck et al., 1995, p. 295).

And yet, in spite of the consensus about the effectiveness of team decision making, there is still vigorous debate as to the processes whereby this happens. Although researchers have demonstrated the link between decision-making outcomes and a host of team variables, they have tended to focus on more visible and measurable features of teams including, but not limited to, variables such as hierarchical relationships, demography (i.e. heterogeneity/homogeneity of membership) (e.g. Gruenfeld et al., 1996; Hambrick & Mason, 1984; Hollenbeck et al., 1995, 1998), and/or the mapping of interaction patterns of communications and information processing (e.g. Bunderson & Sutcliffe, 2002). The very concept of "team as decision maker" is left unspecified. Although there has been debate as to whether it is appropriately modeled as a latent construct or an interpretive metaphor (Klimoski & Mohammed, 1994), the emerging literature on supraindividual cognition, and the plethora of terms such as "collective mind" (Fiol, 1994; Weick & Roberts, 1993), "organizational mind" (Sandelands & Stablein, 1987), and "group mind" (Wegner, 1987), seem to suggest a resolution: team cognition underlies decision making in organizations. We take this as our starting point in this chapter.

Our goal is to add to the conversation on how teams cognate in the process of organizational decision making. A cognitive perspective on business decision making focuses on problem framing, information processing, and issue interpretation; essentially, it involves "sensemaking" (Weick, 1995) at the team level, an implicitly higher level of abstraction than that of the individual level of analysis. As a result, our inquiry begins with a consideration of defining both the appropriate level of analysis and the appropriate mechanisms of transfer, from the micro-level of individual cognition to the more macro-level of team cognition. We accept the received wisdom that, on average, teams tend to make better decisions than individuals; our focus is on the role of "team cognition" or "team mental model" (Klimoski & Mohammed, 1994) in linking processes and outcomes of decision making in organizations. We conclude with implications for future theorizing and research.

This chapter is organized as follows. Initially, we discuss multilevel models of teams as decision-making entities. Next, we apply these models to an examination of team decision making within a particularly critical work context, that of strategic decision making; more specifically, we focus on how top management teams make decisions. In this context, we examine processes and outcomes in team decision making. Finally, we end with ideas on a future agenda for theory and practice on team decision making.

CONCEPTUALIZING TEAMS AS DECISION-MAKING ENTITIES: A MULTILEVEL PERSPECTIVE

An inquiry into team decision making necessarily begins with a model of teams as decision makers. We adopt the lucid definition offered by March (1994, p. 104): "A team is a theoretical construct, a collection of individuals with problems of uncertainty but without conflict of interest or identities." To explicate how teams make decisions, Klimoski and Mohamed (1994, p. 403) observe that "group mind"-like constructs, or, in their terminology, "team mental models," have been advanced to explain variance in team decision making in organizations and, in particular, strategic decision making.

A cognitive approach to team decision making focuses on sensemaking (Weick, 1995), a process whereby individual team members pose a question to themselves along the lines of "What is it that is going on here?" (Goffman, 1974). The answer determines the nature of decision making, the problem(s) to be addressed, the mode of engagement, and the generation of solution(s). Making sense of a dilemma, decision, or situation permits the team to act in some rational manner; thus, meaning or sensemaking is a primary driver of team decisions. The meanings attached to decisions or situations have been variously labeled as frames (Bateson, 1972; Goffman, 1974), enactments (Weick, 1979), schema (Walsh, 1995), or interpretations (Fiol, 1994). At their core, these various terms used to describe cognition involve an understanding of causal maps (antecedents and effects), as well as the stimuli, actions, and consequences that attend decisions (Barr, Stimpert, & Huff, 1992). As Klimoski and Mohamed (1994) note, extending cognition to the team (or collective) level invites a consideration of how micro-level individual constructs such as schema, script, perceptual frame, or mental model can usefully and veridically apply to the macro-level of the team as a decision-making unit.

Although mechanisms for relating individual and team level cognition in decision making are recognized, models of how these transference processes operate are relatively scarce. As in Glynn (1996), we can identify three sets of mechanisms for articulating this micro–macro linkage between a team and its individual members:

1. *Aggregation effects*, whereby team members' individual cognitions aggregate to become those of the team;

2. *Cross-level effects*, whereby individual members' cognitions are shared through team interactions, transformed, codified, and understood (by members) to become those of the team;
3. *Distributed effects*, whereby team decision-making cognition exists in the patterned thoughts and actions in which team members interact and engage with each other but such cognitions are not the sole province of individuals.

Each of these mechanisms of team cognition is built upon a different set of theoretical premises; the models are summarized in Table 8.1.

Aggregation Model of Team Cognition

Existing models of team decision making tend to be predicated largely upon an aggregate movement between levels of analysis (Glynn, 1996; Rousseau, 1985): decision making at the collective level is modeled as the summation or accumulation of individual proclivities for action. In other words, theoretical models tend to depict decision making as originating within individuals, accumulating within dyads or subgroups, and then, depending upon the size of its membership, aggregating to the team level. Measures of central tendency (frequency counts; means) and dispersion (deviations; heterogeneity) operationalize aggregation models. Modeled as an aggregation, team cognition is simply the accumulation of its members' individual mental models. Although an aggregation model affords a rather straightforward assessment of team cognition, it does not capture the multiplicity or diversity of its members' individual models, nor does it recognize how a team mental model may exist apart from those of its members.

A good illustration of this model is advanced by Hollenbeck et al. (1995) in their "multilevel theory of team decision making." According to these authors, the accuracy of team-level decision making is a function of decision-making variables at lower levels of analysis; they summarize:

> Briefly... team decision-making accuracy is determined by constructs that occur at one of four levels: team, dyad, individual, and decision. The theory identifies the most critical variable at each of the three lower levels and *then aggregates these variables at the team level* (Hollenbeck et al., 1998, p. 270, emphasis added).

In this model, the core constructs of decision informity, individual validity, and dyadic sensitivity are modeled at both more micro-levels—the decision, the individual, and the dyadic pair, respectively—as well as that of the team as a whole. Subsequent empirical research has tended to validate this model, demonstrating that these core constructs, at both lower and higher (team) levels of analysis, function to significantly affect team-level decision-making accuracy (Hollenbeck et al., 1998).

An aggregation model is also evident in Bougon, Weick, and Binkhorst's (1977) model of the collective map of orchestral members operationalized as the "simple average of the individuals' maps" (Walsh, Henderson, & Deighton, 1988, p. 195). These and other studies point to the appropriateness of a multilevel approach; an aggregation model of team decision making is perhaps the most parsimonious type in this category. Essentially it emphasizes the composition or structure of a team, as reflected in the patterning of individual attributes, over the processes that attend decision making, such as communication and negotiation.

Table 8.1 Multilevel models of team cognition

Type of model	Key theoretical assumptions	Exemplars	Advantages of model	Limitations of model
Aggregation Model	Mental models of individual team members aggregate to the team level. Team mental model is defined in terms of the accumulation (or summary or average) of its membership. Team cognition is a function of individual capabilities and differences	"Multilevel theory of team decision making" (Hollenbeck et al., 1995, 1998); "Collective Map" (Bougon, Weick, & Binkhorst, 1977)	Theoretically parsimonious; relatively easy to operationalize and measure. Changes in team cognition to enable decision making are achieved through personnel changes and flows	Limited application and generalizability. Theoretically, a team is constrained to be no better than the sum (aggregation) of its component parts (individual members); content of mental models is emphasized over other features, e.g. form, organization, complexity
Cross-level model	Team members' mental models are transferred and encoded to become those of the team. Teams with better process dynamics (interaction patterns; communications, etc.) will tend to develop better models	"Negotiated Beliefs" (Walsh, Henderson, & Deighton, 1988)	Captures the role of team dynamics and mechanisms of information exchange	More difficult and complex to measure; requires a process perspective and methodology. Interventions to enable more effective decision making focus on team dynamics and processes of communications, interaction, socialization, diffusion, institutionalization, and politics, etc.
Distributed model	Team mental model is embedded in the team's systems, routines, norms, symbols, culture, and language. Mental models are more developed to the extent that they encode information that is rich, complex, and isomorphic with needs	"Collective Mind" (Weick & Roberts, 1993; Crowston & Kammerer, 1998; Brockman & Anthony, 1998)	Most veridical assessment of collective cognition at the team level. Team cognition can supersede that of its individual members, either alone or in the aggregate. Decision-making processes shape, and are shaped by, the team's transactive memory (Wegner, 1987)	Least transparent; can be difficult to measure and observe because of the need to capture cognitive and behavioral interaction patterns of team

Although an aggregation model has the advantages of theoretical clarity and operational ease (i.e. assessing central tendencies and variations across individuals), it, like any model, has inherent limitations. Critically, it does not take into account the influences of team dynamics, powerful actors, or environmental context, in crafting how individual cognitions aggregate to become a collective perspective; this issue is addressed more directly in both the cross-level and distributed models of team cognition.

Cross-level Model of Team Cognition

This approach focuses on the upward-oriented and downward-oriented transference between an individual's mental model and that of the team in a decision-making situation. The diffusion of ideas, knowledge, schema, and cognitive maps that enable the flow of decision-making resources is achieved through the conduct of team interactions; further, any shared or consensual mental models are codified and institutionalized in the collective memory of the team, memorialized in decision-making routines, rituals, habits, and practices to become a team-level cognitive construct. In turn, socialization, membership interactions, and team dynamics transfer team understandings and scripted decision-making styles to members, particularly new ones.

A cross-level approach to understanding team cognition focuses at the intersubjective level, capturing the criticality of group processes, interactions, and communications that harvest information from individual members. Team cognition benefits from a culture that permits and encourages diversity in thinking and decision-making styles as well as norms and practices of discussion to process a variety of perspectives. Such diversity in individual members' cognition may either converge to become a shared mental model for decision making or become negotiated through political processes of influence. This is the case for the model of team cognition as a "negotiated belief structure" (Walsh & Fahey, 1986; Walsh, Henderson, & Deighton, 1988). To summarize the approach embedded in a cross-level perspective on team cognition, Walsh (1995, p. 291) offers the following assessment:

> A number of writers examined the work on individual knowledge structures and concluded that when a group of individuals is brought together, each with their own knowledge structure, about a particular information environment, some kind of emergent collective knowledge structure is likely to exist.... The key challenge in considering knowledge structures at the supra-individual level of analysis is to account for the role of social processes in the acquisition, retention and retrieval of information.

Walsh (1995, p. 291) notes that this model has been labeled with a variety of terms, including collective cognitive map (Axelrod, 1976), team mental model (Klimoski & Mohammed, 1994), collective cognition (Langfield-Smith, 1992), hypermap (Bryant, 1983), intersubjectivity (Eden et al., 1981), dominant logic (Prahalad & Bettis, 1986), or collectively produced frames of reference (Bettenhausen & Murnighan, 1985). The contrast between this cross-level model and the aggregation model (discussed previously) is noted by Walsh, Henderson, and Deighton (1988, p. 207), as follows:

> Decisions reflect the schemata employed in the decision making process. It is not just a simple aggregation of schemata, however, but the selectively employed schemata which structure decision environments that are important.... We ... need to investigate how political processes

interact with a group's schematic endowment to affect performance in discrete stages of decision making (i.e. problem definition, alternative generation, alternative evaluation, decision choice, and decision implementation).

A cross-level model thus overcomes one of the restrictions of the aggregation model, by explicitly incorporating the role of team dynamics in forging team cognition. Team interaction, communication, socialization, politics, and other dynamic processes work to shape individuals' cognitions into those of the team that are then applied to making decisions. However, like the aggregation model, a cross-level model still emphasizes the individual level of analysis; a perspective that focuses entirely on the team level, apart from the individual level of analysis, is found in the distributed model of team cognition, to which we now turn.

Distributed Model of Team Cognition

Rather than the transference of mental models that is the focus of a cross-level approach, a distributed model focuses on how team cognition emerges from, and resides in, the patterned interactions of its members (Brown & Dugoid, 1991; Lave & Wenger, 1991) apart from the individual decision makers. The emphasis here is on the team itself and the extent to which it embeds specific models of decision making for the team. The team's cognition exists independent of individual members and is, instead, located or distributed within the structural (roles) and symbolic (language) properties of the team; the focus is on the patterning and dynamism of team interactions and behaviors rather than on individual members' minds (Weick & Roberts, 1993). Cognition is thus "situated" within the team and its decision-making context (Brown & Dugoid, 1991; Lave & Wenger, 1991). This model focuses on how team cognition consists of a set of intersubjectively shared set of meanings that is sustained through the interactions of team members.

A distributed model of team cognition in decision making centers on the creation of meaning, the social construction of reality, and the development of culture, symbolism, and social patterns that exist at a level of abstraction higher than that of individual team members (e.g. Walsh & Ungson, 1991; Weick, 1979). The team consists of interlocked, formalized, and routinized modes of thinking and action that drive decision making. Thus, a team may know more—and make better decisions—than its individual members, either individually or collectively.

> A key implication of distributed cognition is that a group performing a cognitive task may have cognitive properties that differ from the cognitive properties of any individual in the group.... The cognitive properties of the groups are produced by interactions internal to individuals and external to individuals (Thompson & Fine, 1999).

A distributed model of team cognition focuses on the embodiment of knowledge, information, and expertise within the team and, in turn, its role in decision making. A collective mind can emerge from the collective interaction of team members (Weick & Roberts, 1993). Through their interactions, undertaken to develop an understanding and framing of the focal decision, team members develop a more universal or consensual (Fiol, 1994) sense of what makes sense.

Given its location at the team level, preserving what the team knows is key; thus, a transactive memory is critical and "...not traceable to any of the individuals alone, nor can it be found somewhere 'between' individuals. Rather, it is a property of the group" (Wegner, 1987, p. 191). Transactive memory is defined as "a group memory system that details the expertise possessed by group members along with an awareness of who knows what within the group" (Rulke & Rau, 2000, p. 373). Of particular relevance for team decision making, transactive memory systems "should be particularly well developed in intimate relationships in which people share responsibilities, engage in many conversations about different topics, and make joint decisions" (Hollingshead, 1998, p. 659).

Summary: Models of Team Cognition

In the preceding sections, we have outlined three different approaches to modeling team cognition: as the aggregate of individual members' cognition, as the cross-level interaction between individual and collective cognition, and finally as a distributed property of the team as a whole. These three different models have different implications for the way we conceptualize team decision making in organizations.

In our consideration of these variations on team cognition, we chose to focus on strategic decision-making teams, typically those incorporating the organization's top management team (TMT). Our reasons for doing so are multiple. First, these teams make decisions that have not only consequences for the teams themselves but also for the organization. By focusing on organizational outcomes, we heed Klimoski and Mohammed's (1994, p. 428) admonition that, "In the area of strategic decision making, team mental models most likely have their greatest impact, not on the decision phase, but the implementation phase." Thus, examining strategic decision-making teams allowed our central construct of team mental models the greatest transparency. Second, TMTs are the primary focus of much of the organizational literature on management teams. Bunderson and Sutcliffe (2002), in their review of the literature, identified 15 studies published since 1989 that focused on the composition and outcomes of decision making in TMTs. Finally, strategic decision-making teams satisfy a number of the environmental conditions that make the development of collective mind operative and beneficial (Weick & Roberts, 1993): the need for high reliability decisions, nonroutine decisions, and interactive complexity in decision making. We turn now to an examination of how different models of team cognition (aggregation; cross-level; distributed) affect how we research strategic decision making in TMTs.

TEAM COGNITION IN CONTEXT: STRATEGIC DECISION MAKING

When we think of organizational teamwork, one of the most visible teams in organizations is the TMT, which is typically responsible for strategic decision making in the firm. Many studies in the organizational literature seek to investigate how the characteristics and processes of the strategic decision-making team affect the actions and outcomes of the organization (see Bunderson & Sutcliffe (2002) for an overview of the relevant literature). Perhaps strategic decisions have attracted such attention because of their inherent intrigue, dealing as they do with complexity, uncertainty, and consequence in a changing organizational environment. We acknowledge, however, that team decision making in organizations is obviously not limited to organizational elites; often project managers or work teams have decision-making authority to conceive and implement organizational actions. However, for the sake of focus and parsimony, we limit our scope to the TMT level.

We find that March's (1994) two key approaches to decision making reflect the logic that underlies the three conceptualizations of team cognition discussed in the prior section of this chapter. In March's (1994, p. 103) portrayal, individual decision makers can be intendedly rational actors who search for preferred alternatives in a world of limited knowledge and use the logic of consequence. Moving to decision making at the level of the team, a focus on preferred outcomes as a primary driver of the decision-making process suggests that team decisions are an outcome of interactive patterns of communication whereby the team negotiates and enacts a team-level understanding of preferred outcome, and how to reach that outcome. These patterns of communication, negotiation, and enactment are the very processes that are associated with cross-level and distributed models of team cognition.

March (1994, p. 103) also depicts how individual decision makers can be "rule followers," matching appropriate behavior to situations in an attempt to fulfill their identities; in this case, decision making is guided by the logic of appropriateness. Again, moving to team-level decision making, this correspondence between identity and decision rules depends less on team-level processes that craft a shared preference for an outcome (as in an "intendedly rational" approach), and instead, focuses on those individual features that lend identity characteristics to the teams, such as the homogeneity or heterogeneity of compositional characteristics (e.g. functional background, age, gender, tenure). The assumed tight coupling between decision makers' identity and their decision preferences shifts attention toward a team's identity, operationalized in terms of central tendency or dispersion of member characteristics, an approach that reflects an aggregation model of team cognition.

Thus, we observe that both types of decision makers March (1994) identifies—intendedly rational actors and rule-bound role players—reflect cognitive guidance systems (or forms of logic) that embed particular models of decision making. In the following discussion, we shall see how assumptions about these forms of logic in team mental models seem to imply a particular cognitively based logical system of team decision making.

Equipped with March's (1994) insights, we approach the literature to highlight, in depth, a few significant pieces that speak to the interface between team cognition and strategic decision making. Our reading of the critical works led us to observe that, over time, there seemed to be an evolution in theorizing from a focus on team composition and the aggregation of individual TMT member characteristics, to a focus on higher levels of abstraction, embedding more complex processes of team dynamics, information processing, and communication/interaction patterns. It is this historical trajectory, with its movement from more simple to more complex, to a shift in focal level of analysis from individual to collective, that we seek to map. We focus on a few influential pieces to distill significant themes that incorporate different models of team cognition in the study of TMT strategic decision making. We organize our discussion by the three models identified earlier—aggregation, cross-level, and distributed.

TMT Strategic Decision Making as an Aggregation of Member Attributes

In examining the extant literature, it quickly became apparent that much of the debate in this stream of research turns on the advantages and disadvantages of diversity in the composition of the TMT. Investigations into the conceptualization and measurability of a variety of team characteristics have propelled advances in the arena of strategic decision making and mapped their effects on team processes and organizational outcomes.

An inquiry into TMT strategic decision making begins with the influential work of Hambrick and Mason (1984) who theorized that the composition of the executive team would affect the performance outcomes of the organization. Counterposing their ideas against views of strategic processes as "flows of information and decisions, detached from the people involved" (p. 193), they directed attention away from institutional procedures and, instead, toward individual decision makers. Their model construed a profile of the TMT in terms of the composition of the characteristics of team members. The authors defended their approach by reasoning that "If strategic choices have a large behavioral component, then to some extent they reflect the idiosyncrasies of decision makers" (p. 195). To Hambrick and Mason (1984), understanding not only the chief executive but the "entire team increases the potential strength of the theory to predict, because the chief executive shares tasks and, to some extent, power with other team members" (p. 196).

Hambrick and Mason (1984) focused on the role of TMT demographics as a proxy for cognitive attributes. In particular, they emphasized how diversity in team members' age, education, socio-economic roots, functional background, financial position, organizational and team tenure influenced outcomes. The basic model is one that mirror's Ashby's (1952) notion of requisite variety in that the complexity of the decision-making environment should be mirrored in the complexity of the decision-making team. Team processes were not theorized directly, but rather presumed as a latent dynamic that glosses over members' diversity so as to yield rational and coherent decisions. The one team-level variable they consider is heterogeneity, or the amount of dispersion of TMT demography. Building on prior group research, they proposed, for instance, "Homogeneous top management teams will make strategic decisions more quickly than will heterogeneous ones" (p. 203).

Writing at a time when "[n]o such research centering on characteristics of entire top management teams is known to the authors" (p. 196), Hambrick and Mason (1984) articulated a perspective that is essentially an aggregation model. In their conceptualization of the link between team characteristics and strategic outcomes, they propose that a team's mental model is a reflection of the central tendencies of its individual members, assessed through counts or averages of the numbers of executives in one demographic category or another. Focusing on the upper echelon characteristic of functional background, for instance, they write:

> ...assume that two firms each have chief executives whose primary functional backgrounds are in production. In Firm A, three of four other key executives also rose primarily through production-oriented careers, even though they now are serving in nonproduction or generalist roles. In Firm B, the mix of executive backgrounds is more balanced and typical—one from production, one from sales, one from engineering, and one from accounting. Knowledge about the *central tendencies* of the entire top management team improves one's confidence in any predictions about the two firms' strategies. Moreover, the study of an entire team has the added advantage of allowing inquiry into dispersion characteristics, such as homogeneity and balance (Hambrick & Mason, 1984, pp. 196–197, emphasis added).

The focus on decision makers' attributes is predicated upon what March (1994) calls "rule-following," whereby individuals follow rules consistent with their salient identities. Identities are social constructions that relate the decision maker to organizational rules, structures, norms, and institutionalized practices that control decision making by indicating appropriateness. As March explains:

> The logic of appropriateness is tied to the concept of identity. An identity is a conception of self organized into rules for matching action to situations.... When an executive is enjoined to "act like a decision maker," he or she is encouraged to apply a logic of appropriateness to a conception of identity.
>
> Individuals describe themselves in terms of their occupational, group, familial, ethnic, national, and religious identities. Identities are both constructed by individuals and imposed upon them (March, 1994, pp. 62–63).

The logic of appropriateness is operative in an aggregation model of TMT strategic decision making. Doing what is expected of a "good accountant" is what is captured and highlighted in those studies examining the functional composition and diversity of the TMT. The conundrum of TMT functional diversity—that breadth of expertise and perspective is purchased at the expense of team consensus and expedient communication—is consistent with the notion that individuals act in ways that are normatively appropriate with their occupational identity, but in ways that may not be appropriate (or even comprehensible) to those bound by the rules of other occupational identities. Team members with different functional backgrounds thus may claim different logics as the basis for appropriate, credible, and legitimate decisions.

A TMT strategic decision-making model that is based on an aggregation model of team cognition thus capitalizes on both its strengths (particularly in terms of diversity of knowledge, perspective, and experience) and weaknesses, as team members literally occupy different "thought worlds" (Dougherty, 1992) whereby sensemaking (Weick, 1995) is an individual and not a collective (team) level process. With newer methodologies that tap into cognition more directly (than proxy measures such as demographics) and alternative models that incorporate team dynamics more directly (implicating a cross-level approach to team decision making), the field has begun to shift in its approach to modeling TMT strategic decision making so as to allow for the interaction between individual cognition and team processes of dialog, influence, and politics. Keck (1997, p. 144) observes:

> Evidence is emerging (notably Smith et al., 1994) that the relationship among team structure, team process, and firm performance may be much more complex than originally modeled or assumed in previous work. According to Smith et al. (1994), there are three competing models of the effects of team structure on firm performance: 1) the demography model based on the direct effect of team structure on performance, 2) the process model based on the direct effect of team process above and beyond the direct effect of team structure, and 3) the model of team processes as intervening variables.

The influence of Hambrick and Mason's (1984) "general model" (p. 203) cannot be overstated; their ideas set into motion a generation of researchers attempting to map upper echelon characteristics to firms' strategic outcomes that persists to the present. However, a different model of team cognition was emerging.

TMT Strategic Decision Making from a Cross-level Perspective

Partly to overcome some of the conceptual and methodological limitations embedded in an aggregation model of team cognition in strategic decision making, researchers began to focus on explicating the implicit links in the aggregation model, teasing out the implicit processes relating individuals' demographic attributes to decision and organizational outcomes. Kilduff, Angelmar, and Mehra (2000, p. 32) offer this insight:

> According to Hambrick et al. (1996, page 66), the heterogeneous team has a broad potential behavioral repertoire and is able to "conceive and launch actions on many fronts." From this perspective, demographic heterogeneity may well complement rather than determine cognitive heterogeneity... teams heterogeneous on demographic variables may be better able to build on the diverse experience base of the team to validate diverse cognitions, and thus take advantage of innovative suggestions.

The links implicit in the Hambrick and Mason (1984) model, connecting team demography, team process, and firm performance outcomes, were studied more explicitly by Smith et al. (1994) in their widely cited work. In their research, they examined 53 high-technology firms to investigate the roles of team demography and team process in explicating performance (as noted in the Keck (1997) quote above). They empirically examined three models. The first, a demography model, relating TMT member attributes directly to firm performance, is consistent with the aggregation model of Hambrick and Mason (1984), outlined above. The second, a process model, integrating ideas from social psychology, shifts from individual characteristics (of the demography model) to team interactive dynamics, particularly social integration and communication, in terms of both their formality and frequency. The explanatory power of these process factors is examined for their effects above and beyond those of demography. Finally, Smith and his colleagues (1994) investigate a third model, which posits that team process is a mediator between team demography and firm performance. They summarize their results as follows:

> Overall, there was partial support for the intervening model, in which process is a mediator of the relationship between demography and performance, and the process model, in which demography and process variables each affect performance separately. Little support was found for the argument underlying the demography model, in which demography rather than process affects performance (Smith et al., 1994, p. 431).

Their findings attest to the feasibility of a cross-level model of team cognition in strategic decision making; their results speak to the role of team processes in relating the attributes of team members to organizational performance. Although Smith and colleagues (1994) found significant main effects for the demographic variables of tenure, experience, education, and background, an aggregation framework modeling team characteristics in terms of centrality or dispersion of these individual factors underspecifies the relationship between team decision making and organizational performance. In other words, what individual team members bring to the table, by way of personal experience and perspective, as represented in demographic variables, does matter; however, how these individual proclivities are processed within the team adds to their effects on outcomes. Thus, by demonstrating the contribution of team process, above and beyond demography, Smith and colleagues (1994) offer evidence in support of a cross-level model of team decision making.

Given their demonstration that process affects performance, the question then becomes: why? In an extension of this work, Knight et al. (1999) scrutinize more closely the link between team demography and team process. Using data from 76 high-technology firms in the United States and Ireland, Knight and colleagues found that TMT diversity in demography (function, age, education, employment tenure) exerted significant main effects on strategic consensus, but that "the overall fit of the model was not strong. Adding two intervening group process variables, interpersonal conflict and agreement-seeking, to the model greatly improved the overall relationship with strategic consensus" (Knight et al., 1999, p. 445). Thus, beyond the earlier effects found for organizational performance, these researchers demonstrated that group processes similarly played a significant role in influencing team demography to affect team cognition. Further, Simons, Pelled, and Smith (1999, p. 670) support this reasoning in their study. They report: "Our data revealed that debate increased the tendency for diversity to enhance TMT performance. Further, debate—by diversity—interactive effects were strongest for more job-related forms of diversity. Decision comprehensiveness partially mediated these interactive effects." Finally, we note that Ken A. Smith and Ken G. Smith, along with their colleagues, have extensively investigated the effects of demography and process; across several studies, their results support a significant role for team processes in team decision making, thus indicating that a cross-level model that interacts individual cognition with team dynamics is a viable one.

These studies of TMT strategic decision making that incorporate process variables imply that decision makers may not always follow blindly the normative rules associated with their identities. This may be because individual identities are not salient, a notion that has not been tested yet in this literature. Alternatively, however, they do suggest that process variables, particularly those that focus on forging agreement and information sharing among diverse team members, may function either by creating a "team" identity, with a logic of appropriateness that supersedes those of individual members, or by invoking a logic of consequence that focuses not so much on shared identity as shared goal. Both imply different types of decision makers—rational actor versus role actor (March, 1994)—and a different sense of what is shared or held in common by the team, perhaps "partaking in an agreement," with its implications of team consensus or acceptance (Thompson & Fine, 1999). Thus, cross-level models have been effective in illuminating how different assumptions about the bases of decision making—identity and/or rationality—may independently or jointly be embedded in a particular theoretical or empirical approach. Moreover, the cross-level model hints at the emergence of the next perspective in the evolution of team decision making: that at the collective or distributed level.

TMT Strategic Decision Making as Collective Mind

In some ways, this model of team decision making seems to circle back to the original observation that prompted Hambrick and Mason's (1984) work: the criticality of institutionalized flows, patterns, and procedures in the distribution of information and in decision making. It was the lack of agency in this perspective that motivated them to theorize about the role of individual TMT characteristics. Two decades ago, the role of cognition and individual agency in organizing and directing these flows was notably absent; this is no longer so. Current perspectives on TMT decision making, perhaps because of their interest in promoting agency, have minimized the impact of "institutionalized flows, patterns, and procedures." The notion of "collective mind" in team decision making marries the agency, represented by individual level cognition, to the patterns and practices that define "team" and influence decision making by the team.

Weick and Roberts (1993, p. 360) define what is meant by the construct of "collective mind":

> The word "collective," unlike the words "group" or "organization," refers to individuals who act as if they are a group. People who act as if they are a group interrelate their actions with more or less care, and focusing on the way this interrelating is done reveals collective mental processes that differ in their degree of development. Our focus is at once on the individual and the collective, since only individuals can contribute to a collective mind, but a collective mind is distinct from an individual mind because it inheres in the pattern of interrelated activities among many people.

They contend that the "[c]ollective mind is manifest when individuals construct mutually shared fields" (Weick & Roberts, 1993, p. 365). Collective mind springs from individuals' thoughtful contributions, enriched representation of a collective to which their actions connect them, and interrelate and subordinate them; conversely, limitations or deficiencies in individuals' representations of the process and their subordination to team goals can limit the value of their contributions to collective mind (Crowston & Kammerer, 1998, p. 204).

This notion of team cognition is still emergent and has not yet been applied empirically to decision making in TMTs. However, there is much to recommend it. First, a number of the environmental conditions that make the development of collective mind operative and beneficial (Weick & Roberts, 1993) characterize the nature of strategic decision making; as indicated earlier, these include a need for high reliability (and error-free) decisions; nonroutine decisions; and interactive complexity in decision making. Second, the types of interpersonal interactions that reflect the application of a model of collective mind to team decision making—representation of different areas of expertise or knowledge, subordination of personal goals in favor of the attainment of team goals, and heedful interrelating, i.e. the process of keying off other team members—are similar to what one would expect in TMT strategic decision making. Most TMTs are composed of top executives who represent the various functional and/or divisional activities of the firm; the expectation is that the decision outputs will represent what is good for the company and not solely what is in the best interest of individual team members.

Perhaps because it is somewhat antithetical to the American cultural identity of individuated, differentiate self—as well as stereotypes about TMTs as heroic, independent, and insubordinate decision makers—a collective mind model of TMT decision making is not as prevalent as the aggregation or cross-level models. However, the coemergence of new organizational forms that emphasize structures that are more flat, flexible, and networked and strategies that make use of intraorganizational as well as interorganizational networks and alliances to create competitive advantage has had the result of making organizations more interconnected and team-based. We believe that the notion of team cognition at this higher level of abstraction will find wider applicability, consistent with the observations of Brockman and Anthony (1998, p. 210):

> In the strategy context, a collective mind is particularly valuable in helping to surface tacit considerations. For instance, during strategy formulation, the heedful interrelating should help explicate tacit dimensions inherent in the strategic visioning process. During strategy formulation, more strategic alternatives should be identified and then be open for evaluation before becoming strategic objectives. Even for strategy implementation, interrelating may help surface previous experiences of the TMT members that can then be evaluated by the team as alternatives.

Modeling team cognition as collective mind in the process of TMT strategic decision making offers the potential of reconciling several dilemmas in the extant literature. First, it allows researchers to consider the problem of accounting for a persistent firm-level "dominant logic" (Prahalad & Bettis, 1986), even under conditions of TMT change and personnel flows. A view of team cognition as "collective mind" draws attention to how such logic may exist apart from individual members and remain relatively inert over time; thus, it becomes less dependent on the particular attributes of TMT members and more reliant on how such logic is distributed within the substrata of the TMT's institutionalized structural, cultural, and political systems. Second, a collective mind perspective shifts researcher focus away from mapping the functional/demographic diversity of TMT members (an aggregation approach) or the political processes of team influence (a cross-level approach) and toward a fuller integration of the role of team cognition in decision making. Collective mind acknowledges how a diverse set of individual views can contribute to, and be represented in, a team perspective; however, its notion of heedful interrelating offers a counterpoint to explanations that are mired in politics and influence peddling among TMT members. Thus, it allows for variations in TMT strategic decision making and effectiveness without resorting to theorizing about demographic aggregation or building models of upward and downward political and social influence. We offer some extensions on these ideas and how they may build an agenda for future work on team decision making in organizations in our conclusions.

CONCLUSIONS

In this chapter we have identified three models of team-based cognition (aggregation; cross-level; distributed), and related each to specific perspectives on TMT strategic decision making published in the literature. While all three models have their merit and offer explanatory power, we suggest that the notion of distributed cognition and the collective mind offers a promising direction for future research on team decision making. We base this conclusion on several observations.

First, in neither the aggregation nor the cross-level models is the development of the team as intertwined with the team cognition at the collective level. Because the collective mind is "located" in the team process of interrelating (Weick & Roberts, 1993), the development of mind is tightly coupled to the development of group. To create high reliability (or error-free) environments, both mind and team must be mature in their development: "both interrelating and intimacy develop jointly" (Weick & Roberts, 1993, p. 374).

The problems of decoupling the development of mind from collective can be seen in the off-diagonals of Table 8.2, which is derived from Weick and Roberts's (1993, pp. 374–376) discussions. To develop mind without team is to have a shallow and often fleeting pattern of heedful, appropriate, and intelligent team interrelating; its effectiveness may be limited to those types of teams that quickly develop and evaporate, such as ad hoc project teams that assemble to produce films or television shows (e.g. Faulkner & Anderson, 1987; Peters, 1992). Conversely, to develop the collective (team) without an intelligent, heedful mind is to invite dysfunctionality in organizational outcomes, including low reliability, incomprehensibility, and illegitimacy; failure and disaster may result. It is associated with the narrowness and inaccuracies consonant with groupthink in decision making (Janis, 1982).

As suggested in the language of the label itself—"collective mind"—collective and mind become an effective unit when both are well developed. Thus, it is through individuals' contributions, internal representations of the team, and subordination to the goals of the

Table 8.2 Collective mind and group development

	Developed collective mind	Undeveloped collective mind
Developed group	- Interrelating and intimacy develop jointly - Heedful interrelating - Contributions made thoughtfully - Representations are constructed carefully and appreciated by others - High reliability and error reduction Illustrations: Flight operations on aircraft carriers (Weick & Roberts, 1993); teams of software requirements analysts (Crowston & Kammerer, 1998); strategic planning teams (Brockmann & Anthony, 1998)	- Subordination to a system that is envisaged carelessly; overestimation of group's power, morality, and invulnerability - Contributions are made thoughtlessly; self-censorship of deviations, doubts, and counterarguments - Representations are careless; members maintain the false assumption that silence means consent - Heedless interrelating - Comprehension declines - Disasters result Illustrations: Groupthink (Janis, 1982); cults (Galanter, 1989); interactions at NASA prior to the *Challenger* disaster (Starbuck & Milliken, 1988); ethnocentric research groups (Weick, 1979)
Undeveloped group	- Nondisclosive intimacy stressing coordination of action over alignment of cognitions, mutual respect over agreement, trust over empathy, diversity over homogeneity, loose over tight coupling, and strategic communication over unrestricted candor (Eisenberg, 1990) - Shared values, openness, and disclosure are not fully developed - Heedful contributing (e.g. loose coupling, diversity, strategic communication) - Heedful representing (e.g. mutual respect, coordination of action) - Heedful subordination (e.g. trust) Illustrations: Ad hoc project teams (Faulkner & Anderson, 1987; Peters, 1992); temporary systems—in aircraft cockpits (Ginnett, 1990); jazz improvisation (Eisenberg, 1990); in response to crises (Rochlin, 1989) or in high-velocity environments (Eisenhardt, 1989)	

Note: Table is adopted from Weick and Roberts (1993, pp. 374–376).

team that mind is realized and individuals and team become indistinguishable. It is through this connection of heedful interrelating among members of the team that the collective mind becomes functional, transparent, and manifest. As Weick and Roberts (1993, p. 374) explain:

> For the collective mind, the connections that matter are those that link distributed activities, and the ways those connections are accomplished embody much of what we have come to mean by the word "mind." The ways people connect their activities make conduct mindful.

Understanding team cognition as collective mind affords a different perspective on decision-making models as well. The logic of consequence, embedded in the rational actor model of decision making (March, 1994), suggests that, to be effective, the collective mind must represent a commonly held goal to which individuals contribute intelligence and subordinate their personal goals. The logic of appropriateness, embedded in rule-following actors, similarly suggests that individual identities must be subordinated to the collective identity, and new rules of appropriateness need to emerge to guide decision making.

The implications for strategic decision making of a model of team cognition as collective mind depart from that of a cross-level model of team cognition in two important ways. First, a collective mind necessitates the *subordination* of both goals and identities of individuals; a cross-level model necessitates *integration* of individual goals and identities with those of the team. That is, in cross-level models, team processes such as information sharing, consensus seeking, team maintenance, and effective communication encourage the disclosure of individual proclivities and the discovery of overlapping (shared) goals and identities. By contrast, a collective model shifts attention from individual attributes to the distributed patterning of these across the team. The individual becomes less identifiable and the mind of the team exists apart from the individuals; individuals' role is not necessarily to share but to interrelate heedfully, thoughtfully, and carefully.

Our overview of team cognition, in the context of strategic decision making in organizations, offers new perspectives on how we can forge more cooperative behavior within organizations. In this chapter, we have considered three primary avenues: through the aggregation of individual attributes, through the processes of upward and/or downward influence, or through the processes of heedful interrelating that converge a collective mind from distributed cognition. We suggest that, whether building from team members' individual attributes, from interactive team processes that share information and forge agreement on goals and preferences, or from a collective thrust that relates individuals to relate intelligently, teams become effective as decision makers when a perspective on the collective emerges. Informed by these perspectives, future research will hopefully expand on these models and afford richer descriptions on the role of team cognition in decision making.

REFERENCES

Ashby, W. R. (1952). *A Design for a Brain*. New York: Wiley.
Axelrod, R. (1976). *The Structure of Decision*. Princeton: Princeton University Press.
Barr, P. S., Stimpert, J. L., & Huff, A. S. (1992). Cognitive change, strategic action, and organizational renewal. *Strategic Management Journal, 13*, 15–36.

Bateson, G. (1972). *Steps to an Ecology of Mind.* New York: Ballantine Books.
Bettenhausen, E. & Murnighan, J. K. (1985). The emergence of norms in competitive decision making groups. *Administrative Science Quarterly, 20,* 350–372.
Bougon, M., Weick, K., & Binkhorst, D. (1977). Cognition in organizations: an analysis of the Utrecht Jazz Orchestra. *Administrative Science Quarterly, 22,* 606–639.
Brockman, E. P. & Anthony, W. P. (1998). The influence of tacit knowledge and collective mind on strategic planning. *Journal of Managerial Issues, 10,* 204–222.
Brown, J. S. & Dugoid, P. (1991). Organizational learning and communities-of-practice: toward a unified view of working, learning, and innovation. *Organization Science, 2,* 40–57.
Bryant, J. (1983). Hypermaps: a representation of perceptions in conflicts. *Omega, 11,* 575–586.
Bunderson, J. S. & Sutcliffe, K. (2002). Comparing alternative conceptualizations of functional diversity in management teams: process and performance effects. *Academy of Management Journal, 45,* 875–893.
Crowston, K. & Kammerer, E. E. (1998). Coordination and collective mind in software requirements development. *IBM Systems Journal, 37,* 227–245.
Dougherty, D. (1992). Interpretive barriers to successful product innovation in large firms. *Organization Science, 3,* 179–202.
Eden, C., Jones, S., Sims, D., & Smithin, T. (1981). The intersubjectivity of issues of intersubjectivity. *Journal of Management Studies, 18,* 37–47.
Eisenberg, E. (1990). Jamming: transcendence through organizing. *Communication Research, 17,* 139–164.
Eisenhardt, K. M. (1989). Building theories from case study research. *Academy of Management Review, 14,* 532–550.
Faulkner, R. R. & Anderson, A. B. (1987). Short-term projects and emergent careers: evidence from Hollywood. *American Journal of Sociology, 92,* 879–909.
Fiol, C. M. (1994). Consensus, diversity, and learning in organizations. *Organization Science, 5,* 403–420.
Galanter, M. (1989). *Cults.* New York: Oxford University Press.
Ginnett, R. C. (1990). Airline cockpit crew. In J. Richard Hackman (ed.), *Groups That Work (and Those That Don't)* (pp. 427–448). San Francisco: Jossey-Bass.
Glynn, M. A. (1996). Innovative genius: a framework for relating individual and organizational intelligences. *Academy of Management Review, 4,* 1081–1111.
Goffman, E. (1974). *Frame Analysis.* Cambridge, Mass.: Harvard University Press.
Gruenfeld, D. H., Mannix, E. A., Williams, K. Y., & Neale, M. A. (1996). Group composition and decision making: how member familiarity and information distribution affect process and performance. *Organizational Behavior and Human Decision Processes, 67,* 1–15.
Hambrick, D. C. & Mason, P. A. (1984). Upper echelons: the organization as a reflection of its top managers. *Academy of Management Review, 9,* 193–206.
Hollenbeck, J. R., Ilgen, D. R., LePine, J. A., Colquitt, J. A., & Hedlund, J. (1998). Extending the multilevel theory of team decision making: effects of feedback and experience in hierarchical teams. *Academy of Management Journal, 41,* 269–282.
Hollenbeck, J. R., Ilgen, D. R., Sego, D., Hedlund, J., Major, D. A., & Phillips, J. (1995). The multilevel theory of team decision-making: decision performance in teams incorporating distributed expertise. *Journal of Applied Psychology, 80,* 292–316.
Hollingshead, A. B. (1998). Retrieval processes in transactive memory systems. *Journal of Personality and Social Psychology, 74,* 659–671.
Janis, I. (1982). *Groupthink* (2nd edn). Boston: Houghton-Mifflin.
Keck, S. (1997). Top management team structure: differential effects by environmental context. *Organization Science, 8,* 143–156.
Kilduff, M., Angelmar, R., & Mehra, A. (2000). Top management-team diversity and firm performance: examining the role of cognitions. *Organization Science, 11,* 21–34.
Klimoski, R. & Mohammed, S. (1994). Team mental model: construct or metaphor. *Journal of Management, 20,* 403–437.
Knight, D., Pearce, C. L., Smith, K. G., Olian, J. D., Sims, H. P., Smith, K. A., & Flood, P. (1999). Top management team diversity, group process, and strategic consensus. *Strategic Management Journal, 20,* 445–465.

Langfield-Smith, K. (1992). Exploring the need for a shared cognitive map. *Journal of Management Studies, 29*, 349–368.
Lave, J. & Wenger, E. (1991). *Situated Learning*. Cambridge, England: Cambridge University Press.
March, James G. (1994). *A Primer on Decision Making*. New York: Free Press.
Peters, T. (1992). *Liberation Management*. New York: Knopf.
Prahalad, C. K. & Bettis, R. A. (1986). The dominant logic: a new linkage between diversity and performance. *Strategic Management Journal, 7*, 485–501.
Rochlin, G. I. (1989). Organizational self-design is a crisis-avoidance strategy: US naval flight operations as a case study. *Industrial Crisis Quarterly, 3*, 159–176.
Rousseau, D. M. (1985). Issues of level in organizational research. In B. M. Staw & L. L. Cummings (eds), *Research in Organizational Behavior* (Vol. 17, pp. 1–37). Greenwich, Conn.: JAI Press.
Rulke, D. L. & Rau, D. (2000). Investigating the encoding process of transactive memory development in group training. *Group & Organization Management, 25*, 373–396.
Sandelands, L. E. & Stablein, R. (1987). The concept of organization mind. In S. Bacharach & N. DiTomaso (eds), *Research in the Sociology of Organizations* (Vol. 5, pp. 135–161). Greenwich, Conn.: JAI Press.
Simons, T., Pelled, L. H., & Smith, K. A. (1999). Making use of difference: diversity, debate, and decision comprehensiveness in top management teams. *Academy of Management Journal, 42*, 662–673.
Smith, K. G., Smith, K. A., Olian, J. D., Sims, H. P., O'Bannon, D. P., & Scully, J. A. (1994). Top management team demography and process: the role of social integration and communication. *Administrative Science Quarterly, 39*, 412–438.
Starbuck, W. H. & Milliken, F. J. (1988). Challenger: fine-tuning the odds until something breaks. *Journal of Management Studies, 25*, 319–340.
Thompson, L. & Fine, G. A. (1999). Socially shared cognition, affect, and behavior: a review and integration. *Personality & Social Psychology Review, 3*, 278–304.
Walsh, J. P. (1995). Managerial and organizational cognition: notes from a trip down memory lane. *Organization Science, 6*, 280–320.
Walsh, J. P. & Fahey, L. (1986). The role of negotiated belief structures in strategy making. *Journal of Management, 12*, 325–338.
Walsh, J. P., Henderson, C. M., & Deighton, J. (1988). Negotiated belief structures and decision performance: an empirical investigation. *Organizational Behavior and Human Decision Processes, 42*, 194–216.
Walsh, J. P. & Ungson, G. R. (1991). Organizational memory. *Academy of Management Review, 16*, 57–91.
Wegner, D. M. (1987). Transactive memory: a contemporary analysis of group mind. In B. Mullen & G. R. Goethals (eds), *Theories of Group Behavior* (pp. 185–208). New York: Springer.
Weick, K. E. (1979). *The Social Psychology of Organizing* (2nd edn). New York: McGraw-Hill, Inc.
Weick, K. E. (1995). *Sensemaking in Organizations*. Thousand Oaks, Calif.: Sage Publications.
Weick, K. E. & Roberts, K. (1993). Collective mind in organizations: heedful interrelating on flight decks. *Administrative Science Quarterly, 38*, 357.

9

SOCIAL LOAFING IN TEAMS

Christel G. Rutte

Teams are popular in organizations. Only a few decades ago, companies that introduced teams made news, but today organizations that do not use teams are newsworthy. About 80 per cent of US organizations employed teams in 1995 (Robbins, 2001). A recent European survey among 5000 companies revealed that 84 per cent employed teams (Benders et al., 1999). Teams are popular because they are believed to outperform individuals, in particular on tasks requiring multiple skills (Mohrman, Cohen, & Mohrman, 1995; Tjosvold, 1991). Group performance can be high when all team members are cooperative and exert a lot of effort. However, there is a true danger that team members are not cooperative and that working in teams may lead to motivation losses. This phenomenon is also known as social loafing (Latané, Williams, & Harkins, 1979).

Social loafing can be defined as the reduction in individual effort when individuals work on a collective task compared to when they work on an individual or co-action task (Karau & Williams, 1993). In a collective task the individual's own output is combined with the output of other group members. In an individual or co-action task the individual's own output is not combined with the output of others. Erez and Somech (1996) argue on the basis of a study using managers from Israeli kibbutzim and cities working on a simulated judgement task that social loafing is not the rule in groups but the exception. However, Karau and Williams (1993) conducted a meta-analysis of 78 published and unpublished studies and found a reliable social loafing effect across studies: when working on collective tasks people produce less effort than when working on co-action or individual tasks.

Most tasks of organizational teams are collective tasks and therefore social loafing may also occur in organizations. There is evidence that people who work in teams in organizations worry that social loafing in their team may occur. Kirkman et al. (1996) asked 486 employees working in teams, in this case autonomous work teams, what their three most important worries were when they started working as a team. Of 1200 comments that were made, 25 per cent were related to social loafing. Examples of worries were:

> I may have to work harder than others for the same wages. I may have to work harder than others with the same job. I may have to work with slower others and have to pull their weight on top of my own. Maybe other team members will not work as hard as I. Not everybody may

The Essentials *of Teamworking: International Perspectives.*
Edited by M. A. West, D. Tjosvold, and K. G. Smith. © 2005 John Wiley & Sons, Ltd.

do his fair share of the workload. I may become stuck with a bunch of losers who can't pull their own weight (p. 56).

These examples clearly indicate that group members do worry about the possibility that other group members may loaf. In Box 9.1 a case is presented illustrating that social loafing does occur in organizations and what form it may take (Rutte, 1990).

Box 9.1 Case study (Rutte, 1990)

The coding centre of a large Dutch bank employed 118 punch typists. The tasks of the typists were to punch and inspect cheques. The typists worked in pairs: one typist punched, the other inspected. In the morning the supervisor roughly divided the day's work over the pairs. The pairs occupied themselves with the allocated work until lunch. After lunch the supervisor collected all remaining work and redivided it over the pairs. As soon as a pair had finished that work it was free to go home. Thus, the typists functioned as a group in the morning and as individual pairs in the afternoon.

If the total typist group worked hard in the morning, there would have been little work left after lunch to redivide and all typists would have been able to go home early. However, what typically happened in the coding centre was that the typists put in little effort before lunch hoping that the others in the group would work hard. They did exert a lot of effort after lunch on the other hand to be able to go home as early as possible. Because all typists tended to socially loaf before lunch, a lot of work remained and all typists had a lot of work to do in the afternoon. The results were that all went home late, the atmosphere in the coding centre was quarrelsome, and there were frequent accusations of free-riding.

Thus, social loafing is an issue in teams deserving attention. If so many organizations employ teams and social loafing so abounds in collective tasks, then it pays off to understand more about the determinants of social loafing. In this chapter I present a theoretical model that integrates the variables of which research has shown that they influence the tendency to loaf. On the basis of this theoretical model I will present suggestions for interventions to prevent social loafing from occurring.

DETERMINANTS OF SOCIAL LOAFING

The effect that working in teams has on individual motivation and effort has long received attention of social and organizational psychologists. One of the very first experiments dealt with this issue. Ringelmann (1913) compared performance of adults working as a group on a rope-pulling task with performance of adults working individually and noted that performance increasingly deteriorated as group size increased (see, for a recent replication of the Ringelmann effect, Lichacz & Partington, 1997). Ringelmann's results were received with scepticism in the scientific community and dismissed as an artefact: performance decrements were the result of coordination losses between group members and not of motivation losses (Steiner, 1972). Only much later Ingham et al. (1974) convincingly demonstrated that the motivational component of the performance decrement was an important and replicable phenomenon in itself, apart from the coordination problem. This phenomenon was called social loafing (Latané, Williams, & Harkins, 1979).

Since 1974, studies about social loafing have appeared regularly. Most studies are experimental and social psychological in nature, but some of them have been conducted in field settings like the classroom or sports teams (Karau & Williams, 1993). Karau and Williams (2001) found only three studies conducted in business organizations (i.e. Faulkner & Williams, 1996; George, 1992, 1995). Whether studies were conducted in laboratory settings, non-organizational field settings, or organizational field settings, similar results emerged (Karau & Williams, 2001).

Some 10 years ago Shepperd (1993) and Karau and Williams (1993) wrote review articles about the determinants of social loafing. The most important contribution of both these articles was that they aimed, for the first time, to put the various studies in an integrated framework. In both articles the same well-known motivation theory was used for this purpose, Vroom's (1964) expectancy-value theory. I will use the same theory as a starting point in this chapter. Next, I will argue that expectancy-value theory needs to be complemented with insights from Adams's (1965) equity theory. Vroom's theory was developed for individual tasks. When applied to collective tasks, one cannot do without considerations of social comparison of inputs and outcomes of the various group members, for a more complete understanding of the determinants of individual efforts. Adams's equity theory can be of help here. Hereafter a theoretical model will be developed that combines insights from expectancy-value theory with insights from equity theory. But first I will discuss expectancy-value theory.

Expectancy Value

According to Vroom's expectancy-value theory (1964), individual motivation depends on three factors: (a) expectancy, i.e. the expectancy that effort will lead to a certain level of performance, (b) instrumentality, i.e. the extent to which a certain level of performance will lead to an outcome, and (c) value, i.e. the extent to which the outcome is valued. Karau and Williams (1993) develop the collective effort model, extending Vroom's (1964) theory about individual motivation on individual tasks to collective tasks. They argue that instrumentality in particular is more complex for collective tasks than for individual tasks. On individual tasks instrumentality is only determined by the perceived relationship between individual performance and individual outcome. On collective tasks instrumentality is determined by three factors: (a) the perceived relationship between individual performance and group performance, (b) the perceived relationship between group performance and group outcomes, and (c) the perceived relationship between group outcomes and individual outcomes. As a result, working on collective tasks introduces additional contingencies between individual efforts and outcomes.

According to Karau and Williams (1993), individuals will be prepared to exert effort on a collective task if they expect these efforts to be instrumental in acquiring valued outcomes. Several conditions must be fulfilled before individuals deem their efforts to be instrumental. Individual effort must be related to individual performance. Individual performance must be related to group performance. Group performance must lead to a valued group outcome. This valued group outcome must be related to a valued individual outcome. If one or more of these relationships are not present or disturbed, a group member will not deem the exertion of effort instrumental and will not work hard on a task. Likewise group members will not work hard if they do not value the resulting outcomes, irrespective of whether these outcomes are related to individual effort. Valued outcomes can be of a tangible nature, like financial rewards, or intangible, like fun, satisfaction, and feelings of self-esteem or feelings of belonging to the group.

Karau and Williams (1993) predict that, since individual outcomes are less related to individual effort on collective tasks, individuals will generally be inclined to loaf on collective tasks. On the basis of a meta-analysis of a large number of studies, Karau and Williams conclude that this hypothesis is supported. Compared to co-action tasks, individuals tend to reduce their efforts on collective tasks. The extent to which individuals loaf is often not large, but the effect is consistent (in 79 per cent of the compared instances).

The fact that the extent to which individuals loaf is often not large does not imply that it is an unimportant problem. Apparently the phenomenon occurs consistently on collective tasks. Suppose that in most teams in organizations effort reductions of 10 per cent occur, then the phenomenon per team may be limited in scope, but across all teams this may nevertheless constitute a considerable loss for an organization.

Karau and Williams list, on the basis of their meta-analysis, the variables that influence social loafing. These variables are of influence on social loafing because they influence perceived instrumentality or outcome value. Karau and Williams do not detail this any further. The expectancy that individual effort leads to individual performance is a background condition in Karau and Williams's model. If such an expectation does not exist, individuals do not exert effort anyway, whether they work on an individual task or on a collective task. Below, I will further detail the role of the mediating mechanisms of instrumentality and outcome value and formulate specific hypotheses about which variable influences which mediating mechanism. Where relevant I will add selected references that appeared after Karau and Williams wrote their meta-analysis in 1993, to bring their review up to date.

EVALUATION POTENTIAL

Individuals tend to loaf less when their contributions can be evaluated than when they cannot be evaluated (e.g. Gagne & Zuckerman, 1999; George, 1992; Harkins, 1987; Hoeksema-van Orden, Gaillard, & Buunk, 1998; Price, 1987). When the individual contribution of a group member cannot be distinguished from those of others and, as a result, cannot be identified and evaluated, group members can hide in a team. An example of low evaluation potential is a group of service engineers responsible for servicing copy machines for a group of customers. When a copy machine needs repairing each service engineer can put minimal effort into the repair task—just enough to make the copy machine run again—leaving the major repair job for another service engineer next time. The level of effort each service engineer puts into the task cannot be identified and evaluated. This creates the opportunity to blame others if things go wrong ("it was the previous service engineer who did a bad job"). Punishment is less likely and outcomes will be gained despite one's lack of contribution. When group members' contributions are not identifiable and assessable, the tendency to loaf increases, because—in terms of expectancy-value theory—it decreases the instrumentality of contributions. This means that increasing evaluation potential will decrease the tendency to loaf, because it increases instrumentality. Druskatt and Wolff

(1999) studied 44 self-managing undergraduate student groups and 36 self-managing MBA student groups using a repeated measures time-series design. They examined the effect of peer appraisals on social loafing. They found that peer appraisals had a positive impact. The positive effect was not dependent on the ratio of positive to negative feedback, suggesting that being evaluated in itself caused the effect, and not whether the evaluation is positive or negative.

Increased evaluation potential may also lead to increased outcome value. People in general find it pleasing when they are able to evaluate their own performance and see that they performed well. Performing well is a reward in itself, because it increases feelings of self-esteem (Harkins & Szymanski, 1988; Szymanski & Harkins, 1987). Some tasks lend themselves better for evaluation than others. Henningsen, Cruz, and Miller (2000) argued that intellective tasks increase the potential for evaluation when a correct answer is believed to exist. A judgemental task, on the other hand, like jury decision making, has no objective outside standard against which decisions can be evaluated. Henningsen, Cruz, and Miller (2000) therefore predicted and found more social loafing in judgemental than in intellective tasks.

TASK VALUE

Group members tend to loaf less when task value increases (Petty, Cacioppo, & Kasmer, 1985). This implies that intrinsic task motivation, because the task is, for example, important or significant or pleasant, decreases the tendency to loaf. Members of a research and development project team working on an interesting problem, for example, will be less inclined to loaf than members of a team of data typists working away at a pile of data entries, because the first task is intrinsically more motivating than the second. In terms of expectancy-value theory, high task value leads to high outcome value: executing the task is in itself a valuable outcome. George (1992), for example, found in her field study that the extent to which salespeople were intrinsically involved in their task was negatively related to social loafing. Hoeksema-van Orden, Gaillard, and Buunk (1998) had their student participants work on several tasks for 20 hours without sleep in two experiments and found that fatigue increased social loafing. Presumably working on tasks becomes more unpleasant as fatigue increases, thereby reducing intrinsic task motivation. Task motivation may differ for group members. Smith et al. (2001) found that individuals with a high need for cognition are less likely to loaf on cognitively engaging tasks than individuals with a low need for cognition, presumably because individuals with a high need for cognition have higher intrinsic task motivation when the task is cognitively effortful.

GROUP VALUE

Individuals tend to loaf less when group value increases (Hardy & Latané, 1988). This means that high group cohesion or a strong group identity can reduce social loafing. A team consisting of group members who have known each other for some time and who have similar values will have to deal less with social loafing problems than, for example, a team consisting of complete strangers. The effect of group value was indeed found in a study using 59 dyads discussing a controversial issue (Karau & Hart, 1998), and in two experiments using an idea generation task (Karau & Williams, 1997). When group members want to continue their group membership or when their social identity depends to a large extent to membership of the group, they will loaf less. In terms of expectancy-value theory, high group value leads to high perceived outcome value: contributing to the group is a valuable outcome in itself.

REDUNDANCY

The more redundant the contribution of the individual, the more the individual will be inclined to loaf (Harkins & Petty, 1982). This means that having a unique contribution to give to the group reduces the tendency to loaf. In multidisciplinary teams, for example, where all group members have to deliver a specific disciplinary contribution, redundancy will be less of a problem than in monodisciplinary teams where all group members have to deliver the same type of contribution. When group members are interchangeable and somebody else can easily deliver their contribution, group members will be more inclined to reduce their efforts. The upside of this phenomenon is that if somebody else cannot be expected to deliver one's own contribution as well, group members will not be inclined to socially loaf and may even compensate for others' lack of contribution. Karau and Williams (1997, second experiment), for example, found that individuals with a low able co-worker tended to engage in social compensation. Plaks and Higgins (2000) recently found more evidence for this phenomenon in a series of four experiments. In each of the four experiments participants performed worse when there was a good fit between the strengths of their partner and the requirements of the task (making their own contributions redundant), providing evidence for social loafing. To a lesser extent evidence was found for the opposite effect that participants performed better when there was a poor fit between the strengths of their partner and the requirements of the task (making their own contributions non-redundant), providing some evidence for social compensation.

Perceived redundancy may depend on the type of task and on the type of person. Hertel, Kerr, and Messe (2000) had team members with discrepant capabilities work together. They found that motivation gains occurred under conjunctive but not under additive task demands, and suggested that this was due to the fact that increased effort was perceived to be more instrumental in a conjunctive than in an additive task. Huguet, Charbonnier, and Monteil (1999) found that individuals who are high in feelings of self-uniqueness engaged more in social loafing when working on an easy task, and worked harder on a challenging task, compared to individuals low in self-uniqueness. Presumably, individuals high in self-uniqueness believe that their co-workers are less able than themselves to contribute well on a challenging task, and therefore believe their contribution is necessary. The reverse is true when the task is easy (see also Charbonnier et al., 1998). In terms of expectancy-value theory, redundancy of the individual contribution leads to low perceived instrumentality, whereas uniqueness of the individual contribution leads to high perceived instrumentality, thereby influencing the group members' determination of how much effort to expend.

GROUP SIZE

The tendency to loaf is smaller in small groups than in large groups (Latané, Williams, & Harkins, 1979; Petty et al., 1977). This effect was again demonstrated in a recent study investigating whether social loafing occurred in a collaborative educational task in first-year psychology students, comparing groups of three and eight students (North, Linley, & Hargreaves, 2000). Thus, keeping group size limited can reduce social loafing. In terms of expectancy-value theory, a smaller group size leads to higher perceived instrumentality: chances decrease that the valued outcome can be attained without one's own contributions.

COLLECTIVE ORIENTATION

Karau and Williams (1993) note that women compared to men are less inclined to loaf (see, for a recent replication of this finding, Kugihara, 1999). Karau and Williams (1993) also note that Asian cultures compared to Western cultures are less inclined to loaf. Presumably, women compared to men, and Eastern compared to Western cultures, are more collectively oriented. This means that stimulating a prosocial orientation can reduce social loafing. Recently, Duffy and Shaw (2000) investigated the effects of envy in 143 groups over a period of 16 weeks. The occurrence of high levels of envy, or jealousy, in groups can be seen as a sign of lack of collective orientation. The study found that more envy increased social loafing, and reduced group potency, group cohesion, and group performance. In terms of expectancy-value theory, a prosocial orientation leads to higher outcome value: contributing to the group is in itself considered valuable.

EXPECTATIONS ABOUT OTHERS

Individuals are less inclined to loaf when they expect other group members to perform badly (Jackson & Harkins, 1985; Kerr & Bruun, 1981; Williams & Karau, 1991). This means that group members will loaf less when they believe that other group members will contribute insufficiently, for example because of low effort. Williams and Karau (1991) manipulated participants' expectancies about their partners directly, for example by letting the co-worker explicitly announce that "I (don't) think I'm going to work very hard". They found that participants with partners who announced they would work hard socially loafed. Participants with partners who announced they would not work hard socially compensated (see also Williams, Karau, & Bourgeois, 1993; Williams & Sommer, 1997). Hart, Bridgett, and Karau (2001) examined the joint effect of co-worker ability and expected co-worker effort. When co-worker effort was expected to be low, participants socially compensated when they also believed that the partner had low ability. In terms of expectancy-value theory, low expectations about the performance of others lead to high perceived instrumentality: one's own contribution is necessary to attain the valued outcome.

CONTINGENCY BETWEEN INDIVIDUAL AND GROUP PERFORMANCE

Contingency between individual and group performance is not a variable listed in Karau and Williams's (1993) meta-analysis (because it was apparently not investigated until that time), although it is an important variable in their collective effort model. Shepperd and Taylor (1999, experiment 1) directly manipulated this contingency and believed it to influence perceived instrumentality. Their participants were told that the top 10 per cent performing groups on a brainstorm task would receive a prize. Participants in groups who were led to believe that it was very likely that their group would be in the top 10 per cent (high instrumentality) exerted more effort than participants who believed a top 10 per cent position to be highly unlikely (low instrumentality).

198 C. G. Rutte

```
┌─────────────────────┐
│ • Group value       │
│ • Task value        │
│ • Social orientation│
└─────────────────────┘
            ↘
             [Outcome value]
                              ↘
┌─────────────────────┐                [Social loafing]
│ • Evaluation potential │           ↗
└─────────────────────┘
             [Instrumentality]
            ↗
┌─────────────────────────┐
│ • Group size            │
│ • Redundancy            │
│ • Individual–group      │
│   performance contingency│
│ • Group performance–    │
│   outcome contingency   │
└─────────────────────────┘
```

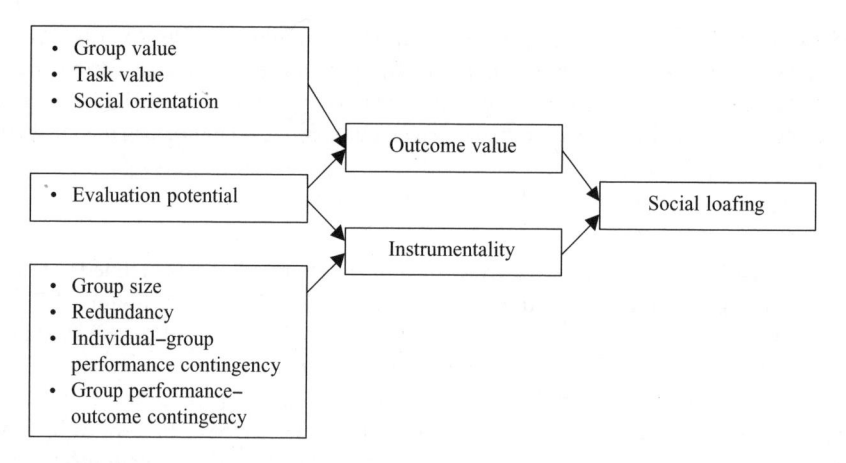

Figure 9.1 Schematic representation of the determinants of social loafing and their mediating variables

CONTINGENCY BETWEEN GROUP PERFORMANCE AND GROUP OUTCOME

Contingency between group performance and group outcome is not a variable listed in Karau and Williams's (1993) meta-analysis (because it was apparently not investigated until that time), although it is again an important variable in their collective effort model. Shepperd and Taylor (1999, experiment 2) directly manipulated this contingency and believed it to influence perceived instrumentality. Half of their participants working on a brainstorm task were led to believe that their group had a 70 per cent chance of winning a prize (high instrumentality), the other half were told their group had only a 1 in 200 chance of winning the prize. Participants in groups who were led to believe that chances to win the prize were high (high instrumentality) exerted more effort than participants who believed those chances to be low (low instrumentality). Thus, the likelihood that a good collective performance will be rewarded reduces social loafing.

Figure 9.1 presents all variables which research has shown to influence social loafing, and the hypothesized relationships with the mediating variables of instrumentality and outcome value. Group size, redundancy, individual–group performance contingency, and group performance–outcome contingency are hypothesized to influence the perceived instrumentality of a contribution and thereby social loafing. Group value, task value, and social orientation are hypothesized to influence the perceived outcome value and thereby social loafing. Evaluation potential is hypothesized to influence social loafing both via outcome value and instrumentality.

Equity

I would like to develop one of the variables that I listed in the previous paragraph a little bit further: expectations about others. According to Karau and Williams (1993), high expectations of others lead to more social loafing than low expectations. I reasoned that this is presumably due to the fact that low expectations of others lead to high perceived instrumentality of one's own contribution. I would like to add that expectations about others may also influence outcome value, albeit outcome value in a different sense than Karau and Williams (1993), Shepperd (1993), and Vroom (1964) use.

The perceived value of an outcome not only depends on the absolute level of the outcome, but also on the point of reference to which the outcome is compared. According to Thibaut and Kelley (1959), outcomes are evaluated by comparing them to a comparison level, an affectively neutral point on a scale of possible outcomes. The comparison level depends among other things on what one knows of the outcomes of others. People compare their own outcomes with those of others and this determines whether their own outcomes are evaluated positively or negatively. Our choice of comparison others is often based on similarity and proximity: we tend to compare ourselves with others who are similar to us or physically close (Festinger, 1954). The point is that team members are likely to not only evaluate the value of their outcomes in an absolute sense, but also relatively. Team members are likely to look at how their own outcomes relate to the outcomes of fellow team members.

Adams (1965) and Walster, Walster, and Berscheid (1978) have extended this reasoning one step further. These authors say that individuals do not only socially compare their outcomes, but also their inputs. Adams (1965) and Walster, Walster, and Berscheid (1978) specifically predict that people strive for equity: the ratio of their own inputs and outcomes should be equal to the ratio of inputs and outcomes of others.

The equity principle is completely non-existent in Vroom's (1964) model. This is understandable considering that Vroom's (1964) model was formulated for individual motivation on individual tasks and not collective tasks. Social comparison is therefore left out of consideration. However, when Vroom's (1964) model is applied to collective tasks, considerations of social comparison of inputs and outcomes cannot be left out of consideration to come to a more complete understanding of the determinants of individual effort.

In a collective task, group members work together to deliver a group performance and, very likely, group members will look at each other and wonder how much each group member contributes. If all group members profit equally from the group's performance, then one may predict on the basis of equity theory that group members will consider it fair that all group members contribute equally. A situation in which contributions are unequal while outcomes are divided equally will be considered unfair. According to equity theory, people are distressed by inequity and they will be inclined to prevent it from occurring, or to seek retribution for it after it has occurred (Greenberg, 1988; Rutte & Messick, 1995; Tyler & Smith, 1998).

Kerr (1983) was one of the first who pointed out the importance of equity in collective tasks. Following Orbell and Dawes (1981), he distinguished two mechanisms that lie at the basis of reduced motivation to contribute in collective tasks. The first is the free-rider mechanism. Free-riders try to take advantage from the fact that the contributions of others may suffice to deliver the required performance and therefore their own efforts are deemed redundant and are withheld. Free-riders profit from the contributions of others without contributing (as much) themselves. The second mechanism is the sucker mechanism. Suckers are those group members who do all or most of the work and do not profit any more than those who did nothing or less. Suckers are those group members on which the free-riders free-ride. The sucker mechanism refers to the phenomenon that people reduce their efforts because they do not want to be a sucker.

Both the free-rider and the sucker mechanism lead, according to Kerr (1983), to a reduction in motivation in group members to contribute to the group. The free-rider mechanism leads to a reduction in motivation because group members perceive their contribution as redundant. This is in agreement with Vroom's (1964) theory in which he deals with perceived instrumentality of contributions. Kerr (1983) points out that if all group members think the same, the required group performance will not be attained. In this sense, working on a collective task has the characteristics of a social dilemma: for each group member it is more rational to defect (i.e. not to contribute) than to cooperate (i.e. to contribute); however, if all group members defect they are all worse off than if all had cooperated (the case in Box 9.1 is a clear example of this).

The sucker mechanism also leads to a reduction in motivation to contribute. People do not like being a sucker. According to Kerr (1983), the equity norm is the most commonly accepted norm for behaviour in work groups. The equity norm makes the sucker role problematic. Why, after all, should one group member contribute more effort than other group members if outcomes are equally divided?

The equity norm also makes the free-rider role problematic, however rational that role may be. Why, after all, should one group member contribute less effort than other group members if outcomes are equally divided? Research has shown that people are more sensitive to inequities when they are to their disadvantage than when they are to their advantage (Walster, Walster, & Berscheid, 1978). Therefore people probably dislike being a sucker more than being a free-rider. But both the free-rider and sucker mechanisms can be active on collective tasks, and both these mechanisms will lead to reductions in motivation and performance.

What is the relevance of all this for expectations about the performance of others? According to Karau and Williams (1993), group members are inclined to increase effort when they expect others to perform badly. This conclusion is at odds with the prediction on the basis of the sucker mechanism. Based on the sucker mechanism, the reverse finding holds: group members are inclined to decrease effort when they expect others to perform badly (Kerr, 1983).

These contradictory findings of expected performance of others on one's own performance can be explained when legitimacy of bad performance is taken into consideration. Some conditions may justify that some group members contribute more to the group's performance than others, for example differences in ability. High able group members have to put in less effort to perform well than low able group members. Because high able group members need to invest less effort for the same performance, it may be justifiable that these group members perform better than low able group members. Under those circumstances a low expectation of the performance of others may lead to an increase in one's own performance. That this reasoning holds has been demonstrated by Kerr and Bruun (1981).

Another condition that may legitimize that some group members perform better than others can be the fact that group members differ in perceived outcome value. Some group members may for instance like the task better. Working on a nice task is a positive outcome value in itself. Because these group members have in this sense more outcomes than group members who do not like the task, it is justifiable that they perform better. Looking at it this way, all variables influencing perceived outcome value (see Figure 9.1) can change the equity judgement.

If there is no legitimization for differences in contributions between group members, group members will avoid becoming a sucker by reducing their contributions. In that case low expectations about performance of others may lead to a reduction in their own

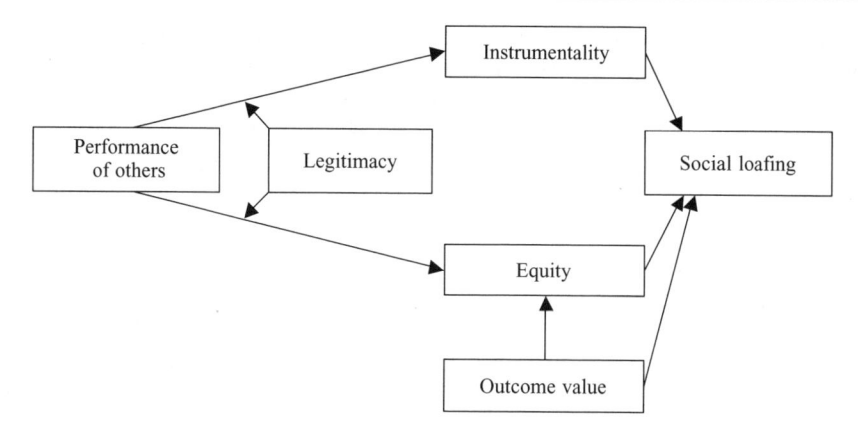

Figure 9.2 Schematic representation of the effect of the expectation about performance of others on social loafing

performance, so that the contributions of the other group members are matched and the situation is fair.

All in all, one may hypothesize that group members have judgements about the fairness of each group member's inputs and outcomes. Perceived unfairness will influence the tendency to loaf. If, for no good reason, other group members are expected to perform badly, then the situation is unfair. Under those circumstances group members will try to reduce unfairness by lowering their own performance and match that of the other group members. Figure 9.2 depicts this reasoning schematically.

Figure 9.2 shows that expectations about the performance of others influence the tendency to loaf, on the one hand via perceived equity and on the other via perceived instrumentality. The weight of each path depends on the perceived legitimacy of the level of performance invested by each group member. The equity judgements about the level of performance invested by each group member are influenced by the perceived outcome value for each group member.

Wilke, Rutte, and van Knippenberg (2000) provide some evidence for the importance of fairness feelings about social loafing in groups. They conducted a field study among 127 members of semi-autonomous teams and found that performance differences between team members led to increased feelings of unfairness. They also found some evidence for our legitimacy hypothesis. They hypothesized that suckers, i.e. team members with relatively high performances, would feel less unfairness when they felt highly rewarded for their efforts. In particular high social rewards and (when the task was unpleasant) high financial rewards appeared to moderate the relationship between performance differences and unfairness feelings for suckers, i.e. for suckers with high rewards performance differences were to a lesser extent associated with feelings of unfairness.

Hart, Bridgett, and Karau (2001) also provide some evidence for our legitimacy hypothesis. They examined the joint effects of expected co-worker effort and co-worker ability. They found that group members who expected co-worker effort to be low, socially loafed when they believed that their partner had high ability, and socially compensated when they believed their partner had low ability. Being a sucker is apparently less problematic with a low than with a high able partner.

Roy, Gauvin, and Limayem (1996) showed that social matching may occur in groups. Undergraduate business school students participated in electronic brainstorming. In one of their experimental conditions, throughout the task, the ideas generated by group members appeared on a public screen. In that condition social matching occurred, i.e. group members adjusted their level of effort to that of the group. All these studies provide some preliminary confirmation for our reasoning that equity plays a role in groups working on collective tasks.

SOLUTIONS

On the basis of the model developed in the previous paragraphs, it is possible to systematically derive possible remedies against social loafing. The mediating mechanisms of instrumentality, outcome value, and equity can be used, alone or in combination, to reduce social loafing.

Outcome Value

When contributions are not rewarded, the outcome value is low and the tendency to contribute diminishes. This suggests one obvious solution: make contributing rewarding. Shepperd (1993) distinguishes four types of rewards: external individual rewards, internal individual rewards, external collective rewards, and internal collective rewards.

Organizations could reward each group member individually. External individual rewards can be financial or social in nature. To reward group members individually, it is necessary to make their individual contributions identifiable and assessable. Each individual's contribution is next linked to an external financial or social reward, e.g. a compliment.

There are internal individual rewards, when an individual judges intrinsic rewards for performing on the task to be present. This is for example the case, according to Shepperd (1993), when individuals have a clear norm or standard against which they can evaluate their performance and find living up to standard performance on the task in itself valuable. Thus, organizations could formulate specific performance goals. There are also individual internal rewards when the group members find the task intrinsically interesting. Organizations could strive therefore to create meaningful or pleasant tasks for their employees.

Organizations could also reward group members collectively. Collective external rewards, i.e. rewarding the group as a group financially or socially, could be such a form of reward. After all, rewarding individual contributions presupposes that individual contributions can be identified and assessed. In real life this will often be difficult, if not impossible. Collective rewards are then an alternative solution. Karau and Williams (1993), however, maintain that collective external rewards will only be effective when there is a direct relationship between the collectively received reward and the individually received reward.

According to Shepperd (1993), there is one final form of reward left: collective internal rewards, such as when individuals identify with, are proud of, or feel obligated towards their group. This will be the case in cohesive groups. When groups are cohesive, individuals value the success of their group as their own success, and this is intrinsically rewarding. This means that organizations could try to increase group cohesiveness, e.g. through careful team composition, to attempt to reduce the tendency to loaf. Karau, Markus, and Williams (2000) suggest that some personality factors may be relevant here. People high in collectivism, need for affiliation, need to belong, and protestant work ethic have the tendency to value collective outcomes and contribute to collective efforts. Having teams composed of members with these characteristics should therefore reduce social loafing.

Instrumentality

Instrumentality refers to the relationship between performance and the acquisition of a valued outcome. Making individuals' contributions indispensable can strengthen this relationship. When individuals' contributions are indispensable they must perform, otherwise the valued outcome cannot be attained. According to Shepperd (1993), there are three ways to convince team members that their contributions are necessary for a sufficient collective performance, i.e. make contributing difficult, unique, or essential.

When contributing is difficult, individuals may become convinced that the task is so complex or difficult that it is unlikely that other group members will duplicate their contributions. As a result, on difficult tasks, group members will loaf less than on simple tasks. Organizations could, thus, increase task difficulty to reduce social loafing, for example by making tasks more complex or by increasing time pressure.

Group members can also be convinced of the necessity of their contribution when their contribution is unique. Organizations could distribute team tasks in such a way to individual group members that they do not overlap, and each group member has a unique contribution to make to the collective performance. As a result, the tendency to loaf will decrease.

Finally, group members can be convinced of the necessity of their contribution by increasing their belief that an adequate collective performance depends on their personal contribution. If, for example, a team leader can make clear to the group that group members differ in ability, then team members who consider themselves able will feel that their contributions are essential. This will decrease the tendency to loaf.

Reducing group size is another possibility organizations can turn to, to increase instrumentality and to reduce social loafing (Karau, Markus, & Williams, 2000). The smaller the group, the less likely each group member's contribution is redundant.

Equity

One can influence perceived equity by making changes in the outcomes of group members, in the inputs, and in the relationship between inputs and outcomes. Organizations can positively influence perceived outcomes by making the task intrinsically motivating, increasing the group's cohesiveness, and giving positive feedback about individual performance. Perceived inputs are influenced by explaining that some group members have, for example, to put in more effort for the same level of performance as others, thereby pointing out that it is legitimate that the performance of some group members is lower than that of others. Organizations can influence the relationship between inputs and outcomes by letting group members know that those who contributed less will be rewarded less or even be punished. All these measures will reduce the tendency to loaf.

CONCLUSION

When individuals work in teams, they all must cooperate for the team to be effective. Group performance can only be high when all team members are cooperative and exert a lot of effort. However, there is a danger that teamwork may lead to motivation losses. In this chapter I presented a framework to organize the results of research on motivation losses in groups. The framework combines insights from Vroom's expectancy-value theory (1964) with insights from Adams's equity theory (1965). Vroom's (1964) theory was developed for individual motivation on individual tasks. On individual tasks, according to Vroom, outcome value and instrumentality determine motivation. Karau and Williams (1993) have argued that working on group tasks negatively influences outcome value and instrumentality, because the link between (group) performance and (individual) outcome is more indirect and because there is potential redundancy of each group member's contribution. In general, working in teams will therefore negatively influence motivation to perform. However, this conclusion of Karau and Williams deserves some comments.

The first is that when one applies Vroom's (1964) theory to collective tasks, amendments from equity theory are necessary for a more complete understanding of the dynamics of individual motivation. Individuals working on collective tasks do not judge their contributions to the collective performance irrespective of the contributions of others. Group members strive for justice. If all receive equal outcomes, contributions should be equal as well. If the ratio of inputs and outcomes is not in balance and is judged unfair by group members, they will influence their own contribution to the collective performance. Working in teams makes free-riding possible. People do not like to be confronted with the free-rider behaviour of others, particularly when there is no legitimization for such behaviour. They will try to avoid being a sucker and reduce their own efforts. When group members start to loaf because they do not want to be a sucker, a downward spiral may be the result: all group members will work increasingly less hard. On the other hand, considerations of fairness may also be a reason for group members to contribute to the group, even if there is no incentive for it in terms of instrumentality and outcome value. In other words, following Vroom (1964) it may be *rational* to loaf, but following Adams (1965) it may be *moral* not to loaf.

A second comment is that Karau and Williams (1993) use Vroom's theory (1964) to organize the determinants of social loafing as they appeared in the literature. Very often, the relevance of these determinants has been demonstrated in experimental laboratory studies. Their conclusion is that working on individual tasks leads to higher productivity than working on collective tasks. This conclusion is at odds with insights from the organizational psychological literature that individual tasks are often more narrow and isolated than group tasks which create their own problems. In a classically structured organization, with individual tasks as building blocks instead of group tasks, several variables presented in the model may be influenced negatively. Evaluation potential, prosocial orientation, group value, task value, perceived redundancy, and perceived contributions of others, all these variables may be negatively influenced when tasks are individual and not collective. In this sense, individual tasks may very well have negative effects on individual performance compared to collective tasks. This chapter is, thus, not a plea against teamwork, but a warning that working in teams is not a panacea, because compared to individual tasks, collective tasks can lead to motivation losses as a result of equity, instrumentality, or outcome considerations. Understanding which variables influence social loafing can help to optimize individual motivation on collective tasks.

Much of the research on social loafing so far has studied small, randomly assembled, ad hoc groups, under controlled experimental conditions, while performing one simple task. Anderson, Lindsay, and Bushman (1999) compared correspondence between laboratory and field study results across a broad range of phenomena, including social loafing. They found considerable correspondence between effect sizes and conclude that laboratory studies may not be as problematic in external validity as often thought. Nevertheless, laboratory groups only exist for a limited time, they have no past and no future and are isolated from the environment instead of being embedded in larger organizations (McGrath, 1991). The nature of this research is reflected in limited theories about groups. Real-world groups, however, often do not have one simple task but need to execute several. Many groups have a past and expect a future. Groups do not exist in isolation, but are embedded in an organization. Group members are not only oriented towards their task, but also towards their individual interest and the maintenance of interpersonal relationships. These circumstances that are normal for many real-life groups are virtually ignored in group research (McGrath, 1991). Relevant research questions in this context are: How do group members deal with social loafing when working on multiple tasks? Is it permissible to loaf on one task if one compensates on another? Are group members equally inclined to loaf when there is a future with the group compared to when there is not? Is it permissible for a group member to loaf on a current task and make up for it on a future task? Is it permissible for a group member to loaf on the present task, because he or she has to work on other tasks with higher priority elsewhere in the organization? Do group members accept social loafing of a co-worker more easily when this co-worker fulfils maintenance or interpersonal roles in the group to compensate?

Erez and Somech (1996) also plead for research using real interactive groups. They are critical about the fact that in most of the research on social loafing participants acted in pseudo-groups, were not allowed to communicate, and did not have specific goals or rewards for performance. In an effort to create more real-life situations, these scholars conducted a study of social loafing in 16 conditions representing four experimental factors: with or without specific goals, with or without communication, with or without rewards, and with or without collectivist values. In all conditions, participants had co-workers they had known for at least six months. Social loafing was found in only one of the 16 conditions. Erez and Somech (1996) conclude that their results demonstrate that social loafing is the exception rather than the rule. It may be concluded that field research on real interactive groups in organizations is necessary, or else laboratory research using more realistic simulations. Comprehensive theoretical models to guide such research are needed. In this chapter I presented a model that will hopefully fulfil a fruitful role in this respect. The model addresses the determinants and dynamics of social loafing. Instrumentality, outcome value, and equity are posed as central mediating mechanisms. The model also offers many starting-points to counter social loafing in practice.

REFERENCES

Adams, J. S. (1965). Inequity in social exchange. In L. Berkowitz (ed.), *Advances in Experimental Social Psychology* (Vol. 2). New York: Academic Press.

Anderson, C. A., Lindsay, J. J., & Bushman, B. J. (1999). Research in the psychological laboratory: truth or triviality? *Current Directions in Psychological Science, 8*(1), 3–9.

Benders, J., Huijgen, F., Pekruhl, U., & O'Kelly, K. P. (1999). *Useful But Unused—Group Work in Europe*. Luxembourg: Office for Official Publications of the European Communities.

Charbonnier, E., Huguet, P., Brauer, M., & Monteil, J. M. (1998). Social loafing and self-beliefs: people's collective effort depends on the extent to which they distinguish themselves as better than others. *Social Behavior and Personality, 26*(4), 329–340.

Druskat, V. U. & Wolff, S. B. (1999). Effects and timing of developmental peer appraisals in self-managing work groups. *Journal of Applied Psychology, 84*(1), 58–74.

Duffy, M. K. & Shaw, J. D. (2000). The Saliery syndrome: consequences of envy in groups. *Small Group Research, 31*(1), 3–23.

Erez, M. & Somech, A. (1996). Is group productivity loss the rule or the exception? Effects of culture and group-based motivation. *Academy of Management Journal, 39*(6), 1513–1537.

Faulkner, S. L. & Williams, K. D. (1996). A study of social loafing in industry. Paper presented at the annual meeting of the Midwestern Psychological Association, Chicago.

Festinger, L. (1954). A theory of social comparison. *Human Relations, 7*, 117–140.

Gagne, M. & Zuckerman, M. (1999). Performance and learning goal orientations as moderators of social loafing and social facilitation. *Small Group Research, 30*(5), 524–541.

George, J. M. (1992). Extrinsic and intrinsic origins of perceived social loafing in organizations. *Academy of Management Journal, 35*, 191–202.

George, J. M. (1995). Asymmetrical effects of rewards and punishments: the case of social loafing. *Journal of Occupational and Organizational Psychology, 68*, 327–338.

Greenberg, J. (1988). Equity and workplace status: a field-experiment. *Journal of Applied Psychology, 73*, 606–613.

Hardy, C. I. & Latané, B. (1988). Social loafing in cheerleaders: effects of teammembership and competition. *Journal of Sport and Exercise Psychology, 10*, 109–114.

Harkins, S. G. (1987). Social loafing and social facilitation. *Journal of Experimental Social Psychology, 11*, 575–584.

Harkins, S. G. & Petty, R. E. (1982). Effects of task difficulty and task uniqueness on social loafing. *Journal of Personality and Social Psychology, 43*, 1214–1229.

Harkins, S. G. & Szymanski, K. (1988). Social loafing and self-evaluation with an objective standard. *Journal of Experimental Social Psychology, 24*, 354–365.

Hart, J. W., Bridgett, D. J., & Karau, S. J. (2001). Coworker ability and effort as determinants of individual effort on a collective task. *Group Dynamics, 5*(3), 181–190.

Henningsen, D. D., Cruz, M. G., & Miller, M. L. (2000). Role of social loafing in predeliberation decision making. *Group Dynamics: Theory, Research, and Practice, 4*(2), 168–175.

Hertel, G., Kerr, N. L., & Messé, L. (2000). Motivation gains in performance groups: paradigmatic and theoretical developments on the Köhler effect. *Journal of Personality and Social Psychology, 79*(4), 580–601.

Hoeksema-van Orden, C. Y. D., Gaillard, A. W. K., & Buunk, B. P. (1998). Social loafing under fatigue. *Journal of Personality and Social Psychology, 75*(5), 1179–1190.

Huguet, P., Charbonnier, E., & Monteil J. M. (1999). Productivity loss in performance groups: people who see themselves as average do not engage in social loafing. *Group Dynamics: Theory, Research, and Practice, 3*(2), 118–131.

Ingham, A. G., Levinger, G., Graves, J., & Peckham, V. (1974). The Ringelmann effect: studies of group size and group performance. *Journal of Experimental Social Psychology, 10*, 371–384.

Jackson, J. M. & Harkins, S. G. (1985). Equity in effort: an explanation of the social loafing effect. *Journal of Personality and Social Psychology, 49*, 1199–1206.

Karau S. J. & Hart, J. W. (1998). Group cohesiveness and social loafing: effects of a social interaction manipulation on individual motivation within groups. *Group Dynamics, 2*(3), 185–191.

Karau, S. J., Markus, M. J., & Williams, K. D. (2000). On the elusive search for motivation gains in groups: insights from the Collective Effort Model. *Zeitschrift für Sozialpsychologie, 31*(4), 179–190.

Karau, S. J. & Williams, K. D. (1993). Social loafing: a meta-analytic review and theoretical integration. *Journal of Personality and Social Psychology, 65*, 681–706.

Karau, S. J. & Williams, K. D. (1997). The effects of group cohesiveness on social loafing and social compensation. *Group Dynamics: Theory, Research, and Practice, 1*(2), 156–168.

Karau, S. J. & Williams, K. D. (2001). Understanding individual motivation in groups: the Collective Effort Model. In M. E. Turner (ed.), *Groups at Work: Theory and Research. Applied Social Research* (pp. 113–141). Mahwah, NJ: Lawrence Erlbaum.

Kerr, N. L. (1983). Motivation losses in small groups: a social dilemma analysis. *Journal of Personality and Social Psychology, 45*, 819–828.

Kerr, N. L. & Bruun, S. E. (1981). Ringelmann revisited: alternative explanations for the social loafing effect. *Personality and Social Psychology Bulletin, 7*, 224–231.

Kirkman, B. L., Shapiro, D. L., Novelli, L., & Brett, J. M. (1996). Employee concerns regarding self-managing work teams: a multidimensional justice perspective. *Social Justice Research, 9*(1), 49–67.

Kugihara, N. (1999). Gender and social loafing in Japan. *Journal of Social Psychology, 139*(4), 516–526.

Latané, B., Williams, K., & Harkins, S. (1979). Many hands make light the work: the causes and consequences of social loafing. *Journal of Personality and Social Psychology, 37*, 822–832.

Lichacz, F. M. & Partington, J. T. (1997). Collective efficacy and true group performance. *International Journal of Sport Psychology, 27*(2), 146–158.

McGrath, J. E. (1991). Time, interaction and performance: a theory of groups. *Small Group Research, 22*, 147–174.

Mohrman, S. A., Cohen, S. G., & Mohrman, A. M. (1995). *Designing Team-based Organizations*. San Francisco: Jossey-Bass.

North, A. C., Linley, A., & Hargreaves, D. J. (2000). Social loafing in a cooperative classroom task. *Educational Psychology, 20*, 389–392.

Orbell, J. & Dawes, R. (1981). Social dilemmas. In G. Stephenson & J. H. Davis (eds), *Progress in Applied Social Psychology* (Vol. 1). Chichester: Wiley.

Petty, R. E., Cacioppo, J. T., & Kasmer, J. A. (1985). Individual differences in social loafing on cognitive tasks. Paper presented at the annual meeting of the Midwestern Psychological Association, Chicago.

Petty, R. E., Harkins, S. G., Williams, K., & Latané, B. (1977). The effects of group size on cognitive effort and evaluation. *Personality and Social Psychology Bulletin, 3*, 579–582.

Plaks, J. E. & Higgins, E. T. (2000). Pragmatic use of stereotyping in teamwork: social loafing and compensation as a function of inferred partner–situation fit. *Journal of Personality and Social Psychology, 79*(6), 962–974.

Price, K. H. (1987). Decision responsibility, task responsibility, identifiability, and social loafing. *Organizational Behaviour and Human Decision Processes, 40*, 330–345.

Ringelmann, M. (1913). Recherches sur les moteurs animés: travail de l'homme. *Annales de l'Institut National Agronomique, 2*(12), 1–40.

Robbins, S. P. (2001). *Organizational Behavior*. Upper Saddle River, NJ: Prentice-Hall.

Roy, M. C., Gauvin, S., & Limayem, M. (1996). Electronic group brainstorming: the role of feedback on productivity. *Small Group Research, 27*(2), 215–247.

Rutte, C. G. (1990). Social dilemmas in organizations. *Social Behaviour: An International Journal of Applied Social Psychology, 5*(4), 285–294.

Rutte, C. G. & Messick, D. M. (1995). An integrated model of perceived unfairness in organizations. *Social Justice Research, 8*(3), 239–261.

Shepperd, J. A. (1993). Productivity loss in performance groups: a motivation analysis. *Psychological Bulletin, 113*, 67–81.

Shepperd, J. A. & Taylor, K. M. (1999). Social loafing and expectancy-value theory. *Personality and Social Psychology Bulletin, 25*(9), 1147–1158.

Smith, B. N., Kerr, N. A., Markus, M. J., & Stasson, M. F. (2001). Individual differences in social loafing: need for cognition as a motivator in collective performance. *Group Dynamics: Theory, Research, and Practice, 5*(2), 150–158.

Steiner, I. (1972). *Group Processes and Productivity*. San Diego, Calif.: Academic Press.

Szymanski, K. & Harkins, S. G. (1987). Social loafing and self-evaluation with a social standard. *Journal of Personality and Social Psychology, 53*, 891–897.

Thibaut, J. W. & Kelley, H. H. (1959). *Interpersonal Relations*. New York: Wiley.

Tjosvold, D. (1991). *Team Organization: An Enduring Competitive Advantage*. Chichester: Wiley.

Tyler, T. R. & Smith, H. J. (1998). Social justice and social movements. In D. T. Gilbert, S. T. Fiske, & G. Lindzey (eds), *The Handbook of Social Psychology* (pp. 595–632). Boston, Mass.: McGraw-Hill.

Vroom, V. H. (1964). *Work and Motivation*. New York: Wiley.

Walster, E., Walster, G. W., & Berscheid, E. (1978). *Equity: Theory and Research*. Boston: Allyn Bacon.

Wilke, M., Rutte, C. G., & Knippenberg, A. van (2000). The resentful sucker: do rewards ease the pain? *European Journal of Work and Organizational Psychology, 9*(3), 307–320.

Williams, K. D. & Karau, S. J. (1991). Social loafing and social compensation: the effects of expectations of co-worker performance. *Journal of Personality and Social Psychology, 61*, 570–581.

Williams, K., Karau, S., & Bourgeois, M. (1993). Working on collective tasks: social loafing and social compensation. In M. A. Hogg & D. Abrams (eds), *Group Motivation: Social Psychological Perspectives* (pp. 130–148). New York: Harvester-Wheatsheaf.

Williams, K. D. & Sommer, K. L. (1997). Social ostracism by coworkers: does rejection lead to loafing or compensation? *Personality and Social Psychology Bulletin, 7*, 693–706.

10

POWER IN GROUPS AND ORGANIZATIONS

Peter T. Coleman and Maxim Voronov

This is a chapter about power in groups and organizations. In the following pages, we suggest that the analysis and exploration of the complexities of organizational power by managers and workers are both necessary and useful. We begin by discussing three of the prominent theoretical perspectives on power from the literatures of social and organizational psychology and critical management studies. We then outline some of the dilemmas and challenges faced by executives, managers, and workers around empowerment, disempowerment, and organizational democracy. Then, building on the seminal works of Follet, Deutsch, Tjosvold, Clegg, Mumby, and others, we offer a framework of organizational power which views power as a multifaceted phenomenon; as thoughts, words, and deeds which are both embedded within and determining of a complex network of relations, structures, and meaning-making processes at different levels of organizational and community life. Such a framework enables us to understand the relational aspects of power and authority within the context of the macro structures and ideologies that give them meaning. It can also help identify those domains in organizations where the potential for sharing cooperative power is, in fact, not disempowering, but genuinely empowering for all concerned. The chapter concludes with a set of practical recommendations for managers that emphasize the benefits of multiple emancipatory initiatives within organizations when implemented with respect to the paradoxes of power.

THEORETICAL PERSPECTIVES ON POWER: CONTROLLING, COOPERATIVE, AND CRITICAL

Power, like other essential organizational phenomena, has been studied through the years from a variety of theoretical perspectives. Each approach has contributed to our understanding of power and influence in organizations; however, each is aspectual, focusing on particular aspects of power at the expense of our understanding of others. Below, we summarize the three primary paradigms of power: controlling, cooperative, and critical.

The Essentials *of Teamworking: International Perspectives.*
Edited by M. A. West, D. Tjosvold, and K. G. Smith. © 2005 John Wiley & Sons, Ltd.

Power-as-control

Morgan (1997) claims that many organizational theorists derive their thinking on power from the definition of power offered by American political scientist Robert Dahl. Dahl (1968) proposed that power involves "an ability to get another person to do something that he or she would not otherwise have done" (p. 158). This ability is often linked with the capacity to overcome the resistance of the other. This type of definition has been influential with many eminent social theorists and researchers, past (Cartwright, 1959; Dahl, 1957; French & Raven, 1959; Lasswell & Kaplan, 1950; Weber, 1947) and present (Hinkin & Schriesheim, 1989; Kipnis, 1976; Mossholder et al., 1998; Pfeffer, 1981; Rahim, 1989; Raven, Schwarzwald, & Koslowsky, 1998; Schriesheim, Hinkin, & Podsakoff, 1991). Power, from this perspective, is seen as a special kind of influence of A over B. This emphasizes the controlling and potentially coercive aspects of person-centered power (A) and views it as both a mechanism for maintaining order and authority and, when abused, a problem to be contained. As such, this perspective is consistent with the technical, mechanistic, and unilateral approaches to organizational life epitomized by Taylor's methods of scientific management.

The study of power-as-control has been immensely important. First, the need for management to maintain a reasonable degree of order and efficiency in organizations is obvious. Furthermore, under certain conditions even coercive power can be a necessary or practical tool. For example, when in conflict with unjust and unresponsive others, or in situations where subordinates are hostile or unmotivated to comply with reasonable demands. In addition, the prevalence in organizations of destructive forms of controlling power through the use of humiliation, fear tactics, and oppression has warranted the need to better comprehend and thereby deter such practices. This approach to the study of power has also led to important advances in the measurement of individual differences such as authoritarianism (Adorno et al., 1950), Machiavellianism (Christie & Geis, 1970), and social dominance orientation (Sidanious & Pratto, 1999), as well as a useful typology of the resources of power often used when asserting power over others (French & Raven, 1959).

Nevertheless, useful as the power-as-control perspective may be, it is limited, conceptually and practically, and ultimately neglects other important aspects of power. Like all theories of power, this perspective contains a set of underlying assumptions and values about the nature of power, the nature of people, and the nature of power relations that limit its applicability (Coleman & Tjosvold, 2000). These include:

1. There is a limited amount of power that exists in any relationship; therefore the more power A has the less power available for B.
2. People use what power they have to increase their power.
3. Power relations are unidirectional; power is located in A and moves from A to B.
4. Due to the scarcity of power as a resource, power relations are intrinsically competitive.
5. Control of another through coercion is the essence of power.

These assumptions, however valid at times, define only a limited view of power.

In practice, a predominantly controlling approach to power is likely to have harmful consequences, producing alienation and resistance in those subjected to the power (Deutsch, 1973). This, in turn, limits the powerholder's ability to use other types of power that are based on trust (such as normative, expert, referent, and reward power), and increases the need for continuous scrutiny and control of subordinates. If the goal of the powerholder is to achieve compliance *and* commitment from her or his subordinates, then reliance on a "power over" strategy will prove to be costly as well as largely ineffective.

Power through Cooperation

Mary Parker Follett, writing in the 1920s, offered a different perspective on power. Follett argued that even though power in organizations was usually conceived of as "power-over" others, it would also be possible to develop the conception of "power-with" others. She envisioned this type of power as jointly developed, coactive and noncoercive (see Follett, 1973). Cooperative power, then, is that type of power that brings about constructive outcomes for all. It motivates people to search out each other's abilities and to appreciate their contributions, to negotiate and influence each other to exchange resources that will help them both be more productive, and to encourage each other to develop and enhance their valued abilities. In fact, Follett suggested that one of the most effective ways to limit the use of coercive power strategies was to develop the idea, the capacity, and the conditions that foster cooperative power. As such, she was able to rise above the dualistic power struggles between labor and management that had threatened the survival of many organizations during her time. She did so by encouraging both groups to see the value of working together to improve their mutual situation. This was Follett's attempt to temper scientific management practices with her own "science of the situation," where labor and management collaborated to define acceptable rates of productivity and social justice (Boje & Rosile, 2001). Thus, cooperative power was consistent with the values and intentions of the emerging human relations school of management.

The empirical research on cooperation and power, although not abundant, has largely supported Follett's propositions. In a series of studies on power and goal interdependence (Tjosvold, 1981, 1985a, b; Tjosvold, Johnson, & Johnson, 1984), researchers found that differences in goal interdependence (task, reward, and outcome goals) affected the likelihood of the constructive use of power between high- and low-power persons. Cooperative goals, when compared to competitive and independent goals, were found to induce "higher expectations of assistance, more assistance, greater support, more persuasion and less coercion and more trusting and friendly attitudes" between superiors and subordinates (Tjosvold, 1997, p. 297). Similar effects have been found with members of top management teams. In a recent study with 378 executives from 105 organizations in China, perceived cooperative goals were found to reinforce mutually enhancing interactions and promote team recognition of abilities, which in turn resulted in a strategic advantage for the company (Tjosvold, Chen, & Liu, 2001). Coleman (in press) found that people with both chronic and primed cooperative cognitive orientations to power were more willing to share resources and involve others in decision-making processes than those with competitive orientations. In another experiment, powerholders who were led to believe that power was expandable in a given context (compared to a limited and thus competitive resource) developed cooperative relationships and provided support and resources to their subordinates, especially when employees lacked the ability rather than the motivation to perform well (Tjosvold, Coleman, & Sun, in press). These studies support the assertion that, under cooperative conditions, people want others to perform effectively and use their joint resources to enhance each other's power and promote common objectives.

The underlying values and assumptions of cooperative power are in contrast to those of power-as-control. These include:

1. It is possible to create power and enhance everyone's situation through mutually cooperative efforts.
2. Under certain conditions, people will share their power with others.
3. Power relations are bidirectional and mutually interdependent.
4. Often, promotively interdependent goals exist between A and B, as does the opportunity for mutually satisfying outcomes to be achieved.
5. People's power can be positively affected by harmonious relations with others and through their openness to the influence of others (Coleman & Tjosvold, 2000).

Again, these assumptions define the boundaries and limitations of this perspective.

The cooperative perspective on power has not gone without criticism. From the realist camp, concerns have been voiced that this view of power offers us a well-intentioned pipe dream, an idealistic vision of something ultimately unattainable. Given the ruthless jungle of the marketplace and of most organizational environments, they argue, the possibilities for mutual enhancement through cooperative power are severely limited. Even under the best circumstances, mutual power enhancement is a fragile process, highly susceptible to suspicion and ruptures in trust between the parties. And at their extreme, cooperative and participatory processes can be pathological, leading to inefficiency, irresponsible leadership practices, chronic consensus seeking, and nepotism (see Deutsch, 1985, for an extensive discussion of the problems of cooperation and equality).

However, it is the critical theorists and postmodernists that deliver the most scathing critique of the cooperative approach to power (see Alvesson & Willmott, 1992a, b; Boje & Rosile, 2001; Townley, 1993). They raise four primary concerns. First, they argue that the power achieved through cooperative and participatory practices by those in low power in organizations is restricted to those practices that are instrumental to the enhanced achievement of organizational goals, which subordinates do not participate in determining, and the improvement of organizational performance. Thus, these practices restrict the experiences of autonomy and opportunities for development that would result in a genuine sense of empowerment for these individuals (see, for example, Barker, 1993; Ezzamel & Willmott, 1998; Ezzamel, Willmott, & Worthington, 2001). Second, because of the persuasiveness of the empowerment ideologies used to justify cooperative and participatory management practices, employees often abandon the need to critically reflect on and challenge the many injustices and inequities (such as sexual and racial discrimination) which pervade most organizations. This notion was preceded by Marx's concern over the development of a false consciousness among workers (Marx, 1844). In other words, emphasizing micro-level cooperative practices in organizations can often mask the pressing need for macro-level reform (see Barker, 1993; Mumby & Stohl, 1991).

Third, some critics contend that the well-intended human relations and participative management initiatives often become appropriated by management and used as subtle forms of control. For example, Mumby and Stohl (1991) demonstrated how team-based work designs can construct the illusion of worker autonomy and draw the workers' attention away from the structure imposed on them by the management. As the structure becomes a given, conflicts among workers begin to be perceived by them as merely interpersonal ones and unrelated to management's policies and objectives. Norms are then established to govern each worker's obligations toward the team, and efforts are undertaken to enforce those norms, instead of reflecting upon and possibly questioning the agenda dictated from above. Thus, rather than offering workers more autonomy and discretion, such cooperative team-based work arrangements often result in more intensive monitoring than would have been possible under the traditional work arrangements. Instead of freeing workers from traditional vertical monitoring, improved management information systems have strengthened vertical control, and the new team-based arrangements add horizontal peer monitoring (Sewell, 1998; Sewell & Wilkinson, 1992), which can be a great deal more intrusive, coercive, and abusive than the traditional work processes (Barker, 1993, 1999). Finally, the critical and postmodern theorists argue, the overemphasis on the A to B relational power processes of both the controlling and cooperative perspectives tends to decontextualize the theoretical discussion of power, which is often largely predetermined by the historical and normative context of communications and meaning-making typically controlled by elites in organizations (Alvesson & Willmott, 1992a).

Critical Perspectives on Power

Critical management studies (CMS) have sought to challenge the assumption that management is a neutral and value-free activity concerned with attaining the instrumental goals of organizations that serve a common good. Reynolds (1998, p. 190) writes:

> Managing is not a neutral or disinterested activity. The socially intrusive nature of managing means involvement in and having effects on the lives of others and on their future and the future conditions of wider society. The essential stuff of management is the construction of particular power relations through which these processes are instigated and maintained.

Although mainstream humanist approaches to management also aspire to foster fairer organizational practices, they generally focus on curbing more blatant abuses and do not question the taken-for-granted assumptions of management. CMS is concerned with the "questioning of taken-for-granteds, both about practice and its social and institutional context.... Identifying and questioning both purposes, and conflicts of power and interest" (Reynolds, 1998, p. 192). It aims to expose and reform the mundane and frequently unnoticed practices that privilege some groups (and individuals) at the expense of others (e.g. how many seemingly neutral aspects of engineering work tend to privilege men over women; see Fletcher, 1999).

CMS's critique targets not only managers (and others who create and sustain the kind of practices that CMS seeks to expose and reform) but also many mainstream management research projects. Critical researchers have pointed out that mainstream management research tends to take the managerial or pro-elite point of view. The aim of mainstream research is to help managers and elites attain their goals, such as overcoming resistance to change or more readily attaining maximum productivity. Employees' needs are considered solely from an instrumental perspective. Furthermore, mainstream organizational scholars are criticized for assuming the privileged position of "objective" and disinterested purveyors of pure knowledge while in reality manufacturing knowledge that is political and serves those at the top of the hierarchy.

CMS has taken seriously the role of language in shaping and maintaining social reality. Language is not viewed as a transparent or neutral carrier of meaning. In other words, language does not merely represent reality out there but constitutes what we take to be reality out there and opens and constrains the ways in which we act upon this reality (Gergen, 1992). CMS also contends that an orderly reality is not natural but is a result of power plays that suppress the inherent contradictions, inconsistencies, and conflicts of interest in organizations. Power is embedded within the organizational structure, and mundane and taken-for-granted organizational practices both express and reproduce this power structure.

When organization is viewed as a conversation (Ford, 1999), or a story (Boje, 1991, 1995), the critical question is: whose story? Wallemacq and Sims (1998) write: "Storytelling is not a universal privilege. A key indicator of power in organizations is who has the right to tell stories" (p. 123). Although the conversation that constitutes organization includes many voices, some voices are louder than others. Voices compete for dominance for the right—the privilege—to frame the organizational reality for others and to define meaning for all (Salzer-Mörling, 1998; Wallemacq & Sims, 1998).

Clegg (1989) uses the pool-table metaphor to illustrate the difference between conventional theories of power and ones proposed by critical and postmodern theorists. The former conceptualizes the players A and B playing on a carefully calibrated table, where neither party has an advantage (for example, A over B or A with B). The latter assume that the playing field is uneven. Players find themselves thrown into a game in which the playing field has been skewed to the benefit of one of the parties, and this privilege makes it easier for that party to accomplish its goals. In this view power does not reside solely within the A–B relation. Instead, the two are embedded within a predefined set of rules and meanings that have been fixed. That is not to exclude the possibility that social actors may be invested in maintaining the existing power relations (see Potter, 1996; Wetherell & Potter, 1992, for related discussions). Thus, as reality is not a given but is continuously constructed and reconstructed, so too are power relations, which cannot be separated from reality construction. As Tsoukas (2000) writes, "social reality is causally independent of actors (hence realists have a point) and, at the same time, what social reality is depends on how it has been historically defined, the cultural meanings and distinctions which have made this reality as opposed to that reality (hence constructivists also have a point)" (p. 531). Since it is argued that meanings do not inhere in situations but are assigned to them, as things are defined and assigned meaning, some people find themselves in positions of power, while others find themselves subordinated (Mumby & Stohl, 1991). Power then is not only a personal or a relational variable. More dramatically, it emerges as meanings are defined.

As the meaning of such things as what constitutes historical "fact," or the standards of fairness and value become fixed, alternative meanings and possibilities are suppressed. Mumby and Stohl (1991) described the case of a male secretary who was ostracized in his organization because he violated the notions of what it meant to be a secretary (i.e. necessarily a woman) and what it meant to be a man (i.e. necessarily an executive). Thus, a male secretary becomes an "impossibility" in such a setting because the meanings associated with "masculinity" and with the profession of "secretary" become fixed, and are seen as mutually exclusive (Mumby & Stohl, 1991).

Organizations oftentimes suffer from narrowly fixed meanings of "how work should be done," which privileges some groups in relation to others. For instance, engineering firms tend to value problem solving a great deal more than problem prevention (e.g. Fletcher, 1999; Wright, 1996). These are stereotypically masculine ways of conducting work. Yet all that such practices accomplish is a constant operation in a crisis mode. At the same time the value of relational practices, such as organizational citizenship behaviors (OCBs), is overlooked (Fletcher, 1999). Performance tends to be assessed indirectly by measuring commitment, as expressed in willingness to work long hours and to put work above family, a masculine trait (Bailyn, 1993a, b; Eaton & Bailyn, 1999; van Maanen & Kunda, 1989). While penalizing many employees (female and male), who may need greater flexibility of work schedules in order to better meet their many obligations, this rigid insistence on long hours does not benefit organizations (Bailyn, 1993a, b).

Like the two previously discussed power paradigms, CMS has not escaped its share of criticism. Whereas mainstream management research has been accused of taking the managerial perspective and of failing to address the needs of those with less power, CMS has tended to marginalize managerial interests. Both critical theory and postmodernism tend to take the workers' point of view and to portray the needs of managers as illegitimate. Another criticism frequently directed at CMS is its intellectualism and apparent impracticality (Alvesson & Willmott, 1992a, b). It appears to see power and oppression everywhere, yet seems unable to locate it anywhere in particular. This leaves managers with a clear sense of the negative impact of current organizational arrangements, but with little sense of how to begin to create alternatives.

Nord and Jermier (1992) have pointed out that many managers find critical social science appealing. What has been neglected is that non-elites are not the only ones who are oppressed by the prevalent power arrangements. As Alvesson and Willmott (1992a) note, "Caught between contradictory demands and pressures, they [managers] experience ethical problems, they run the risk of dismissal, they are 'victims' as well as perpetrators of discourses and practices that unnecessarily constrain their ways of thinking and acting" (p. 7). McCabe (2000, 2002), for instance, offers two intensive case studies of an automotive plant and an insurance company, respectively, to show that not only do the managers exercise or attempt to exercise power over others, but that often their own identities are also constructed and constrained by these power relations. Thus, those with relatively higher power should not be viewed as exempt from the operations and consequences of power (see also Alvesson, 2002, Chapter 5, for a related discussion of leadership).

However, as a result of its frequently hostile tone and abstract and inaccessible language, CMS often appears irrelevant to managers. They often do not find it interesting, because it does not appear to be interested in them. If CMS is to be heard, it must adopt a more compassionate approach and seek to liberate all groups of people from oppressive social arrangements, rather than privileging the "underdog" (workers) while creating a new one (management). Furthermore, in keeping with its democratic ideals, CMS must learn to communicate its concepts in a clear and less intellectualized manner and to demonstrate its practical relevance to a wider audience.

Two Powers?

In reviewing the three perspectives on power, it becomes evident that there is much greater similarity between the power-as-control and cooperative power perspectives than between either of these perspectives and the critical one. The first two camps view power as relational, while the critical camp views relationships as embedded within and expressive of systems of meaning-making. Even the ontological and epistemological assumptions of these researchers and methodologies used are quite different. We suggest that rather than deciding which group is "right" or "wrong," it may be more instructive to recognize that conventional (i.e. power as control and co-power) and critical researchers speak of different things when discussing power. We offer the distinction between *primary* and *secondary* power as a heuristic to illuminate that distinction.

Primary power refers to the socio-historical process of reality construction. This is the process by which our sense of reality, as we know it, is constructed. As Chia (2000, p. 513) writes,

> Social objects and phenomena such as "the organization", "the economy", "the market" or even "stakeholders" or "the weather", do not have a straightforward and unproblematic existence independent of our discursively-shaped understandings. Instead, they have to be forcibly carved out of the undifferentiated flux of raw experience and conceptually fixed and labeled so that they can become the common currency for communicational exchanges. Modern social reality, with its all-too-familiar features, has to be continually constructed and sustained through such aggregative discursive acts of reality-construction.

Thus, primary power defines the domain. A manager is able to give orders and to expect them to be followed because the role of a manager has been historically constructed so as to include notions of order giving. It is important to recognize that the various sources of power (e.g. French & Raven, 1959) are not concrete but socially constructed. "Legitimacy," for example, is not objective but is created through management of meaning, and thus legitimacy requires power to be demonstrated (Hardy & Phillips, 1998). Only once the domain has been defined does it become possible for power as conceived of in conventional theories to be exercised (Hardy, Palmer, & Phillips, 2000).

Secondary power refers to the exercise of power in the conventional sense—the ability to get one's goals met. This can take a coercive or positive form. However, it involves working in a domain that has already been largely defined. Thus, the various strategies that managers may use to obtain their employees' compliance or commitment would constitute secondary power. The manager indeed has a choice whether to attempt to sell her or his ideas to the employees or to force them to obey. However, it is primary power that has made entertaining the options possible.

The two forms of power then are interconnected. Primary power opens and constrains the possibilities for exercising secondary power. Secondary power can be seen as expressing and reproducing the primary power relations. Individuals' identities are constituted by primary power, and these identities determine how much secondary power these individuals can exercise. However, secondary power can also contribute to transforming primary power. Revolutions or hostile takeovers are dramatic examples of secondary power being used in an attempt to transform primary power.

However, it is secondary power that most easily lends itself to the most popular management research methods, such as surveys and experiments. These methods carry a set of epistemological assumptions: there is an a priori social reality that is independent of the researchers' methodology; research uncovers, rather than constructs, reality; theory is a mirror, which putatively reflects the reality out there. Thus, both power-as-control and cooperative power researchers have focused on secondary power. The processes by which secondary power is exercised are crucial to understand. However, it is also important to better understand the operation of primary power.

Critical researchers have to a great extent concentrated on primary power, which is better investigated by methods that carry a different set of epistemological assumptions: the world out there cannot be separated from the research process; researchers are a part of the phenomena that they are investigating and as a result the research process constructs rather than uncovers reality; theory is better viewed as a lens, rather than as a mirror, and should be evaluated not on how accurately it represents the world out there but on what kind of insights it offers and what possibilities for action it opens up. Thus, most of CMS research uses ethnographies and case studies to collect data.

The primary/secondary power distinction helps us recontextualize conventional and critical research on power in a more productive way, such that the merits of each can be appreciated.

The Paradoxes of Emancipation

A serious limitation of many organizational approaches to empowerment, democratization, and emancipation is their rather one-sided view of power-sharing as unquestionably "good." When implemented, these initiatives often have unintended, paradoxical effects and consequences. Costs to the emancipated individuals and groups as well as to the organizations and the larger society must be measured along with the gains (Alvesson & Willmott, 1992b; Deutsch, 1985). Thus, the following paradoxes of emancipation should be thoroughly considered when these practices are applied in organizational change initiatives.

First, it must be recognized that emancipation can be anxiety-provoking for many individuals. Alvesson and Willmott (1992b) write, "A critical questioning of beliefs and values might not only facilitate more rational thinking, recognition and clarification of neglected needs, ideas about fairness, and so on, but, in doing so, may estrange the individual from the tradition that has formed his or her very subjectivity" (p. 447). Thus, emancipation may result in a profound sense of identity loss, confusion, general distrust, and depression (Fay, 1987). Others have suggested that the disempowered, when made to recognize their oppressed state, feel a deep sense of humiliation and resentment toward those who brought on such recognition (see Lindner, 2001). These difficult psychological experiences serve to exacerbate the more mundane anxieties associated with the fear of change, leading to an increased investment in the status quo (see Schein, 1993, for a related discussion).

Emancipation can also negatively affect organizational efficiency and productivity—at least temporarily—as individuals begin to question and challenge the duties, roles, and expectations previously taken for granted. This questioning can lead to a sense of ambivalence, role confusion, and inefficient performance. Management may in turn penalize these employees, leading to further disruptions of work. In addition, the implementation of more inclusive decision-making practices and decentralization of authority may increase the time it takes to make important decisions (Coleman, 2002; Whyte & Blasi, 1982) and negatively impact the organization's bottom line. Thus, increasing the ecological consciousness, level of participation, and free choice of employees, although beneficial, could ultimately result in bankruptcy and unemployment (Alvesson & Willmott, 1992b).

Another potential trap of emancipatory practices is that even if they begin by opening up understanding and encouraging reflection on taken-for-granteds, they can end up locking people into another form of fixed, unreflective thinking (Alvesson, 1996). For instance, one of the main arguments of CMS is that those in the lower echelons of the hierarchy are often "duped" by those at the top into believing that they are empowered, while in reality still being controlled from above through ideology. However, there remains a possibility that in trying to relieve the oppressed of their false consciousness, CMS is merely replacing one ideology with another. How does a CMS-inspired scientist or practitioner make people who think they are empowered realize that they are not? Does s/he not still bring this knowledge "from above"? Following its own ideals, then, CMS must refrain from "telling people what to do," while at the same time attempting to alter the apparently natural way that people have been "doing things"—sometimes all their lives.

Furthermore, when focusing on the oppressive nature of dominant ideologies, structures, and practices, it is sometimes easy to overlook the "loopholes" in the operations of power that are available to those in low power. These are microemancipatory processes "in which attention is focused on concrete activities, forms, and techniques that offer themselves not only as means of control, but also as vehicles for liberation" (Alvesson & Willmott, 1992b, p. 446). Sometimes, managerial initiatives aimed at increasing cultural control "trigger suspicion, resistance, and critical reflections" (Alvesson & Willmott, 1992b, p. 446; see also Collinson, 1994). These initiatives, then, have the paradoxical effect of fostering the opposite of their objectives. For example, a number of scholars (e.g. Collinson, 1994; Ezzamel, Willmott, & Worthington, 2001; Knights & McCabe, 2000) have documented how workers can and often do resist management's initiatives designed to increase their control over workers.

Finally, it is crucial to also examine what drives the empowerment initiatives themselves. Many of the "new" approaches to management, such as just-in-time and total quality management, are, again, frequently driven by an economic, rather than emancipatory agenda. Although both concerns are certainly legitimate, the two should not be confused, and "empowerment" should not become a marketing ploy for selling a new financial strategy to employees, for as several researchers have shown, employees tend to be better at sensing the true agenda than managers think (Collinson, 1994; Covaleski et al., 1998; Ezzamel, Willmott, & Worthington, 2001; Knights & McCabe, 2000; McCabe, 2000).

The preceding cautions are not intended to dismantle the emancipatory and empowerment agenda of organizational scholars and practitioners. Instead, the aim is to encourage critical examination on the part of such initiatives, so they can better avoid the pitfalls that have characterized much of mainstream organizational research and practice (Alvesson, 1996). In practice, however, this is a demanding task. As Deutsch (1985, p. 244) writes,

> I am further persuaded that even the nearest thing to common visions of an earthly utopia—a small, well-functioning, worldly, cooperative, egalitarian community—has to work hard and thoughtfully on a continuing basis to preserve its democracy, cooperativeness and egalitarianism as well as to survive. The inherent tendency of such communities is to break down; it takes sustained effort to prevent this from happening.

A CRITICAL–POSTMODERN FRAMEWORK OF ORGANIZATIONAL POWER

In this section, we present a brief overview of our framework of organizational power that builds on the controlling, cooperative, and critical perspectives in a manner that is mindful of the multifaceted and paradoxical nature of power and emancipation. The objective of such an approach is to offer a more comprehensive view of organizational power that is also concrete, useful, and applicable to organizational phenomena. The framework centers on an image of *power as exercised within a complex and contradictory network of*

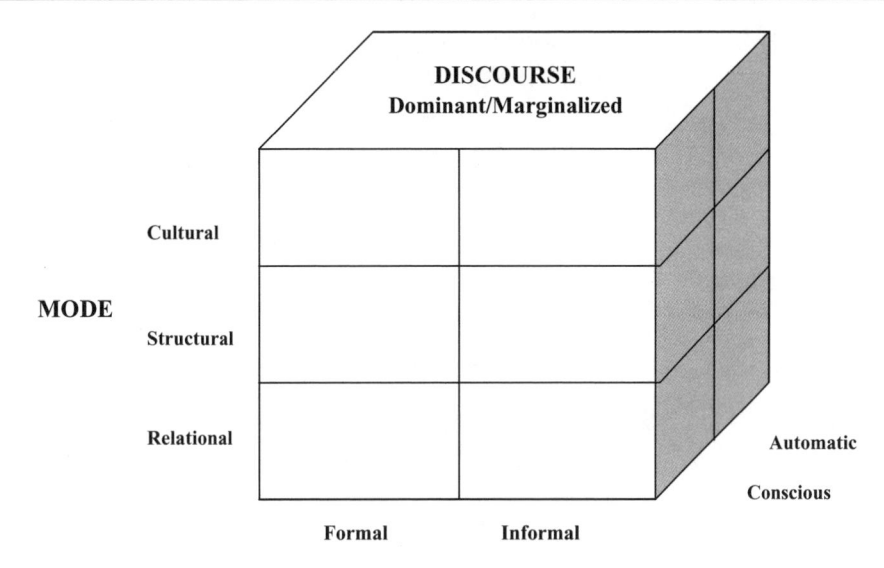

Figure 10.1 A critical–postmodern framework of organizational power

relations, structures, and meaning-making processes at different levels of organizational and community life. It prioritizes the construction and management of meaning and ideology as a central mechanism of power (by defining what is good, normal, ideal, deviant, etc.), but heeds the important roles that structural and relational variables also play. The framework acknowledges both the destructive and constructive potentialities inherent in the exercise of power, but can help to identify targeted and concrete opportunities for democratization, emancipation, and constructive change in organizational–community systems.

Dimensions of the Framework

We begin by articulating the four dimensions of our critical–postmodern framework of organizational power (CFOP): multimodal analysis, formal/informal activities, conscious/automatic activities, and oppositional discourses (ideologies and practices; see Figure 10.1). Each of these dimensions could be considered "meta-theoretical" because of their usefulness in enhancing the understanding of phenomena across different theoretical orientations.

MULTIMODAL ANALYSIS

A variety of scholars interested in the study of power in social systems have approached it from a multimodal perspective (see Alvesson & Willmott, 1992b; Boje & Rosile, 2001; Clegg, 1989; Deutsch, 1973; Foucault, 1980; Marshak, 1998). Each of these approaches has differed, but all have argued for the value of conceptualizing complex power dynamics through different modes in social systems, as well as understanding the relationships between the modes.

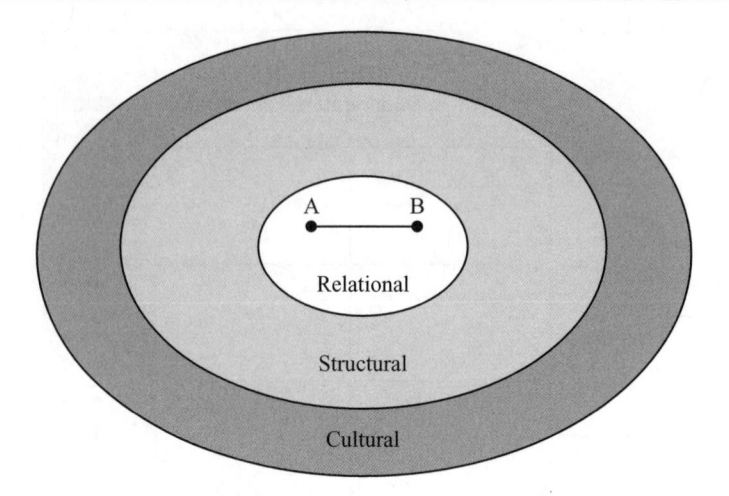

Figure 10.2 Nested levels of organizational power

The CFOP conceptualizes power in organizations through three nested modes: the relational, the structural, and the cultural (see Figure 10.2). Each mode can be affected by and can affect variables in the other modes, but each mode differs to the degree that it is associated with primary vs secondary power.

Power in the *relational* mode considers those factors and dynamics between people and between groups of people at the most micro-level of work and interaction. This can include all nature of interactive exchanges and behaviors including verbal and nonverbal communication, the management of conflict, and interpersonal or intergroup attempts at control, countercontrol, and resistance. This is power as conceptualized by many power-as-control and cooperative power scholars and corresponds to our notion of secondary power.

Power in the *structural* mode is concerned with macro-level systems of strategy, technology, work and organization design, decision making, reward, and punishment. Power in this mode is a mixture of primary and secondary power, in that it reproduces primary power relations, but changes in a system through this mode (including changes in rules, policies, procedures, goals, and incentives) can directly affect the character of the interactions in the relational mode.

Finally, power in the *cultural* mode considers those taken-for-granted aspects of organizational life: assumptions, ideologies, habits, and practices, which construct, express, and challenge the status quo of power in the system. These processes are pervasive, operating at both micro- and macro-levels, and correspond directly to primary power.

Thus, the power and authority relations between a manager and his/her subordinate will be affected by their unique relational dynamics (for example, the flexibility, temperament, and inducibility of each party in relation to the other), which are to some degree shaped by contextual structures (cooperative goals and incentives, labor/management policies, decentralized decision-making designs), which are largely determined by the taken-for-granted meaning of such structures and relations in that organization (employees who are not "team-players" are problematic, strike-busters are scabs, women managers should be empathetic, etc.).

FORMAL/INFORMAL ACTIVITIES

Over the past few decades, there has been a trend in organizational life toward more egalitarian and inclusive structures and policies (Burke, 1986). For example, many organizations have attempted to decentralize authority and power and promote more delegation and participative decision making. Similarly, there has been an ongoing attempt in organizations to implement diversity programs in order to meet EEOC regulatory standards and be more respectful and responsive to an increasingly diverse and "globalized" workforce and marketplace. However, many of these initiatives fail.

Current research on organizational citizenship behaviors (Organ & Bateman, 1991) and emotional labor (van Maanen & Kunda, 1989) has shed light on some of the obstacles these democracy and diversity initiatives face. This work has highlighted the central importance of *informal* or "extra-role" organizational practices for understanding and changing organizational processes and performance. Moghaddam (1997) contends that, despite the implementation of new decentralized and inclusive formal policies and structures, informal organizational practices often remain unaffected and ultimately hinder the desired changes in organizational culture.

Understanding the mechanisms through which these informal processes are sustained and affect power relations and intergroup dynamics can be extremely beneficial to executives, managers, and workers alike. Such an understanding can help shed light on:

(a) the nature and value of the system's resistance to the implementation of new policies;
(b) how their own actions may inadvertently perpetuate these undesirable informal practices;
(c) how informal practices sometimes benefit certain identity groups (e.g. racial or ethnic groups) over others and cause tension in the system;
(d) how they can become more effective in implementing desired systemic changes.

CONSCIOUS/AUTOMATIC ACTIVITIES

Contemporary research on social cognition has indicated that there are important forms of thought and action that are not under our control in that they are autonomous and detached from our will and intentions (Bargh, 1996). These thoughts and actions are believed to have been made cognitively accessible from previous experiences, and to be triggered by stimuli in the environment. For instance, stereotypes of low-power social groups (women, the elderly, ethnic minorities, etc.) have been shown to become active automatically in response to the perception of a group's distinct physical features in an individual (Fiske, 1993). In fact, there are very few research phenomena in mainstream social psychology that have not been shown to occur at least partially automatically (Bargh, 1996). Typically, however, these phenomena are considered to be affected by a combination of conscious and automatic processing. Current research on stereotyping (see Devine, 1989; Operario & Fiske, 2001), intergroup bias (Dovidio, Kawakami, & Beach; 2001), attitudes and persuasion (Chaiken, Giner-Sorolla, & Chen, 1996), and even the management of death-related anxieties (Pyszczynski, Greenberg, & Solomon, 1999) offer such dual-process theories. Thus, when analyzing the exercise of power in organizations, we must consider the role of both conscious and automatic processes in maintaining the status quo and creating change.

OPPOSITIONAL DISCOURSES

We use the term *discourse* to refer to all processes of meaning-making in organizations, which are typically accomplished through self-reflection and interpersonal communication between people. Power operates through discourse by framing the reality of organizational members in particular ways. Before reality can be acted upon, it has to be defined, and power manifests itself—perhaps most dramatically—in being able to define things (Alvesson, 1996), for certain definitions invite or even demand particular actions. For example, the emphasis on "teamwork" is becoming widespread in contemporary organizations. Although this notion is a social construction, it is often assumed to be a given, natural and unproblematic. The reification of teamwork can obscure the systemic nature of power by emphasizing power at the relational level and encouraging power negotiations to occur between individual actors within the team (Mumby & Stohl, 1991). Group norms start emerging, certain individuals assume leadership, and team-based sanctioning mechanisms develop only after the reification of the notion that "teamwork is the way we do work here" has made such activities possible.

We will address two of the many aspects of discourse: ideology and what we call organizational power practices (OPPs). Ideologies are various competing metanarratives that provide the frames of reference that individuals use to interpret reality. An example of such competing ideologies is what Sidanius and Pratto (1999) call "legitimizing myths." These can be hierarchy-enhancing (e.g. racism, sexism, meritocracy) or functioning to reproduce inequalities and hierarchies, or hierarchy-attenuating (e.g. civil rights, feminism, egalitarianism) or functioning to promote equality and to flatten the various hierarchies.

The other aspect of discourse, the OPPs, operate in ways that are automatic and virtually imperceptible. This refers to mundane and taken-for-granted social practices, such as rules of politeness, the way work is routinely done, and so on, that appear neutral and natural but in fact systematically reproduce hierarchies based on gender, race, sexual orientation, and so forth. These practices will be discussed in greater detail below.

Organizational cultures are often portrayed as monolithic and uniform systems of values, beliefs, attitudes, and practices. However, such coherence and integration are not natural but instead result from the suppression of alternative discourses, "where the managerial monologue seems to orchestrate the polyphony into one coherent voice...a process of homogenization of meanings" (Salzer-Mörling, 1998, p. 117; see also Alvesson, 1996). The process by which conflicting interests and contradictory values, beliefs, attitudes, and practices are suppressed and the illusion of consensus is produced is referred to as *discursive closure* (Alvesson & Deetz, 2000). Because ideological control is usually approached from an instrumental perspective—it is a much more efficient mode of controlling organizations than direct supervision (Deetz, Tracy, & Simpson, 2000)—discursive closure is not only common, but is often seen as desirable.

There are multiple reasons why this type of ideological control in organizations is problematic. First, it should be questioned on ethical grounds. Controlling another human being's subjectivity is perhaps more abusive than direct coercion. Here employees end up controlling themselves on behalf of management, as was suggested in the critique of the phenomena of work teams above (see also Deetz, 1995; Deetz, Tracy, & Simpson, 2000). Second, it can have detrimental long-term effects on organizational well-being. Homogenization of meanings facilitates managerial control and reduces blatant conflicts, but it does little for organizational performance. There appears to be increasing evidence for Kenneth Gergen's assertion that "if everything is running smoothly, the organization is in trouble" (1992, p. 223). Discursive closure achieves control at the expense of effective decision making, as dramatically illustrated by such fiascoes as the Bay of Pigs invasion (Janis, 1983) or the Watergate scandal (Deetz, Tracy, & Simpson, 2000). As organizations are becoming increasingly diverse, many of them find it tempting to continue "doing business as usual," or to use minorities and women to break into new markets instead of allowing diversity to change the organizational culture and work process (Thomas & Ely, 1996). As a result, such organizations fail to reap the benefits of diversity.

The final point against discursive closure is the practical impossibility of attaining a complete homogenization of meaning. As discussed before, every attempt at increased control can also facilitate resistance. Oppositional discourses may become marginalized, dormant, or temporarily silenced, but never die. The suppressed voices can find outlet in ways that are detrimental to an organization's goals. For instance, Collinson (1994) shows how workers at an assembly plant resisted management's attempts at ideological control through various subversive activities, such as using work time and equipment to produce products (car parts, sleds for their children) for their own use (for other examples, see Ezzamel, Willmott, & Worthington, 2001; Knights & McCabe, 2000).

Because ideological control tends to present certain values, interests, and practices as "common sense," those that do not endorse such values, interests, and practices come to be perceived as problematic and become marginalized by the dominant groups. Over time, polarized identities are created and sustained on both sides of these differences (Sampson, 1993a, b), often leading to protracted social conflicts between groups.

Putting it All Together

The four dimensions of the CFOP are presented in Table 10.1. To illustrate the four dimensions of power that comprise the framework, we present a brief analysis of a research workgroup in which we both participate. The workgroup conducts research on conflict resolution and power and consists of one professor, four doctoral students, and seven master's students. The group meets weekly for two hours to plan, review, and present research conducted by its members. Formally, it is designed to facilitate cooperative, team-based work, with positively interdependent tasks and goals. However, in practice the group members have a combination of competitive, cooperative, and independent goals. The data in Table 10.1 were collected using detailed observations of group meetings for two weeks and conducting interviews with several members.

Table 10.1 presents some examples from the research group to illustrate the different dimensions of the CFOP. Space limitations do not permit us to discuss examples of all the dimensions in detail. Since this chapter has emphasized the importance of the cultural mode, we will briefly discuss the examples that illustrate that dimension.

The cultural mode focuses on seemingly "normal" activities and seeks to understand how they function to construct and reproduce a certain version of reality that privileges some people at the expense of others. Looking at the top-right four cells, we observe that the group favors theoretical arguments over personal experiences as a strategy for contributing to the group (dominant/conscious/formal cell). In other words, members who are best able to use

Table 10.1 Twenty-four types of organizational power

			Mode				
			Relational		Structural		Cultural	
			Formal	Informal	Formal	Informal	Formal	Informal
Oppositional Discourses	Dominant	Conscious	Professor establishes a vision for the research	Professor offers general academic advice to students	Inclusion of MA and Ph.D. students in workgroup	Professor encourages teamwork	Privileging theory over personal experience to make a point	Using intellectualized language
		Automatic	Connecting world affairs to research	Expressing concern for members who are ill	Professor opens and closes each meeting	Evaluation of fellow student's work	Professor summarizes and integrates conflicting strands of discussions	Ph.D. students interrupting others when speaking
	Marginal	Conscious	Students offering a marginalized theoretical interpretation (e.g. post-modern)	Students inviting professor to informal get-togethers	MA students initiating a project	Students expressing contrary opinions of the work to other students in hallway	Offering a personal experience to make a point	MA students changing the topic in the group
		Automatic	Cognitively disengaging (doodling) when in disagreement with speaker	Students chronically arriving late to meetings	Students meeting independently with other students to initiate new projects	Students sharing concerns with each other re the work—independent of professor	Students presenting their work with air of confidence and independence	MA students interrupting others when speaking

their knowledge of various theories to support their arguments—usually the professor and doctoral students—are more likely to be heard and to influence the direction of discussions. This is understandable in an academic research setting; however it is important to recognize that this practice tends to neglect the considerable value of the practical insight brought to the group by the experienced practitioners in the group. As such, psychological jargon and social science concepts are preferred over personal rumination (dominant/conscious/informal). Again, given their academic training, the professor and doctoral students in the group are more likely to be able to use this type of language than the master's students.

When seeking to move the discussion forward, the professor sometimes integrates conflicting points made by several students into a coherent narrative (dominant/automatic/formal), which allows him to move the discussion in his desired direction. Due to their relatively privileged position in the group, the doctoral students tend to interrupt the other students when speaking more than the master's students (dominant/automatic/informal).

Both of these practices have a negative impact on the MA student-practitioner's experience of autonomy and ability to contribute to the research.

As argued above, there are always oppositional discourses that can be more or less audible. Looking at the bottom-right four cells, we note the marginalized discourses in our group. Personal experience is not valued as highly as theory and research to make points (marginal/conscious/formal). Attempts at switching discussion topics made by master's students are rarely successful (marginal/conscious/informal). It is relatively uncommon for students who report the progress of their research not to seek reassurance from the professor. They typically make eye contact with him, leave pauses in sentences for him to fill in information, and so on. However, on occasion an elite member of the Ph.D. group may present his or her work with a greater sense of independence and confidence (marginal/automatic/formal). As common as interrupting by doctoral students may be, it is highly uncommon for master's students to interrupt others (marginal/automatic/informal).

Putting the examples together, it becomes apparent that despite the cooperative, team-based structure of the group there is a clear hierarchy and a dominant culture within the research group. We are not suggesting that finding a hierarchy in the research group is unexpected or undesirable. Given the normative expectation at universities, the resulting hierarchy and culture would be considered "legitimate." However, it is *where* and *how* the hierarchy manifests, is maintained, and the consequences of such a culture that are of interest. Our analysis allowed us to observe how practices that appeared harmless on the surface, positioned the professor at the top of the hierarchy and claimed a privileged spot for the doctoral students and the academically trained at the expense of the master's students and practitioners in the group. This arrangement, although typical of university settings, was having unintended consequences for our work; shutting down some of the valuable insights from practice that could inform our research. Of course, explicitly identifying these processes, on this or other hierarchies of difference (such as those based on race, gender, sexual orientation, nationality, class, etc.), can come at some costs to the efficient functioning of the group.

Practical Implications

We began this chapter with an image of power as a multifaceted phenomenon exercised within a complex and contradictory network of relations, structures, and meaning-making processes at different levels of organizational and community life. Thus, any practical implications emerging from our discussion must address the same degree of complexity, contradiction, and scope. We support the position that it is insufficient to conduct meaningful organizational change solely at the relational level (Boje & Rosile, 2001) or at either one of the more macro-levels (Deetz, Tracy, & Simpson, 2000; Moghaddam, 1997). Instead, we advocate a program of *multiple emancipatory initiatives*, in which different groups of stakeholders at different levels attempt separate initiatives. These initiatives may combine controlling, cooperative, and critical activities, and can serve as a safeguard against institutionalizing new interests at the expense of others. Ideally, a plurality of actions helps ensure representation and voice for all stakeholders, including consumers, workers, investors, suppliers, host communities, the general society, and the world ecological community (Deetz, 1995). Social responsibility and consideration of the stakeholders' well-being is not only the "right" thing to do but is also important for the long-term economic sustainability of the organization.

In service of such a program, we offer the CFOP (see Figure 10.1 and Table 10.1) as an analytic and diagnostic tool for use in identifying organization-specific patterns and tendencies around power, dominance, and change. However, like any diagnostic tool, the CFOP has the potential to be abused by members of both dominant and marginalized groups. Thus, we recommend that it be utilized through a process of participatory action research (PAR). PAR is a methodology that places social transformation and empowerment at the center of the research process (Brydon-Miller, 1997; Lykes, 1997). Originating from Kurt Lewin's action research methodology (Lewin, 1946), and the emancipatory work of Paulo Freire (1970), Marxists (Oquist, 1978), feminists (Maguire, 1987), and various critical theorists (Comstock & Fox, 1993; Habermas, 1971), PAR attempts to achieve positive social change by addressing the concerns of all stakeholders, which includes the fundamental causes of oppression. It is "at once a process of research, education, and action to which all participants contribute their unique skills and knowledge and through which all participants learn and are transformed" (Brydon-Miller, 1997, p. 661). When combined with the CFOP, PAR can facilitate an increase in awareness around power and dominance and an openness to learning and influence for all members of the organization.

However, we again stress that any emancipatory initiative must be implemented with an understanding of the paradoxical nature of such initiatives. This requires recognition of the merits and the trade-offs of both sides of emancipation. The needs for stability, adaptability, and reform cannot be seen as mutually exclusive, but must be recognized as part of a dynamic whole. In other words, *a key to fostering constructive change processes in organizations is in managing these basic tensions and reframing them in a manner that influences their direction.* These processes will need to respond to resistance (closed mind-sets, vested interests, practices, structures, identities, etc.), but do so in a more balanced manner. Thus we must look for approaches that seek sufficient control *and* equal participation, that meet short-term *and* long-term objectives, and that create value for laborers *and* managers alike. Morgan (1997) suggests that this can be achieved through the creation of *new contexts* based on *new understandings* of paradox and *new actions*. He contends that the fact that these tensions are perceived as contradictory in the first place is germane to the problem. Thus, we need to develop new contexts and approaches that reframe the tensions between control and emancipation as natural and complementary, and respond to them with new actions (experiments, prototypes) which enable stakeholders to manage the tensions constructively.

The following are some examples of the types of initiatives that can be undertaken by separate groups of stakeholders within the relational, structural, and cultural modes of the organization to mobilize a program of multiple emancipatory initiatives.

Relational Initiatives

Tjosvold, Andrews, and Struthers (1991) provided a series of recommendations for establishing strong cooperative links and constructive power relations in organizations by developing: (a) a common direction and vision, (b) mutual tasks, (c) assessment of joint productivity, (d) shared rewards contingent upon success, (e) complementary responsibilities and roles that require collaboration, and (f) team identity and supportive culture (p. 297). Coleman and Tjosvold (2000) added: (g) mutual recognition and appreciation of each other's strengths, (h) reciprocal exchange of resources, (i) openness to development and learning, and ideally (j) a shared value base that emphasizes human dignity, human equality, nonviolence, reciprocity, respect of diverse others, and a common good (Deutsch, 2000; Rawls, 1996). These are primarily structural and cultural interventions aimed at fostering promotively interdependent relations. Training in the knowledge, attitudes, and skills necessary for cooperative work and constructive conflict resolution are also basic to promoting positive relational dynamics. These activities can create the conditions and capacities for cooperative power to develop where people want others to perform effectively and use their joint resources to promote common objectives. However, concerns over the disempowering effects of relational strategies must be addressed through additional co-power initiatives within the structural and cultural modes.

Structural Initiatives

Boje and Rosile (2001) proposed two major democratization initiatives within the structural mode. Based on the works of Mary Parker Follett (1973) and Stuart Clegg (1989), they advocate co-power reforms in both corporate governance and at the organization–community interface (see also Deutsch's (1985) discussion of worker capitalism and worker-owned collectives). First, they recommend cooperative forms of joint democratic governance for management and labor. They write (p. 68):

> Follett, however, favored workers' councils, including direct representation of workers on boards of directors and departments and the training of workers in the financial affairs of the entire firm. The cooperative and guild movements also stressed worker participation in the governance of the whole firm; employees were to become co-owners of production, not just design participants. Empowerment through co-ownership is not the same as empowerment through participative approaches to work design that afford more team participation or worker control over the pace and layout of work.

Second, Boje and Rosile (2001) cite the value of the current charter movement, a grassroots movement to return control of local corporate charters back to the communities in which they are situated. This is an attempt to make corporations in this age of globalization more accountable for "spreading mass poverty, environmental devastation, and social disintegration...weakening our capacity for constructive social and cultural innovation" (Korten, 1995, p. 268). They argue for a movement to firms that are locally controlled and accountable to emphasize the need for corporations to serve public and ecological well-being. They envision a global system of localized economies that celebrate and support local diversity, which ultimately enriches the whole. Both of these initiatives—corporate governance and corporate charter movements—situate the mechanisms of co-power within the macro-structural mode where their effects are profound and lasting.

Cultural Initiatives

Emancipatory initiatives targeted at organizational culture are the most central to our framework, for it is within this mode that meaning, status, and dominance are constructed, maintained, and ultimately challenged. Although it is often difficult to determine how or where to intervene in a mode as pervasive and mercurial as culture, we suggest three methods: through the identification and discussion of organizational power practices (OPPs), through training in critical reflection, and by creating a climate which values oppositional and marginalized voices.

IDENTIFYING AND EXPLORING ORGANIZATIONAL POWER PRACTICES

Not knowing whether or when to smile, to laugh out loud, or to nod in solemn agreement in a meeting can adversely affect one's status within that group. We call this type of taken-for-granted practice *organizational power practices (OPPs)* because they can serve to privilege some individuals in relation to others along important dimensions of difference. To be sure, it can be argued that all aspects of organizational behavior are to some extent structured by and reproduce power relations (Alvesson, 1996; Townley, 1993)—including the organizational members' emotional experience of work (see Hancock & Tyler, 2001, Chapter 5, for a review). However, because it is impossible and impractical to identify the many ways in which every action is connected to power, we offer OPPs as an analytic concept through which to better understand power relations. In other words, OPPs can help us to determine which social practices are most essential to power relations in a given context. Thus, *OPPs are the social practices that are most relevant to operations of power in a given context*. We offer several "rules of thumb" about OPPs.

Point 1: OPPs are group-specific; what is an OPP within a certain group may not be an OPP within another. For example, Collinson (1994) described a case where, in the spirit of a corporate culture campaign, management sought to de-emphasize hierarchy by encouraging workers to call managers by their first names. Thus, calling a manager by his/her first name was a hierarchy-attenuating OPP from management's perspective. However, the workers were determined to resist the corporate culture initiative, which they perceived as a management trick designed to increase productivity, and in order to do so sought to distance themselves from management. Thus, from the workers' perspective addressing a manager by his/her first name did not constitute an effective OPP.

We can see here how the social practices within the cultural mode can resist attempts at reform within the relational and structural modes. Managers' OPPs are attempts at creating a new organizational structure (structural mode), which is more in keeping with the ideology of "flat organizations" (cultural level). The workers' refusal to perform such OPPs prevents the desired structure from taking shape and fuels the oppositional discourse, such as "No, we are not all equal here."

Point 2: OPPs can be conscious or automatic. Sometimes people are conscious of the OPPs in a given system or subsystem and try to perform them. For example, the various subversive activities in which the workers in Collinson's (1994) study engaged were for the most part performed deliberately and intentionally. However, many—if not most—OPPs are automatic and do not require much thought. OPPs are learned by living in a system and observing others perform OPPs that eventually become part of an individual's repertoire to be used in appropriate situations. People are usually efficient in reading the power relations in a particular context and acting as the situation demands. For instance, at a meeting we usually know whether or not and when to speak up and how to do it. Some people will not speak at all. Other people may interrupt others, while others patiently wait for their turn to speak.

Point 3: OPPs can enhance current power relations or subvert the power structure—sometimes simultaneously. Since most mundane practices are somehow linked to power, when engaging in any behavior that is seen as appropriate to one's position (e.g. superior giving a subordinate advice and the subordinate receiving it), the status quo of power is maintained. However, some attempts at control from above backfire and stimulate awareness and resistance on the part of those below. Those with less power may then develop OPPs that revolve around subverting managerial control (Collinson, 1994). On the other hand, resistance can also reproduce the status quo. In Collinson's (1994) study the workers voluntarily distanced themselves from management and thwarted the potential for genuine improvement in their conditions through obtaining more information about the decision-making processes and attempting to influence them.

Point 4: An individual's OPPs depend on her or his status relative to others in a particular group. Fletcher (1999) discusses how in the engineering firm that she studied more "masculine" and aggressive patterns of behavior were valued. However, women who attempted to act "more masculine" in order to fit in were frequently informally sanctioned for not acting "feminine enough." Thus, different roles and statuses carry with them particular OPPs, and successful performance of OPPs is conditional upon the individuals' correct reading of their particular roles and statuses in any given interaction (Hardy, Palmer, & Phillips, 2000; Voronov & Coleman, 2001).

Point 5: The category of interest will drive which OPPs are noted and investigated. Power hierarchies are often constructed around a wide range of social categories, such as gender, race, sexual orientation, and so on. Thus, which social practices are construed as OPPs will depend on the kind of power hierarchy one seeks to investigate. For example, when trying to uncover gender inequities in an organization, one may note the privileging of more masculine behaviors in a given situation (e.g. Fletcher, 1999). The OPPs here then would be the taken-for-granted social practices that construct and reproduce a gender hierarchy.

To sum up, OPPs are an analytic tool that allows us to see the links between the social practices within the cultural mode and the relational and structural modes. OPPs emphasize the importance of the informal and taken-for-granted social practices for the maintenance of the status quo of power. Thus, a successful culture change demands more than formal restructuring; the informal practices and communication must also express the new vision (Deetz, Tracy, & Simpson, 2000).

TRAINING AND SUPPORTING CRITICAL REFLECTION

Many human resource training programs utilize self-reflection as a mechanism to increase awareness of personal beliefs, values, attitudes, problem-solving strategies, and other behavioral tendencies. However, very few such programs include *critical reflection* as an integral part of their curriculum. Critical reflection is distinct from self-reflection in four ways:

1. It is principally concerned with developing the capacity to question "common sense" assumptions.
2. Its focus is social, political, and historical rather than individual.
3. It pays particular attention to the analysis of power relations, hierarchies, and privilege.
4. It is concerned with emancipation and, as such, is ideological (Reynolds, 1998).

The ability to critically reflect is essential for all members of contemporary organizations. We understand that all employees may not be in the position to act upon the system to make it reflect critical–postmodern ideals. However, having learned to engage in critical reflection, they may be more likely to seize the available opportunities to change aspects of organizational functioning toward a more inclusive and democratic end—given the practical and political limitations that they face. The idea of OPPs can be particularly useful for such critical reflection training, because it offers a way to see the operations of power more concretely and without falling into the trap of many CMS writings where dominance is thought to be everywhere but cannot be identified anywhere.

FOSTERING A CLIMATE FAVORABLE TO MARGINALIZED VOICES

Engaging in participatory action research on OPPs and offering training in critical reflection can go a long way in assessing the value and consequences of the dominant system of power in any organization. However, we have repeatedly emphasized the need to be mindful of the costs and consequences of such emancipatory initiatives, as well as the reactive tendencies to close out previously privileged discourses. Thus, we recommend viewing emancipation not as an outcome, but as an ongoing process of critical reflection, exploration, and restructuring. A commitment to a process of questioning the taken-for-granteds in any organization can help establish a climate where all voices are valued and where the true value of diversity can flourish.

REFERENCES

Adorno, T. W., Frenkel-Brunswick, E., Levinson, D. J., & Sanford, R. N. (1950). *The Authoritarian Personality*. New York: Harper and Brothers.
Alvesson, M. (1996). *Communication, Power and Organization*. Berlin: Walter de Gruyter.
Alvesson, M. (2002). *Understanding Organizational Culture*. London: Sage.
Alvesson, M. & Deetz, S. (2000). *Doing Critical Management Research*. London: Sage.
Alvesson, M. & Willmott, H. (1992a). Critical theory and management studies: an introduction. In M. Alvesson & H. Willmott (eds), *Critical Management Studies* (pp. 1–20). London: Sage.
Alvesson, M. & Willmott, H. (1992b). On the idea of emancipation in management and organization studies. *Academy of Management Review, 17*, 432–464.
Bailyn, L. (1993a). *Breaking the Mold: Women, Men, and Time in the New Corporate World*. New York: The Free Press.
Bailyn, L. (1993b). Patterned chaos in human resource management. *Sloan Management Review*, Winter, pp. 77–83.
Bargh, J. A. (1996). Automaticity in social psychology. In E. T. Higgins & A. W. Kruglanski (eds), *Social Psychology: Handbook of Basic Principles*. New York: Guilford Press.
Barker, J. R. (1993). Tightening the iron cage: concertive control in self-managing teams. *Administrative Science Quarterly, 38*, 408–437.
Barker, J. R. (1999). *The Discipline of Teamwork: Participation and Concertive Control*. Thousand Oaks, Calif.: Sage.
Boje, D. M. (1991). The storytelling organization: a study of story performance in an office-supply firm. *Administrative Science Quarterly, 36*, 106–126.
Boje, D. M. (1995). Stories of the storytelling organization: a postmodern analysis of Dysney as a "Tamara-Land". *Academy of Management Journal, 38*, 997–1035.
Boje, D. M. & Rosile, G. A. (2001). Where's the power in the empowerment? Answers from Follett and Clegg. *The Journal of Applied Behavioral Science, 37*, 90–117.

Brydon-Miller, M. (1997). Participatory action research: psychology and social change. *Journal of Social Issues, 53*(4), 657–666.

Burke, W. W. (1986). Leadership as empowering others. In S. Srivastra & associates (eds), *Executive Power: How Executives Influence People and Organizations*. San Francisco: Jossey-Bass.

Cartwright, D. (1959). *Studies in Social Power*. Ann Arbor, Mich.: Institute for Social Research.

Chaiken, S., Giner-Sorolla, R., & Chen, S. (1996). Beyond accuracy: defense and impression motives in heuristic and systematic information processing. In P. M. Goldwitzer & J. A. Bargh (eds), *The Psychology of Action: Linking Cognition and Motivation to Behavior* (pp. 553–587). New York: Guilford Press.

Chia, R. (2000). Discourse analysis as organizational analysis. *Organization, 7*, 513–518.

Christie, R. & Geis, F. L. (1970). *Studies in Machiavellianism*. New York: Academic Press.

Clegg, S. (1989). *Frameworks of Power*. Thousand Oaks, Calif.: Sage.

Coleman, P. T. (2002). Change, paradox, complexity and meaning: a meta-framework for working seemingly intractable conflict. Working Paper, The International Center for Cooperation and Conflict Resolution, Teachers College, Columbia University.

Coleman, P. T. (in press). Implicit power theories: impact on perceptions of power and power sharing decisions. *Journal of Applied Social Psychology*.

Coleman, P. T. & Tjosvold, D. (2000). Positive power: mapping the dimensions of constructive power relations. Unpublished manuscript.

Collinson, D. (1994). Strategies of resistance: power, knowledge and subjectivity in the workplace. In J. M. Jermier, D. Knights, & W. R. Nord (eds), *Resistance and Power in Organizations* (pp. 25–68). London: Routledge.

Comstock, D. & Fox, R. (1993). Participatory research as critical theory: the North Bonneville, USA experience. In P. Park, M. Brydon-Miller, B. Hall, & T. Jackson (eds), *Voices of Change: Participatory Research in the United Sates and Canada*. Westport, Conn.: Bergin and Garvey Press.

Covaleski, M. A., Dirsmith, M. W., Heian, J. B., & Samuel, S. (1998). The calculated and the avowed: techniques of discipline and struggles over identity in Big Six public accounting firms. *Administrative Science Quarterly, 43*, 293–327.

Dahl, R. P. (1957). The concept of power. *Behavioral Science, 2*, 201–218.

Dahl, R. P. (1968). Power. In D. L. Sills (ed.), *International Encyclopedia of the Social Sciences* (Vol. 12). New York: Macmillan.

Deetz, S. (1995). *Transforming Communication, Transforming Business: Building Responsive and Responsible Workplaces*. Cresskill, NJ: Hampton Press, Inc.

Deetz, S., Tracy, S. J., & Simpson, J. L. (2000). *Leading Organizations through Transition: Communication and Cultural Change*. Thousand Oaks, Calif.: Sage.

Deutsch, M. (1973). *The Resolution of Conflict*. New Haven, Conn.: Yale University Press.

Deutsch, M. (1985). *Distributive Justice: A Social–Psychological Perspective*. New Haven, Conn.: Yale University Press.

Deutsch, M. (2000). Justice and conflict. In Morton Deutsch & Peter T. Coleman (eds), *The Handbook of Conflict Resolution: Theory and Practice* (pp. 41–64). San Francisco: Jossey-Bass.

Devine, P. G. (1989). Stereotypes and prejudice: their automatic and controlled components. *Journal of Personality and Social Psychology, 56*, 5–18.

Dovidio, J. F., Kawakami, K., & Beach, A. (2001). Reducing intergroup bias: the benefits of recategorization. In R. Brown & S. Gaertner (eds), *Blackwell Handbook of Social Psychology: Intergroup Processes* (pp. 22–44). Malden, Mass.: Blackwell Publishers.

Eaton, S. C. & Bailyn, L. (1999). Work and life strategies of professionals in biotechnology firms. *The Annals of the American Academy of Political and Social Science, 562*, 159–173.

Ezzamel, M. & Willmott, H. (1998). Accounting for teamwork: a critical study of group-based systems of organizational control. *Administrative Science Quarterly, 43*, 358–396.

Ezzamel, M. Willmott, H., & Worthington, F. (2001). Power, control and resistance in "The factory that time forgot". *Journal of Management Studies, 38*, 1053–1079.

Fay, B. (1987). *Critical Social Science*. Cambridge, UK: Polity Press.

Fiske, Susan T. (1993). Social cognition and social perception. *Annual Review of Psychology, 44*, 155–194.

Fletcher, J. (1999). *Disappearing Acts: Gender, Power, and Relational Practice at Work.* Cambridge, Mass.: The MIT Press.

Follett, M. P. (1973). Power. In E. M. Fox & L. Urwick (eds), *Dynamic Administration: The Collected Papers of Mary Parker Follett* (pp. 66–87). London: Pitman.

Ford, J. D. (1999). Organizational change as shifting conversations. *Journal of Organizational Change Management, 12*, 480–500.

Foucault, M. (1980). *Power/knowledge.* New York: Pantheon.

Freire, P. (1970). *Pedagogy of the Oppressed.* New York: Seabury Press.

French, J. R. P., Jr & Raven, B. (1959). The bases of social power. In D. Cartwright (ed.), *Studies in Social Power*, (pp. 150–167). Ann Arbor: University of Michigan Press.

Gergen, K. J. (1992). Organization theory in the postmodern era. In M. Reed & M. Hughes (eds), *Rethinking Organization: New Directions in Organization Theory and Analysis* (pp. 207–226). London: Sage.

Habermas, J. (1971). *Knowledge and Human Interests.* Boston: Beacon.

Hancock, P. & Tyler, M. (2001). *Work, Postmodernism and Organization: A Critical Introduction.* London: Sage.

Hardy, C., Palmer, I., & Phillips, N. (2000). Discourse as a strategic resource. *Human Relations, 53*, 1227–1248.

Hardy, C. & Phillips, N. (1998). Strategies of engagement: lessons from the critical examination of collaboration and conflict in an organizational domain. *Organization Science, 9*, 217–230.

Hinkin, T. R. & Schriesheim, C. A. (1989). Development and application of new scales to measure the French and Raven (1959) bases of power. *Journal of Applied Psychology, 74*, 561–587.

Janis, I. L. (1983). Groupthink. In J. R. Hackman, E. E. Lawler, & L. W. Porter (eds), *Perspectives on Behavior in Organizations* (2nd edn, pp. 378–384). New York: McGraw-Hill.

Kipnis, D. (1976), *The Powerholders.* Chicago: University of Chicago Press.

Knights, D. & McCabe, D. (2000). Bewitched, bothered and bewildered: the meaning and experience of teamworking for employees in an automobile company. *Human Relations, 53*, 1481–1517.

Korten, D. C. (1995). *When Corporations Rule the World.* San Francisco: Berrett-Koehler.

Lasswell, H. D. & Kaplan, A. (1950). *Power and Society.* New Haven, Conn.: Yale University Press.

Lewin, K. (1946). Action research and minority problems. *Journal of Social Issue, 2*(4), 34–46.

Lewin, K. (1947). Frontiers in group dynamics. *Human Relations, 1*, 5–41.

Lindner, E. (2001). Humiliation and the human condition: mapping a minefield. *Human Rights Review, 2*(2), 46–63.

Lykes, M. B. (1997). Activist participatory research among the Maya of Guatemala: constructing meanings from situated knowledge. *Journal of Social Issues, 53*(4), 725–746.

McCabe, D. (2000). Factory innovations and management machinations: the productive and repressive relations of power. *Journal of Management Studies, 37*, 931–953.

McCabe, D. (2002). "Waiting for dead men's shoes": towards a cultural understanding of management innovation. *Human Relations, 55*, 505–536.

Maguire, P. (1987). *Doing Participatory Research: A Feminist Approach.* Amherst, Mass.: Center for International Education, University of Massachusetts.

Marshak, R. J. (1998). A discourse on discourse: redeeming the meaning of talk. In D. Grant, T. Keenoy, & C. Oswick (eds), *Discourse and Organization* (pp. 15–30). Thousand Oaks, Calif.: Sage.

Marx, K. (1844). *Critique of the Hegelian Philosophy of Right.* Deutsche–französische Jahrbücher.

Moghaddam, F. M. (1997). Change and continuity in organizations: assessing intergroup relations. In C. S. Granrose & S. Oskamp (eds), *Cross-cultural Workgroups* (pp. 36–58). Thousand Oaks, Calif.: Sage.

Morgan, G. (1997). *Images of Organization* (2nd edn). London: Sage.

Mossholder, K. W., Bennett, N., Kemery, E. R., & Wesolowski, M. A. (1998). Relationships between bases of power and work reactions: the mediational role of procedural justice. *Journal of Management, 24*(4), 533–552.

Mumby, D. K. & Stohl, C. (1991). Power and discourse in organization studies: absence and the dialectic of control. *Discourse and Society, 2*, 313–332.

Nord, W. R. & Jermier, J. M. (1992). Critical social science for managers? Promising and perverse possibilities. In M. Alvesson & H. Willmott (eds), *Critical Management Studies* (pp. 202–222). London: Sage.
Operario, D. & Fiske, S. T. (2001). Stereotypes: content, structures, processes, and context. In R. Brown & S. Gaertner (eds), *Blackwell Handbook of Social Psychology: Intergroup Processes* (pp. 22–44). Malden, Mass.: Blackwell Publishers.
Oquist, P. (1978). The epistemology of action research. *Acta Sociologica, 21*(2), 143–163.
Organ, D. W. & Bateman, T. S. (1991). *Organizational Behavior* (4th edn). Boston: Irwin.
Pfeffer, J. (1981). *Power in Organizations*. Marshfield, Mass.: Pitman.
Potter, J. (1996). *Representing Reality: Discourse, Rhetoric and Social Construction*. Thousand Oaks, Calif.: Sage.
Pyszczynski, T., Greenberg, J., & Solomon, S. (1999). A dual-process model of defense against conscious and unconscious death-related thoughts: an extension of terror management theory. *Psychological Review, 106*(4), 835–845.
Rahim, M. A. (1989). Relationships of leader power to compliance and satisfaction with supervision: evidence from a national sample of managers. *Journal of Management, 15*, 545–556.
Raven, B. H., Schwarzwald, J., & Koslowsky, M. (1998). Conceptualizing and measuring a power/interaction model of interpersonal influence. *Journal of Applied Social Psychology, 28*(4), 307–332.
Rawls, J. (1996). *Political Liberalism*. New York: Columbia University Press.
Reynolds, M. (1998). Reflection and critical reflection in management learning. *Management Learning, 29*, 183–200.
Salzer-Mörling, M. (1998). As God created the Earth... A saga that makes sense? In D. Grant, T. Keenoy, & C. Oswick (eds), *Discourse and Organization* (pp. 104–118). Thousand Oaks, Calif.: Sage.
Sampson, E. E. (1993a). *Celebrating the Other: A Dialogic Account of Human Nature*. Boulder, Colo.: Westview Press.
Sampson, E. E. (1993b). Identity politics: challenges to psychology's understanding. *American Psychologist, 48*, 1219–1230.
Schein, E. H. (1993). How can organizations learn faster? The challenge of entering the green room. *Sloan Management Review*, Winter, 85–92.
Schriesheim, C. A., Hinkin, T. R., & Podsakoff, P. M. (1991). Can ipsative and single-item measures produce erroneous results in field studies of French and Raven's (1959) bases of power? An empirical investigation. *Journal of Applied Psychology, 76*, 106–114.
Sewell, G. (1998). The discipline of teams: the control of team-based industrial work through electronic and peer surveillance. *Administrative Science Quarterly, 43*, 397–428.
Sewell, G. & Wilkinson, B. (1992). "Someone to watch over me": surveillance, discipline and the just-in-time labour process. *Sociology, 26*, 271–289.
Sidanius, J. & Pratto, F. (1999). *Social Dominance*. Cambridge University Press.
Thomas, D. A. & Ely, R. J. (1996). Making differences matter: a new paradigm for managing diversity. *Harvard Business Review*, September–October, 79–90.
Tjosvold, D. (1981). Unequal power relationships within a cooperative or competitive context. *Journal of Applied Social Psychology, 11*, 137–150.
Tjosvold, D. (1985a). The effects of attribution and social context on superiors' influence and interaction with low performing subordinates. *Personnel Psychology, 38*, 361–376.
Tjosvold, D. (1985b). Power and social context in superior–subordinate interaction. *Organizational Behavior and Human Decision Processes, 35*, 281–293.
Tjosvold, D. (1997). The leadership relationship in Hong Kong: power, interdependence and controversy. In K. Leung, U. Kim, S. Yamaguchi, & Y. Kashima (eds), *Progress in Asian Social Psychology* (Vol. 1). New York: Wiley.
Tjosvold, D., Andrews, I. R., & Struthers, J. T. (1991). Power and interdependence in workgroups. *Group and Organization Studies, 16*(3), 285–299.
Tjosvold, D., Chen, G., & Liu, C. H. (2001). Interdependence, mutual enhancement and strategic advantage: top management teams in China. Paper, Social Interdependence Theory Conference, July, Minneapolis.

Tjosvold, D., Coleman, P. T., & Sun, H. (in press). Effects of power concepts on using power to affect performance in China. *Group Dynamics: Theory, Research, and practice.*

Tjosvold, D., Johnson, D. W., & Johnson, R. T. (1984). Influence strategy, perspective-taking, and relationships between high and low power individuals in cooperative and competitive contexts. *Journal of Psychology, 116,* 187–202.

Townley, B. (1993). Foucault, power/knowledge, and its relevance for human resource management. *Academy of Management Review, 18,* 518–545.

Tsoukas, H. (2000). False dilemmas in organization theory: realism or social constructivism? *Organization, 7,* 531–535.

Van Maanen, J., & Kunda, G. (1989). "Real feelings": emotional expression and organizational culture. In L. L. Cummings & B. M. Staw (eds), *Research in Organizational Behavior* (pp. 43–103). Greenwich, Conn.: JAI Press.

Voronov, M. & Coleman, P. T. (2001). Expanding the horizons of organizational discourse: social reductions, gender, and power in technical fields. Manuscript under review.

Wallemacq, A. & Sims, D. (1998). The struggle with sense. In D. Grant, T. Keenoy, & C. Oswick (eds), *Discourse and Organization* (pp. 119–133). Thousand Oaks, Calif.: Sage.

Weber, M. (1947). *The Theory of Social and Economic Organization.* New York: Oxford University Press.

Wetherell, M. & Potter, J. (1992). *Mapping the Language of Racism: Discourse and the Legitimation of Exploitation.* New York: Columbia University Press.

Whyte, F. W. & Blasi, J. R. (1982). Worker ownership, participation and control: toward a theoretical model. *Policy Sciences, 4,* 137–163.

Wright, R. (1996). The occupational masculinity of computing. In C. Cheng (ed.), *Masculinities in Organizations* (pp. 77–96). Thousand Oaks, Calif.: Sage.

11

MANAGING THE RISK OF LEARNING
PSYCHOLOGICAL SAFETY IN WORK TEAMS

Amy C. Edmondson

INTRODUCTION

This chapter explores how members of organizational work teams can overcome the interpersonal risks they face every day at work, to help themselves, their teams, and their organizations to learn. Over the past few years I have been developing a model of learning in the work group setting that stems from the underlying premise that people are (both conscious and unconscious) impression managers—reluctant to engage in behaviors that could threaten the image others hold of them. Although few of us are without concern about others' impressions, our immediate social context can mitigate—or exacerbate—the reluctance to relax our guard. In field studies in several organizational contexts, I have found enormous differences across teams in people's willingness to engage in behavior for which the outcomes are both uncertain and potentially harmful to their image.

An extensive literature on organizational culture examines how norms, values, and beliefs arise in organizations to reduce the anxiety people feel confronting ambiguity and uncertainty (Schein, 1985). In times of significant organizational or environmental change the potential for anxiety is increased because people must take action without knowing whether things will work out as expected. Organizational culture, for all its complexity, cannot fully mitigate the anxiety and uncertainty that accompany novel behaviors or activities. For example, a team launching a new product targeted for unfamiliar customers faces unavoidable technical and business risk. This can provoke feelings of anxiety in the team, but these risks can be minimized by formal risk assessment methods and explicit discussion. At the same time, all individuals in organizations constantly face more subtle interpersonal risks that provoke anxiety and yet tend to remain tacit and undiscussed.

Some years ago I became intrigued by the small risks people face every day at work, when interacting with others and facing change, uncertainty, or ambiguity. To take action in such situations involves learning behavior, including asking questions, seeking help, experimenting with unproven actions, or seeking feedback. Although these activities are associated with such desired outcomes as innovation and performance (e.g. Edmondson, 1999; West, 2000),

---

The Essentials *of Teamworking: International Perspectives.*
Edited by M. A. West, D. Tjosvold, and K. G. Smith. © 2005 John Wiley & Sons, Ltd.

engaging in them carries a risk for the individual of being seen as ignorant, incompetent, or perhaps just disruptive. Most people feel a need to manage this risk to minimize harm to their image, especially in the workplace and especially in the presence of those who formally evaluate them. This is both instrumental (promotions and other valued rewards may be dependent on impressions held by bosses and others) and socio-emotional (we prefer others' approval rather than disapproval). One solution to minimizing risk to one's image is simply to avoid engaging in interpersonal behaviors for which outcomes are uncertain. The problem with this solution is that it precludes learning. Another solution—to create conditions in which perceived interpersonal risk is reasonably low—is explored in this chapter.

Most people in organizations are being evaluated—whether frequently or infrequently, overtly or implicitly—in an ongoing way. The presence of others with more power or status makes the threat of evaluation especially salient, but it by no means disappears in the presence of peers and subordinates. This salience of evaluation in organizations intensifies the problem of image risk that people also confront in everyday lives (de Cremer, Snyder, & Dewitte, 2001; Snyder, 1974; Turnley & Bolino, 2001). Here I posit four specific risks to image that people face at work: being seen as ignorant, incompetent, negative, or disruptive. Each is triggered by particular behaviors through which individuals and groups learn.

First, when individuals ask questions or seek information, they run the risk of being seen as ignorant. Most of us can think of a time when we hesitated to ask a question because it seemed that no one else was asking, or perhaps we believed that the information was something we were expected to know already.

Second, when admitting (or simply calling attention to) mistakes, asking for help, or accepting the high probability of failure that comes with experimenting, people risk being seen as incompetent, whether in a narrow, particular domain, or more broadly. Reluctance to take such *interpersonal* risks can create *physical* risks in high-risk industries such as nuclear power, where admitting mistakes and asking for help may be essential for avoiding catastrophe (Carroll, 1998; Weick & Roberts, 1993). Similarly, this phenomenon is particularly troubling in organizations where lives are at stake, such as in hospitals. Reluctance to report mistakes in the health care setting is widely reported (e.g. Leape et al., 1991). Although this silence limits the ability of hospitals as organizations to improve through collective learning from mistakes, a goal most health care professionals would heartily endorse, the perceived need for impression management to protect one's professional image is extremely high in medicine.

Third, to learn and improve—as individuals and collectives—it is essential to reflect critically on current and past performance. The risk of being seen as negative often stops people from delivering critical assessments of a group or individual's performance, which limits the thoroughness and accuracy of collective reflection (Edmondson, 2002). Moreover, people strive to maintain their own and others' face, a tendency that inhibits sharing negative feedback. It is well known that bad news rarely travels well *up* the hierarchy, such that in the presence of supervisors and bosses, the risk of being seen as negative has been shown to be more acute than it might otherwise be (Reed, 1962).

Fourth, to avoid disrupting or imposing upon others' time and goodwill, people will avoid seeking feedback, information, or help (Brown, 1990). In particular, individuals are often reluctant to seek feedback about their performance. Despite the gains that can be obtained from feedback (Ashford & Cummings, 1983), many fail to take advantage of the opportunity. Although this can be driven by avoidance of the possibility of hearing something we do not want to hear, it also stems from a wish not to be seen as lacking in self-sufficiency, or as intrusive.

I have used the term "psychological safety" (Edmondson, 1999, 2002) to capture the degree to which people perceive their work environment as conducive to taking these interpersonal risks. In psychologically safe environments, people believe that if they make a mistake others will not penalize them or think less of them for it. They also believe that others will not resent or penalize them for asking for help, information, or feedback. This belief fosters the confidence to take the risks described above and thereby to gain from the associated benefits of learning.

I argue that creating conditions of psychological safety is essential to laying a foundation for effective learning in organizations. I further propose that structuring a collective learning process at the team or group level is a second critical element for effective organizational learning, and that a compelling goal is necessary for motivating this collective learning process. Although human beings are endowed with both desire and ability for learning, collections of interdependent individuals, whether small groups or large organizations, do not learn automatically. Not only does interpersonal risk inhibit some of the necessary behaviors, but organizational routines tend to endure and have a permanence of their own, independent of the actors who engage in them (Gersick & Hackman, 1990; Levitt & March, 1988). Moreover, traditions and beliefs about the appropriateness of the status quo inhibit learning and change (Levitt & March, 1988). Thus, an important aim of this chapter is to describe a collective learning process I observed taking place in similar ways across different contexts in a number of organizational work teams I have studied over the past few years. Teams are defined as work groups that exist within the context of a larger organization, have clearly defined membership, and share responsibility for a team product or service (Alderfer, 1987; Hackman, 1987).

In what follows, I describe the construct of psychological safety, the process of team learning, the role of the team leader, and how these constructs are related—drawing from my own and others' research. I first discuss psychological safety and how it differs from the related notion of interpersonal trust, and then describe team learning as an iterative process of action and reflection. I argue that compelling goals are necessary to motivate this deliberate, effortful process, and that psychological safety enhances the power of such goals. Without a goal, there is no clear direction to drive toward and no motivation to do so. However, without psychological safety, the risks of engaging wholeheartedly in this learning process are simply too great. The team leader can shape and strengthen the collective learning process both directly and indirectly by fostering psychological safety, and, in turn, setting goals. This chapter thus introduces a new theoretical model, depicted in Figure 11.1, in which psychological safety moderates the positive relationship between learning goals and

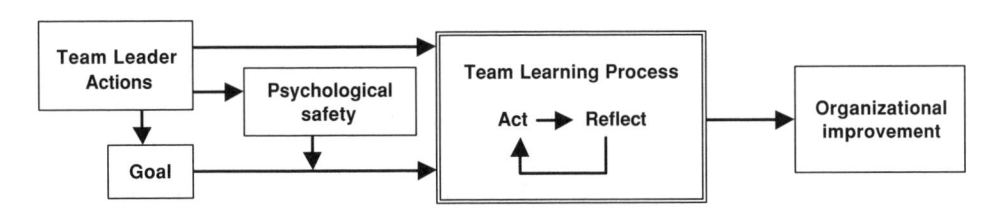

Figure 11.1 Model of team learning process

effortful learning behavior to accomplish them. I conclude with implications for future research and practice.

PSYCHOLOGICAL SAFETY: A COGNITIVE GROUP-LEVEL CONSTRUCT

Psychological safety describes individuals' perceptions about the consequences of interpersonal risks in their work environment. It consists of taken-for-granted beliefs about how others will respond when one puts oneself on the line, such as by asking a question, seeking feedback, reporting a mistake, or proposing a new idea. I argue that individuals engage in a kind of tacit calculus at micro-behavioral decision points, in which they assess the interpersonal risk associated with a given behavior (Edmondson, 1999). In this tacit process, one weighs the potential action against the particular interpersonal climate, as in "If I do this here, will I be hurt, embarrassed, or criticized?" A negative answer to this tacit question allows the actor to proceed. In this way, an action that might be unthinkable in one work group can be readily taken in another, due to different beliefs about probable interpersonal consequences.

The construct of psychological safety has roots in early research on organizational change, in which Schein and Bennis (1965) discussed the need to create psychological safety for individuals if they are to feel secure and capable of changing. More recently, Schein (1985) argued that psychological safety helps people overcome the defensiveness, or "learning anxiety," that occurs when people are presented with data that disconfirm their expectations or hopes, which can thwart productive learning behavior. However necessary the need for a comfortable learning environment, psychological safety does not imply a cozy environment in which people are necessarily close friends, nor does it suggest an absence of pressure or problems. Team psychological safety is distinct from group cohesiveness, as research has shown that cohesiveness can reduce willingness to disagree and challenge others' views, such as in the phenomenon of groupthink (Janis, 1982)—implying a lack of interpersonal risk-taking. Psychological safety describes a climate in which the focus can be on productive discussion that enables early prevention of problems and the accomplishment of shared goals because people are less likely to focus on self-protection.

Psychological Safety Versus Trust

The importance of trust in groups and organizations has long been noted by researchers (Kramer, 1999). Trust, defined as the expectation that others' future actions will be favorable to one's interests, makes one willing to be vulnerable to those actions (Mayer, Davis, & Schoorman, 1995; Robinson, 1996). The nature of this vulnerability is more narrowly defined for psychological safety than for trust. The concepts of psychological safety and trust have much in common; they both describe intrapsychic states involving perceptions of risk or vulnerability, as well as making choices to minimize negative consequences, and, as explored below, both have potential positive consequences for work groups and organizations. This section describes conceptual differences between these related constructs, to argue that they are complementary but distinct interpersonal beliefs. Three elements of psychological safety are described to distinguish it from trust—the timeframe, the object of focus, and level of analysis.

TEMPORAL IMMEDIACY

The tacit calculus inherent in perceptions of psychological safety considers the very short-term interpersonal consequences one expects from engaging in a specific action. For example, a nurse facing the decision of whether to ask a physician in the unit about a medication dosage she suspects is erroneous may be so focused on the potential immediate consequences of asking this question, such as being scolded and humiliated for being ignorant, that she temporarily discounts the longer-term consequence of *not* speaking up—that is, the harm that may be caused to a patient. Although the differential weighting of consequences in this example is clearly not rational, I have heard countless similar stories in field studies in markedly different organizational contexts. For example, nurses in one of several hospital teams in a study of medication error, after embarrassing past encounters with the nurse manager, were inclined to avoid speaking up about mistakes for fear of getting "put on trial," thereby unwittingly discounting the longer-term consequences of silence for patients and for the team (Edmondson, 1996). The construct of trust, in contrast, pertains to anticipated consequences across a wide temporal range, including the relatively distant future.

FOCUS ON "SELF" VERSUS "OTHER"

Trust involves giving others the benefit of the doubt—indicating a focus on *others'* potential actions or trustworthiness. In contrast, in discussing psychological safety, the question is whether others will give *you* the benefit of the doubt when, for instance, you have made a mistake or asked an apparently stupid question. For example, a member of a production team I studied in a manufacturing company reported, "I don't have to wear a mask in this team... it's easy to be myself." When people describe their situation at work in this way, they are revealing a sense of psychological safety, a sense of comfort expressing their true selves. The focus is internal, in contrast to the focus on others' future actions implicit in the construct of trust.

LEVELS OF ANALYSIS

An individual's sense of psychological safety in the workplace is likely to be shaped by ongoing interpersonal interactions among close coworkers. Although words and actions of top management may contribute to perceptions of psychological safety (e.g. Detert, 2002), as might individual differences in temperament (Tynan, 1999), the most salient influence is the perceptions of those individuals with whom an individual works most closely. Because psychological safety describes beliefs about interpersonal interaction, those interactions that are best situated to affect these beliefs are contained within a local work group or team. Moreover, members of teams tend to hold similar perceptions about psychological safety—that is, about "the way things are around here"—because they are subject to the same set of objective influences (for example, in having a common manager or a similar level of access to organizational resources), as well as because many of their beliefs develop out of shared experiences. Thus, team members of a nurse who reported being "made to feel like a two year old" when reporting a drug error independently reported similar feelings of discomfort about speaking up, for example commenting that "nurses are blamed for mistakes" and "[if you make a mistake here,] doctors bite your head off." These nurses, either from personal or vicarious experience, came to the conclusion that, on their team, reporting mistakes was interpersonally penalized. Consistent with this line of reasoning, in two studies I have found significant variance in psychological safety at the group level of analysis (Edmondson, 1996, 1999). In contrast, trust pertains primarily to a dyadic relationship, even if that dyad is sometimes conceptualized as consisting of large entities.

Others have studied both interpersonal trust and psychological safety; for example, in a recent study, May, Gilson, and Harter (1999) showed that coworker trust had a significant positive effect on psychological safety. Kahn (1990) found that "interpersonal relationships [in an architecture firm he studied] promoted psychological safety when they were supportive and trusting." Informants in his study felt free to share ideas and concepts about designs when they believed that any criticism would be constructive rather than destructive. The belief that others see one as competent (an aspect of respect) is particularly salient in this context; those who feel that their capability is in question are more likely to feel judged or monitored and thus may keep their opinions to themselves for fear of harming their reputation (Edmondson & Moingeon, 1998). In sum, if relationships within a group are characterized by trust and respect, individuals are likely to believe they will be given the benefit of the doubt—a defining characteristic of psychological safety.

Outcomes of Psychological Safety

Psychological safety can increase the chances of effortful, interpersonally risky, learning behavior, such as help seeking, experimentation, and discussion of error. Empirical support for this was found in the manufacturing company study, referenced earlier, in which I collected both qualitative and quantitative data on 51 teams of four types (management, new product development, staff services, and production) (Edmondson, 1999). These data were analyzed to show that psychological safety promoted team learning, which in turn facilitated team performance in teams throughout the organizational hierarchy.

In a more recent field study of 16 operating room teams learning to use an innovative (and extremely challenging) new technology for minimally invasive cardiac surgery, Edmondson, Bohmer, and Pisano (2000) found that psychological safety allowed nonsurgeons to speak up—despite facing long-standing status barriers—with observations, questions, or concerns about the new technology. Established hierarchical roles and routines in the operating were renegotiated to allow the technology to be implemented successfully (Edmondson, Bohmer, & Pisano, 2001). Rather than only waiting for the chief surgeon to issue commands, all team members (nurses, perfusionists, and anesthesiologists) had to speak up about and act upon crucial information from each other. Teams that were able to establish a degree of psychological safety were better able to renegotiate the ingrained hierarchy within the surgical team, and speaking up was a predictor of successful implementation of the technology. One of the successful implementers, for example, reported team members speaking up, even if it meant correcting a superior. One scrub nurse volunteered a story about her own error and how her junior, a circulating nurse, pointed it out to her:

> We all have to share the knowledge. For example, in the last case, we needed to reinsert a guidewire and I grabbed the wrong wire and I didn't recognize it at first. And my circulating nurse said, "Sue, you grabbed the wrong wire." This shows how much the different roles don't matter. We all have to know about everything. You have to work as a team.

In contrast, unsuccessful implementers reported great difficulty in doing this. For example, a nurse in one hospital explained that it was difficult to speak up when she suspected that something might be wrong:

> I'd tell the adjunct. Or, I might whisper to the anesthesiologist, "does it look like [the clamp] migrated?" In fact I've seen that happen. It drives me crazy. They are talking about it—the adjunct is whispering to the anesthesiologist, "It looks like it moved" or "There is a leak in the ASD" or something, and I'm saying "You've got to tell him! Why don't you tell him?" But they're not used to saying anything. They are afraid to speak out. But for this procedure you have to say stuff.

Research has also found that psychological safety can stimulate innovation. For example, West and Anderson (1996) studied top management teams in British hospitals and found that organizational support for innovation enabled both "participative safety" and participation, which led to proposing more innovations. In other studies, participative safety allowed teams both to generate and integrate innovations into practice (D'Andrea-O'Brien & Buono, 1996). Similarly, in the study of cardiac surgery teams, teams with greater psychological safety were also more likely to engage in process innovation—another factor associated with successful implementation of the technology in their hospitals (Edmondson, Bohmer, & Pisano, 2000, 2001).

Removing the fear of speaking up can promote innovation by freeing people up to suggest novel or unorthodox ideas. For example, in one of the cardiac surgery teams we studied, where unobtrusive measures revealed the presence of psychological safety (see Edmondson, Bohmer, & Pisano, 2001), a nurse spontaneously suggested solving a particular problem experienced in the new technology by using a long-forgotten piece of equipment—a clamp nicknamed the "iron intern." The nurse's brainstorm ultimately became a part of that team's routine. This kind of creative innovation can be contrasted with the views of members of other teams. For example, an anesthesiologist in an operating room team lacking psychological safety told the researchers that, although team members saw opportunities for change and experimentation, "It is best not to stick your neck out. Innovation is tolerated at best." The latter team ranked among the least successful implementers of the new technology, while the former was one of the most successful.

THE COLLECTIVE LEARNING PROCESS IN TEAMS

Mitigating the inherent risks of speaking up through psychological safety is only part of enabling teams to learn. Learning as a team also requires coordination and some degree of structure, to ensure that insights are gained from members' collective experience and also used to guide subsequent action. Individual learning is thought of as an iterative process in which actions are taken, reflected upon, and modified in an ongoing way (Kolb, 1984; Schön, 1984). This iterative process does not happen automatically in a team (Edmondson, Bohmer, & Pisano, 2001; West, 2000). This section describes the somewhat structured process through which teams learn and then discusses factors that contribute to this process, again drawing from three field studies to illustrate these factors.

Collective Learning as an Iterative Process

First, organizational learning researchers have described the need for reflection-in-action, or "double-loop learning" (Argyris & Schön, 1978), for effective organizational adaptation. Reflection-in-action is the critical examination of a process, such that it can be subsequently adjusted according to new data and knowledge. One component of reflection-in-action is analogic thinking (Hargadon, 1998). Analogic thinking—merging diverse pools of knowledge and integrating past and present experiences—is a learning strategy particularly relevant to new product development teams and others that are confronted with a learning challenge.

The team learning process consists of iterative cycles of action, reflection, and adjustment. What is being learned, made more effective, or disseminated are routines for conducting work that accomplishes goals. Although some organizational routines are simple and carried out by one person, most require coordinated action from multiple people. The knowledge needed to carry out these routines is stored in many different forms and locations, including procedure manuals, physical equipment and layout, and individual minds. Through repeated action and reflection, teams access this knowledge and learn how to best use it. In developing this conceptualization of team learning, I draw both from the literature (e.g. West, 2000) and from empirical evidence. In particular in studying cardiac surgery teams, those that successfully implemented a new technology in their hospitals tended to engage in a qualitatively different process—one characterized by iterative trial and reflection—than unsuccessful teams (Edmondson, Bohmer, & Pisano, 2001).

West (2000) stated that reflexive learning teams possess self-awareness and the *agency* to enable change. Periods of reflection in teams are structured around the questions: "What are we learning? What can we do better? What should we change?" and are followed by planning and implementation, or action. Some teams engage in reflection on a daily basis; others reflect at a natural break in the project, such as at "half-time" for sports teams (Katz, 2001); still others reflect when a project is completed, as in the "after action reviews" conducted by the US Army following military exercises (Garvin, 2000). The chronological midpoint of a project is a crucial time for reflection and change; anticipating "half-time" allows team members to work toward mini-deadlines and makes long-term projects approachable (Gersick, 1988). Furthermore, resolution is more easily obtained if it occurs "in the moment" because fidelity to data is likely to be greater.

Team reflection does not necessarily indicate extensive sessions to thoroughly analyze team process or performance, but instead can be quick and pragmatic. For example, a production team responsible for technical support in the manufacturing company included short daily meetings to check on team progress. Observing one of these meetings, I was struck by the quick task-focused updates, in which members described problems or solutions that had arisen within the past day or two, and others asked questions and offered suggestions. For example, after one member described "printer problems with those labels" and asked, "Who can we ask for help?" another member responded "How about asking the vendors who make the labels? They probably know how to fix it," and the team leader offered to make a phone call—closing the loop and dealing with the problem before it escalated in magnitude. Knowing that they would have a chance to reflect on triumphs and worries, the daily check-in contributed to this team's success within the organization.

For other teams it may be more appropriate to wait for outcomes to be available before reflecting on the team process. In a study of design firm teams, for example, Busby (1999) found that periods of collective retrospection after project completion produced cognitive and (to a lesser extent) behavioral learning. Increases in shared understanding (cognitive learning) were the most trenchant outcomes of these more extensive reflective sessions, and this shared understanding allowed team members to act and reflect in a coordinated manner.

Summary of the Team Learning Process

Across varying forms of team reflection (which differ in the frequency at which it occurs, at what point(s) in the project it happens, and what its outcomes might be) are some common themes: collaborating, making changes (whether mid-course or for subsequent projects), and expecting to encounter problems that will require changes. Reflection-in-action can lead to increased success in new technology implementation (Edmondson, Bohmer, & Pisano, 2001) and in product development. Reporting on a study of learning in new product development teams, Lynn et al. (1998, p. 8) concluded, "The key to developing really new products successfully is the degree to which teams are able to learn from prior steps—frequently in unpredictable ways—and act on that information."

LEARNING GOALS

Learning behavior is effortful. Something must motivate individuals to exert the effort to engage in learning behavior and drive groups to adopt the discipline to enact a collective learning process. A compelling shared goal motivates teams by establishing positive pressure or stress. A compelling goal for learning is one that is both meaningful (achieving it would in some way help the team or the organization accomplish something of generally agreed upon value) and sufficiently challenging to incur some doubt about its feasibility—but not so much doubt as to evoke feelings of helplessness (Csikszentmihalyi, 1994; Locke, 2001). For example, surgeon leaders of the more successful teams presented the new technology as an opportunity to help patients (by dramatically reducing the size of the surgical wound) and also stressed the difficulty of the challenge, explaining that it would require everyone on the team's active participation to pull it off. This emphasis on the goal and on the outcomes of their effort helped the team go through the arduous learning process.

The motivational power of goals is well established in the literature (Locke, 2001). Research has also shown that goal interdependence enables efficiency in group problem solving (Tjosvold, 1990), a kind of learning behavior. Other research (Frink & Ferris, 1998) suggests that goal setting and the effort invested in reaching goals are positively correlated to perceptions of accountability and performance evaluation. Goals also keep a team "on track" by establishing a benchmark against which its members can measure progress.

The Role of Shared Goals in Team Learning

Goals must be reasonably well defined and understood by all team members to foster reflection-in-action. For example, in a study of geographically dispersed product development teams (Sole & Edmondson, 2002), one team was working to develop a radical new material for a large Asian manufacturer. Distant team members had had no direct contact with this customer yet needed to understand its market strategy to estimate the longer-term commitment required for the team and its company. Other team members were located near the customer site and seemed to be in a good position to have the necessary information. After waiting for some time for the requested information, the distant team members' frustrations escalated:

> [We thought] our colleagues weren't putting priority and effort into it, when actually [we later learned] there was a void with the customer being able to articulate that themselves.

An intermediary familiar with both companies became involved and through his probing discovered that the customer itself had not yet established sales, marketing, or distribution plans, nor identified people responsible for these activities. A research scientist on the dispersed development team described this realization as an "ah-ha" moment:

> That was probably one of the biggest issues, because the customer themselves, for the longest time, didn't have their own strategy clear and *we didn't know it*.

The distant team members had made two assumptions: first that a *shared* team goal existed and second that the team members in contact with the customer had data relevant to achieving that goal. From these assumptions came attributions of noncompliance, leading to negative emotions within the team. Through better articulation of the team's shared goals (which would begin to suggest strategies for obtaining the information needed to achieve them), this miscommunication would have been less likely to happen. In fact, the act of goal setting can be as or more important than the goal itself, because it creates shared understanding of the team's task and suggests implications for how to work together.

Psychological Safety as a Moderator

Social psychologists have investigated relationships between objective goals and intrapsychic and interpersonal states in a group. For example, Dirks (1999) showed that trust moderates the relationship between goals and performance: when there is a low level of trust in a group, contributions of group members were limited to achieving personal rather than cooperative goals. This can inhibit group-level learning and get in the way of accomplishing a desired organizational change (Edmondson & Woolley, 2003). Similarly, in this chapter I propose that psychological safety moderates the positive relationship between a compelling goal and team learning. When psychological safety is high, this relationship is likely to be strong; when it is low, the motivating effects of goals are inhibited, as, despite the desire to learn, interpersonal risk may inhibit the necessary behavior. This hypothesis is consistent with existing theories of task motivation which maintain that behavior and performance are driven by needs, goals, and rewards (Dirks, 1999; Kanfer, 1990). Consistent with this, Figure 11.1 presented learning as motivated by goals, not by psychological safety itself. Psychological safety, when present, may enhance the motivating effects of goals on behavior, just as trust has been shown to moderate the effects of task (cognitive) conflict on relationship (affective) conflict (Simons & Peterson, 2000). In this study, trust reduced the likelihood of relationship conflict in top management teams, such that task conflict (productive disagreement over the content of one's decisions and ideas that deepen cognitive understanding of the problem) was able to help the team produce better solutions. Termed "creative abrasion" by Leonard-Barton (1995), task conflict thus may have to exist within a cushion of psychological safety to enable a learning climate of discussion, innovation, and productive group thinking. Otherwise such conflict is destructive—characterized by aggression, harsh language, and the threat of humiliation in front of others. Similarly, Barsade and her colleagues (2001) found that psychological safety moderates the effect of conflict on anger. Psychological safety allows groups to set high goals and work toward them through cycles of learning and collaboration.

In this way, psychological safety allows the interpersonal risks of learning to be mitigated. It has very real consequences for the way learning occurs—or fails to occur—in work teams of all kinds, and thus organizations. As depicted in Figure 11.1, team leader actions are predicted to influence goals, psychological safety, and the team learning process, while psychological safety moderates the relationship between a compelling team goal and a team learning process—enhancing or inhibiting the effect of goals on team learning.

THE ROLE OF TEAM LEADERS IN PSYCHOLOGICAL SAFETY, LEARNING PROCESS, AND GOALS

Factors that shape the team learning process include power relationships and how team leaders manage them. Above, I argued that psychological safety facilitates freedom and openness to engage in the interpersonally risky behaviors needed for learning, and also, perhaps paradoxically, that an effective team learning process is structured and guided, through deliberate action (West, 2000). Managing this apparent tension is the job of a team leader. Further, team leaders help to articulate or highlight a shared goal for the team.

The actions and attitudes of the team leader are thus important determinants of the team learning process. First, team leaders are a critical influence on psychological safety; second, they can deliberately work to structure a learning process, and third, team leaders play a role in shaping, or at least communicating, the team's goal. In this section, I develop implications for team leaders related to managing all three elements of team learning.

Creating Psychological Safety

Team leaders have a powerful effect on psychological safety. Researchers have shown that team members are particularly aware of the behavior of the leader (Tyler & Lind, 1992), and leaders' responses to events and behaviors influence (in a way either beneficial or detrimental to the group) other members' perceptions of appropriate and safe behavior (Winter, Sarros, & Tanewski, 1997). Leaders can create environments for learning by acting in ways that promote psychological safety. Autocratic behavior, inaccessibility, or a failure to acknowledge vulnerability all can contribute to team members' reluctance to incur the interpersonal risks of learning behavior (Edmondson, 1996; Edmondson, Bohmer, & Pisano, 2001). And, when team leaders are selected solely on the basis of technical expertise, such as skill and knowledge about a topic, they may lack the interpersonal skills necessary to seek others' input, invite feedback and ideas, and create an interpersonal climate in which others are willing to speak up with ideas and concerns.

ACCESSIBILITY

Leaders encourage team members to learn together by being accessible and personally involved. In one of the cardiac surgery teams that promoted organizational learning (in the form of successfully implementing the challenging new technology), an operating room nurse implicitly made this association by describing the surgeon leading her team as "very accessible. He's in his office, always just two seconds away. He can always take five minutes to explain something, and he never makes you feel stupid." In striking contrast, the surgeon in one of the less successful teams requested that nonphysician team members go through his residents (junior physicians who are still in training) rather than speak to him directly. Through their behaviors, these two surgeons conveyed very different messages to their teams. The first surgeon increased the likelihood that people would come to him with questions or problems, and, more importantly, would speak up quickly and openly in the operating room, with questions and observations, while the other surgeon made this more difficult (Edmondson, Bohmer, & Pisano, 2001).

ACKNOWLEDGING FALLIBILITY

To create psychological safety, team leaders also can demonstrate tolerance of failure, such as by acknowledging one's own fallibility, taking interpersonal risks, and religiously avoiding punishing others for well-intentioned risks that backfire. Self-disclosure by team leaders is one way to do this (Gabarro, 1987). For example, one surgeon team leader repeatedly told his team: "I need to hear from you because I'm likely to miss things." The repetition of this phrase was as important as its meaning: people tend not to hear—or not to believe—a message that contradicts old norms when they hear it only once. Soliciting feedback suggests to others that their opinion is respected; it may also contribute to establishing a norm of active participation.

Other vivid examples of purposefully refraining from penalizing failure exist in the management literature. For example, Brand (1998) reiterates the tale of how innovation at 3M was fostered by a culture of leaders and management tolerant of mistakes: the adhesive used in the now ubiquitous Post-it notes was the botched version of another product development project. The motto of product-design firm IDEO is "Fail often, so you'll succeed sooner" (Katz, 2001, p. 61). Similarly, Cannon and Edmondson (2001) describe the "Mistake of the Month" ritual at a public relations firm, in which certain meetings opened with a review of mistakes—a lighthearted way to acknowledge the learning value in mistakes, and even for building a sense of community.

PSYCHOLOGICAL SAFETY VERSUS ACCOUNTABILITY

In supporting a climate of psychological safety, are leaders sacrificing team member accountability? I argue that this is a false trade-off. First, it is inaccurate to equate psychological safety with the removal of consequences for lack of performance. My research suggests that skilled team leaders can reward excellence, sanction poor performance, and at the same time embrace the imperfection and error that are inevitable under conditions of uncertainty and change. Psychological safety is nurtured without sending the message that "anything goes." In this way, team leaders and other immediate supervisors of work must communicate clear expectations about performance and accountability, without communicating that they are closed to, or unwilling to hear, bad news. Psychological safety means no one will be punished or humiliated for errors, questions, or requests for help, in the service of reaching ambitious performance goals. To make this work, team leaders must inspire team members to embrace error and deal with failure in a productive manner. This balancing act may be difficult to enact without some natural leadership ability or training, or may require excellent interpersonal skills, and perhaps even humor (Filipowicz, 2002).

Managing Process

To encourage learning, the leader must impose structure on the team to ensure that reflection follows action and that changes are both suggested and implemented accordingly (Edmondson, 2002). This structured learning process will benefit from the leader's explicit request for input from the team. Team and organizational-level learning both necessarily depend on individually held knowledge, and there is a large body of valuable, untapped knowledge within the organization (Macdonald, 1995). Leaders must seek out this internal knowledge especially from lower-status team members (such as nurses and technicians in the context of the cardiac surgery operating room) who might otherwise be reluctant to speak. Team leaders can play a role in drawing members' thoughts out by setting up reflective sessions where task and time pressures are temporarily removed.

POWER

Leaders can manage power from both directions, first by empowering those in lower-power positions to speak up and second by minimizing the domineering tendencies of higher-power individuals. For example, in a qualitative study of four production teams in a manufacturing company, Brooks (1994) described one in which the leader, Dave, used his position as an engineer as an advantage over lower-status technicians in the team. Dave and another engineer dominated meetings and regularly belittled their teammates' contributions. The leader's style so swayed the group that Brooks characterized them as the "lost team," unable to set goals or make any real efforts to achieve them. Dominant individuals like Dave can be useful in prompting team reflection but should not be allowed to dictate the form of subsequent action (Wageman & Mannix, 1998). Power differences can and must be managed to enhance team learning and performance. Suppressing the input of team members reduces opportunities for learning, with such consequences as less robust data or poorly articulated, constructed, and executed projects.

Research on power differentials explains such scenarios as the relative presence or potency of power in a group influences willingness to participate and the type of knowledge produced (Brooks, 1994; Dirks, 1999; Lee et al., 2001). Other research suggests that fear (on an individual or organizational level) impedes collective learning by marring what Rifkin and Fulop (1997) term a "learning space." Fear in people holding subordinate positions within the team causes concealment of one's identity, blocking "mutual self-disclosure" (Rifkin & Fulop, 1997) and hindering the process of team learning. Psychological safety, however, can counteract the debilitating forces of power.

STRUCTURING A PROCESS

The second way leaders contribute to structuring the learning process is by guiding the team through preparation and early, sometimes experimental, efforts. The challenge of learning behaviors such as talking about errors, experimenting, and learning how to gather data from varied sources is affected by team composition. Knowledge differences, credentials, length of tenure, gender, and rank within the organization can threaten collective learning, yet many teams are successful learners in spite of these inequalities. Leaders can help this come about: in addition to building psychological safety, they can lead training and practice sessions, use direct, actionable language, and articulate norms for working together. Vignettes from several field studies illustrate these aspects of the team learning process.

STRUCTURE VERSUS INNOVATION

At first glance it may seem that leaders must sacrifice innovation by imposing the structure of a learning process. On the one hand, ensuring that action and reflection occur in a timely and productive way requires the imposition of structure, schedule, and guidance. On the other hand, this process not only allows spontaneity, creativity, and process innovation, it can promote it (West, 2000). Enabling innovation thus may require being flexible while imposing structure, another skillful balancing act that involves prodding the team to reflect, while remaining open to what transpires in the reflection process.

Setting Team Goals

IMPOSING VERSUS PARTICIPATING

The leader's role in setting team goals also involves a tension between setting direction unilaterally and allowing group participation in shaping goals. Clear, compelling goals are considered an essential prerequisite for team effectiveness (Hackman, 1987), and imposing a goal from above is often considered effective practice. This imposition can come at the cost of valuable input from members who may know more about certain facets of the team's work than the leader does. One factor driving this balance is the role a given team plays in executing the organization's strategy. If a team's job is defined by organizational imperatives, its specific goals may be set by senior management but perhaps further developed by the team leader and team members. An externally imposed goal may also be required if a team's work must be integrated with the work of other teams. This integration can either be planned in advance, when enough is known to do so, or coordinated through interaction across team boundaries throughout different teams' progress on their tasks. In this model, a network of teams in the organization shares knowledge and works cooperatively toward organizational goals in an iterative learning process. For most teams, team members' input is more important and more useful for figuring out how goals will be achieved rather than what the goals are—that is, input is directed into means not ends (Hackman, 1987). Finally, effective goals for learning must balance radical ("stretch") and incremental (finite, foothold) goals to measure progress along the way to achieving goals that seem ambitious if not impossible to achieve at the outset.

IMPLICATIONS FOR THEORY AND PRACTICE

The model presented in this chapter extends previous theory on team learning by introducing the role of a compelling goal that is both meaningful and challenging as a driver of the team learning process, and by arguing that psychological safety moderates this relationship. I draw from the literature and from several field studies to illustrate and demonstrate the plausibility of relationships in the model. These examples are by no means offered as conclusive evidence of the hypothesized relationships, however, and empirical research is needed to test and extend the model depicted in Figure 11.1.

The Role of Psychological Safety in Team Learning

Field studies in various settings—health care delivery, product development, production, and management—suggest that, in situations where collaboration is critical to learning, certain conditions must be present for teams to learn and to work together effectively—especially psychological safety and (not unrelated) an open, coaching-oriented team leader. The construct and effects of psychological safety have growing support in the literature (e.g. Barsade, Gibson, & Putzel, 2001; Edmondson, 1999, 2002; Kahn, 1990); however, further research is needed to build on the studies referenced above.

IMPLICATIONS OF PSYCHOLOGICAL SAFETY AS A MODERATOR

Previously, I have discussed psychological safety as a mechanism that translates supportive inputs into outcomes (Edmondson, 1999). This conceptualization makes sense, given inputs that directly help build psychological safety, but it is incomplete in that it bypasses the issue of motivation. The model presented in this chapter thus may be more accurate and complete. Proposing psychological safety as a moderator is meant to help explain the differential impact of goals on outcomes and why teams learn and improve at varying rates. These propositions are offered to encourage additional work to support a new theory of work motivation in teams, with a focus on motivators and detractors.

PSYCHOLOGICAL SAFETY'S LIMITATIONS

Psychological safety is an explanatory construct—a set of intangible interpersonal beliefs and predictions—rather than a managerial lever or action. There are actions leaders can take to build psychological safety, as discussed above, but psychological safety cannot be mandated or altered directly. In this sense, theory and practice related to psychological safety must be advanced by research that investigates effects of leader behavior and other organizational factors on psychological safety and on more tangible outcomes related to performance and job satisfaction.

Research on explanatory constructs like trust and psychological safety (both intrapsychic states) has a particular burden: to be relevant to practitioners the concepts must be unpacked into specific, actionable steps and they must be related to other critical variables such as goals and task design. Such research must balance the development of theoretical bodies of knowledge and the investigation of "real world" problems (King, Keohane, & Verba, 1994).

Implications for Practice

A few practical suggestions can be gleaned from the ideas and studies reviewed in this chapter. First, we can return to a suggestion raised by Peter Senge (1990) in his influential book on organizational learning, where he argued that managers lack, yet need, management "practice fields," where they can participate together in simulated experiences, make and learn from mistakes without actual harm to the organization, and conduct experiments.

PRACTICE FIELDS

Leaders of teams can orchestrate explicit sessions for off-line "practice," in which the team is able to learn from simulated experiences or from thought experiments, without risk of harming their real work. Six of the eight successful cardiac surgery teams we studied used a form of this technique, by engaging in a thorough team practice session, in the form of a dry run, while six of the eight unsuccessful teams did not engage in a dry run. In these explicit practice sessions, team members walked through the procedure in "real time," discussing what moves each person would be making if a real patient had been present. Through this kind of off-line practice, the teams were able to anticipate technical problems that might arise during surgery and also to get comfortable in new interpersonal roles and relationships (Edmondson, Bohmer, & Pisano, 2001). Similarly, other recent research found that leader briefings and team training influenced mental model accuracy and were integral to team performance in new environments (Marks, Zaccaro, & Mathieu, 2000). Practice fields are also likely to foster psychological safety, not only because real financial or medical consequences are removed, but because they convey to the members of the team that learning is important and that getting it right the first time is understood to not always be possible. Team leaders are most often in a position to suggest and implement practice fields as a tool in promoting team learning.

DIRECT LANGUAGE

In addition to setting a context for learning that encourages participation from all members, using direct, actionable language also contributes to an effective learning process (Argyris, 1993). Teams cannot afford to shirk critiques—the risk of sounding negative, criticizing the boss, or making the company appear fallible. For example, management teams often face strategic decisions in which they must reflect on the company's current situation and suggest changes. The challenge in such discussions is to be objective and blunt about problems and about what is not working. In many such team discussions, however, the language is anything but direct and clear. For example, a top management team I studied engaged in a series of meetings for the explicit purpose of developing a new strategy. In these conversations, I observed a persistent pattern of using metaphor to evade stating a critical assessment of the team's progress. To illustrate, one member commented,

> Listening to Bob talk about the ship, I'd like to explore the difference between the metaphor of the ship and how the rudder gets turned and when, in contrast to a flotilla, where there's lots of little rudders and we're trying to orchestrate the flotilla. I think this contrast is important. At one level, we talk about this ship and all the complexities of trying to determine not only

its direction but also how to operationalize the ship in total to get to a certain place, versus allowing a certain degree of freedom that the flotilla analogy evokes.

Although metaphors such as this can provoke new ideas and creativity, they can also obscure the real issues and preclude direct or contentious discussion. In this team, members rarely inquired to clarify the meaning of each other's words, or to seek to identify areas of disagreement. The team continued to discuss the company and its situation abstractly in this way, avoiding disagreement and postponing resolution of the self-assessment process, and members tended not to challenge each other's abstract language. By the end of six months, little progress and no decisions had been made. The team's abstract ruminations did not translate easily into action (Edmondson, 2002).

NORMS

Finally, team leaders and members can explicitly seek to define objectives and agreed upon norms for how to work toward them. For example, in the study of geographically dispersed product development teams cited above, we found some teams establishing clear norms for working together and an explicit process for learning from each other (Sole & Edmondson, 2002). One team held weekly "virtual" meetings via telephone to share recently collected data. In contrast, another team had no established routine for collecting and distributing information, ultimately contributing to mistrust and frustration in the team. Another way in which the first team encouraged collective learning was by being explicit about goals and taking inventory of members' capacities and strengths—and weaknesses—what they *needed* to know. Based on the results of this informal inventory, the team exercised flexibility and brought in someone not officially on the team to fill gaps in their knowledge and expertise.

Similarly, differences in technology implementation success in the cardiac surgery study could be accounted for in part by how the team leader framed the learning challenge. Successful implementers viewed technology implementation as a team learning project; unsuccessful implementers viewed it as a technical challenge. These different frames led to different norms for team member interaction, which ultimately allowed or disallowed a structured team learning process of testing, reflecting, and modifying the procedure, in an ongoing, participative way.

CONCLUSION

This chapter has drawn from teams in many contexts to model the collective learning process in teams. One the one hand, these teams may seem too diverse to allow useful comparisons and to develop general insights. The challenges encountered on the factory floor, in the operating room, and around the glass-topped tables in a management team's conference room differ substantively. On the other hand, all of the teams studied—whether geographically dispersed product development teams or co-located nursing teams—struggled with the need for learning and all struggled with issues of power, trust, and psychological safety. In each, it appeared that team leaders were in positions to play a critical role in shaping the learning process. The model and guidelines presented above provide team leaders with a supportive framework for understanding and responding to the dynamics of the collective learning process.

Team leaders can be seen to occupy an increasingly sophisticated and challenging role, especially when they lead teams that need to learn. These leaders, found throughout the organization, must continually clarify the meaning and importance of the team's goal, make sure that goal is serving the organization's strategic aims, and remain open to input from other team members about ways in which the goal must be modified to meet new changes in the team's environment. This means setting challenging goals and specific direction without engaging in authoritarian action that stifles participation. It means allowing team members the latitude for innovation while providing the structure needed for learning. To do this, I argue, requires enough structure to ensure inclusiveness and teamwork without restricting the spontaneity and creativity that can produce unexpected synergies—structure without rigidity. It means creating a climate of psychological safety that allows people to feel safe taking risks, while also setting high standards that require enormous effort and preclude settling into a comfort zone—safety without complacency.

ACKNOWLEDGEMENTS

The research described in this chapter was supported by the Division of Research at Harvard Business School. The chapter benefited from the superb research assistance of Laura Feldman, and helpful comments and suggestions from Michael West improved the text immensely.

REFERENCES

Alderfer, C. P. (1987). An intergroup perspective on organizational behavior. In J. W. Lorsch (ed.), *Handbook of Organizational Behavior*. Englewood Cliffs, NJ: Prentice-Hall.

Argyris, C. (1993). *Knowledge for Action: A Guide to Overcoming Barriers to Organizational Change*. San Francisco: Jossey-Bass.

Argyris, C. & Schön, D. (1978). *Organizational Learning: A Theory of Action Perspective*. Reading, Mass.: Addison-Wesley.

Ashford, S. J. & Cummings, L. L. (1983). Feedback as an individual resource: personal strategies of creating information. *Organizational Behavior and Human Performance, 32*, 370–398.

Barsade, S. G., Gibson, D. E., & Putzel, R. (2001). *To Be Angry or Not to Be Angry in Groups: Examining the Question*. Washington, DC: Academy of Management.

Brand, A. (1998). Knowledge management and innovation at 3M. *Journal of Knowledge Management, 2*(1), 17–22.

Brooks, A. K. (1994). Power and the production of knowledge: collective team learning in work organizations. *Human Resource Development Quarterly, 5*(3), 213–235.

Brown, R. (1990). Politeness theory: exemplar and exemplary. In I. Rock (ed.), *The Legacy of Solomon Asch: Essays in Cognition and Social Psychology* (pp. 23–37). Hillsdale, NJ: Lawrence Erlbaum Associates.

Busby, J. S. (1999). The effectiveness of collective retrospection as a mechanism of organizational learning. *Journal of Applied Behavioral Sciences, 31*(1), 109–129.

Cannon, M. D. & Edmondson, A. C. (2001). Confronting failure: antecedents and consequences of shared beliefs about failure in organizational work groups. *Journal of Organizational Behavior, 22*, 161–177.

Carroll, J. S. (1998). Organizational learning activities in high-hazard industries: the logics underlying self-analysis. *Journal of Management Studies, 35*(6), 699–717.

Csikszentmihalyi, M. (1994). *Flow: The Psychology of Optimal Experience*. New York: Simon and Schuster.

D'Andrea-O'Brien, C. & Buono, A. F. (1996). Building effective learning teams: lessons from the field. *S.A.M. Advanced Management Journal, 61*(3), 4–10.

De Cremer, D., Snyder, M., & Dewitte, S. (2001). "The less I trust, the less I contribute (or not)?" The effects of trust, accountability and self-monitoring in social dilemmas. *European Journal of Social Psychology, 31*, 93–107.

Detert, J. R. (2002). Speaking up at Hi-Co. Harvard Business School Working Paper.

Dirks, K. T. (1999). The effects of interpersonal trust on work group performance. *Journal of Applied Psychology, 84*(3), 445–455.

Edmondson, A. (1996). Learning from mistakes is easier said than done: group and organizational influences on the detection and correction of human error. *Journal of Applied Behavioral Sciences, 32*(1), 5–32.

Edmondson, A. (1999). Psychological safety and learning behavior in work teams. *Administrative Science Quarterly, 44*, 350–383.

Edmondson, A. (2002). The local and variegated nature of learning in organizations: a group-level perspective. *Organization Science, 13*(2), 128–146.

Edmondson, A., Bohmer, R. M. J., & Pisano, G. (2000). Learning new technical and interpersonal routines in operating room teams: the case of minimally invasive cardiac surgery. In B. Mannix, M. Neale, & T. Griffith (eds), *Research on Groups and Teams* (pp. 29–51). Greenwich, Conn.: JAI Press.

Edmondson, A., Bohmer, R. M. J., & Pisano, G. (2001). Disrupted routines. *Administrative Science Quarterly, 46*(4), 685–716.

Edmondson, A. C. & Moingeon, B. (1998). From organizational learning to the learning organization. *Management Learning, 29*(1), 5–20.

Edmondson, A. C. & Woolley, A. (2003). Understanding outcomes of organizational learning interventions. In M. Easterby-Smith et al. (eds), *International Handbook on Organizational Learning and Knowledge Management*. London: Blackwell.

Filipowicz, A. (2002). The impact of humor on performance in task-based interactions: a theoretical model. Harvard University Working Paper.

Frink, D. D. & Ferris, G. R. (1998). Accountability, impression management, and goal setting in the performance evaluation process. *Human Relations, 51*(10), 1259–1283.

Gabarro, J. J. (1987). The development of working relationships. In J. Lorsch (ed.), *Handbook of Organizational Behavior* (pp. 172–189). Englewood Cliffs, NJ: Prentice-Hall.

Garvin, D. A. (2000). *Learning in Action*. Boston: Harvard Business School Press.

Gersick, C. J. G. (1988). Time and transition in work teams: toward a new model of group development. *Academy of Management Journal, 31*, 9–41.

Gersick, C. J. G. & Hackman, J. R. (1990). Habitual routines in task-performing teams. *Organizational Behavior and Human Decision Processes, 47*, 65–97.

Hackman, J. R. (1987). The design of work teams. In J. Lorsch (ed.), *Handbook of Organizational Behavior* (pp. 315–342). Englewood Cliffs, NJ: Prentice-Hall.

Hargadon, A. B. (1998). Firms as knowledge brokers: lessons in pursuing continuous innovation. *California Management Review, 40*(3), 209–227.

Janis, I. L. (1982). *Groupthink: Psychological Studies of Policy Decisions and Fiascos*. Boston: Houghton Mifflin.

Kahn, W. A. (1990). Psychological conditions of personal engagement and disengagement at work. *Academy of Management Journal, 33*(4), 692–724.

Kanfer, R. (1990). Motivation theory and industrial and organizational psychology. In M. D. Dunnette & L. M. Hough (eds), *Handbook of Industrial and Organizational Psychology* (Vol. 1, p. 755). Palo Alto, Calif.: Consulting Psychologists Press, Inc.

Katz, N. (2001). Sports teams as a model for workplace teams: lessons and liabilities. *Academy of Management Executive, 15*(3), 56–67.

King, G., Keohane, R., & Verba, S. (1994). *Designing Social Inquiry*. Princeton, NJ: Princeton University Press.

Kolb, D. A. (1984). *Experiential Learning: Experience as the Source of Learning and Development*. Englewood-Cliffs, NJ: Prentice-Hall.

Kramer, R. M. (1999). Trust and distrust in organizations: emerging perspectives, enduring questions. *Annual Review of Psychology, 50,* 569–598.

Leape, L. L., Brennan, T. A., Laird, N., Lawthers, A. G., Localio, A. R., Barnes, B. A., Hebert, L., Newhouse, J. P., Weiler, P. C., & Hiatt, H. (1991). The nature of adverse events in hospitalized patients: results of the Harvard Medical Practice Study II. *New England Journal of Medicine, 324,* 377–384.

Lee, F., Edmondson, A., Thomke, S., & Worline, M. (2001). Promoting experimentation in organizational knowledge creation: effects of status, values and rewards. Manuscript under review.

Leonard-Barton, D. (1995). *Wellsprings of Knowledge: Building and Sustaining the Sources of Innovation.* Boston: Harvard Business School Press.

Levitt, B. & March, J. G. (1988). Organizational learning. *Annual Review of Sociology, 14,* 319–340.

Locke, E. A. (2001). Motivation by goal setting. In R. T. Golembiewski (ed.), *Handbook of Organizational Behavior* (pp. 43–56). New York: Marcel Dekker, Inc.

Lynn, G. S., Mazzuca, M., Morone, J. G., & Paulson, A. S. (1998). Learning is the critical success factor in developing truly new products. *Research Technology Management, 41*(3), 45–51.

Macdonald, S. (1995). Learning to change: an information perspective on learning in the organization. *Organization Science, 6,* 557–568.

Marks, M. A., Zaccaro, S., & Mathieu, J. E. (2000). Performance implications of leader briefings and team-interaction training for team adaptation to novel environments. *Journal of Applied Psychology, 85*(6), 971–986.

May, D. R., Gilson, R. L., & Harter, L. (1999). Engaging the human spirit at work: exploring the psychological conditions of meaningfulness, safety and availability. Chicago, Ill., National Meeting of the Academy of Management.

Mayer, R. C., Davis, J. H., & Schoorman, F. D. (1995). An integrative model of organizational trust. *Academy of Management Review, 20*(3), 709–734.

Reed, W. H. (1962). Upward communication in industrial hierarchies. *Human Relations, 15,* 3–15.

Rifkin, L. F. & Fulop, W. D. (1997). Representing fear in learning in organizations. *Management Learning, 28*(1), 45–63.

Robinson, S. L. (1996). Trust and breach of the psychological contract. *Administrative Science Quarterly, 41*(4), 574–599.

Schein, E. H. (1985). *Organizational Culture and Leadership.* San Francisco: Jossey-Bass.

Schein, E. H. & Bennis, W. (1965). *Personal and Organizational Change through Group Methods.* New York: Wiley.

Schön, D. (1984). *The Reflective Practitioner.* New York: Basic Books.

Senge, P. (1990). *The Fifth Discipline: The Art and Practice of the Learning Organization.* New York: Doubleday.

Simons, T. L. & Peterson, R. S. (2000). Task conflict and relationship conflict in top management teams: the pivotal role of intra-group trust. *Journal of Applied Psychology, 85*(1), 102–111.

Snyder, M. (1974). Self-monitoring of expressive behavior. *Journal of Personality and Social Psychology, 30*(4), 526–537.

Sole, D. & Edmondson, A. (2002). Bridging knowledge gaps: learning in geographically dispersed cross-functional development teams. In N. Bontis & C. W. Choo (eds), *The Strategic Management of Intellectual Capital and Organizational Knowledge: A Collection of Readings* (pp. 587–604). New York: Oxford University Press.

Tjosvold, D. (1990). Making technological innovations work. *Human Resources, 43,* 1117–1131.

Turnley, W. H. & Bolino, M. C. (2001). Achieving desired images while avoiding undesired images: exploring the role of self-monitoring in impression management. *Journal of Applied Psychology, 86*(2), 351–360.

Tyler, T. R. & Lind, E. A. (1992). A relational model of authority in groups. In M. Zanna (ed.), *Advances in Experimental Psychology.* New York: Academy.

Tynan, R. (1999). The impact of threat sensitivity and face giving on upward communication. Paper presented at the Academy of Management Conference, Chicago, Ill.

Wageman, R. & Mannix, E. A. (eds) (1998). *Uses and Misuses of Power in Task-performing Teams. Power and Influence in Organizations.* Thousand Oaks, Calif.: Sage.

Weick, K. E. & Roberts, K. H. (1993). Collective mind in organizations: heedful interrelating on flight decks. *Administrative Science Quarterly, 38,* 357–381.

West, M. A. (2000). Reflexivity, revolution, and innovation in work teams. In M. M. Beyerlein, D. A. Johnson, & S. T. Beyerlein (eds), *Advances in Interdisciplinary Studies of Work Teams* (Vol. 5, pp. 1–29). Greenwich, Conn.: JAI Press.

West, M. & Anderson, M. (1996). Innovations in top management teams. *Journal of Applied Psychology, 31*(6), 680–693.

Winter, R. P., Sarros, J. C., & Tanewski, G. A. (1997). Reframing managers' control orientations and practices: a proposed organizational learning framework. *The International Journal of Organizational Analysis, 5*(1), 9–24.

12

COOPERATION AND TEAMWORK FOR INNOVATION

Michael A. West and Giles Hirst

INTRODUCTION

Innovations commonly involve changes to an array of processes and are rarely the result of the activity of one individual. Thus for an innovation to be implemented effectively, teamwork and cooperation are essential. We develop a model which uses an input–process–output structure (see Figure 12.1), to examine the factors likely to influence innovation implementation in work groups. This structure segments variables into inputs of teams such as the task the team is required to perform (e.g. provide health care, make landmines, or sell mobile phones), the composition of the group (such as functional, cultural, gender, and age diversity), and the organizational context (e.g. manufacturing, health service, large or small, organic, the demands it places on the team). Group processes mediate the relationships between inputs and outputs and include levels of participation, support for innovation, leadership, and the management of conflict. These processes create climates of, for example, safety and trust or threat and anxiety. The model proposes that team leaders play a crucial role in moderating the effects of organizational and team context upon team processes and thereby upon innovation outputs. Outputs include the number of innovations, magnitude of innovation, radicalness (changes to the status quo), novelty, and effectiveness of innovation in achieving the desired end. We will consider each of these elements of the framework below. But first it is important to define what is meant by innovation.

Innovation is the introduction of new and improved ways of doing things. A fuller, more explicit definition of innovation is "... the intentional introduction and application within a job, work team or organization of ideas, processes, products or procedures which are new to that job, work team or organization and which are designed to benefit the job, the work team or the organization" (West & Farr, 1990). Innovation is restricted to *intentional* attempts to bring about benefits from new changes; these might include economic benefits, personal growth, increased satisfaction, improved group cohesiveness, better organizational communication, as well as productivity and economic gains. Various processes and products may be regarded as innovations. They include technological changes such as new products,

---

The Essentials *of Teamworking: International Perspectives.*
Edited by M. A. West, D. Tjosvold, and K. G. Smith. © 2005 John Wiley & Sons, Ltd.

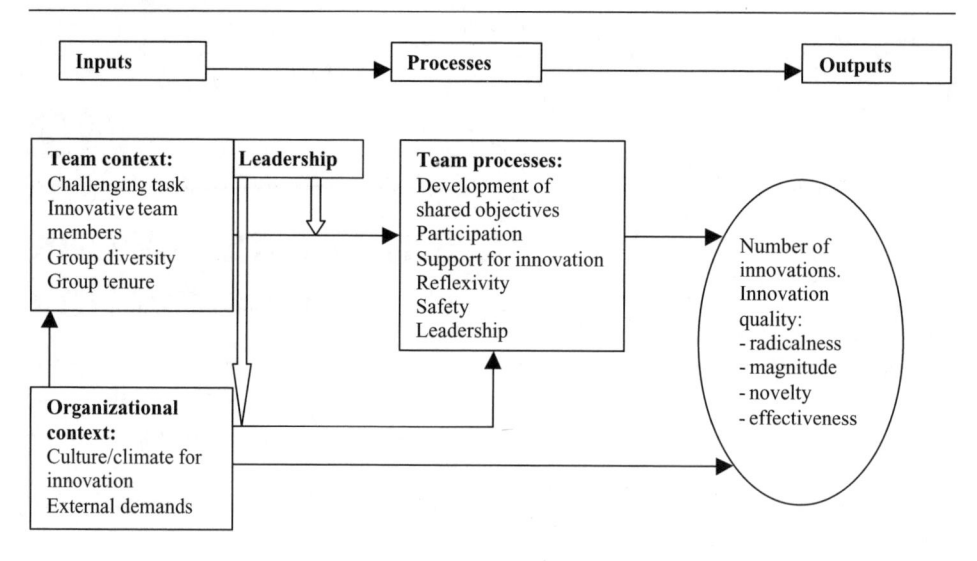

Figure 12.1 An input–process–output model of work group innovation

but may also include new production processes, the introduction of advanced manufacturing technology, or the introduction of new computer support services within an organization. Administrative changes are also regarded as innovations. New human resource management (HRM) strategies, organizational policies on health and safety, or the introduction of teamwork are all examples of administrative innovations within organizations. Innovation implies novelty, but not necessarily absolute novelty (West & Farr, 1990). Innovation encompasses both creative idea generation and idea implementation. What input, process, and output factors related to cooperation and teamwork therefore influence levels and qualities of innovation in work groups? Elsewhere we have examined a broad range of input and process factors (illustrated in Figure 12.1) (see West, 2002). Here we consider those inputs and processes most closely related to concepts of cooperation and teamwork that influence innovation. We begin by examining aspects of team and organizational context: team diversity, team tenure, and organizational climate and culture. In the second part of the chapter we examine how team processes influence levels of team innovation.

TEAM CONTEXT

Group Member Diversity

Are groups composed of very different people (professional background, age, organizational tenure) more innovative than those whose members are similar? This question is prompted by the notion that if people who work together in groups have different backgrounds, personalities, training, skills, experiences, and orientations, they will bring usefully differing perspectives to the group. This divergence of views will create multiple perspectives, disagreement, and conflict. If this informational conflict is processed in the interests of effective decision making and task performance rather than on the basis of motivation to win or prevail, or conflicts of interest, this in turn will generate improved performance and more innovative actions will be the result (De Dreu, 1997; Hoffman & Maier, 1961; Pearce & Ravlin, 1987; Porac & Howard, 1990; Tjosvold, 1985, 1991, 1998).

Of the different classification systems for diversity (e.g. Jackson 1992, 1996; Maznevski, 1994) most differentiate between task-oriented diversity in attributes that are relevant to the person's role or task in the organization (e.g. organizational position and specialized knowledge), and those that are simply inherent in the person and "relations oriented" (e.g. age, gender, ethnicity, social status, and personality) (Maznevski, 1994). Jackson (1992) believes that the effects of diversity on team performance are complex: task-related and relations-oriented diversity have different effects that depend also on the team task. For tasks requiring creativity and a high quality of decision making, Jackson says that "the available evidence supports the conclusion that team [task] diversity is associated with better quality team decision-making" (Jackson, 1996, p. 67), citing evidence provided by Filley, House, and Kerr (1976), Hoffman (1979), McGrath (1984), and Shaw (1981).

The most significant study of innovation in teams to date is a UNESCO-sponsored international effort to determine the factors influencing the scientific performance of 1222 research teams (Andrews, 1979; see also Payne, 1990). Diversity was assessed in six areas: in projects; interdisciplinary orientations; specialities; funding resources; R&D activities; and professional functions. Overall, diversity accounted for 10 per cent of the variance in scientific recognition, R&D effectiveness, and number of publications, suggesting that diversity does influence team innovation.

There is some evidence that heterogeneity in both relations-oriented and task-oriented domains is associated with group innovation, including heterogeneity in personality (Hoffman & Maier, 1961), training background (Pelz, 1956), leadership abilities (Ghiselli & Lodahl, 1958), attitudes (Hoffman, Harburg & Maier, 1962; Willems & Clark, 1971), gender (Wood, 1987), occupational background (Bantel & Jackson, 1989), and education (Smith et al., 1994).

The dominant explanation for the positive effects of diversity on team innovation is that diversity of information, experience, and skills produces more comprehensive and effective decision making. In essence, diversity increases the amount and variety of information accessible for a team's collective problem solving. However, another explanation for the (still debated) effects of task-oriented diversity on team innovation is that functional diversity might influence work group performance as a result of the higher level of external communication which group members initiate, precisely because of their functional diversity (Zenger & Lawrence, 1989). Mohrman, Cohen, and Mohrman (1995) have pointed out that there are likely to be innovation benefits of good linkages between groups and teams and across departments within organizations. The cross-disciplinarity, cross-functionality, and cross-team perspectives that such interactions can produce are likely to generate the kinds of dividends related to innovation that heterogeneity within teams could offer.

In a study of 45 new product teams in five high-technology companies, Ancona and Caldwell (1992) found that when a work group recruited a new member from a functional area in an organization, communication between the team and that area went up dramatically. This would favour innovation through the incorporation of diverse ideas and models gleaned from these different functional areas. Consistent with this, the researchers discovered that the greater the group's functional diversity, the more team members communicated outside the work group's boundaries and the higher ratings of innovation they received from supervisors. The UNESCO research described above also showed that the extent of communication between research teams had strong relationships with scientific recognition of the teams, R&D effectiveness, number of publications, and the applied value of their work. Keller (2001) studied 93 R&D teams. He found that functional diversity increased external communication and thereby enhanced project performance. However, functional diversity also reduced internal communication and cohesiveness. Keller concluded that it is necessary to manage the creative tension between reduced team identification and enhanced organizational integration. Although Keller did not measure whether diversity increased the breadth of team knowledge, his findings illustrate how diversity can impact on both internal and external processes. Further we hypothesize that there are opportunities to advance our understanding of the internal processes by which diversity operates by including measures of team mental models. For example, diversity provides a greater range of knowledge and information as well as differing mental models, i.e. different perspectives and approaches. We propose that divergent mental models and differing social identification, as opposed to diverse information, promote conflict and reduce cohesion.

Although power and status in groups are likely to be associated with innovation in organizations (West, 1987; West & Anderson, 1996), status diversity, in contrast, is likely to threaten integration and safety in the group. The threat occasioned by disagreeing with high-status members is likely to restrict public speculation by lower-status group members. Such status differentials, as much social psychological research has shown, will retard integration because of the barriers to cohesiveness and shared orientation they create. For example, De Dreu (1995) has shown that power and status asymmetries in groups produce hostile interaction patterns in contrast to groups in which there is power balance. Such hostility is clearly likely to inhibit creativity and innovation (West, 2002).

So does diversity predict group innovation? The research evidence suggests that functional or knowledge diversity in the team is associated with innovation. However, when diversity begins to threaten the group's safety and integration (such as status or age diversity) then creativity and innovation implementation will be likely to suffer. Where diversity reduces group members' clarity about and commitment to group objectives, levels of participation (interaction, information-sharing, and shared influence over decision making), task orientation (commitment to quality of task performance), and support for new ideas, then it is likely that innovation attempts will be resisted. Diversity will also be affected by temporal factors, since over time the experience of diversity in a group will be softened into familiarity. We therefore turn to consider how the tenure or age of a work team is likely to affect innovation.

However, the critical influence on how diversity affects group processes, we propose, is leadership within the team. Leaders who effectively integrate diverse perspectives and manage conflict effectively (by, for example, emphasizing shared objectives and vision) are likely to enhance the influence of diversity upon innovation implementation in teams. Leadership processes that inhibit the integration of diverse perspectives (for example by exacerbating conflict between team members) will reduce or nullify the effect of diversity upon group processes and, thereby, team innovation.

Group Tenure

In order to encourage innovation should we try to keep work teams together over time or constantly ensure a change of membership and therefore maintain its diversity? Katz (1982) suggested that project newcomers would increase creativity since they may challenge and thereby improve existing methods and knowledge. He suggested too that the longer groups have been together, the less they communicate with key information sources, scan the environment, and communicate internally within the group and externally. Members of such groups (he proposed) tend to ignore and become increasingly isolated from sources that provide the most critical kinds of feedback, evaluation, and information. This suggests that without changes in membership, groups may become less innovative as time goes by. Indeed some research on diversity in teams (Bantel & Jackson, 1989; Jackson, 1996) suggests that longer tenure might be associated with increasing homogeneity and therefore low levels of innovation. The tenure of a group may result in lower requisite diversity for meeting the demands of the environment as a result of the increasing similarity of group members' attitudes, skills, and experiences through their close association (which symbolic interactionist approaches would suggest is likely).

However, tenure homogeneity has been positively related in some studies to frequency of communication, social integration within the group, and innovation (O'Reilly & Flatt, 1989). This may be because the longer people work together, they more they create a predictable and therefore safer social psychological environment. Such safety may enable the exploration and risk taking necessary for innovation (Edmondson, 1996).

The resolution of these positions may lie not in issues of tenure, diversity, and safety per se, but in the balance between these factors. It may be that tenure, diversity, and psychosocial safety interact in their influence on innovation. Where long tenure leads to high safety this will lead to creativity and innovation, all other things being equal, since it will be safer to take risks and to continually introduce diverse perspectives (see, for example, the discussion on minority influence below and the chapter by Nemeth and Nemeth-Brown, in press). Similarly, individual and group level variables may interact. For example, teams which have worked together for long periods of time may have developed stable norms, understanding of each other's skills, and efficient collaborative approaches. For these teams membership change (either the introduction of new members or their departure) may impact on morale as well as on communication. Conversely, newly formed teams with less crystallized team norms and more fluid work assignments may be more able to adapt to membership changes. Another possibility is that the longer teams work together the more likely they are to develop and apply ways of working that enable them to achieve shared objectives, to implement appropriate participation strategies, and effective communication and decision-making processes, which in turn lead to innovation (West & Anderson, 1996). And leadership processes will play a crucial role in determining whether tenure translates into innovation.

The task a team is required to perform determines to a large extent the level of innovation a team can implement. High levels of autonomy ceded to the group over the performance of its work, interdependence in the work of the team members, and task identity (the team performs a whole task) together will influence the level of innovation. At the same time the characteristics of group members (innovativeness, ability to work in teams, the diversity of skills, perspectives, and knowledge they bring to the task, and the length of time for which the members have worked together) will influence the level of innovation. The reader can consider his or her own team and ponder on the extent to which the task demands innovation. Is the team composed of people who have a propensity to innovate (Bunce & West, 1995, 1996)? And do the team members embody a diversity of knowledge, skills, and perspectives which, when combined, lead to ideas for new and improved ways of working? Are the team members skilled at integrating their perspectives, activities, and knowledge, thus enabling interdependent team working? Have they worked together for a long enough period of time that they are reasonably efficient at decision making and achieving a shared representation of their work and ways of working? And finally, are the leadership processes in the team such that these factors that favour innovation are enhanced? If so, we would argue that the likelihood is that the team has the capacity to be highly innovative, but this capacity can be constrained or enabled by the organization within which the team works in powerful ways. It is to a consideration of the organizational context for team innovation that we turn to next.

ORGANIZATIONAL CONTEXT

How do organizations enable or inhibit team innovation? In this section, we suggest that the culture and the climate of the organization powerfully determine whether teams will attempt to introduce innovation.

Organizational Culture and Climate

Organizations create an ethos or atmosphere within which creativity is either nurtured and blooms in innovation, or is starved of support. Supportive and challenging environments are likely to sustain high levels of creativity (Mumford & Gustafson, 1988; West, 1987), especially those which encourage risk taking and idea generation (Cummings, 1965; Delbecq & Mills, 1985; Ettlie, 1983; Hage & Dewar, 1973; Kanter, 1983; Kimberley & Evanisko, 1981). Employees frequently have ideas for improving their workplaces, work functioning, processes, products, or services (Nicholson & West, 1988; West, 1987), but where climates are characterized by distrust, lack of communication, personal antipathies, limited individual autonomy, and unclear goals, implementation of these ideas is inhibited.

Creative, innovative organizations are those where employees perceive and share an appealing vision of what the organization is trying to achieve—one therefore that is consistent with their values (West & Richter, in press). Innovative organizations have vigorous and mostly enjoyable interactions and debates between employees at all levels about how best to achieve that vision. Conflicts are seen as opportunities to find creative solutions that meet the needs of all parties in the organizations rather than as win–lose situations. And people in such organizations have a high level of autonomy, responsibility, accountability, and power—they are free to make decisions about what to do, when to do it, and who to do it with. Trust, cooperativeness, warmth, and humour are likely to characterize interpersonal and intergroup interactions. There is strong practical support for people's ideas for new and improved products, ways of working, or of managing the organization. Senior managers are more likely than not to encourage and resource innovative ideas, even when they are unsure of their potential value (within safe limits). Such organizations will almost certainly find themselves in uncertain, dynamic, and demanding environments, whether this is due to competition, scarcity of resources, changing markets or legislation, or to global and environmental pressures. After all, that is why innovation has always occurred—humans have adapted their organizations and ways of working to the changing environments they find themselves in.

The leaders of teams will play an important part in buffering team members from the negative effects of organizational climate upon team innovation. A leader who fights for the autonomy of his or her team in an organization that is highly controlling will moderate the effects of organizational culture upon team innovation. Equally, a team leader who dominates the team, whether or not the organizational context is supportive of innovation and team autonomy, will be likely to dramatically reduce the positive influence of a supportive organizational culture upon group processes (such as team member participation in decision making) and thereby levels of team innovation.

Other indicators of culture include the size, age, and structure of the organization. The greater the complexity and more differentiated the organization's structure (in terms of departments, groupings, etc.) the easier it is to cross knowledge boundaries and the greater the number of sources from which innovation can spring. Collaborative idea development across an organization is often cited as a precondition for organizational innovation (Allen, Lee, & Tushman, 1980; Kanter, 1983; Monge, Cozzens, & Contractor, 1992; Zaltman, Duncan, & Holbeck, 1973). There is support for the notion that high centralization is a negative predictor of innovation (Burns & Stalker, 1961; Hage & Aiken, 1967; Shepard, 1967) and Lawrence and Lorsch's (1967) case studies showed that tightly coupled interdepartmental relationships fostered new product development in organizations. However, our research in manufacturing organizations (West et al., 2000) also suggests that centralization may be necessary to ensure innovation implementation. Zaltman, Duncan, and Holbeck (1973) call this the innovation dilemma. Decentralization at local level is necessary for creative ideas to be developed, but centralization may be required for the effective implementation of those ideas in the wider organization. The failure of many organizations to innovate may be a consequence of a failure to recognize this inherent tension.

The resolution of the dilemma may be team-based organizations (Mohrman, Cohen, & Mohrman, 1995). Teams provide the sources for ideas (especially cross-functional teams) while the team-based organization also offers simultaneously centralized and distributed decision-making structures that enable successful innovation. Indeed, the extent of team-based working in organizations appears to be a good predictor of innovation (Agrell & Gustafson, 1996; Mohrman, Cohen, & Mohrman, 1995; West et al., 2000).

What of size and age as cultural indicators? Large organizations have difficulty changing their forms to fit changing environments. Yet organizational size has been a positive predictor of both technological and administrative innovations (Kimberly & Evanisko, 1981). Innovative agility is more a characteristic of smaller organizations (Rogers, 1983; Utterback, 1974). Size may be a surrogate measure of several dimensions associated with innovation such as resources and economies of scale. However, in large organizations, decentralization and specialization are not sufficient to ensure innovation. Integration across groups, departments, and specialisms is also necessary for communication, and sharing of disseminated knowledge, and this requires some centralization or else the sophisticated development of team-based structures. More recent research, examining all 35 US firms that produced microprocessors between 1971 and 1989, showed that smaller organizations were more likely to be the sources of innovation (Wade, 1996). And younger organizations appear to be more innovative, all other things being equal. The longer human social organizations endure, the more embedded become their norms and the more resilient to change become their traditions. Consequently, mature organizations will have difficulty innovating and adapting (Kimberly & Evanisko, 1981; Pierce & Delbecq, 1977). Our data from a 10-year study of 110 UK manufacturing organizations revealed that younger organizations (years since start-up) were likely to innovate in products, production technology, production processes, work organization, and people management (West et al., 2000). Evidence from US studies also suggests younger organizations are the predominant sources of innovation (Wade, 1996).

Amabile's componential model of creativity and innovation (Amabile, 1988, 1997) provides a link between the work environment, individual and team creativity, and organizational innovation. The organizational work environment is conceptualized as having three key characteristics: *organizational motivation to innovate* describes an organization's basic orientation toward innovation, as well as its support for creativity and innovation. *Management practices* include the management at all levels of the organization, but most importantly the level of individual departments and projects. Supervisory encouragement and work group support are two examples of relevant managerial behaviour or practices. *Resources* are related to everything that an organization has available to support creativity at work. Amabile proposes that the higher the concurrent levels of these three aspects of the organizational environment, the more the innovation in organizations. The central statement of the theory is that elements of the work environment will impact individual and team creativity by influencing expertise, task motivation, and creativity skills. The influence of intrinsic task motivation on creativity is considered essential: even though the environment may have an influence on each of the three components, the impact on task motivation is thought to be the most immediate and direct. Furthermore, creativity is seen as a primary source of organizational innovation.

In a study examining whether and how the work environments of highly creative projects differed from the work environments of less creative projects, Amabile and colleagues found that five dimensions consistently differed between high-creativity and low-creativity projects (Amabile et al., 1996). These were challenge, organizational encouragement, work group support, supervisory encouragement, and organizational impediments.

Challenge is regarded as a moderate degree of workload pressure that arises from the urgent, intellectually challenging problem itself (Amabile, 1988; Amabile et al., 1996). The authors carefully distinguish challenge from excessive workload pressure, which is supposed to be negatively related to creativity, and suggest that time pressure may add to the perception of challenge in the work if it is perceived as a concomitant of an important, urgent project. This challenge, in turn, may be positively related to intrinsic motivation and creativity.

Organizational encouragement refers to several aspects within the organization. The first is encouragement of risk taking and idea generation, a valuing of innovation from the highest to the lowest levels of management. The second refers to a fair and supportive evaluation of new ideas; the authors underline this by referring to studies that showed that whereas threatening and highly critical evaluation of new ideas was shown to undermine creativity in laboratory studies, in field research it was shown that supportive, informative evaluation can enhance the intrinsically motivated state that is most conducive to creativity. The third aspect of organizational encouragement focuses on reward and recognition of creativity; in a series of studies, Amabile and colleagues showed that reward perceived as a bonus, a confirmation of one's competence, or a means of enabling one to do better, more interesting work in the future can stimulate creativity, whereas the mere engagement in an activity to obtain a reward can be detrimental towards it (see Amabile et al., 1996). The final aspect refers to the important role of collaborative idea flow across the organization, participative management, and decision making, in the stimulation of creativity.

Work group support indicates the encouragement of activity through the particular work group. The four aspects thought to be relevant for this are team member diversity, mutual openness to ideas, constructive challenging of ideas, and shared commitment to the project; whereas the former two may influence creativity through exposing individuals to a greater variety of unusual ideas, the latter two are thought to increase intrinsic motivation.

Supervisory encouragement stresses the aspects goal clarity, open supervisory interactions, and perceived supervisory or leader support. Whereas goal clarity might have an effect on creativity by providing a clearer problem definition, Amabile et al. argue that open supervisory interactions as well as perceived supervisory support may influence creativity through preventing people from experiencing fear of negative criticism that can undermine the intrinsic motivation necessary for creativity.

In reporting the last of the five factors, organizational impediments, Amabile et al. (1996) refer to a few studies indicating that internal strife, conservatism, and rigid, formal management structures represent obstacles to creativity. The authors suggest that because these factors may be perceived as controlling, their likely negative influence on creativity may evolve from an increase in individual extrinsic motivation (a motivation through external factors but not the task itself) and a corresponding decrease in the intrinsic motivation necessary for creativity. However, research on impediments to creativity, in comparison to research on stimulants of creativity, is still comparatively limited.

In conclusion, therefore, we suggest that the organizational culture or climate provides a context which determines the level of group innovation both directly and via their impact on team inputs and team processes. Clearly the culture will influence the group's task (the amount of autonomy they are given), the group's composition (cross-functional teams are more likely in organic organizations), and group processes (team members are more likely to be supportive of innovation in a culture which recognizes and rewards ideas for new and improved ways of doing things). We cannot treat work teams as isolated islands if we wish to understand creativity and innovation at work. The organizational context plays a powerful part in influencing both the level and type of innovation. But, we shall argue below, the most important factors are the interaction and socio-emotional processes that occur within teams.

TEAM PROCESSES

Task characteristics, group diversity, and organizational context will all influence team processes affecting the development and redevelopment of shared objectives, levels of participation, management of conflict, support for new ideas, and leadership (West, 1990, 1994; West & Anderson, 1996). These processes, if sufficiently integrated (i.e. there are shared objectives, high levels of participation, constructive, cooperative conflict management, high support for innovation, and leadership which enables innovation), will foster creativity and innovation implementation. Moreover, effective group processes will be both sustained by and increase the level of psychosocial safety in the group.

Developing Shared Objectives

In the context of group innovation, clarity of team objectives is likely to facilitate innovation by enabling focused development of new ideas, which can be filtered with greater precision than if team objectives are unclear. Theoretically, clear objectives will only facilitate innovation if team members are committed to the goals of the team since strong goal commitment will be necessary to maintain group member persistence for implementation in the face of resistance among other organizational members. Pinto and Prescott (1987), in a study of 418 project teams, found that a clearly stated mission was the only factor which predicted success at all stages of the innovation process (conception, planning, execution, and termination). Where group members do not share a commitment to a set of objectives (or a vision of the goals of their work) the forces of disintegration created by disagreements (and lack of safety), diversity, and the emotional demands of the innovation process are likely to inhibit innovation.

Participation in Decision Making

Participation leads to a more complete understanding of potential problems, as useful information is shared (Rodgers & Hunter, 1991) leading to the cross-fertilization of ideas, spawning innovation (Mumford & Gustafson, 1988). Kivimaki et al. (2000) found that, based on a sample of 493 employees, participative communication was the strongest predictor of innovation effectiveness out of eight aspects of organizational communication ($r = 0.60$) and of patents produced ($r = 0.19$). The researchers concluded that understanding opposing ideas and information enables employees to see the limitations in their views and incorporate other perspectives, leading to high-quality decision making and innovation. Further high participation in decision making means less resistance to change and therefore greater likelihood of innovations being implemented (Bowers & Seashore, 1966; Coch & French, 1948; Lawler & Hackman, 1969).

Conflict

Many scholars believe that the management of competing perspectives is fundamental to the generation of creativity and innovation (Mumford & Gustafson, 1988; Nemeth & Owens, 1996; Tjosvold, 1998). Such processes are characteristic of task-related conflict (as opposed to conflicts of relationship and process conflict; see De Dreu, 1997). They can arise from a common concern with quality of task performance in relation to shared objectives. Task conflict includes the appraisal of, and constructive challenges to, the group's performance. In essence, team members are more committed to performing their work effectively and excellently than they are either to bland consensus or to personal victory in conflict with other team members over task performance strategies or decision options.

Dean Tjosvold and colleagues (Tjosvold, 1982, 1998; Tjosvold & Field, 1983; Tjosvold & Johnson, 1977; Tjosvold, Wedley, & Field, 1986) have presented cogent arguments and strong supportive evidence that such constructive (task-related) controversy in a cooperative group context improves the quality of decision making and creativity (Tjosvold, 1991). Constructive controversy is characterized by full exploration of opposing opinions and frank analyses of task-related issues. It occurs when decision makers believe they are in a cooperative group context, where mutually beneficial goals are emphasized, rather than in a competitive context where decision makers feel their personal competence is confirmed rather than questioned, and where they perceive processes of mutual influence rather than attempted dominance.

For example, the most effective self-managing teams in a manufacturing plant that Alper and Tjosvold (1993) studied were those which had compatible goals and promoted constructive controversy. The 544 employees who made up the 59 teams completed a questionnaire which probed for information about cooperation, competition, and conflict within the teams. Teams were responsible for activities such as work scheduling, housekeeping, safety, purchasing, accident investigation, and quality. Members of teams which promoted interdependent conflict management (people cooperated to work through their differences), compared to teams with win/lose conflict (where team members tended to engage in a power struggle when they had different views and interests), felt confident that they could deal with differences. Such teams were rated as more productive and innovative by their managers. Apparently, because of this success, members of these teams were committed to working as a team.

Another perspective on conflict and innovation comes from minority influence theory. A number of researchers have shown that minority consistency of arguments over time is likely to lead to change in majority views in groups (Maass & Clark, 1984; Nemeth, 1986; Nemeth & Chiles, 1988; Nemeth & Kwan, 1987; Nemeth & Owens, 1996; Nemeth & Wachtler, 1983) (for an account of this research and an assessment of how it relates to group creativity, see the excellent chapter by Nemeth and Nemeth-Brown, in press).

De Dreu and De Vries (1997) suggest that a homogeneous workforce in which minority dissent is suppressed will reduce creativity, innovation, individuality, and independence (De Dreu & De Vries, 1993; see also Nemeth & Staw, 1989). Disagreement about ideas within a group can be beneficial and some researchers even argue that team task or information-related conflict is valuable, whether or not it occurs in a collaborative context, since it can improve decision making and strategic planning (Cosier & Rose, 1977; Mitroff, Barabba, & Kilmann, 1977; Schweiger, Sandberg, & Rechner, 1989). This is because task-related conflict may lead team members to re-evaluate the status quo and adapt their objectives, strategies, or processes more appropriately to their situation (Coser, 1970; Nemeth & Staw, 1989; Roloff, 1987; Thomas, 1979). However, De Dreu and Weingart (Chapter 8 this volume) suggest that high levels of conflict in teams, regardless of whether the conflict is focused on relationships or task, will inhibit team effectiveness and innovation.

In a study of newly formed postal work teams in the Netherlands, De Dreu and West found that minority dissent did indeed predict team innovation (as rated by the teams' supervisors), but only in teams with high levels of participation (De Dreu & West, 2001). It seems that the social processes in the team necessary for minority dissent to influence the innovation process are characterized by high levels of team member interaction, influence over decision making, and information sharing. This finding has significant implications for our understanding of minority dissent in groups operating in organizational contexts.

Overall, therefore, moderate task-related (as distinct from emotional or interpersonal) conflict and minority dissent in a participative climate will lead to innovation by encouraging debate (requisite diversity) and to consideration of alternative interpretations of information available, leading to integrated and creative solutions.

Support for Innovation

Innovation is more likely to occur in groups where there is support for innovation, and innovative attempts are rewarded rather than punished (Amabile, 1983; Kanter, 1983). Support for innovation is the expectation, approval, and practical support of attempts to introduce new and improved ways of doing things in the work environment (West, 1990). Within groups, new ideas may be routinely rejected or ignored, or attract verbal and practical support. Such group processes powerfully shape individual and group behaviour (for reviews see e.g. Brown, 2000; Hackman, 1992), and those which support innovation will encourage team members to introduce innovations. In a longitudinal study of 27 hospital top management teams, we found that support for innovation was the most powerful predictor of team innovation of any of the group processes so far discussed (Anderson & West, 1998; West & Anderson, 1996).

Reflexivity

Team reflexivity is the extent to which team members collectively reflect upon the team's objectives, strategies, and processes as well as their wider organizations and environments, and adapt them accordingly (West, 1996, p. 559). There are three central elements to the concept of reflexivity—*reflection*, *planning*, and *action or adaptation*. Reflection consists of attention, awareness, monitoring, and evaluation of the object of reflection (West, 2000). Planning is one of the potential consequences of the indeterminacy of reflection, since during this indeterminacy courses of action can be contemplated, intentions formed, plans developed (in more or less detail), and the potential for carrying them out is built up. High reflexivity exists when team planning is characterized by greater detail, inclusiveness of potential problems, hierarchical ordering of plans, and long- as well as short-range planning. More detailed implementation intentions or plans are more likely to lead to innovation implementation (Frese & Zapf, 1993; Gollwitzer, 1996). Indeed the work of Gollwitzer and colleagues suggests that goal-directed behaviour or innovation will be initiated when the team has articulated implementation intentions. This is because planning creates a conceptual readiness for, and guides team members' attention towards, relevant opportunities for action and means to accomplish the team's goal. Action refers to goal-directed behaviours relevant to achieving the desired changes in team objectives, strategies, processes, organizations, or environments identified by the team during the stage of reflection.

Reflexivity can relate to team objectives, strategies, internal processes, development of group psychosocial characteristics, and external relations as well as the external environment. As a consequence of reflexivity, the team's reality is continually renegotiated during team interaction. Understandings negotiated in one exchange between team members may be drawn upon in a variety of ways in order to inform subsequent discussions and offer the possibility of helpful and creative transformations and meanings (Bouwen & Fry, 1996). Research with BBC television programme production teams, whose work fundamentally requires creativity and innovation, provides support for these propositions (Carter & West, 1998). Dunbar (1996) studied four renowned science laboratories tracing the processes underlying scientific discoveries and found that scientific breakthroughs tended to occur when groups reflected on potential causes for negative or inconsistent findings. The findings mirror West's studies of team reflexivity. Reflection was more effective if it occurred in teams, as individuals tended to discount anomalous findings. Secondly, reflection stimulated the reframing of cognitive representations of tasks and questioning of commonly held assumptions, leading to the proposal of alternative, novel, and innovative approaches.

Group Psychosocial Safety

Group psychosocial safety refers to shared understandings, unconscious group processes, group cognitive style, and group emotional tone (Cohen & Bailey, 1997). Examples include norms, cohesiveness, team mental models (members share an understanding of the nature of the group's task, its task processes, how team members are required to work together, and the organizational context), and group affect. In groups with high levels of psychosocial safety, it is suggested, there will be high creativity. Creative ideas arise out of individual cognitive processes and, though group members may interact in ways which offer cognitive stimulation via diversity, creative ideas are produced as a result of individual cognitions. Evidence suggests that, in general, creative cognitions occur when individuals are free from pressure, feel safe, and experience relatively positive affect (Claxton, 1997, 1998). Moreover, psychological threats to face or identity are also associated with more rigid thinking (Cowen, 1952). Time pressure can also increase rigidity of thinking on work-related tasks such as selection decisions (Kruglansky & Freund, 1983). Another example of stress inhibiting the flexibility of responses is offered by Wright (1954), who asked people to respond to Rorschach inkblot tests. Half of the people were hospital patients awaiting an operation and half were "controls". The former gave more stereotyped responses, and were less fluent and creative in completing similes (e.g. "as interesting as..."), indicating the effects of stress or threat upon their capacity to generate creative responses.

Jehn (1995) found that norms reflecting the acceptance of conflict within a group, promoting an open and constructive atmosphere for group discussion, enhanced the positive effect of task-based conflict on individual and team performance for 79 work groups and 75 management groups. Members of high performing groups were not afraid to express their ideas and opinions. Such a finding further reinforces the notion that safety may be an important factor in idea generation or creativity.

Edmondson (1996) found major differences between newly formed intensive care nursing teams in their management of medication errors. In some groups, members openly acknowledged and discussed their medication errors (giving too much or too little of a drug, or administering the wrong drug) and discussed ways to avoid their occurrence. In others, members kept information about errors to themselves. Learning about the causes of these errors, as a team, and devising innovations to prevent future errors, were only possible in groups of the former type. Edmondson gives an example of how, in one learning-oriented team, discussion of a recent error led to innovation in equipment. An intravenous medication pump was identified as a source of consistent errors and so was replaced by a different type of pump. She also gives the example of how failure to discuss errors and generate innovations led to costly failure in the Hubble telescope development project. In particular, Edmondson (1996, 1999) argues that learning and innovation will only take place where group members trust other members' intentions. This manifests in a group level belief that well-intentioned action will not lead to punishment or rejection by the team, which Edmondson calls "team safety": "The term is meant to suggest a realistic, learning oriented attitude about effort, error and change—not to imply a careless sense of permissiveness, nor an unrelentingly positive affect. Safety is not the same as comfort; in contrast, it is predicted to facilitate risk" (Edmondson, 1999, p. 14).

LEADERSHIP

Leaders of groups can seek ideas and support their implementation among members; leaders may promote only their own ideas; or leaders may resist change and innovation from any source. The leader, by definition, exerts powerful social influences on the group or team, and therefore affects team performance (Beyerlein, Johnson, & Beyerlein, 1996; Brewer,

Wilson, & Beck, 1994; Komaki, Desselles, & Bowman, 1989). For example, research in Canadian manufacturing organizations reveals that CEOs' ages, flexibility, and perseverance are all positively related to the adoption of technological innovation in their organizations (Kitchell, 1997). We propose that leadership processes moderate the effects of inputs (team and organizational contexts) upon team processes and thereby affect the level and quality (magnitude, radicalness, and novelty) of the innovation (see Figure 12.1).

In any discussion of team leadership it is important to acknowledge that leadership processes are not necessarily invested in one person in a team. In most work teams there is a single and clearly defined team leader or manager and his or her style and behaviour had a considerable influence in moderating the relationships between inputs and processes. But leadership processes can be distributed such that more than one or all team members take on leadership roles at various points in the team's activities. Consider, for example, the breast cancer care team responsible for diagnosis, surgery, and postoperative treatment of patients. At various points the oncologist, surgeon, and breast care nurse are likely to (and it is appropriate that they should) take leadership roles in the team (Haward et al., 2002).

Recent theories of leadership depict two dominant styles: transformational and transactional. Transactional leaders focus on transactions, exchanges, contingent rewards, and punishments to change team members' behaviour (see Schriesheim & Kerr, 1977; Yammarino, 1996; Yukl, 1994). This style reflects an emphasis on the relationship between task-oriented leader behaviour and effective group member performance. Transformational leaders influence group members by encouraging them to transform their views of themselves and their work. They rely on charisma and the ability to conjure inspiring visions of the future (e.g. Bass, 1990; Burns, 1978; House & Shamir, 1993). Such leaders use emotional or ideological appeals to change the behaviour of the group, moving them from self-interest in work values to consideration of the whole group and organization. Although the reader may be tempted to the conclusion that only the transformational style will produce innovation, it is likely that both of these styles will influence creativity and innovation by moderating the relationship between inputs and processes. Inspiration or reward could lead to individual propensity to innovate being translated into innovation implementation. Rewards used by the leader will influence group creativity and innovation where these rewards are directed towards encouraging individual and group innovation, such as performance-related pay for new product development successes.

Team leadership studies (cf. Barry, 1991; Kim, Min, & Cha, 1999; McCall, 1988) have adopted role-based approaches to measure the specific leadership behaviours that team leaders perform in order to facilitate and direct teamwork. The basic premise of these studies is that team leaders must be competent at performing a diverse array of leadership activities. The most comprehensive framework was developed by McCall (1988) and recently reported and tested by Hoojberg and Choi (2000). This framework is based on the competing values theory that leaders must grapple with very different roles, which can be categorized within the quadrant of internal versus external as well interpersonal versus personal. The most striking finding of Hoojberg and Choi's (2000) research is that there are systematic differences in the structure of these roles depending on which stakeholder's perspective is assessed. More parsimonious frameworks tend to highlight the extent to which leaders foster teamwork, organize and direct project work, manage relationships with external stakeholders, and stimulate creativity and innovation. Barry (1991) conducted a detailed qualitative study of engineering and product development teams and identified four leadership roles that are critical to ensuring teams tackle the challenges of R&D work. Yukl (2002) refined this taxonomy, drawing upon empirical studies of knowledge work teams, to identify four roles: boundary spanning, facilitative leadership, innovation-stimulating leadership, and task management. We describe the four roles and summarize empirical support for each below.

- Leadership boundary spanning involves the management of external relationships, including coordinating tasks, negotiating resources and goals with stakeholders as well as scanning for information and ideas. Waldman and Atwater (1994) conducted a study of 40 R&D project teams; they found, out of a range of leadership behaviours examined (including transformation leadership and goal-setting behaviour), that boundary spanning (in particular championing the project) was the strongest predictor ($r = 0.22$) of research managers' ratings of project performance.

- Facilitative leadership refers to whether the leader encourages an atmosphere conducive to teamwork, ensuring team interactions are equitable and safe, encouraging participation, sharing of ideas, and open discussion of different perspectives. Kim, Min, and Cha (1999) surveyed 87 R&D teams in six Korean organizations; they found that the leader's performance of the team builder role was a significant predictor of team ratings of performance.

- A leader who acts as an innovator envisions project opportunities and new approaches by questioning team assumptions and challenging the status quo. Keller (1992) found that leaders who questioned approaches and suggested innovative ways of performing tasks were more likely to lead effective teams. Likewise Kim, Min, and Cha (1999) found that the leader's technical problem-solving ability, in particular appraisal of problems and identification of new ideas, was significantly correlated with project performance ($r = 0.35$).

- Directive leaders drive structured and ordered performance of project work by communicating instructions, setting priorities, deadlines, and standards. Yukl, Wall, and Lepsinger (1990) found that leaders who clarified tasks, communicated instructions, set priorities, deadlines, and standards, were most effective. Based on a sample of 296 groups, Kim and Yukl (1995) found, from a comprehensive list of managerial activities, planning and organizing were the strongest predictors of subordinate ratings of leadership effectiveness. Clear direction setting enables the focused development of ideas which can be assessed with greater precision than if team members are unclear (West & Anderson, 1996).

Of the four roles described, three pertain to leadership activities directed towards stimulating and managing cooperation within the team, whereas the fourth role, leadership boundary spanning, measures the extent to which the leader manages team relationships and coordination with the external environment. Thus while the nature and content of the roles differ, all roles require leader actions to stimulate and direct cooperation between individuals/groups to perform effectively and develop innovations.

Knorr et al. (1979) found that the team leader's professional status, ability to plan and coordinate activities, integrate the team, and encourage career promotion predicted the climate for innovation in the team as well as its overall performance. McDonough and Barczak (1992) examined the relationships between a leader's cognitive problem-solving style and the team's cognitive problem-solving style in product development teams. Cognitive problem-solving style was characterized as either adaptive (conforms to commonly accepted procedures) or innovative (searches for novel solutions). When the technology they were required to use was familiar to the team, the leader's style was unimportant. However, when the technology was unfamiliar, teams whose leaders had an innovative cognitive style developed new products faster than other teams. For product innovation in familiar situations, it seems leaders can withdraw from the team, but when the situation is unfamiliar, a non-conforming leader enables the team to consider a variety of options.

No discussion of leadership in social or industrial/organizational (I/O) psychology should neglect the impressive programme of work carried out by Norman Maier and his colleagues in the 1960s and 1970s. Maier (1970) conducted a series of experiments with (mostly student) groups exploring the influence of different leadership styles on problem solving and creativity. The results suggested that the leader should encourage "problem mindedness" in groups on the basis that exploring the problem fully is the best way of eventually generating a rich vein of solution options. The leader can delay a group's criticism of an idea by asking for alternative contributions and should use his or her power to protect individuals with minority views, so that their opinions can be heard (Maier & Solem, 1962; see also Osborn, 1957). Maier (1970) argued that leaders should delay offering their opinions as long as possible, since propositions from leaders are often given undue weight and tend either to be too hastily accepted or rejected, rather than properly evaluated, a finding since replicated in a variety of applied studies. Maier (1970) concludes that leaders should function as "the group's central nervous system": receive information, facilitate communication, relay messages, and integrate responses—in short, integrate the group. The leader must be receptive to information, but not impose solutions. The leader should be aware of group processes; listen in order to understand rather than to appraise or refute; assume responsibility for accurate communication; be sensitive to unexpressed feelings; protect minority views; keep the discussion moving; and develop skills in summarizing (Maier, 1970).

Leadership processes have a considerable influence in determining whether the inputs (such as team task, team member characteristics, organizational culture and climate, and demands on the team) are translated into group processes that support innovation implementation or smother both creativity and innovation. In this chapter we have proposed that they play a major role in moderating the relationship between input variables and group processes, and thereby innovation implementation. Generally, leadership is a topic that has been neglected in the study of group creativity and innovation since Maier's seminal work. As we move into an era when the imperatives for innovation in organizations are intense, it is important that social and I/O psychologists stretch their research to achieve a better understanding of how leaders influence creativity and innovation in teams.

CONCLUSIONS

Based upon the premise that cooperation and teamwork are fundamental for innovation, we developed an input–process–output framework examining how measures of teamwork, as well as factors impacting on teamwork, influence innovation. The inputs included team composition and organizational context. We identified a range of team processes including clarity of objectives, participation, and the climate supporting innovation. Thirdly, we proposed that leadership moderated the relationship between inputs and outputs.

Guided by this framework, we conducted a review of relevant literatures. The following themes emerged from this review. Task-oriented diversity acts as a double-edged sword, reducing cooperation and cohesion while providing teams with a greater range of perspectives, information as well as links to the external environment. Organizational contextual factors such as age and size and structural factors such as centralization influence team processes as well as team innovation. Leaders play a key role in buffering the team from the pernicious effects, or enhancing in the team the nurturing effects, of organizational culture. Team leaders also can ensure that team member and task characteristics influence group processes in a way that leads to rather than inhibits innovation. The relationship between team processes and innovation tends to be strong and positive. Although the nature of these processes varies considerably, virtually all include some measure of cooperative task performance, interaction, or social support processes within the group. Cooperation is core to team innovation.

While research has highlighted the importance of teamwork and cooperation, much of this research has adopted a static perspective (Marks, Mathieu, & Zacarro, 2001). Few studies take into account temporal factors which may change across a project's life cycle and a team's development. Punctuated equilibrium theory (cf. Gersick, 1988) predicts that teams have stable and relatively fixed routines and norms which are punctuated by radical change. More traditional theoretical orientations, which adopt stage-based models of teamwork (cf. Tuckman, 1965), suggest that these norms develop over time and after conflicts within teams; groups go through an ordered series of phases. One perspective (e.g. Marks, Mathieu, & Zacarro, 2001) to emerge is that there are times when irrespective of a project's progress or the stages of a team's development high levels of cooperation and teamwork are critical. Periods when high levels of project obstacles are encountered may necessitate intense cooperation and commitment. Failure to perform during these periods of high stress may have a disastrous effect on team performance and innovation. Based on similar assumptions but a different categorization system, Marks, Mathieu, and Zacarro (2001) contrast transition (i.e. periods of time when teams are evaluating or planning actions to attain goals) and action phases (periods when teams are performing activities leading to goal attainment). In essence the authors assert that different processes are important during action as opposed to transition phases. For example, mission analysis and the development of shared objectives are essential during transition phases, whereas during the action phases coordination and cooperation are essential. On the basis of these observations we believe that research in this area should track team development and team innovation in order that we can better understand these dynamic relationships. Sustained high levels of innovation are unlikely, and possibly counterproductive, in any team. Understanding when and how cooperation enables team innovation and when and how team innovation is helpful for effectiveness is important in future research.

For creativity and innovation implementation to emerge from group functioning over time—for groups to be sparkling fountains of ideas and changes—the context must be demanding but there must be strong group integration processes, good leadership, and a high level of intragroup safety. This requires that members have the integration abilities to work effectively in teams; and that they develop a safe psychosocial climate and appropriate group processes (clarifying objectives, encouraging participation, constructive controversy, reflexivity, and support for innovation). Such conditions are likely to produce high levels of group innovation, but crucially, too, the well-being which is a consequence of effective human interaction in challenging and supportive environments.

REFERENCES

Agrell, A. & Gustafson, R. (1996). Innovation and creativity in work groups. In M. A. West (ed.), *The Handbook of Work Group Psychology* (pp. 317–344). Chichester: Wiley.

Allen, T. J., Lee, D. M., & Tushman, M. L. (1980). R&D performance as a function of internal communication, project management, and the nature of work. *IEEE Transactions, 27*, 2–12.

Alper, S. & Tjosvold, D. (1993). Cooperation theory and self-managing teams on the manufacturing floor. Paper presented at the International Association for Conflict Management, Eugene, Ore.

Amabile, T. M. (1983). The social psychology of creativity: a componential conceptualization. *Journal of Personality and Social Psychology, 45*, 357–376.

Amabile, T. M. (1988). A model of creativity and innovation in organizations. In B. M. Staw & L. L. Cummings (eds), *Research in Organizational Behavior* (Vol. 10, pp. 123–167). Greenwich, Conn.: JAI Press.

Amabile, T. M. (1997). Motivating creativity in organizations: on doing what you love and loving what you do. *California Management Review, 40*(1), 39–58.

Amabile, T. M., Conti, R., Coon, H., Lazenby, J., & Herron, M. (1996). Assessing the work environment for creativity. *Academy of Management Journal, 39*, 1154–1184.

Ancona, D. F. & Caldwell, D. F. (1992). Bridging the boundary: external activity and performance in organisational teams. *Administrative Science Quarterly, 37*, 634–665.

Anderson, N. & West, M. A. (1998). Measuring climate for work group innovation: development and validation of the Team Climate Inventory. *Journal of Organizational Behavior, 19*, 235–258.

Andrews, F. M. (ed.) (1979). *Scientific Productivity*. Cambridge: Cambridge University Press.

Bantel, K. A. & Jackson, S. E. (1989). Top management and innovations in banking: does the demography of the top team make a difference? *Strategic Management Journal, 10*, 107–124.

Barry, D. (1991). Managing the boss-less team: lessons in distributed leadership. *Organizational Dynamics*, Summer, 31–47.

Bass, B. M. (1990). *Bass and Stogdill's Handbook of Leadership* (3rd edn). New York: Free Press.

Beyerlein, M. M., Johnson, D. A., & Beyerlein, S. T. (eds) (1996). *Advances in the Interdisciplinary Study of Work Teams* (Vol. 2) *Knowledge Work in Teams*. London: JAI Press.

Bouwen, R. & Fry, R. (1996). Facilitating group development: interventions for a relational and contextual construction. In M. A. West (ed.), *The Handbook of Work Group Psychology* (pp. 531–552). Chichester: Wiley.

Bowers, D. G. & Seashore, S. E. (1966). Predicting organizational effectiveness with a four-factor theory of leadership. *Administrative Science Quarterly, 11*, 238–263.

Brewer, N., Wilson, C., & Beck, K. (1994). Supervisory behaviour and team performance amongst police patrol sergeants. *Journal of Occupational and Organizational Psychology, 67*, 69–78.

Brown, R. J. (2000). *Group Processes: Dynamics within and between Groups*. London: Blackwell.

Bunce, D. & West, M. A. (1995). Changing work environments: innovative coping responses to occupational stress. *Work and Stress, 8*, 319–331.

Bunce, D. & West, M. A. (1996). Stress management and innovation interventions at work. *Human Relations, 49*, 209–232.

Burns, J. M. (1978). *Leadership*. New York: Harper & Row.

Burns, T. & Stalker, G. M. (1961). *The Management of Innovation*. London: Tavistock.

Carter, S. M. & West, M. A. (1998). Reflexivity, effectiveness and mental health in BBC-TV production teams. *Small Group Research, 5*, 583–601.

Claxton, G. L. (1997). *Hare Brain, Tortoise Mind: Why Intelligence Increases When You Think Less*. London: Fourth Estate.

Claxton, G. L. (1998). Knowing without knowing why: investigating human intuition. *The Psychologist, 11*, 217–220.

Coch, L. & French, J. R. (1948). Overcoming resistance to change. *Human Relations, 1*, 512–532.

Cohen, S. G. & Bailey, D. E. (1997). What makes teams work: group effectiveness research from the shop floor to the executive suite. *Journal of Management, 23*, 239–290.

Coser, L. A. (1970). *Continuities in the Study of Social Conflict*. New York: Free Press.

Cosier, R. & Rose, G. (1977). Cognitive conflict and goal conflict effects on task performance. *Organizational Behavior and Human Performance, 19*, 378–391.

Cowen, E. L. (1952). The influence of varying degrees of psychological stress on problem-solving rigidity. *Journal of Abnormal and Social Psychology, 47*, 420–424.

Cummings, L. L. (1965). Organizational climates for creativity. *Journal of the Academy of Management, 3*, 220–227.

De Dreu, C. K. W. (1995). Coercive power and concession making in bilateral negotiation. *Journal of Conflict Resolution, 39*, 646–670.

De Dreu, C. K. W. (1997). Productive conflict: the importance of conflict management and conflict issue. In C. K. W. De Dreu & E. van de Vliert (eds), *Using Conflict in Organizations* (pp. 9–22). London: Sage.

De Dreu, C. K. W. & De Vries, N. K. (1993). Numerical support, information processing, and attitude to change. *European Journal of Social Psychology, 23*, 647–662.

De Dreu, C. K. W. & De Vries, N. K. (1997). Minority dissent in organizations. In C. K. W. De Dreu & E. Van De Vliert (eds), *Using Conflict in Organizations* (pp. 72–86). London: Sage.

De Dreu, C. K. W. & West, M. A. (2001). Minority dissent and team innovation: the importance of participation in decision-making. *Journal of Applied Psychology, 68*, 1191–1201.

Delbecq, A. L. & Mills, P. K. (1985). Managerial practices that enhance innovation. *Organizational Dynamics, 14*, 24–34.

Dunbar, K. (1996). How scientists really reason: scientific reasoning in real-world laboratories. In R. J. Sternberg & J. E. Davidson (eds), *The Nature of Insight* (pp. 365–395). Cambridge, Mass.: MIT Press.

Edmondson, A. C. (1996). Learning from mistakes is easier said than done: group and organizational influences on the detection and correction of human error. *Journal of Applied Behavioral Science, 32*, 5–28.

Edmondson, A. C. (1999). Psychological safety and learning behavior in work teams. *Administrative Science Quarterly, 44*, 350–383.

Ettlie, J. E. (1983). Organizational policy and innovation among suppliers to the food-processing sector. *Academy of Management Journal, 26*, 27–44.

Filley, A. C., House, R. J., & Kerr, S. (1976). *Managerial Process and Organizational Behavior*. Glenview, Ill.: Scott Foresman.

Frese, M. & Zapf, D. (1993). Action as the core of work psychology: a German approach. In H. C. Triandis, M. D. Dunnette, & L. M. Hough (eds), *Handbook of Industrial and Organizational Psychology* (2nd edn, Vol. 4, pp. 271–340). Palo Alto, Calif.: Consulting Psychologists Press.

Gersick, C. J. G. (1988). Time and transition in work teams: toward a new model of group development. *Academy of Management Journal, 31*(1), 9–41.

Ghiselli, E. E. & Lodahl, T. M. (1958). Patterns of managerial traits and group effectiveness. *Journal of Abnormal and Social Psychology, 57*, 61–66.

Gollwitzer, P. M. (1996). The volitional benefits of planning. In P. M. Gollwitzer & J. A. Bargh (eds), *The Psychology of Action: Linking Cognition and Motivation to Behaviour* (pp. 287–312). New York: Guilford Press.

Hackman, J. R. (1992). Group influences on individuals in organisations. In M. D. Dunnette & L. M. Hough (eds), *Handbook of Industrial and Organizational Psychology* (Vol. 3). Palo Alto, Calif.: Consulting Psychologists Press.

Hage, J. & Aiken, M. (1967). *Social Change in Complex Organizations*. New York: Random House.

Hage, J. & Dewar, R. (1973). Elite values versus organizational structure in predicting innovation. *Administrative Science, 18*, 279–290.

Haward, B., Amir, Z., Borrill, C. S., Dawson, J. F., Sainsbury, R., Scully, J., & West, M. A. (2002). Breast cancer teams: the impact of constitution, new cancer workload, and methods of operation on their effectiveness. Unpublished paper, Leeds, UK: Epidemiology and Health Services Research, University of Leeds.

Hoffman, L. R. (1979). Applying experimental research on group problem solving to organizations. *Journal of Abnormal and Social Psychology, 58*, 27–32.

Hoffman, L. R., Harburg, E., & Maier, N. R. F. (1962). Differences and disagreement as factors in creative group problem solving. *Journal of Abnormal and Social Psychology, 64*, 206–214.

Hoffman, L. R. & Maier, N. R. F. (1961). Sex differences, sex composition, and group problem-solving. *Journal of Abnormal and Social Psychology, 63*, 453–456.

Hoojberg, R. & Choi, J. (2000). Which leadership roles matter to whom? An examination of rater effects on perceptions of effectiveness. *Leadership Quarterly, 11*(3), 341–364.

House, R. J. & Shamir, B. (1993). Toward the integration of transformational, charismatic, and visionary theories. In M. M. Chemers & R. Ayman (eds), *Leadership Theory and Research: Perspectives and Directions* (pp. 81–107). San Diego, Calif.: Academic Press.

Jackson, S. E. (1992). Consequences of group composition for the interpersonal dynamics of strategic issue processing. *Advances in Strategic Management, 8*, 345–382.

Jackson, S. E. (1996). The consequences of diversity in multidisciplinary work teams. In M. A. West (ed.), *Handbook of Work Group Psychology* (pp. 53–75). Chichester: Wiley.

Jehn, K. A. (1995). A multimethod examination of the benefits and detriments of intragroup conflict. *Administrative Science Quarterly, 40*, 256–282.

Kanter, R. M. (1983). *The Change Masters: Corporate Entrepreneurs at Work*. New York: Simon & Schuster.

Katz, R. (1982). The effects of group longevity on project communication and performance. *Administrative Science Quarterly, 27*, 81–104.

Keller, R. T. (1992). Transformational leadership and the performance of research and development research groups. *Journal of Management, 18*(3), 489–501.

Keller, R. T. (2001). Cross-functional project groups in research and new product development: diversity, communications, job stress and outcomes. *Academy of Management Journal, 44*(3), 547–555.

Kim, H. & Yukl, G. (1995) Relationships of managerial effectiveness and advancement to self-reported leadership–reported leadership behaviors from the multiple-linkage model. *Leadership Quarterly, 6*(3), 361–377.

Kim, Y., Min, B., & Cha, J. (1999). The roles of R&D team leaders in Korea: a contingent approach. *R&D Management, 29*(2), 153–165.

Kimberley, J. R. & Evanisko, M. J. (1981). Organizational innovation: the influence of individual, organizational and contextual factors on hospital adoption of technological and administrative innovations. *Academy of Management Journal, 24*, 689–713.

Kitchell, S. (1997). CEO characteristics and technological innovativeness: a Canadian perspective. *Canadian Journal of Administrative Sciences, 14*, 111–125.

Kivimaki, M., Lansisalmi, H., Elovainio, M., Heikkila, A., Lindstrom, K., Harisalo, R., Sipila, K., & Puolimatka, L. (2000). Communication as a determinant of organizational innovation. *R&D Management, 30*(1), 33–42.

Knorr, K. D., Mittermeir, R., Aichholzer, G., & Waller, G. (1979). Leadership and group performance: a positive relationship in academic research units. In F. M. Andrews (ed.), *Scientific Productivity* (pp. 95–117). Cambridge: Cambridge University Press.

Komaki, J. L., Desselles, M. L., & Bowman, E. D. (1989). Definitely not a breeze: extending an operant model of effective supervision to teams. *Journal of Applied Psychology, 74*, 522–529.

Kruglansky, A. W. & Freund, T. (1983). The freezing and unfreezing of lay influences: effects on impressional primacy, ethnic stereotyping and numerical anchoring. *Journal of Experimental Social Psychology, 12*, 448–468.

Lawler, E. E., III & Hackman, J. R. (1969). Impact of employee participation in the development of pay incentive plans: a field experiment. *Journal of Applied Psychology, 53*, 467–471.

Lawrence, P. R. & Lorsch, J. W. (1967). *Organization and Environment: Managing Differentiation and Integration*. Boston: Harvard Business School.

Maass, A. & Clark, R. D. (1984). Hidden impacts of minorities: fifty years of minority influence research. *Psychological Bulletin, 95*, 428–450.

McCall, M. W., Jr (1988). Developing leadership. In J. L. Galbraith, E. E. Lawler, III, & associates (eds), *Organizing for the Future: The New Logic for Managing Complex Organizations* (pp. 256–284). Jossey-Bass Series.

McDonough, E. F., III & Barczak, G. (1992). The effects of cognitive problem-solving orientation and technological familiarity on faster new product development. *Journal of Product Innovation Management, 9*, 44–52.

McGrath, J. E. (1984). *Groups, Interaction and Performance*. Englewood Cliffs, NJ: Prentice-Hall.

Maier, N. R. (1970). *Problem Solving and Creativity: In Individuals and Groups*. Monterey, Calif.: Brooks Cole.

Maier, N. R. & Solem, A. R. (1962). Improving solutions by turning choice situations into problems. *Personnel Psychology, 15*, 151–157.

Marks, M. A., Mathieu, J. E., & Zaccaro, S. E. (2001). A temporally based framework and taxonomy of team processes. *Academy of Management Review, 26*(3), 356–376.

Maznevski, M. L. (1994). Understanding our differences: performance in decision-making groups with diverse members. *Human Relations, 47*, 531–552.

Mitroff, J., Barabba, N., & Kilmann, R. (1977). The application of behaviour and philosophical technologies to strategic planning: a case study of a large federal agency. *Management Studies, 24*, 44–58.

Mohrman, S. A., Cohen, S. G., & Mohrman, A. M. (1995). *Designing Team-based Organizations: New Forms for Knowledge Work*. San Francisco: Jossey-Bass.

Monge, P. R., Cozzens, M. D., & Contractor, N. S. (1992). Communication and motivational predictors of the dynamics of organizational innovation. *Organizational Science, 3*, 250–274.

Mumford, M. D. & Gustafson, S. B. (1988). Creativity syndrome: integration, application and innovation. *Psychological Bulletin, 103*, 27–43.

Nemeth, C. (1986). Differential contributions of majority and minority influence. *Psychological Review, 93*, 23–32.

Nemeth, C. & Chiles, C. (1988). Modelling courage: the role of dissent in fostering independence. *European Journal of Social Psychology, 18*, 275–280.

Nemeth, C. & Kwan, J. (1987). Minority influence, divergent thinking and the detection of correct solutions. *Journal of Applied Social Psychology, 9*, 788–799.

Nemeth, C. & Nemeth-Brown, B. (in press). Better than individuals? The potential benefits of dissent and diversity for group creativity. In P. Paulus & B. Nijstad (eds), *Group Creativity*. New York: Oxford University Press.

Nemeth, C. & Owens, P. (1996). Making work groups more effective: the value of minority dissent. In M. A. West (ed.), *Handbook of Work Group Psychology* (pp. 125–142). Chichester: Wiley.

Nemeth, C. & Staw, B. M. (1989). The trade offs of social control and innovation within groups and organizations. In L. Berkowitz (ed.), *Advances in Experimental Social Psychology* (pp. 175–210). New York: Academic Press.

Nemeth, C. J. & Wachtler, J. (1983). Creative problem solving as a result of majority vs minority influence. *European Journal of Social Psychology, 13*, 45–55.

Nicholson, N. & West, M. A. (1988). *Managerial Job Change: Men and Women in Transition*. Cambridge: Cambridge University Press.

O'Reilly, C. A. & Flatt, S. F. (1989). Executive team demography, organizational innovation, and firm performance. Paper presented at the Academy of Management Conference, Washington, DC.

Osborn, A. F. (1957). *Applied Imagination*. New York: Scribner's.

Payne, R. L. (1990). The effectiveness of research teams: a review. In M. A. West & J. L. Farr (eds), *Innovation and Creativity at Work: Psychological and Organizational Strategies* (pp. 101–122). Chichester: Wiley.

Pearce, J. A. & Ravlin, E. C. (1987). The design and activation of self-regulating work groups. *Human Relations, 40*, 751–782.

Pelz, D. C. (1956). Some social factors related to performance in a research organization. *Administrative Science Quarterly, 1*, 310–325.

Pierce, J. L. & Delbecq, A. (1977). Organizational structure, individual attitude and innovation. *Academy of Management Review, 2*, 27–33.

Pinto, J. K. & Prescott, J. E. (1987). Changes in critical success factor importance over the life of a project. *Academy of Management Proceedings*, New Orleans, 328–332.

Porac, J. F. & Howard, H. (1990). Taxonomic mental models in competitor definition. *Academy of Management Review, 2*, 224–240.

Rodgers, R. & Hunter, J. E. (1991). Impact of management by objectives on organizational productivity. *Journal of Applied Psychology, 76*(2), 322–336.

Rogers, E. M. (1983). *Diffusion of Innovations* (3rd edn). New York: Free Press.

Roloff, M. E. (1987). Communication and conflict. In C. R. Berger & S. H. Chaffee (eds), *Handbook of Communication Science* (pp. 484–534). Newbury Park, Calif.: Sage.

Schriesheim, C. A. & Kerr, S. (1977). Theories and measures of leadership: a critical appraisal of current and future directions. In J. G. Hunt & L. L. Larson (eds), *Leadership: The Cutting Edge* (pp. 9–45). Carbondale, Ill.: Southern Illinois University Press.

Schweiger, D., Sandberg, W., & Rechner, P. (1989). Experimental effects of dialectical inquiry, devil's advocacy, and other consensus approaches to strategic decision making. *Academy of Management Journal, 32*, 745–772.

Shaw, M. E. (1981). *Group Dynamics: The Psychology of Small Group Behavior*. New York: McGraw-Hill.

Shepard, H. A. (1967). Innovation-resisting and innovation-producing organizations. *Journal of Business, 40*, 470–477.

Smith, K. G., Smith, K. A., Olian, J. D., Sims, H. P. Jr, O'Brannon, D. P., & Scully, J. A. (1994). Top management team demography and process. The role of social integration and communication. *Administrative Science Quarterly, 39*, 412–438.

Thomas, K. W. (1979). Organizational conflict. In S. Kerr (ed.), *Organizational Behaviour* (pp. 151–184). Columbus, Ohio: Grid Publishing.

Tjosvold, D. (1982). Effects of approach to controversy on superiors' incorporation of subordinates' information in decision making. *Journal of Applied Psychology, 67*, 189–193.

Tjosvold, D. (1985). Implications of controversy research for management. *Journal of Management, 11*, 21–37.

Tjosvold, D. (1991). *Team Organization: An Enduring Competitive Advantage*. Chichester: Wiley.

Tjosvold, D. (1998). Co-operative and competitive goal approaches to conflict: accomplishments and challenges. *Applied Psychology: An International Review, 47*, 285–342.

Tjosvold, D. & Field, R. H. G. (1983). Effects of social context on consensus and majority vote decision making. *Academy of Management Journal, 26*, 500–506.

Tjosvold, D. & Johnson, D. W. (1977). The effects of controversy on cognitive perspective-taking. *Journal of Education Psychology, 69*, 679–685.

Tjosvold, D., Wedley, W. C., & Field, R. H. G. (1986). Constructive controversy, the Vroom–Yetton Model, and managerial decision-making. *Journal of Occupational Behaviour, 7*, 125–138.

Tuckman, Bruce W. (1965). Developmental sequence in small groups. *Psychological Bulletin, 63*, 384–399.

Utterback, J. M. (1974). Innovation in industry and the diffusion of technology. *Science, 183*, 620–626.

Wade, J. (1996). A community level analysis of sources and rates of technological variation in the microprocessor market. *Academy of Management Journal, 39*, 1218–1244.

Waldman, D. A. & Atwater, L. E. (1994). The nature of effective leadership and championing processes at different levels in a R&D hierarchy. *The Journal of High Technology Management Research, 5*(2), 233–245.

West, M. A. (1987). Role innovation in the world of work. *British Journal of Social Psychology, 26*, 305–315.

West, M. A. (1990). The social psychology of innovation in groups. In M. A. West & J. L. Farr (eds), *Innovation and Creativity at Work: Psychological and Organizational Strategies* (pp. 309–333). Chichester: Wiley.

West, M. A. (1994). *Effective Teamwork*. Leicester: British Psychological Society.

West, M. A. (1996). Reflexivity and work group effectiveness: a conceptual integration. In M. A. West (ed.), *Handbook of Work Group Psychology* (pp. 555–579). Chichester: Wiley.

West, M. A. (2000). Reflexivity, revolution, and innovation in work teams. In M. M. Beyerlein, D. A. Johnson, & S. T. Beyerlein (eds), *Advances in Interdisciplinary Studies of Work Teams: Product Development Teams* (pp. 1–29). Stamford, Conn.: JAI Press.

West, M. A. (2002). Sparkling fountains or stagnant ponds: an integrative model of creativity and innovation implementation in work groups. *Applied Psychology: An International Review, 51*, 355–424.

West, M. A. & Anderson, N. (1992). Innovation, cultural values and the management of change in British hospitals. *Work and Stress, 6*, 293–310.
West, M. A. & Anderson, N. (1996). Innovation in top management teams. *Journal of Applied Psychology, 81*, 680–693.
West, M. A. & Farr, J. L. (1990). Innovation at work. In M. A. West & J. L. Farr (eds), *Innovation and Creativity at Work: Psychological and Organizational Strategies* (pp. 3–13). Chichester: Wiley.
West, M. A. & Richter, A. (in press). Climates and cultures for innovation and creativity at work. In C. Ford (ed.), *Handbook of Organizational Creativity*. London: Sage.
West, M. A., Patterson, M., Pillinger, T., & Nickell, S. (2000). Innovation and change in manufacturing. Working paper, Aston Business School, Aston University, Birmingham, UK.
Willems, E. P. & Clark, R. D., III (1971). Shift toward risk and heterogeneity of groups. *Journal of Experimental and Social Psychology, 7*, 302–312.
Wood, W. (1987). Meta-analytic review of sex differences in group performance. *Psychological Bulletin, 102*, 53–71.
Wright, M. (1954). A study of anxiety in a general hospital setting. *Canadian Journal of Psychology, 8*, 195–203.
Yammarino, F. J. (1996). Group leadership: a levels of analysis perspective. In M. A. West (ed.), *Handbook of Work Group Psychology* (pp. 189–224). Chichester: Wiley.
Yukl, G. A. (1994). *Leadership in Organizations*. Englewood Cliffs, NJ: Prentice-Hall.
Yukl, G. A. (2002). *Leadership in Organizations* (5th edn). New Jersey: Prentice-Hall.
Yukl, G. A., Wall, S., & Lepsinger, R. (1990). Preliminary report on validation of the Managerial Practices Survey. In K. E. Clark & M. B. Clark (eds), *Measures of Leadership*. New Jersey: Leadership Library of America.
Zaltman, G., Duncan, R., & Holbeck, J. (1973). *Innovations and Organizations*. London: Wiley.
Zenger, T. R. & Lawrence, B. S. (1989). Organizational demography: the differential effects of age and tenure distributions on technical communication. *Academy of Management Journal, 32*, 353–376.

13

WHEN EAST AND WEST MEET
EFFECTIVE TEAMWORK ACROSS CULTURES

Kwok Leung, Lin Lu, and Xiangfen Liang

INTRODUCTION

Asia, especially East Asia, has emerged from poverty and underdevelopment into a symbol of rapid economic development in the last century (Chen, 1995). Accounting for half of the annual growth in world trade, Asia today has become the third largest business partner in the world. Although the Asian economic crisis in 1997–98 put an end to the high-growth era, some countries have restructured their economy successfully and are once again on the path of growth. With China becoming the economic locomotive for the region, East–West encounters and collaborations are bound to increase.

Positive East–West interactions are only a recent phenomenon. Not too long ago, Asia was a land of mystery to Westerners, and Asians saw the West as synonymous with gunboat diplomacy. The mysterious veil of Asia has now been lifted by globalization, and gunboat diplomacy has long been replaced by multilateral dialogues and economic rationality. Nonetheless, deep-seated cultural differences persist, and East–West contact is sometimes marked by frustration and tension. Considerable research has been conducted to examine how teamwork and cooperation can be encouraged in East–West contact (e.g. Baran, Pan, & Kaynak, 1996; Berger, 1996; Dunung, 1998; Hofstede, 1980, 1995; Mo, 1996). In this chapter, a framework based on the notion of cultural tuning will be introduced for understanding and facilitating teamwork between East and West. A review of the cultural and social characteristics of Asian countries is then given to provide the background for the final section, which describes how the cultural tuning framework can be applied to overcome barriers to effective teamwork between Asians and Westerners in the workplace.

East–West Encounters

A myriad of problems can stifle East–West collaboration, and most people find it hard to rely on a set of simple principles to guide their actions in diverse situations. Different East–West encounters seem to involve different problems and call for different solutions. For

---

The Essentials *of Teamworking: International Perspectives.*
Edited by M. A. West, D. Tjosvold, and K. G. Smith. © 2005 John Wiley & Sons, Ltd.

example, when Sage Publications was planning to operate in India, they faced a wide range of challenges, including the political relationship between the US and India, the instability of the Indian currency, governmental bureaucracy, involvement of unions in resisting some Western management practices, and incongruence in nonverbal communication between Americans and Indians (Whiting & Reardon, 1994). Very different problems surfaced in the case of the Aladdin and Dunes Hotel in Las Vegas, a US–Japan collaboration. Americans found the emphasis on consensus by Japanese too slow and cumbersome in the fast-moving casino environment (Ricks, 1993).

To help practitioners deal with the complexities of cross-cultural encounters, some general guidelines have been proposed. Trompenaars (1993), in the best-seller *Riding the Waves of Culture*, emphasizes three basic principles in handling culture differences: awareness, respect, and taking advantage of cultural differences. On a more practical level, Berger (1996) has proposed five guidelines for intercultural encounters:

1. Be patient and persistent in communicating with speakers using a second language;
2. Recognize cultural differences, but resist stereotypes;
3. Recognize cultural differences in norms about politeness and communication style;
4. Be aware of status differences;
5. Be sensitive about the influence of people's loyalty toward their own cultural group.

CULTURAL TUNING

These types of guidelines are often derived from anecdotes and experiences, and lack a firm conceptual foundation. To overcome these problems, Leung (in press) has recently introduced a framework of cultural tuning for effective intercultural interaction, the essence of which is to facilitate two cultural groups to use the same frame of reference in communication and interaction.

Cultural tuning involves three rules, and the first is the holistic rule. Ashmos and George (1987), in their systems theory, argue for a holistic approach to organizational theory because all elements in the universe are interrelated and interdependent, and they should be studied in the context of their interconnections. In terms of East–West interactions, we also argue that all important elements that are directly or indirectly related to an interaction, such as norms, motives, and cognitive processes, must be considered simultaneously. In fact, cultural psychologists argue that cultural elements cannot be understood in the abstract and in isolation (e.g. Greenfield, 2000), and a holistic perspective is essential to the understanding of another cultural group. The holistic rule avoids the problems of misunderstanding and misinterpretation in intercultural interaction created by a narrow focus. For instance, although cultural differences account for numerous intercultural problems, a given problem may be triggered by socioeconomic differences, and will remain unresolved if both parties only focus on cultural issues.

The second rule in the cultural tuning framework is the synergistic rule, which stipulates that the effort of both cultural groups is necessary for effective collaboration. Unilateral initiatives without a corresponding effort from another cultural group are typically inadequate in sustaining effective cross-cultural interactions. For instance, a key element in the "graduated reciprocation in tension-reduction" (GRIT) proposed by Osgood (1962) for thawing the cold war between the US and USSR is reciprocity. Conciliatory moves, when reciprocated, will lead to a positive spiral toward disarmament and peace. Obviously, for such a scheme to work, joint effort is needed.

The third rule is the learning rule, which stipulates that each intercultural encounter should be viewed as a new learning process. In cross-culture settings, cultural membership is only a fuzzy cue at best for interpreting the behavior of members of other cultural groups because of significant individual variations within a culture. For instance, the fact that a person is from a materialistic culture does not necessarily imply that this person is materialistic. One frequent failure in cross-cultural encounters is the overgeneralization of cultural characteristics. Mechanical applications of cultural knowledge are likely to be misleading, and cultural knowledge should only provide the basis for initial hypotheses, which may be proven wrong by subsequent observations. Also, factors other than culture may also play a significant role in shaping people's behavior. Thus, a learning approach, which involves a careful evaluation and revision of initial hypotheses, is key to veridical judgments.

The cultural tuning framework has not been tested systematically, but some support has been provided by Kelman (1999), who found that intense, interactive problem-solving sessions between Arabs and Jewish Israelis were able to reduce their conflict. In these sessions, the two groups focused on the underlying causes and dynamics of their conflict and were motivated to understand the fears and needs of each other. Kelman (1999) also noted that learning is a major outcome of the interaction and a critical factor for promoting intercultural understanding and accommodation. It is clear that the three cultural tuning rules are observed in these sessions. The two groups were asked to take a holistic view of their conflict from a broad perspective, engage in an open, sincere dialogue, and exchange synergistically to arrive at mutual understanding and accommodation, and learn from the exchange and revise their views and judgments.

To sum it up, the holistic perspective together with the synergistic and learning rules of cultural tuning should give rise to a common frame of reference, which will facilitate constructive dialogue and effective interaction between two cultural groups. A similar notion, "microculture," has been discussed by Kimmel (2000), which arises from mutual adaptation and active engagement by two cultural groups. In the cultural tuning framework, this new culture is labeled as a common *cultural platform*, which serves as the basis for productive intercultural interaction.

Before we discuss how the cultural tuning framework can be applied to improve East–West teamwork, we first provide a brief overview of Asia. The holistic perspective requires a broad understanding of East–West differences in social, cultural, economic, and political domains, which is given below.

AN OVERVIEW OF ASIA

Being the largest continent on Earth, Asia is home to three-fifths of the human population. Very diverse languages, religions, cultures, and socioeconomic–political conditions can be found in this vast continent, which are briefly reviewed below.

East Asia

The major countries in this region are China, Japan, and Korea.

CHINA

China is the most populous country in the world. China's trade has been expanding at a rate double that of world trade, and it is now among the world's top 10 trading nations, accounting for 4 percent of total world trade, compared to 1 percent in 1980. Since China opened up for foreign investments in 1979, it has become a popular destination for foreign direct investment (FDI), second only to the US (Lounsbury & Martin, 1996). Joint ventures have remained the preferred choice of FDI, with the total sales volume of the 500 top Sino-foreign joint ventures rising to US$72 billion in 1998 (Liu & Pak, 1999).

China is certainly on its way to becoming a major global economic player, but its integration into the global economy is not problem-free. Many Western businesses have suffered from clashes with the communist-influenced Chinese business ideology (Tung, 1988), as well as disagreements in how interpersonal relationships should be managed (Hsu, 1970). A prominent Chinese value is *guanxi* or interpersonal connections (Hwang, 1987), which shapes Chinese behaviors in many domains (Osland, 1989). To succeed in a competitive environment, Chinese people believe in the development of *guanxi* to support and protect each other from adversity. With *guanxi*, one becomes an "insider" of a network and cooperation can proceed smoothly (Lee & Lo, 1988; Leung, Bond, & Schwartz, 1995). Lack of an understanding of the *guanxi* dynamics by non-Chinese often leads to intercultural problems. For instance, Chinese often see American businesspersons as insufficiently familiar with Chinese business practices and the *guanxi* dynamics (Brunner, Koh, & Lou, 1992).

JAPAN

Japan has ascended to the second largest economy in the world from a war-torn economy after World War II. However, Japan began to slide into recession in the early 1990s, marked by a sharp drop in stock and estate prices. Japanese workers, known to be disciplined, efficient, and high quality, began to question the grueling, stressful work demand imposed on them.

Japanese people are famous for borrowing or learning from other cultures, but their enthusiasm for borrowing does not mean a constant dilution of the Japanese culture. Gannon (1994, p. 255) noted that Japanese "have always been aware of the difference between things foreign and native, and early on they recognized the value of borrowing from others while maintaining their Japaneseness." For instance, English speakers may recognize many English pronunciations in the Japanese language, but the meaning may be quite different.

Japan is known for its group orientation inherited from its agricultural past when rice farming required routine but diligent and communal work. In fact, even leadership in Japan takes on a collectivistic tone, as Sakaiya (1993, p. 78) noted that "what Japan looked for in its leaders was neither decisiveness nor foresight, but a gentleness that helped rice cultivation proceed smoothly and a spirit of self-sacrifice to take the lead in getting to work."

SOUTH KOREA

South Korea lies on the southern part of the Korean Peninsula and is heavily populated with about 45 million people. Like Japan, Korea is homogeneous in terms of language, culture, and heritage. The Korean War in 1953 separated South Korea from communist North Korea. Soon after the Korean War, the country took off economically, with its manufacturing industries as the spearhead. South Korea was crippled by the financial crisis in 1997 (Dunung, 1998), but it has returned to the road of recovery because of decisive and effective structural reforms.

Koreans are under the influence of Confucianism and Buddhism, but a large percentage of Koreans are now Christians. South Korea is a fast-changing country, and seemingly contradictory behaviors coexist. Examples are harmony vs change, face-saving vs aggressiveness, and emotional community vs impersonal achievement, a pattern described as "dynamic collectivism" (Cho & Park, 1998).

THE CONFUCIAN HERITAGE

Confucianism originates from China, but it is the cultural root of all East Asian countries. Yum (1991) noted that in Korea, Confucianism was adopted as the official philosophy of the Yi dynasty for 500 years, and in Japan, it was adopted by the Tokugawa shogunate for 250 years. To understand East Asian cultures, some knowledge of the Confucian philosophy is essential.

Five principles constitute the foundation of Confucian doctrines: *ren* (benevolence), *yi* (righteousness), *li* (propriety), *zhi* (wisdom), and *xin* (trustworthiness). Confucianism is relationship-oriented, with five central relations: emperor–subject, father–son, brother–brother, husband–wife, and friend–friend, the so-called five cardinal relations (*wu lun*). In essence, Confucianism emphasizes the acceptance of social hierarchies, with an emphasis on deference to authorities, who should show benevolence to their subordinates (Bond & Hwang, 1986). Diligence is emphasized, and so is harmony with nature and other people. In dealing with others, it is important to maintain *ren* (benevolence), *yi* (righteousness), *li* (propriety), and *xin* (trustworthiness).

While Confucianism was often credited for the phenomenal growth prior to the Asian financial crisis, a more balanced view of its effects on economic growth has been promulgated. Alon and Kellerman (1999, p. 7) provide a summary of this position:

> While the Asian ideals of hard work, respect for learning, and collectivism over individualism brought them unparalleled growth, many analysts now believe that these cultural factors led to the abuses of collusion, lack of transparency, poor banking practices, and corruption that precipitated large weaknesses in many of these countries' economies and continue to forestall recovery.

Southeast Asia

Southeast Asia is a complex region, where diversity is wide-ranging. Buddhism, Islam, Christianity, and Hinduism coexist peacefully, and large variations in size, geography, history, language, and economic development can also be found. Four major countries are reviewed below, i.e. Indonesia, Malaysia, the Philippines, and Thailand, all of which are members of the Association of Southeast Asian Nations.

THAILAND

Unlike East Asian countries, Thailand has a heterogeneous population, with 75 percent ethnic Thais and 14 percent Chinese. The dominant religion is Buddhism, with over 95 percent Buddhists in the population. The country has a long history of free trade and private enterprise, and has a diverse industrial base. Before the Asian financial crisis Thailand enjoyed a rather long period of growth, and is now grappling with serious economic, financial, social, and political problems.

The research on the "Nine Thai Values orientation" has shed some light on Thai culture (Komin, 1990, 1995). Two indigenous concepts, *kreng jai* and *jai yen,* are important for understanding the emphasis of Thais on smooth interpersonal relationships. According to Komin (1990, p. 691), *kreng jai* is "to be considerate, to feel reluctant to impose upon another person, to take another person's feelings into account, or to take every measure not to cause discomfort or inconvenience for another person." In contrast, *jai yen* literally means "cool heart," which arises from a Buddhist ideal (Roongrengsuke & Chansuthus, 1998). Both *kreng jai* and *jai yen* practices can be observed in Thais' daily interaction. When disagreement may result in destructive conflict, the concern for *kreng jai*, aided by *jai yen*, often leads to harmonious solutions.

INDONESIA

Indonesia is the world's largest Islamic nation, with approximately 80 percent of the population being Muslims (Kayam, 1996). However, Earl (1994, p. 105) noted its diversity by concluding that "Indonesia is a place of extraordinary contrast, with people being drawn to European fashion houses and car manufacturers as much as traditional *Wayang* puppet theatres."

Indonesia's economic performance in the three decades before the Asian financial crisis was considered among the best in Southeast Asia, with a GDP growth averaging 7 percent annually since 1970 (Harvie, 2000; www.worldbank.com). However, the Asian financial crisis has sent Indonesia into a deep economic, financial, political, and social crisis, from which the country has yet to recover. The pace of the recovery depends very much on whether the nation can achieve the necessary political stability for implementing economic reforms, and whether it will get necessary international financial support (Harvie, 2000).

The culture in Indonesia, like other Southeast Asian countries, emphasizes group harmony, which is best illustrated by the notions of *musyawarah* and *mufakat* in conflict resolution. *Musyawarah* refers to a decision-making process in which opinions from all parties are considered in order to arrive at an agreement (Benton & Setiadi, 1998). Once the results are accepted by all the people involved, *mufakat* (consensus), the final objective of *musyawarah*, is achieved.

MALAYSIA

Malaysia has an ethnically mixed population of around 23 million people with 62 percent Malays and other indigenous groups, 27 percent Chinese, 8 percent Indian, and 3 percent others. Dominant religious beliefs include Islam, Hinduism, Buddhism, and Christianity. Islam is the official religion, but freedom of religion is allowed. Ethnic relationships are generally harmonious. Malaysia made a quick economic recovery from the Asian financial crisis, and most of the capital controls imposed by the government in response to the crisis have been relaxed.

Malays are well known for their modesty, self-effacement, politeness, and courtesy. Historically, Malays lived in a *kampung* (village) with a strong sense of community, where the *adat* (norms) are important. A strong and cohesive community results in a strong emphasis on order and respect for the elders. Malays were governed by a sultanate system, characterized by patronage and feudalistic traditions. Despite the fading out of this system, the value of tolerating authoritarianism, especially when it is accompanied by benevolence, is still prevalent. Another popular attitude among Malays is *tidak apa*, a Malay phrase meaning "it's alright," "never mind," or "don't worry," which aptly describes the easy-going Malays. It is also noted that Malaysians strive to be "honest, generous, respectful, sincere, righteous, and caring" (Mansor, 1998, p. 157).

THE PHILIPPINES

The Philippines consist of a cluster of over 7000 tropical islands, with farming and fishing as the traditional sources of livelihood. Compared to other Southeast Asian countries, the economic development of the Philippines has been slow because of ineffective economic policies and political instability. However, the Philippines are currently pursuing export-led economic growth and the expansion of the private sector. Despite the adverse impact of the Asian financial crisis, structural reforms over the past decade, particularly improved financial market control, have reduced the economic vulnerability of the country.

Spain colonized the Philippines from the 1550s to the 1890s, when they were ceded to the US after the Spanish–American War. The US remained in control until the independence in 1956. Filipinos are of Malay stock, with Islamic, Hindu, Chinese, Spanish, and American influence. Racial relationships in the Philippines are generally harmonious. The Chinese in the Philippines, as elsewhere in Southeast Asia, dominate the economic arena. Filipino society is family-oriented, and Filipino extended families include kinship ties and unrelated others, such as godfathers and wedding sponsors. Smooth interpersonal relationships play a key role in Filipino social life, and sincerity and sensitivity toward others are regarded as important attributes. Considerable gender equality exists in the Philippines, with many women in senior positions in different sectors.

South Asia

South Asia consists of large countries such as India and Pakistan and a few other smaller ones. We provide a brief review of India, the major country in this region.

INDIA

India is the seventh largest in territory and the second most populous country in the world. More than four-fifths of its people are Hindu, and the rest include Muslims, Christians, Sikhs, Buddhists, and Jains. With a vast array of religions and languages and dialects, people are differentiated from each other in terms of their religion and language rather than their ethnic origin. India is a developing country, which constantly struggles with overpopulation, natural disasters, political unrest, and religious tensions. However, the country has survived many crises, and maintained a growth rate ranging from 5 to 6 percent since 1991. India's economy is currently the fifth largest in the world and was designated by the Clinton administration as one of the world's 10 big emerging markets (MacClure, 1995). Its software industry is especially noteworthy, growing at a very high rate.

The *karma* doctrine, i.e. achieving a better afterlife, is central in the Hindu value system. Unlike the Western value system, *karma* stipulates that the "pursuit of economic objectives and involvement with the material world are discouraged as they are considered distractions that could detract an individual from attaining salvation" (Gopalan & Rivera, 1997, p. 163). In addition, the notion of *dharma* (duty) requires people to perform their duties as defined by their particular role in life (Sinha, 1978). *Dharma* is conceptually broader than the Western idea of duty in that it includes the totality of social, ethical, and spiritual harmony. It is generally believed that social conflict, oppression, and unrest originate in nonadherence to *dharma* by those in positions of power, and that it is their actions that have created the cycle of disharmony. Finally, Indian society is hierarchical as reflected in its traditional caste system, in which people are divided into four castes, which will be discussed in detail in a later section.

CULTURAL CHARACTERISTICS OF ASIA

The previous section reviewed the cultural, social, and economic conditions in Asia. In this section, we provide an integrative review of the cultural characteristics of Asians and how East–West differences in these characteristics may strain their collaboration. The first part focuses on cultural values because there are significant East–West differences, and Chen, Bishop, and Scott (2000) note that cultural values will influence the willingness and ability to work in teams. The second part focuses on social–economic conditions that may impact East–West collaborations.

Cultural Values

Despite the diversity in Asia, based on Hofstede's (1980, 1991) framework, two commonalities are obvious in the previous review: Asian cultures are collectivistic and high in power distance.

GROUP ORIENTATION

Collectivism refers to a preference for a tightly knit social network in which individuals can expect their relatives, clan, or other in-group members to look after them in exchange

Table 13.1 Individualism scores

The West	Scores	The East	Scores
USA	91	Hong Kong	25
Great Britain	89	Japan	46
Canada	80	South Korea	18
Netherlands	80	Thailand	20
Italy	76	Indonesia	14
Spain	51	Malaysia	26
Finland	63	The Philippines	32
Germany	67	India	48

Note: Adapted from Hofstede (1980, 1991).

Table 13.2 Power distance scores

The West	Scores	The East	Scores
USA	40	Hong Kong	68
Great Britain	35	Japan	54
Canada	39	South Korea	60
Netherlands	38	Thailand	64
Italy	50	Indonesia	78
Spain	57	Malaysia	104
Finland	33	The Philippines	94
Germany	35	India	77

Note: Adapted from Hofstede (1980, 1991).

for their loyalty and commitment (Hofstede, 1980; Triandis, 1995). Western countries are individualistic, and people live in a loosely knit social network and only take care of themselves and their immediate families. In contrast, Asian countries are collectivistic, a view that is supported by numerous empirical findings (e.g. Boisot & Child, 1996; Triandis, McCusker, & Hui, 1990). For instance, research has shown that the most frequent way of handling problems in Japan was through coworkers' advice, while in Britain and the US it was the reliance on one's own experience and prior training (Luthans, Marsnik, & Luthans, 1997). In the following, several collectivistic attributes that are relevant for East–West collaboration are reviewed.

Relationship networks in Asia

A major feature of Asian collectivism is the ubiquitous relationship networks. It is often argued that the capitalist economies of East and Southeast Asia are organized through business networks, which provide an "institutional medium of economic activity" (Hamilton, 1996). A good interpersonal relationship is viewed as fundamental to success in business, and Asians often go out of their way to maintain extensive interpersonal networks.

Westerners operating in Asia may sometimes be frustrated by the low performance of their suppliers and subordinates, without knowing that perhaps their lack of networks has handicapped their ability to obtain results. Networks operate outside a firm as well, and through stable networks, firms support each other by sharing resources and information, and hedging risk. Examples of such business networks include Japanese *kaisha*, a group of firms functioning in alliance to maximize competitiveness (Woronoff, 1996), Korean *chaebol*, diversified family-owned business groups, and Chinese family businesses (Carney & Gedajlovic, in press).

To illustrate the subtle influence of these networks, take planning in Japan as an example. Firms often draw up 10- or even 20-year plans, but these plans are symbolic, and the main objective is to reassure customers, suppliers, and partners that the firm is committed to long-term relationships with them.

The demarcation between in-groups and out-groups is embedded in Asian relationship networks. In-group members often receive preferential treatment, whereas out-groups are treated with caution, and sometimes even as targets of exploitation. For instance, Indians are sensitive to the in-group–out-group boundary, and people from the family, kinship, the same caste, the same religion, or even the same language group are considered in-groups. Gopalan and Rivera (1997, p. 165) noted that "Attitudes towards members of the out-group range from suspicion to outright hostility, and violent clashes frequently erupt between members of different castes." This type of parochialism often hinders intergroup communication and collaboration, stifling teamwork in culturally mixed groups. For effective teamwork, Westerners cannot ignore the need to develop in-group ties with their Asian coworkers and business partners.

The supremacy of harmony

Westerners are often struck by the extensive effort by Asians to preserve harmony in in-groups. Because of the emphasis on in-group harmony, teamwork and group incentives often work better in Asian countries than in the West (Hofstede, 1980; Luthans, Marsnik, & Luthans, 1997). Take Japan as an example: to arrive at a consensus, decisions are often made with the *ringi* system, which requires all parties affected by a decision to be consulted (Brake et al., 1995). In traditional Indonesian villages, as mentioned before, *musyawarah* is a consultative decision-making process for conflict resolution, in which all voices and opinions are heard (Mulder, 1992). Like the *ringi* system, the objective of *musyawarah* is to achieve *mufakat* (consensus).

One consequence of the emphasis on harmony is the prevalence of conflict avoidance in Asia. Asians are more inclined toward conflict avoidance, whereas Westerners are more inclined toward a competitive conflict style (Morris et al., 1998). Asians are also more in favor of mediation and compromises, whereas Westerners are more in favor of win–lose settlements (Leung, 1997). Leung, Koch, and Lu (2002) argue that Asians' concern for harmony may be driven by instrumental concerns because disharmony may damage one's self-interest. One function of conflict avoidance is to protect the face of other people (Kirkbride, Tang, & Westwood, 1991). An affront may be viewed as an insult, and if done in public, it is a serious challenge to the target's face. In the West, criticizing an idea is common in meetings, but in Asia, criticizing someone publicly, especially a senior person, may result in severe retaliation. The notion of face is often associated with China, but similar concepts can be found in various Asian languages. In South Korea, *inhwa* and *kibun* are used to mean "face," and in Malay, face is referred to as *maruah* and *air muka*. Westerners working in Asia need to be sensitive about maintaining the face of their Asian colleagues for maintaining smooth working relationships.

High-context communication

Effective communication is a key to successful teamwork, and cultural differences in communication present significant challenges to East–West collaboration. Asian cultures are characterized by the high-context communication style, whereas in the West, low-context communication is the norm. Brake, Walker, and Walker (1995) noted that in high-context cultures, a major purpose of communication is for forming and developing relationships rather than for exchanging facts and information. Furthermore, communication in high-context societies goes beyond verbal expressions, and such nonverbal behaviors as eye contact, special gestures, and even silence are important means of information exchange. These nonverbal communicative behaviors present no problem in intracultural communication, but across cultural lines they are likely to be misinterpreted. For instance, silence during negotiation does not signal passivity in Japan (Brake, Walker, & Walker, 1995), and

Westerners often mistake it as a lack of response or an indication of consent (Graham & Sano, 1984). A different type of misunderstanding may arise when Asians misread an American's direct, adversarial arguments as an indication of unreasonableness and lack of respect (Morris et al., 1998).

Another characteristic of high-context communication is indirectness, as a direct expression of disagreement and objection may damage the face of the receiver. In Korea, for example, formal meetings are not regarded as a place for debates, but are instead for expressing group harmony and mutual trust (Cho & Park, 1998). Westerners who are not sensitive to the connotation of indirect messages may find themselves caught in a web of misunderstanding and miscommunication in Asia.

POWER DISTANCE

Asians are high in power distance, which refers to a tendency to accept an uneven distribution of power and status and to regard hierarchical social systems as desirable (Hofstede, 1980). In the organizational context, high power distance fosters a structural hierarchy and centralization, and discourages participation in decision making. In Asia, workers often wait for their bosses to make decisions (Mo, 1996), and delegation or participation is uncommon (Hofstede, 1980, 1991). Several major characteristics of the high power distance in Asia are reviewed below.

Social hierarchies

Social hierarchies are prevalent in Asia. Because East Asian countries are often discussed in the literature, two countries outside of East Asia, India and Thailand, are chosen to illustrate the social hierarchies in Asia.

The Hindu caste system is unique in India, which assigns people into four castes: the *Brahmins* (priests, poets, and intellectuals), the *Kshatriyas* (warriors, rulers, and statesmen), the *Vaishyas* (traders, merchants, bankers, and artisans), and the *Shudras* (laborers and menials). Based on these castes, occupations were hereditary and marriages took place within the same castes. Despite active campaigns against the social hierarchies, many high positions are still held by people from higher castes, while low-level jobs are occupied almost exclusively by people from lower castes.

In Thailand, *Sakdina*, prominent in the Ayudhya period, is probably the origin of social hierarchies in modern Thailand. *Sakdina (sakdi* means power, and *na* means fields) is a system of social stratification that gives each person a rank or "degree of power" and a portion of land based on that rank (Keyes, 1987). In this system, all residents are sorted into a hierarchy and are graded in terms of their bureaucratic distance from the king. Each person within the *Sakdina* hierarchy is expected to respect the dignity of others according to their rank. The influence of *Sakdina* on Thai social and work life is still significant.

A major consequence of social hierarchies in the workplace is the importance given to employee participation in decision making (Newman & Nollen, 1996). In Asia, employees may be unwilling to make decisions without explicit endorsement or direction from their superiors, posing a frequent challenge to East–West collaboration. When Western managers leave initiatives and decision-making authority to Asian employees, it is possible that they may be confused and even doubt the leadership of the Western managers. If Western managers fail to understand the tendency of Asians to look to authorities for support and instructions, they may see the unwillingness of Asians to take charge as an excuse to evade responsibility and to avoid work.

Respect for authority

Respect for seniority and authority is emphasized in Asia. For instance, in traditional Indonesian villages, *musyawarah*, a consultative process for conflict resolution described above, is managed by the village elders. In the workplace, seniority is often used as a criterion in compensations and promotion decisions. Asians' deference to authority figures may seem unnatural to Westerners, but failure to take into account these social dynamics will hinder their collaboration with Asians. Challenging a senior person in public may backfire into a personal dispute, and omission of social practices that respect the seniority and status of others may engender unnecessary ill feelings. In short, egalitarian managerial practices that bring results in the West may not work in an Asian context (Newman & Nollen, 1996).

Leadership

Leadership in Asia shows characteristics of high power distance. Take *Phradetphrakhun*, a traditional Thai leadership style, as an example. *Phradet* (autocratic leadership) calls for a strict leadership style that demands loyalty and service, and provides clear directions and decisions. *Phrakhun* (benevolence) ensures loyalty and commitment by providing desired rewards, protection, and personal care to followers that sometimes extend to their family members (Roongrengsuke & Chansuthus, 1998). A similar style of leadership is also observed in China (Westwood & Chan, 1992). Western managers, who are unfamiliar with this leadership style, may be seen as businesslike and cold by their Asian employees. In a similar vein, Western subordinates may also find their Asian superiors autocratic and unnecessarily inquisitorial about their private life.

Socioeconomic Differences

While collectivism and power distance provide the common thread running through diverse Asian countries, socioeconomic conditions vary drastically throughout the continent, and have significant impact on East–West collaboration. Several major dimensions are reviewed below.

LANGUAGE BARRIERS

English is the lingua franca of the business world, but English proficiency varies in Asia. English is widely used in India, the Philippines, Hong Kong, and Singapore, but rarely used in countries such as Japan and Korea. Although young Asians are learning more English than their parents, the paralyzing effect of language barriers on East–West collaboration cannot be underestimated. The involvement of interpretation complicates intercultural interaction by adding errors to the communication and reducing its fidelity, especially in competitive situations such as in a negotiation. In addition, in intercultural communication, cultural values often tint the decoding of meaning on the part of the receiver (Beamer,

1992), and lead to subtle misrepresentation and misinterpretation. For example, unlike in English, the word "collectivism" (*ji ti zhu yi*) in Chinese connotes unselfishness and noble devotion, while "individualism" (*ge ren zhu yi*) has a negative ring of egoism and selfishness. These subtle differences in meaning may cause difficulties in communication and collaboration.

ECONOMIC DEVELOPMENT

Asia has been a high growth area in the past several decades. Intraregional trade in Asia first surpassed that of US–Asia trade in 1986, and has grown to 43 percent of the total trade in the region in 1992 (Baran, Pan, & Kaynak, 1996). Japan started the trend of high growth, then followed by the dragons and tigers, and currently China is the growth engine of the region. Nevertheless, very diverse economic conditions exist in Asian countries.

DIFFERENTIAL COMPENSATIONS

When Westerners work with locals in developing countries in Asia, the typical arrangement is that Westerners are paid according to their home labor market conditions, whereas locals are paid according to the local labor market. This arrangement is sensible, but creates a huge gap between the pay of Westerners and locals. In fact, it is well documented that local staff are often frustrated by the huge gap between their compensations and those of expatriate managers, resulting in animosity between these two groups (Gladwin & Walter, 1980).

Leung et al. (1996) investigated this phenomenon in international joint ventures in China, and found that comparison with overseas expatriates in terms of compensations did not add to the prediction of the job satisfaction of local staff, whereas comparison with other local employees was able to account for additional variance. Furthermore, locals regarded their pay as fair even in light of the very high salary of the expatriate staff. To explain these results, Leung et al. argued that because Chinese employees were aware of the economic differences between China and developed nations, they would not use expatriate employees as their referent group to assess the fairness of their compensations. However, in a follow-up study three years later, Leung, Wang, and Smith (2001) found that, in sharp contrast to previous results, comparison with expatriates was significant in predicting the job attitudes of locals, and that they also regarded their pay as highly unfair in comparison with that of expatriates. Leung, Wang, and Smith (2001) suggest that this shift is likely to be caused by the familiarity with expatriates and a perception that the gap between the know-how of expatriates and locals is narrowing. They warn that this change in attitudes will pose a serious threat to teamwork between locals and expatriates.

JOINT VENTURES AND TECHNOLOGY TRANSFER

Joint ventures have been a major form of Western investments in developing countries in Asia, such as China and India. On the one hand, joint ventures enhance East–West cooperation and benefit both partners in terms of higher market share and lower costs for the Western partners, and capital injection and technology transfer for the Asian partners. However, the technology gap between Western and local partners often leads to conflict and mistrust. Technology transfer from Western firms can equip the local partners with the know-how for their long-term development and independence. But to avoid local competition, Western firms are keener to transfer production know-how than engineering or innovation capabilities, particularly when the intent of the joint venture is to capture local market share (Kim, 1998). Consequently, issues surrounding technology transfer are often thorny topics in joint venture negotiations. For example, foreign investors invariably find it difficult to persuade Chinese partners to accept many of the typical commercial provisions found in their standard technology transfer contracts used elsewhere, because the Chinese parties prefer their own laws that give them more access to Western technology (Peerenboom, 1998). In fact, because of the long-term implications of technology transfer, some Western investors have shifted their concern from short-term profitability to issues of management control and long-term competitiveness in Asia. Technology transfer may prove to be a structural issue that is hard to be resolved in some East–West collaboration.

THE APPLICATION OF CULTURAL TUNING TO ENHANCING EAST–WEST TEAMWORK

Holistic Perspective

Given that Asian cultural characteristics and socioeconomic conditions deviate drastically from those of the West, teamwork and cooperation between the East and the West are complex. In many cases, it is hard to determine the main cause of a conflict among a myriad of potential causes that span across cultural, economic, and linguistic domains. In fact, a problem may result from the interaction of several factors. It is exactly for this reason that we advocate a holistic perspective in our cultural tuning framework. Take the case of a Western expatriate manager who is sent to a newly established Asian subsidiary, say, in China. Assume that many workers are late for work, and she tries to resolve the problem with a local human resource (HR) manager without success. Her failure may be caused by many reasons. First, the language barrier between the expatriate manager and the local workers may prevent her from understanding the difficulties encountered by local workers as well as communicating her management values to them. Second, the norm against lateness may be weak in this particular setting. In many state-owned enterprises, punctuality is not emphasized. Third, to avoid conflict, the HR manager may not want to punish and reprimand workers who are consistently late. Fourth, the expatriate is soft and polite in her tone, and the HR manager mistakes it as a lack of seriousness of the problem. Finally, unreliable public transport may be the culprit. We can add more potential causes to the list, but the point is obvious that without a holistic perspective, the chance of identifying the major causes of any given problem is limited.

A real case is used to illustrate the holistic rule, which requires consideration of a broad range of issues in approaching an intercultural problem. Electronic Associates, Inc. (EAI), an American developer and manufacturer of computer systems for dedicated and general-purpose simulation applications, were trying to sell their products to Chinese clients in the late 1970s, shortly after China opened its doors to the West. One Chinese client was interested in their products, but demanded frequent presentations and explanations from EAI staff, including even minor technical details. To make things worse, the Chinese client was reluctant to reveal to EAI information about their business activities. The communication process dragged on for a very long period of time, with constant demand for more information from EAI, but without any signal from the Chinese client about a purchase contract. Naturally, EAI staff were frustrated, and many interpretations of the fastidious behavior of the Chinese client are possible. EAI staff may invoke cultural explanations (Chinese are indirect in their communication style, or they are suspicious of out-groups because of their collectivistic orientation), or economic explanations (they are collecting market information to find the best deal). These two interpretations, if endorsed, are likely to result in lukewarm responses to the inquiries of the Chinese client. A holistic perspective, however, demands a comprehensive search for likely interpretations, and a sociological explanation is also possible. The Chinese just started their contact with the West, and because of the lack of experience, they might become extremely cautious. In any event, according to Sanders, EAI's vice president for marketing, they were patient and thorough in their responses to the inquiries of the Chinese client, and eventually their persistence was rewarded by a sizeable contract (see Tung, 1982, for details of this case).

The Synergistic Rule

Once a holistic view is adopted, the next concern is how to manage a culturally diverse team. Three approaches are identified in managing international operations (Taylor, Beechler, & Napier, 1996). The exportive strategy attempts to completely export the management practices of the parent firm to the target country. The adaptive strategy requires the expatriate managers to adapt themselves to the local customs or practices. The integrative strategy orients toward identifying the best practices regardless of their cultural origin. A major problem of this type of framework lies in its unilateral focus. One may try the exportive strategy, only to be charged with chauvinism and imposition. The adaptive strategy is likely to be well received by the locals, but it may not generate desirable behavior. It is easy to adapt to, say, a lack of punctuality by ignoring it, but productivity may suffer. Finally, the integrative strategy sounds excellent in theory but, in practice, it is hard to identify and agree on what the best practices are across cultural groups.

The synergistic rule argues for a joint effort in building a culturally diverse team, because unilateral effort is typically suboptimal. In fact, the integrative strategy discussed above would work best if it is done in a synergistic fashion. A good case to illustrate this point comes from a rare, but increasingly common, case, in which Huali, a Chinese company, purchased an R&D department of Philips (http://www.cctv.com/financial/dialogue). To show concern to the newly acquired team, the president of Huali sent daily e-mails from China to a Canadian who was in charge of a technical project in Vancouver. In China, concern is often expressed by frequent inquiries, and close supervision is less resisted. However, the Canadian, who is from an individualistic and low power distance culture, saw the frequent inquiries as a sign of mistrust and decided to resign. Shocked by this incident, the president learnt about the cultural differences and decided to resolve the problem constructively. He explained his intentions to his Canadian subordinate, and finally they reached an agreement that involved synergistic adjustments from both sides. The president would stop sending frequent e-mails to the Canadian subordinate, and the latter would report to the president regularly about the progress of the project. This case clearly illustrates that a satisfactory resolution of an intercultural problem requires the joint effort of all the cultural groups involved.

The Learning Rule

There is no standard, preset solution to intercultural problems because every problem may be unique in some way, and intracultural variations may be huge and defy the application of cultural generalizations. The learning rule is proposed to take into account the idiosyncrasies of problems in cross-cultural teamwork. Under this rule, each case should be analyzed individually, and the search for an optimal solution should be regarded as a learning process. To illustrate this rule, consider a case described by Roongrengsuke and Chansuthus (1998), in which an American senior manager was trying to set up a management-by-objective (MBO) system in an American–Thai joint venture in Thailand. However, he could not get his Thai production manager, who had worked in the US for 10 years previously, to give him concrete objectives. After failing to deliver the objectives a few times, the production manager finally told his American boss that a lot of people resisted the MBO system and saw it as a way to make them work harder. His advice was to implement the system slowly, and focus on helping the staff understand the benefits of the MBO system to them. The American manager rejected the advice, and in fact, he regarded him as ineffective and uncommitted to his plan.

If we explore this case from the learning perspective, we can see that the American manager had been frustrated by the low priority given to objective results and efficiency in the Thai environment. It is probably true that on the average, factories in Thailand are not as efficient as similar factories in the US. Thus, this American manager developed an expectation that if he cannot improve productivity, the stumbling block must be the lack of a positive attitude toward efficiency and getting results on the part of the Thai employees. However, in this specific situation, the Thai production manager actually supported the MBO system and had positive experience with it when he worked in the US. He just did not believe that a quick implementation would be productive. Instead of putting pressure on the production manager and other local staff, a more productive approach for the American manager to take is to learn more about the resistance and objections of the local staff, and to explore innovative strategies to get results without sacrificing team morale and cohesiveness.

CONCLUSIONS AND DIRECTIONS FOR FUTURE RESEARCH

The review makes it clear that for effective East–West collaboration, a holistic perspective is essential. While previous research typically focuses on one aspect of East–West collaboration, such as the structural conflict triggered by technology transfer from the West to developing countries in Asia, or the behavioral conflict triggered by the different importance attached to face, in real-life settings, however, all hurdles, cultural and socioeconomic as well as structural and behavioral, have to be overcome. Omission of one aspect may nullify all effort that intends to forge effective cross-cultural teamwork. It is in this spirit that the holistic framework of cultural tuning is proposed. Perhaps effective cross-cultural teamwork can be likened to an iron chain, the strength of which is defined by its weakest link. One major lesson made clear by this review is that we cannot ignore any hurdle in East–West collaboration, because every hurdle counts.

Directions for Future Research

While much has been learned about East–West collaboration in the past several decades, this review has also raised a number of important gaps for future research, which are reviewed below.

More Research outside of East Asia

It is clear that research activities are driven by economic prominence, and this is why most research on Asia concentrates in East Asia. For theoretical reasons, research has to branch out to Southeast and South Asia. Such questions as whether power distance may take different forms in South Asia cannot be answered with research on East Asia only. A related issue is that research on East–West collaboration often uses Americans as the Western group, and we know relatively little about how Asians interact with Europeans. Research on East–West collaboration simply has to take on a more global outlook.

The Role of Governments

Most cross-cultural research focuses on elements of subjective culture, such as values and beliefs. However, Asian countries have been a popular destination of Western investment, and complaints are often raised about bureaucratic hurdles and inefficient governments. Lasserre and Probert (1994) surveyed over 800 expatriate managers in the Asia Pacific region about risks of doing business in the region. They noted that the role of government varies and they listed three levels of government in terms of their strategic importance to business interests. Korea, China, Malaysia, and Indonesia are listed at the top for governmental importance; Japan occupies the middle ground together with the Philippines and Thailand; while in Taiwan, Singapore, and Hong Kong the authorities exert negligible influence over business affairs. We do not know much about how government policies and interventions affect East–West collaboration, a topic that deserves serious attention in the future.

More Attention to Context

Throughout the chapter, the diversity of Asia has been repeatedly highlighted. Because of differences in economic development, issues confronting Westerners in China are quite different from those they encounter in Japan, despite the common Confucian heritage of the two countries. Cross-cultural interaction is sensitive to contextual elements, and a full understanding of the dynamics involved cannot be achieved by general knowledge about cultures alone. Furthermore, the fact that Asians are characterized by high sensitivity toward the social context (e.g. Chua & Gudykunst, 1987) adds to the importance of contexts. An obvious area for future research is to examine how culture interacts with contextual factors in influencing cross-cultural teamwork.

Broadening the Conceptual Basis

The theoretical framework guiding research on East–West collaborations owes much to the classic work of Hofstede (1980), which is based on work values. Indeed, Leung et al. (2002) noted that the vast majority of cross-cultural research is guided by value frameworks. For the field to progress, we are in sore need of alternative conceptual tools to inform our empirical work. Leung et al. (2002) have proposed that general beliefs, or social axioms, may provide a new perspective on cultural similarities and differences. While values refer to the importance people attach to a set of goals, social axioms refer to general beliefs about how the social world functions. Leung et al. (2002) identified five social axioms that are generalizable across five cultural groups: Hong Kong, Japan, US, Venezuela, and Germany. For instance, cynicism refers to the belief that the social world is malevolent. Peoples are likely to take advantage of others if they are given the opportunity. In addition to values, cultures also vary systematically along dimensions of social axioms, and it would be interesting to examine the teamwork problems that may occur between two cultural groups that differ in, say, their degree of cynicism. Thus, a productive research avenue would be to explore how East–West differences in social axioms may affect teamwork between these two cultural groups.

REFERENCES

Alon, I. & Kellerman, E. A. (1999). Internal antecedents to the 1997 Asian economic crisis. *Multinational Business Review, 7*, 1–12.

Ashmos, D. P. & George, P. H. (1987). The systems paradigm in organization theory: correcting the record and suggesting the future. *Academy of Management Review, 12*, 607–621.

Baran, R., Pan, Y., & Kaynak, E. (1996). Research on international joint ventures in East Asia: a critical review and future directions. *Journal of Euro-Marketing, 4*, 7–22.

Beamer, L. (1992). Learning intercultural communication competence. *The Journal of Business Communications, 29*, 285–303.

Benton, S. & Setiadi, B. N. (1998). Mediation and conflict management in Indonesia. In K. Leung & D. Tjosvold (eds), *Conflict Management in the Asia Pacific: Assumptions and Approaches in Diverse Cultures* (pp. 223–253). Singapore: John Wiley & Sons (Asia).

Berger, M. (1996). *Cross-cultural Team Building: Guidelines for More Effective Communication and Negotiation*. London: The McGraw-Hill Companies.

Boisot, M. & Child, J. (1996). From fiefs to plans and network capitalism: explaining China's emerging economic order. *Administrative Science Quarterly, 41*, 600–628.

Bond, M. H. & Hwang, K. K. (1986). The social psychology of Chinese people. In M. H. Bond (ed.), *The Psychology of the Chinese People* (pp. 213–266). Hong Kong: Oxford University Press.

Brake, T., Walker, D. M., & Walker, T. (1995). *Doing Business Internationally: The Guide to Cross-cultural Success*. New York: Irwin.

Brunner, J. A., Koh, A., & Lou, X. (1992). Chinese perceptions of issues and obstacles confronting joint ventures. *Journal of Global Marketing, 6*, 97–127.

Carney, M. & Gedajlovic, E. (in press). Context, configuration and capability: organizational design and competitive advantage in Asian firms. In K. Leung & S. White (eds), *Handbook of Asian Management*. New York: Kluwer.

Chen, M. (1995). *Asian Management Systems: Chinese, Japanese and Korean Styles of Business*. London: International Thomson Business Press.

Chen, X. M., Bishop, J. W., & Scott, K. D. (2000). Teamwork in China: where reality challenges theory and practice. In J. T. Li, A. S. Tsui, & E. Weldon (eds), *Management and Organization in the Chinese Context*. New York: Macmillan Press.

Cho, Y. & Park, H. (1998). Conflict management in Korea: the wisdom of dynamic collectivism. In K. Leung & D. Tjosvold (eds), *Conflict Management in the Asia Pacific: Assumptions and Approaches in Diverse Cultures* (pp. 15–48). Singapore: John Wiley & Sons (Asia).
Chua, E. & Gudykunst, W. B. (1987). Conflict resolution styles in low and high context cultures. *Communication Research Reports, 4*, 32–37.
Dunung, S. P. (1998). *Doing Business in Asia: The Complete Guide*. San Francisco: Jossey-Bass.
Earl, G. (1994). Indonesia from strangers to partners. In S. Mills (ed.), *The Australian Financial Review Asian Business Insight*. Sydney: Financial Review Library.
Gannon M. J. (1994). *Understanding Global Cultures: Metaphorical Journeys Through 17 Countries*. London: Sage Publications.
Gladwin, T. N. & Walter, I. (1980). *Multinationals under Fire: Lessons in the Management of Conflict*. New York: John Wiley & Sons.
Gopalan, S. & Rivera J. B. (1997). Gaining a perspective on Indian value orientations: implications for expatriate managers. *The International Journal of Organizational Analysis, 5*, 156–179.
Graham, J. L. & Sano, Y. (1984). *Smart Bargaining: Doing Business with the Japanese*. Cambridge, Mass.: Ballinger.
Greenfield, P. M. (2000). Three approaches to the psychology of culture: where do they come from? Where can they go? *Asian Journal of Social Psychology, 3*, 223–240.
Hamilton, G. G. (1996). *Asian Business Networks*. Berlin: Walter de Gruyter.
Harvie, C. (2000). Indonesia: the road from economic and social collapse. In T. V. Hoa (ed.), *The Asia Crisis: The Cures, Their Effectiveness and the Prospects After* (pp. 110–139). New York: St Martin's Press.
Hofstede, G. (1980). *Culture's Consequences: International Differences in Work Related Values*. Beverly Hills, Calif.: Sage.
Hofstede, G. (1991). *Cultures and Organizations: Software of the Mind*. London: McGraw-Hill.
Hofstede, G. (1995). The cultural relativity of the quality of life concept. In G. Redding (ed.), *International Cultural Differences*. Dartmouth Publishing Company Limited, UK.
Hsu, F. L. K. (1970). *American and Chinese: Passage to Differences* (3rd edn). Honolulu: University Press of Hawaii.
Hwang, K. K. (1987). Face and favor: the Chinese power game. *American Journal of Sociology, 92*, 944–974.
Kayam, U. (1996). On foreign influence: the Indonesia case. *The Indonesian Quarterly, 24*, 214–220.
Kelman, H. C. (1999). Interactive problem solving as a metaphor for international conflict resolution: lessons for the policy process. *Peace and Conflict: Journal of Peace Psychology, 5*, 201–218.
Keyes, C. F. (1987). *Thailand: Buddhist Kingdom as Modern Nation-state*. Boulder, Colo.: Westview Press.
Kim, L. (1998). Technology policies and strategies for developing countries: lessons from the Korean experience. *Technology Analysis and Strategic Management, 10*, 311–323.
Kimmel, P. R. (2000). Culture and conflict. In M. Deutsch & P. T. Coleman (eds), *The Handbook of Conflict Resolution: Theory and Practice* (pp. 453–474). San Francisco: Jossey-Bass.
Kirkbride, P. S., Tang, S. F. Y., & Westwood, R. I. (1991). Chinese conflict preferences and negotiations behavior: cultural and psychological influences. *Organization Studies, 12*, 265–386.
Komin, S. (1990). Culture and work-related values in Thai organizations. *International Journal of Psychology, 25*(4), 681–704.
Komin, S. (1995). Socio-cultural influences in managing for productivity in Thailand. In Kwang-Kuo Hwang (ed.), *Easternization: Socio-cultural Impact on Productivity*. Tokyo: Asian Productivity Organization.
Lasserre, P. & Probert, J. (1994). Competing on the Pacific Rim: high risks and high returns. *Long Range Planning, 27*(2), 12–35.
Lee, K. H. & Lo, T. W. C. (1988). American businesspeople's perception of marketing and negotiating in the People's Republic of China. *International Marketing Review*, Summer, 41–51.
Leung, K. (1997). Negotiation and reward allocations across cultures. In P. C. Earley & M. Erez (eds), *New Perspectives on International Industrial and Organizational Psychology* (pp. 640–675). San Francisco: Jossey-Bass.

Leung, K. (in press). Effective conflict resolution for intercultural disputes. In T. Gärling, G. Backenroth-Ohsako, B. Ekehammar, & L. Jonsson (eds), *Diplomacy and Psychology: Prevention of Armed Conflicts After the Cold War*.

Leung, K., Bond, M. H., Reimel de Carrasquel, S., Muñoz, C., Hernández, M., Murakami, F., Yamaguchi, S., Bierbrauer, G., & Singelis, T. M. (2002). Social axioms: the search for universal dimensions of general beliefs about how the world functions. *Journal of Cross-Cultural Psychology, 33*, 286–302.

Leung, K., Bond, M. H., & Schwartz, S. H. (1995). How to explain cross-cultural differences: values, valences, and expectancies? *Asian Journal of Psychology, 1*, 70–75.

Leung, K., Koch, T. P., & Lu, L. (2002). A dualistic model of harmony and its implications for conflict management in Asia. *Asia Pacific Journal of Management, 19*, 201–220.

Leung, K., Smith, P. B., Wang, Z. M., & Sun, H. F. (1996). Job satisfaction in joint venture hotels in China: an organizational justice analysis. *Journal of International Business Studies, 27*, 947–962.

Leung, K., Wang, Z. M., & Smith, P. B. (2001). Job attitudes and organizational justice in joint venture hotels in China: the role of expatriate managers. *International Journal of Human Resource Management, 12*, 926–945.

Liu, H. & Pak, K. (1999). How important is marketing in China? *European Management Journal, 17*, 546–554.

Lounsbury, P. & Martin, D. (1996). China retains its FDI allure. *China Business Review, 23*, 5.

Luthans, F., Marsnik, P. A., & Luthans, K. W. (1997). A contingency matrix approach to IHRM. *Human Resource Management, 36*, 183–199.

MacClure, J. (1995). India: strong tradition, new frontiers. *Canadian Business Review, 22*, 40–43.

Mansor, N. (1998). Managing conflict in Malaysia: cultural and economic influences. In W. Leung & D. Tjosvold (eds), *Conflict Management in the Asia Pacific: Assumptions and Approaches in Diverse Culture*. Singapore: John Wiley & Sons (Asia).

Mo, Y. H. (1996). Orientation values with eastern ways. *People Management, 2*, 28–31.

Morris, M. W., Williams, K. Y., Leung, K., Larrick, R., Mendoza, M. T., Bhatnagar, D., Li, J. F., Kondo, M., Luo, J. L., & Hu, J. C. (1998). Conflict management style: accounting for cross-national differences. *Journal of International Business Studies, 29*, 729–747.

Mulder, N. (1992). *Individual and Society in Java: A Cultural Analysis* (2nd rev. edn). Yogyakarta: Gajah Mada University Press.

Newman, K. L. & Nollen, S. D. (1996). Culture and congruence: the fit between management practices and national culture. *Journal of International Business Studies, 27*, 753–779.

Osgood, C. E. (1962). *An Alternative to War or Surrender*. Urbana: University of Illinois Press.

Osland, G. (1989). Doing business in China: a framework for cross-cultural understanding. *Marketing Intelligence and Planning, 8*, 4–14.

Peerenboom, R. (1998). China: China's new contract law fails to address concerns of foreign technology providers: a missed opportunity? *East Asian Executive Reports, 20*, 9–16.

Ricks, D. A. (1993). *Blunders in International Business*. Cambridge: Blackwell Business.

Roongrengsuke, S. & Chansuthus, D. (1998). Conflict management in Thailand. In W. Leung & D. Tjosvold (eds), *Conflict Management in the Asia Pacific: Assumptions and Approaches in Diverse Culture* (pp. 167–222). Singapore: John Wiley & Sons (Asia).

Sakaiya, T. (1993). *What is Japan: Contradictions and Transformations*. Translated by S. Karpa. New York: Kodansha International.

Sinha, J. B. P. (1978). Power in superior–subordinate relationships: the Indian case. *Journal of Social and Economic Studies, 6*, 205–218.

Taylor, C., Beechler, S., & Napier, N. (1996). Toward an integrative model of strategic international human resource management. *Academy of Management Review, 21*, 959–985.

Triandis, H. C. (1995). *Individualism and Collectivism*. Boulder, Colo.: Westview Press.

Triandis, H. C., McCusker, C., & Hui, C. H. (1990). Multimethod probes of individualism and collectivism. *Journal of Personality and Social Psychology, 59*, 1006–1021.

Trompenaars, F. (1993). *Riding the Waves of Culture: Understanding Cultural Diversity in Business*. London: Nicholas Brealey.

Tung, R. L. (1982). *US–China Trade Negotiations*. New York: Pergamon Press.

Tung, R. L. (1988). Towards a conceptual paradigm of international business negotiations. In R. D. Famer (ed.), *Advances in International Comparative Management* (Vol. 3, pp. 203–219). Greenwich, Conn.: JAI Press.

Westwood, R. I. & Chan, A. (1992). Headship and leadership. In R. I. Westwood (ed.), *Organisational Behaviour: Southeast Asian Perspectives* (pp. 118–143). Hong Kong: Longman.

Whiting, V. R. & Reardon, K. K. (1994). Strategic alliance in India: Sage Publications. In R. T. Moran, D. O. Braaten, & J. E. Walsh (eds), *International Business Case Studies: For the Multicultural Marketplace*. London: Gulf Publishing Company.

Woronoff, J. (1996). *Japan as Anything but Number One*. Wiltshire: Antony Rowe Ltd.

Yum, J. O. (1991). The impact of Confucianism on interpersonal relationships and communication patterns in East Asia. In L. A. Samovar & R. E. Porter (eds), *Intercultural Communication: A Reader* (6th edn). Belmont, Calif.: Wadsworth.

INDEX

3M 246

Academy of Management (journal) 40
accessibility 246
accountability
 group 139, 151–2, 169
 individual 139, 145
 organizational 227
 and psychological safety 246–7
acquisition and development of team mental models (ADTMM) 106
ACT cognitive skill acquisition model 106–7
Adams, J. S. 193, 204
adaptability 153–4, 159, 160, 162
advanced cognitive engineered intervention technologies approach (ACE-IT) 84–5
agency 184, 242
agreement 6, 8, 13–14, 24–5
alignment 155–6
Amabile, T. M. 264–5
ambiguity 81, 235
 task 111–12
analogic thinking 242
anarchic social situations 22
anxiety 83, 217, 235
 regarding conflict 20–1
 regarding group attachment 47, 48, 49, 50
appropriateness, logic of 180, 181–2, 184, 188
Arabs 283
Asia
 cross-cultural teamwork 281–2, 283–98
 cultural characteristics 288–94
 overview 283–8
Asian economic crisis 1997–98 281, 286
Asians 197
assimilation 26
attachment 37–8, 45–9, 50
attraction–selection model 108
attribution 20, 80–1
authority, respect for 292
autonomy 26, 161–2, 212–13, 225, 261–3

avatars 85
avoidance behaviors
 regarding conflict 19, 21, 59, 64, 65, 290
 regarding group attachment 47, 48, 49, 50

'bargaining power' 12–13
bargains 8, 12–13
belligerence 10, 12, 13
biases 20
 hostile attribution bias 81
 ingroup 42–3
Blader, S. L. 39
Boje, D. M. 227
boundary workers 162
Buddhism 285–6
Bull's-Eye diagram 154
burden of proof principle 109
burnout 57, 58, 60

career coaching 92
caste system 288, 291
categorization 42, 43
Center for the Study of Work Teams 149
centralization 263
challenge 264
change 165, 168, 235, 238
charter movement 227
chief executive officers (CEOs) 270
China 281, 284–5, 289–90, 292–7
civil society 28
class struggles 2–3
Clegg, Stuart 209, 227
Coats, S. 46–7
coercion 6, 12, 13, 210
cognition
 distributed 100
 see also team cognition
cognitive problem-solving style 272
cognitive rigidity 22, 269
cohesiveness, group 238
Cold War 31, 282–3

collaboration 6
  as conflict management strategy 59, 62–3, 64, 65
  and schema congruence 76
collaborative task analysis 84–5
collective identities 184, 188
collective learning 237
  double-loop learning 242
  goals of 243–9
  interpersonal risks of 235–52
  as iterative process 241–3, 247–8
  and practice fields 250
  and reflection-in-action 242–4
  summary of 243
collective mind 176, 178–9, 184–8
collectivism 113, 288–9
  dynamic 285
Collinson, D. 228, 229
command-and-control organizations 160
commitment 110, 111, 122, 162
commonality 98, 99
communication
  amongst different specialties 158
  and competitive processes 5
  and cooperation 5
  high-context 290–1
  and innovation 259–60
  see also language
competition
  and coercion 6
  and conflict 2–3, 4–10, 22
  definition 2, 132
  early studies 4
  features of 6, 10
competitive social interdependence 131, 132–7, 143, 145
complementarity 98–9, 100, 101, 103
compliance 38–9, 75
componental model of creativity and innovation 264
conflict 1–31
  anxiety regarding 20–1
  applicability of Western models of 8, 29–30
  approach–approach type 5
  approach–avoidance type 5
  avoidance 19, 21, 59, 64, 65, 290
  avoidance–avoidance type 5
  competitive contexts of 2–3, 4–10, 22
  compulsively revealing versus compulsively concealing 22
  conceptual progress in the study of 30
  constructive 1, 8–10, 71, 72–9, 83, 85–7, 142–5, 262, 266–7
  constructive management 8, 18–22, 26, 30
  contingency model of 56–8, 60–7
  cooperative contexts of 2, 4–10, 16, 18–19, 28–9, 40, 142–5
  de-escalating 30–1
  definition 2, 58, 72
  destructive 1–2, 8–10, 25–30
  empirical progress in the study of 30–1
  escalating spirals 20, 21–2, 23
  ethnic 8, 25–9, 30
  excessive involvement in 21
  facing 19
  firm, fair and friendly approach to 20
  and game theory 7
  and group efficacy 39–41, 55, 61–3, 65–6, 71–9, 83, 85–7
  hard–soft 21
  identity conflicts 8, 25–9
  and individual well-being 60–1, 65
  inner displaced as external 22, 23–4
  integrative/win–win bargaining 13
  intellectual–emotional 21
  and inter-party agreements 8, 13–14
  intervention in protracted/intractable 8, 22–5
  intractable/destructive 8, 22–9, 30
  and malignant social processes 22–3
  methodological progresses in the study of 30
  minimizing 21–2
  misinterpretation 75–6
  mixed-motive 18–19
  and moral personhood 22
  nonnegotiable issues 24–5
  nonrealistic 72
  perceptions/interpretations of 73–4, 75–7
  and psychological safety 244–5
  pure cooperative 18–19
  realistic 72
  relationship 41
  religious 8, 25–9
  resolution 1–31
  rigid–loose 21
  self-awareness of personal reactions to 20–2
  six dimensions of dealing with 21–2
  social psychological research themes 8–30
  socio-emotional 72, 73, 76–8, 80–2, 86
  technological progress in the study of 31
  third party mediation of 8, 15–18, 30
  types 18–19, 58–9, 63–7
  and violence 19
  win–lose 18–19, 22
  winning 8, 10–13
  zero-sum 18–19
  see also constructive controversy; interests, conflicts of; task conflict
conflict management strategies
  avoiding 19, 21, 59, 64, 65, 290
  cognitive 71–87
  collaborating 59, 62–3, 64, 65

conceding 59, 65
constructive 8, 18–22, 26, 30
contending 59, 65
definition 59
and group performance 55, 59, 62–7
and power 59, 65
and rights 59, 64–5
typology 59
see also conflict, resolution
Confucianism 285
consequence, logic of 188
constructive controversy 59, 63, 86–7, 143–5, 266
constructive normative behavior 79, 80
context
  and competitive conflict 2–3, 4–10, 22
  and cooperative conflict 2, 4–10, 16, 18–19, 28–9, 40, 142–5
  and cross-cultural teamwork 297
  environmental 114–16, 120, 160
  high-context communication 290–1
  team 257, 258–62, 273
  team task 99–100, 110–12, 114–16
  see also organizational context
contingency theory of task conflict and performance 55–67
control
  concertive 169
  power as 209–11, 215–17, 220, 225
  see also command-and-control organizations
cooperation
  basic elements of 131, 137–42
  and conflict 2, 4–10, 16, 18–19, 28–9, 40, 142–5
  and constructive conflict 142, 143–4, 145
  definition 131–2
  discretionary behaviors 39
  early studies of 4
  effect on team member efforts 133, 134–5, 136
  and effort to achieve 132–5, 144–5
  elements of 131, 137–42
  features of 5–6, 7, 9–10
  and group efficacy 39–40, 132–8, 141–5
  and group processing 141–2, 145
  and group trust 38–9, 40–1
  and group-to-individual transfer 134
  and individual accountability 139, 145
  and individualistic effort 132–7, 143, 145
  and innovation 257–74
  mandatory behaviors 39
  outcomes of 132–7, 144–5
  and positive interdependence 137–8, 139, 145
  and positive relationships 135–6, 144–5
  and promotive (face-to-face) interactions 139–40, 145
  and psychological health 136–7, 145
  and social skills 140–1, 142, 145
  team members' 37–50
  and team mental models 97
  training for 131–45
  and trust 142–3, 145
cooperative goals 79, 83, 84, 211
coordination 55
corporate governance 227
cost/benefit analysis 151
creative abrasion 245
creativity *see* innovation
critical incident technique 105
critical management studies (CMS) 213–18
critical reflection 229–30
critical–postmodern framework of organizational power (CFOP) 218–30
  conscious/automatic activities 221
  cultural initiatives 227–30
  dimensions 219–23
  example 223–5
  formal/informal activities 221
  multimodal analysis 219–20
  oppositional discourses 222–5
  participatory action research for 226
  practical implications 225–6
  relational initiatives 226–7
  structural initiatives 227
cross-cultural teamwork 281–98
  and context 297
  and cultural overgeneralizations 283
  and cultural tuning 282–3, 294–6
  and cultural values 288–92, 298
  and governments 297
  guidelines for 282
  and social axioms 298
  and socioeconomic difference 292–4
cross-training 84
cultural difference 8, 29–30
  see also cross-cultural teamwork
cultural platforms 283
cultural tuning 282–3, 294–6
  holistic perspective 282, 283, 294–5, 296
  learning rule 283, 296
  synergistic rule 282–3, 295–6
cultural values 288–92, 298
culture
  collectivist 113, 288–9
  individualistic 113, 288, 289
  see also organizational culture
customers 163

Dahl, Robert 210
Darwin, Charles 2, 3
De Best Waldhober, M. 61
De Dreu, C. K. W. 61, 63

decentralization 221, 263
decision making
    and cooperation 39–40
    cultural influences on 291–2
    day-to-day operational 161–2, 163
    and groupthink 102
    and innovation 266
    and rules 180, 181–2, 188
    strategic 179–86
    by teams 39–40, 161–3, 173–88, 266
democratization 217, 221
design
    job 159
    organizational/team 165, 166
destructive groups 137
Deutsch, M. 209, 218, 227
Deutsch's crude law of social relations 9–10, 14
devil's advocacy 78
dharma 288
dialectical enquiry 78
disagreement 6
discourses
    dominant 223, 224
    oppositional 222–5
discursive closure 222–3
disempowerment 6, 209, 217, 227
disruptive behavior 236–7
distress 57
distributed cognition 100
distributive justice 13–14, 30
diversity, team 82–3, 181, 182, 184
    and innovation 257, 258–60
    measurement 108–9, 122
double-loop learning 242

East Asia 281, 283–5, 297
East–West relations 281–2, 283–98
economic development 293
economic orientations 14
Edmonson, A. C. 269
EEOC regulations 221
effort
    coordination of 6
    of implementation in team-based
        organization 156–7
    individualistic 132–7, 143, 145
    to achieve 132–5, 144–5
Electronic Associates, Inc. (EAI) 294–5
elicitive approach 29
emancipatory initiatives 225–30
    paradox of 209, 217–18, 226
empathy 20, 25
empiricism 4
employee engagement 162, 169
empowerment 6, 17, 162–3, 209, 212, 217–18, 227, 247

environment
    context 114–16, 120, 160
    workspace 112–13, 165, 168
envy 197
equity theory 13, 14, 193, 198–202, 203, 204
ethnicity 197
evaluations 236
evolution 2, 3
expectancy-value theory 193–9, 204
expectations, and social loafing 197, 198–202
experience 82
expert teams 91–3, 96, 107, 114, 116–20
experts 112, 117
extremism 28

face, notion of 290, 291
failure/fallibility, tolerance of 246
fairness 59, 61, 64–5
    see also equity theory; justice
fairness accountability theory 50
fairness heuristic theory 44, 50
fear 247
feedback
    failure to ask for 236–7
    group 140
    individual 140–1, 142
feedback loops 50
field theory 4–7
financial goals 155
financial management 165, 167
Fisher, Ronald 25–6
flexibility 153–4, 160, 162, 164–5
Follett, Mary Parker 209, 211, 227
foreign direct investment (FDI) 284
frame of reference 81, 84, 85
free-rider mechanism 199–200, 204
Freud, Sigmund 2, 3
friendliness 5–6
fundamental attribution error 20

game theory 7
gamesmanship orientation 23
gender differences
    and power relations 229
    and social loafing 197
globalization 227, 281
goals
    commitment to 110, 111, 122
    cooperative 79, 83, 84, 211
    definition 110
    financial 155
    and innovation 265–6
    interdependent 79, 83–4, 131–2, 137–8, 140–2, 157, 211, 243
    learning 243–9
    organizational 248
    process 141

setting 243–4, 248–9
shared 243–4
subordination of individual to the group 186–8
and team mental models 102–3, 110, 111, 122
and team-based organization 149, 155, 157
governments 297
graduated reciprocation in tension-reduction (GRIT) 31, 282
group performance/efficacy
conflict and 39–40, 41, 61–3, 65–7
contingency theory of 55–67
cooperation and 39–40, 132–8, 141–5
and individual well-being 56–8
and level of task uncertainty 56–7, 63–5
potential 137
see also team performance/efficacy
group processing 141–2, 145
Group Task Circumplex 111
groups
accountability 139, 151–2, 169
attachment to 37–8, 45–50
attractiveness 43
cohesiveness 238
collective esteem of 43, 44
compliance 38–9
cooperation of individual members 37–50
identification 38, 42–3, 45, 47–8, 50
identity 26–7, 37–8, 41–5, 48–9, 184, 188
in-group/out-group differentials 289–90
ingroup biases 42–3
inputs 201, 203, 257–65, 270, 272–3
orientation 288–91
outcomes 193–4, 198, 202–3
outputs 257–8, 272–3
and procedural justice 43–5, 49–50
and relationship conflict 41
salience 43
self-esteem of individual members 44
and task conflict 41
tenure 260–2
training for cooperative 131–45
trust in 37–8, 39–50, 42–3
see also teams
groupthink 102, 238
guanxi (interpersonal connections) 284
Gurr, T. R. 26

Hambrick, D. C. 181, 183, 184
harmony 290, 291
Harris Semiconductor 156
helpfulness 5–6
Hewlett-Packard 154
hierarchical task analysis (HTA) 103, 105
hierarchies
social 291–2
training information structures 118–19

holistic perspective (cultural tuning) 282, 283, 294–5, 296
Hong Kong 297
hostile attribution bias 81

identification
group 38, 42–3, 45, 47–8, 50
social 42–3
identity
collective 26–7, 37–8, 41–5, 48–9, 184, 188
conflicts and 8, 25–9
individual 180, 181–2, 188
organizational 42
see also Social Identity Theory
IDEO 246
ideology 222
ignorance 10, 11, 13, 236
image risk, in teams 235–52
disruptive behavior 236–7
ignorance 236
incompetence 236
negativity 236
impression management 235–6
in-groups 289–90
incompetence 236
India 282, 287–8, 289–90, 291, 292, 293
indirectness 291, 295
individual differences 45, 48–9, 82–3
individualistic cultures 113, 288, 289
individualistic effort 132–7, 143, 145
individuals
accountability 139, 145
inputs 199, 201
outcomes 193–4, 199, 201, 204
performances 193, 197, 198
and social loafing 193–4
well-being of 56–8, 60–1, 65
see also team members
Indonesia 286, 290, 292, 297
influence 109–10
information sharing 165
informational factors 44
injustice 27, 61
innovation 241, 248
and challenge 264
componential model of 264
cooperation in teams for 257–74
definition 257
examples of 257–8
and group inputs 257–65, 270, 272–3
and group outputs 257–8, 272–3
and organizational context 257–8, 262–5, 273
organizational encouragement of 264
organizational impediments to 265
and supervisory encouragement 264, 265
support for 264, 267–8
and team context 257–62, 273

innovation (*cont.*)
   and team leadership 260, 261, 262–3, 264, 265, 269–72, 273
   and team processes 257–8, 265–9, 272–4
   team-based support systems for 165, 168
   and work group support 264
instinctivism 3, 4
instrumentality 193–4, 196–9, 200, 202–4
integrated product teams (IPTs) 160
integration 165, 168
integrative negotiation 62, 144
intensive care units 64
interaction
   oppositional/contrient 132
   promotive 132, 139–40, 145
interactional justice 44
interests
   being ignorant of 11
   conflicts of 6, 143, 144, 145
   respect for 19
   shared 19
interpersonal attraction 135–6
interpersonal risks
   and learning in teams 235–52
   tacit calculus of 238, 239
interpersonal sensitivity factors 44
interpersonal trust 237, 238–40
investment 284
Islam 286
Israelis 283

jai yen 286
Japan 282, 284, 285, 289, 290, 292, 293, 297
job design 159
joint ventures 293–4
just-in-time production 218
justice
   distributive 13–14, 30
   establishment 28
   interactional 44
   procedural 38, 40–1, 43–5, 48–50
   see also fairness; injustice

Karau, S. J. 191, 193–4, 196, 197, 198, 199, 200, 202, 204
karma 288
Kennedy experiment 31
Kerr, N. L. 199–200
knowledge
   breadth-first 119–20
   declarative 107–8
   depth-first/linear 119–20
kreng jai 286
Kressel, Kenneth 15, 17–18

labor
   division of 6
   emotional 221
language
   barriers 292–3, 294
   direct 250–1
   indirect 291, 295
   and reality 213–14
   see also communication
'last clear chance' 11
leadership
   cultural influence on 284, 291–2
   Japanese 284
   see also management; team leadership; top management team
learning
   anxiety regarding 238
   collective 235–52
   from mistakes 236, 237
   goals of 243–9
   and interpersonal risks 235–52
   organizational 237
   and psychological safety 237–41
   team-based support systems for 165, 167–8
learning rule 283, 296
learning space 247
Lewin, Kurt 4–5
'line of sight' 155–6
Lockheed Martin Electronics and Missiles 160
logic of appropriateness 180, 181–2, 184, 188
logic of consequence 188

Maier, Norman 272
Malaysia 286–7, 290, 297
management
   emancipatory initiatives of 209, 218
   facilitative leadership styles 169
   and innovation 264
   as partners to the workforce 169
   and power 213, 215–16, 218, 220, 223, 228
   team-based support systems for 165, 166
   see also leadership; team leadership; top management team
management-by-objective (MBO) 296
marginalized voices 224–5, 230
marital counseling 23–5
Marx, Karl 2–3
masculine behavior, privileging of 229
Mason, P. A. 181, 183, 184
means interdependence 137
mediation 8, 15–18, 30, 144
   framework for 16
   peer 144
   skill set for 16–17
   social–emotional 17
   styles 17–18

task-oriented 17
transformational 17
medicine 239–41, 243, 250, 269, 270
memory, transactive 179
mental models
  faulty/inaccurate 119–20
  individual 94, 103–5, 121–2, 175–6
  multiple 94–5, 101
  overlap 101–2, 116–17, 121, 122–3
  shared 93–4, 101, 102, 121
  working 117
  see also team mental model
metaphors 250–1
microcultures 283
mind, collective 176, 178–9, 184–8
minority influence theory 267
misjudgments/misperceptions 20, 22, 81
mistakes, learning from 236, 237
MIT Research Center for Group Dynamics 5
monitoring 213
morality 22
motivation
  expectancy-value theory of 193
  and social loafing in teams 191–3, 199–200, 203–4
  task 264
mufakat 286
Mumby, D. K. 209, 210–11
Murphy, L. 46–7
musyawarah 286, 290, 292
myths, legitimizing 222

needs, team 91–2
negativity 236
negotiation, integrative 62, 144
normative behavior, constructive 79, 80
norms 13, 251
nurses 239–41

obstructiveness 5
openness behaviors 80, 83, 84
organizational citizenship 39, 214–15, 221
organizational context 112–13
  alignment 155
  cultural 113
  and innovation in teams 257–8, 262–5, 273
  physical 112–13
  and team-based organization 149–50, 155
  see also organizational culture
organizational culture 113, 235
  definition 160–1
  enforced homogenization of 222–3
  and innovation 262–5
  and power 220, 222, 224, 227–30
  and team-based organization 160–2
organizational encouragement 264

organizational identity 42
organizational learning 237
organizational power 209–30, 221, 263
  see also critical–postmodern framework of organizational power
organizational power practices (OPPs) 222, 228–9
organizational road maps 157
organizational structure
  centralization 263
  decentralization 221, 263
  flat 163, 165, 228
  and innovation 263
  and team-based organization 162–4
organizational support systems 164–9
  flexibility of 164–5
  list of 165–9
  in traditional organizations 164
organizational systems 164–9
organizational teams 55–67
organizations
  accountability 227
  age 263
  change 235, 238
  as conversations 214
  design 165, 166
  goals 248
  performance/efficacy 181, 182, 184, 217
  project-team-based 152
  size 263
  team decision making in 173–88
  and team needs 91–2
  tenure 109
  see also team-based organization
other
  humanization of 28
  powerful 20
  understanding in conflict resolution 25
out-groups 289–90
outcome interdependence 137
outcome values 193–204

participation 266, 267
participative safety 241
participatory action research (PAR) 226
path of relevance principle 110
peer mediation 144
peer pressure 169
performance 6
  individual 193, 197, 198
  management 165, 166–7
  organizational 181, 182, 184, 217
  see also group performance/efficacy; team performance/efficacy
person perception 82–3
person-oriented attributes 108–9, 122

personal responsibility 139
perspective taking 20, 83
Philippines 287, 292, 297
Phradetohrakhun 292
physical workspace 112–13, 165, 168
planning 110–11
　pre-planning 110, 122
　process-planning 110–11, 122
pluralism 26
position rotation 84
positions 19
positive interdependence 132, 137–8, 139, 145
postmodern perspectives of power 214, 215, 218–30
power
　bargaining power 12
　coercive 210
　and conflict management strategies 59, 65
　as control 209–11, 215–17, 220, 225
　through cooperation 209, 211–13, 215–17, 220, 225, 227
　critical 209, 213–17, 218–30, 225
　cultural mode 220, 224, 227–30
　and emancipation 209, 217–18, 225–6
　enhancing personal in competitive situations 6
　in groups 209–30
　and innovation 260
　organizational 209–30
　pool-table metaphor 214
　primary 216–17, 220
　and psychological safety 247
　relational mode 220, 224, 226–7
　secondary 216, 217, 220
　social construction of 216
　structural mode 220, 224, 227
　team leaders and 247
　theoretical perspectives on 209–18
　see also critical–postmodern framework of organizational power
power distance 288, 289, 291–2
power sharing 26, 209, 217
powerful people, confrontation 20
practice fields 250
preconceptions 107
problem mindedness 272
problem-solving styles 272
procedural justice 38, 40–1, 43–5, 48–50
products 163
project-team-based organizations 152
promotive (face-to-face) interactions 132, 139–40, 145
proportionality 13, 14
prosocial orientation 197, 198
Pruitt, Dean 15
psychological health 136–7, 145

psychological mode 3–4
psychological safety 237–41, 244–52
　creation 245–7
　and direct language 250–1
　focus on self versus other 238, 239
　and innovation 261, 268–9
　levels of analysis 238, 239–40
　limitations 249
　as moderator 244–5, 249
　and norms 251
　outcomes of 240–1
　and practice fields 250
　role in team learning 249
　and team leaders 245–8, 250, 251–2
　temporal immediacy 238, 239
　versus trust 238–40
psychosomatic complaints 60, 61
punctuated equilibrium theory 273

reality
　and language 213–14
　and power 213–14, 216
　social construction of 213–14, 216, 222
redundancy 196, 198, 200, 203
reflection-in-action 242–4
reflexivity 242–4, 268
relational model (procedural justice) 44
relationships
　networks 289–90
　positive in cooperative group work 135–6
research and development (R&D) 270–1
resources
　and innovation 264
　interdependence 137, 138
　scarce 64–5
respect 19, 28
responsibility
　personal 139
　team level 161
responsibility forces 138
rewards
　external/internal collective 202
　external/internal individual 202
　and innovation 264
　interdependence 137, 138
　and social loafing in teams 202
right-based conflict management strategies 59, 64–5
rigid thinking 22, 269
ringi 290
risks
　interpersonal in teams 235–52
　physical 236
Roberts, K. 184–5, 186, 188
role differentiation 158
role reversal 20

Rosile, G. A. 227
rules 108, 114, 116
   and decision making 180, 181–2, 188
   production/'how to' 116

Sage Publications 282
Sakdina hierarchies 291
schemas 71, 72, 74–87
   accuracy 74–5, 76–9, 80–7
   congruence 74, 75, 76–87
   content 79–81, 82–5, 86, 87
   forms 74–87
   stereotypical 80
   and team decision making 174, 177–8
   of team influence 110
   and team member characteristics 82–3
   and technology 84–5
   and training 83–4
security, mutual 28
self-as-group-member 46
self-awareness 20–2, 242
self-categorization theory 108
self-concept 42
   see also social identity theory
self-esteem 135, 136–7
self-focused people 83
self-fulfilling prophecies 23
self-interest model 50
self-reflection 229–30
self-regulation 107, 114
self-respect 19
Senge, Peter 250
sensemaking 173–4, 182
Shepperd, J. A. 202, 203
similarity–attraction theory 108
Singapore 297
skills
   acquisition 96–7, 105–17
   sets 158
Smith, E. R. 46–7
social axioms 298
social Darwinism 3, 4
social dependence 131
social dilemmas 42, 49, 200
social identification 42–3
Social Identity Theory 26–7, 30, 37–8, 41–5, 43–5, 48
social independence 131
social interdependence theory 131, 151
   basic premise 132
   cathexsis 132
   competitive social interdependence 131, 132–7, 143, 145
   cooperative social interdependence 131–45
   external validity 145

   goal interdependence 79, 83–4, 131–2, 137–8, 140–2, 157, 211, 243
   inducibility 132
   means interdependence 137
   negative interdependence 132
   outcome interdependence 137
   positive interdependence 132, 137–8, 139, 145
   resource interdependence 137, 138
   reward interdependence 137, 138
   substitutability 132
   and team work 157–8
social loafing 137, 139, 191–205
   case study 192
   and collective orientation 197, 198
   definition 191
   determinants of 192–202
   equity theory of 193, 198–202, 203, 204
   and evaluation potential 194–5
   expectancy-value theory of 193–9, 204
   and expectations about others 197, 198–202
   external validity of studies 204–5
   group members' concern regarding 191–2
   and group performance/outcomes 198
   and group size 196–7, 198
   and group value 195–6, 198
   and individual/group performance 197, 198
   and instrumentality 193–4, 196–9, 200, 202–4
   and redundancy 196, 198, 200, 203
   rewarding strategies for 202
   solutions to 202–3
   and task value 195, 198
social matching 202
social norms 13
social psychology
   conflict resolution 2–31
   empiricism 4
   field theory 4–7
   game theory 7
social relations, Deutsch's crude law of 9–10, 14
social skills
   group 140, 140–1, 142, 145
   interpersonal 140
social support 135–6
socio-political–economic mode 3–4
socioeconomic difference 292–4
South Asia 287–8, 297
South Korea 284–5, 290, 291, 292, 297
Southeast Asia 285–7, 297
speaking up, fear of 240–1
specialization 263
stage-based models of teamwork 273
state policy 26
status characteristics (SCs) 109–10, 112, 122, 229, 260
stereotypes 80, 221

Stohl, C. 210–11
strategic decision making 179–86
stress 57–8, 60–1, 269
stress hormones 60
stress response 57–8
stressors 57
sucker mechanism 199, 200–1, 204
superego 3
suppliers, strategic alliances with 160
support 135–6, 264
survival of the fittest 2, 3
synergistic rule 282–3, 295–6

Taiwan 297
task analysis
　collaborative 84–5
　hierarchical (HTA) 103, 105
task conflict 41, 72–3
　contingency theory of 55–67
　and innovation 266, 267, 273
　and psychological safety 244–5
　and schemas 76–8, 79–80, 81–2, 86
　and task-content 58–9, 61, 63, 64–5
　and task-process 58–9, 61, 64–5
task type 103, 122, 123
　classification schemes 111
　and cooperative group work 133–4, 135
　difficulty 87, 110, 111–12
　and innovation 261
　and social loafing 196, 203
task-oriented attributes 108
tasks
　ambiguity 111–12
　complexity 87, 110, 111–12
　context 99–100, 110–12, 114–16
　critical incident technique 105
　individual/co-action 191, 204
　motivation 264
　performance 55–67
　and social loafing 191–4, 196, 199–200, 203–4
　uncertainty 56–7, 63–5
　value 195, 198
　see also team tasks
team cognition 71–87
　aggregation model 175–7, 179–82, 186, 188
　cross-level model 176–80, 182–4, 186, 188
　and decision making 173–86
　distributed model 176, 178–80, 184–8
　high congruence 74
　as negotiated belief structure 176, 177
　and schema similarity 71, 72, 74–87
　and strategic decision making 179–86
team congruence
　and commonality 98
　and complementarity 98–9
　and distributed cognition 100

　and team mental models 98–9, 100, 101
　see also team member schema congruence
team context
　group member diversity 82–3, 181, 182, 184, 257, 258–60
　group tenure 260–2
　and innovation in teams 257–62, 273
team decision making 39–40, 161–3, 173–88, 266
　aggregation effects 174–7, 179–82, 186, 188
　cross-level effects 175–80, 182–4, 186, 188
　distributed effects 175, 177–80, 184–8
　micro–macro linkage between teams and members 174–5
　multilevel theory of 174–9
　in organizations 173–88
　strategic 179–86
team enhanced action mediators (TEAMs) 85
team leadership
　accessibility 246
　acknowledgment of fallibility 246
　facilitative 271
　and goal setting 248
　and innovation 260–5, 269–72, 273
　innovation-stimulating 271
　leadership boundary spanning 271
　and the learning process 247–8
　and practice fields 250
　problem-solving style of 272
　and psychological safety 245–8, 250, 251–2
　task-management/directive leadership 271
　team–manager interactions 116–17, 121, 122, 123
　transactional 270
　transformational 270
　see also leadership; management; top management team
team member diversity
　and innovation 257, 258–60
　measurement 108–9, 122
　and schemas 82–3
team member schema accuracy 74–5, 76–9, 80–7
　and team member characteristics 82–3
　and technology 84–5, 87
　and training 83–4
team member schema congruence 74, 75, 76–80, 81–7
　and constructive normative behavior 79, 80
　and cooperative goal interdependence 79, 83, 84
　and openness behaviors 80, 83, 84
　and team member characteristics 82–3
　and technology 84–5, 87
　and training 83–4

team member schema similarity (TMSS) 74–87
　team member schema accuracy 74–87
　team member schema congruence 74–87
team members
　and decision making 174–88
　expert 112, 117
　functional backgrounds of 181, 182
　and social loafing 191–205
　status of 109–10, 112, 122, 229, 260
　see also individuals
team mental models (TMMs) 91–123
　abstract nature 102
　applied considerations 117–20
　attributes 97–100
　bottom-line improvements 117–18
　and the challenges of modern teams 120
　and commonality 98, 99
　and complementarity 98–9, 100, 101, 103
　components 102–3
　and cooperation 97
　and decision making in organizations 174–9
　declarative phase 107–13
　definition 93–4
　developmental nature 120
　distinction from mental models 94
　and distributed cognition 100
　dynamic nature 106, 120
　ecological validity 120
　and environmental context 114–16, 120
　equipment models 95–6
　expert teams 91–3, 96, 107, 114, 116–20
　feedback cycles 107
　future research 121–3
　hierarchical 95
　and the hierarchical nature of team tasks 103, 105
　and individual mental models 94, 103, 104, 105, 121, 122
　knowledge compilation phase 107, 113–16
　measurement 100–1
　mental models overlap 101–2, 116–17, 121, 122–3
　multiple constructs 101
　and multiple mental models 94–5, 101
　past frameworks 95–6
　problems with the construct 96
　procedural phase 107, 116–17
　representations of 100–5
　and self-regulation 107, 114
　skill acquisition and 96–7, 105–17
　and taskwork track 95
　and team members 107–10
　and team productivity/efficacy 97–100, 117–18
　and team task context 99–100, 110–12
　and team–manager interactions 116–17, 121, 122, 123

　and teamwork track 95
　theoretical challenges 100–5
　utility 93, 96–7, 98, 117–18
team performance/efficacy 191
　and cognitive conflict management 71–87
　and social loafing 191, 193, 197–9, 203–4
　and team mental models 97–100, 117–18
　and team needs 91–2
　and team-based organization 149–52, 156, 157, 165
team processes
　and conflict 266–7
　and decision making 266
　and innovation in teams 257–8, 265–9, 272–4
　and organizational performance 181, 182, 184
　and psychological safety 268–9
　reflexivity 268
　and shared objectives 265–6
　team organization around 163
　team process mental models 103
team safety 269
team tasks
　context 99–100, 110–12, 114–16
　hierarchical nature of 103, 105
　planning 110–11
　visualization of 116
team-based organization (TBO) 149–70
　and adaptability 153–4, 159, 160, 162
　and alignment 155–6
　components 157–69
　as continuing improvement process 153
　definition 150–7
　and effort of implementation 156–7
　and the environment 160
　and innovation 263
　interfacing with traditional organizations 163–4
　key tenets 150–7, 169
　lack of a common language for 169–70
　and organization leaders 156
　and organizational culture 160–2
　and organizational road maps 157
　and organizational structure 162–4
　and organizational systems 164–9
　and team performance 149–52, 156, 157, 165
　teams as the basic units of accountability and work 151–2, 169
　and teams leading teams 152
　using an array of teams 152–3, 154, 162, 165
　using teams only when appropriate 152, 159, 163, 165
　and work 157–9
teams
　accuracy 74–87, 98
　action phases 273

teams (*cont.*)
  appropriateness of work for 152, 159, 163, 165
  cooperation for innovation 257–74
  cross-cultural 281–98
  definition 174
  diversity 82–3, 108–9, 122, 181–2, 184, 257–60
  empowerment 162–3
  expert 91–3, 96, 107, 114, 116–20
  external relations 115–16, 120, 122–3
  flexibility 153–4
  fluent expert 117
  goals 102–3, 110, 111, 122, 265–6
  high performance 91, 117
  integrated product (IPTs) 160
  integration teams 162
  leading teams 152
  management teams 152, 156, 162–3, 169, 241, 250–1, 268
  –manager interactions 116–17, 121, 122, 123
  needs 91–2
  objectives 265–6
  organizational 55–67
  and organizational context 112–13
  parallel 162
  popularity of 191
  power in 209–30
  project teams 162
  reflexivity 268
  role differentiation in 99
  rules of 108, 114, 116
  size 196–7, 198
  social loafing in 137, 139, 191–205
  stage-based models 273
  transition phases 273
  types 87, 152–3, 154, 162, 165
  using an array of 152–3, 154, 162, 165
  virtual 84–5, 251
  work teams 162
  see also groups
technology
  and schemas 84–5, 87
  and team mental models 120, 121
  transfer 293–4
tenure
  group 260–2
  organizational 109
Thailand 285–6, 291, 292, 296, 297
theory of constraints (TOC) 156
tidak apa 287

top management team (TMT) 152, 156, 162, 163
  use of direct language 250–1
  and innovation 241, 250–1, 268
  and psychological safety 241, 250–1
  and team decision making 179–86
  and team-based organization 152, 156, 162, 163, 169
  and trust 244–5
total preventive maintenance (TPM) 156
total quality management 218
toughness 10, 11, 13
training
  for conflict resolution 8, 18–22, 31
  for cooperative group work 131–45
  for critical reflection 229–30
  for expert teams 118–20
  and schemas 83–4
transactive memory 179
trust 37–8, 39–50
  and cooperative group work 142–3, 145
  and feedback loops/reciprocal causality 50
  and goal achievement 244
  interpersonal 237, 238–40
  mutual 28–9
  and schema accuracy 83
  versus psychological safety 238–40
trusting behavior 143
trustworthy behavior 143
Tyler, T. R. 39

uncertainty 235–6
understanding, shared 99–102, 105, 116–17
United Nations Educational, Scientific, and Cultural Organization (UNESCO) 259–60

values
  cultural 288–92, 298
  outcome 193–204
  task 195, 198
van Dierendonck, D. 61
verbal training 84
violence 19
virtual teams 84–5, 251
Vroom, V. H. 193, 199, 200, 204

Weick, K. E. 184–5, 186, 188
well-being, individual 56–8, 60–1, 65
Williams, K. D. 191, 193–4, 196, 197, 198, 199, 200, 202, 204

Xerox 156